NOV 1 9 2007

Cancer Activism

Cancer Activism

Gender, Media, and Public Policy

KAREN M. KEDROWSKI

MARILYN STINE SAROW

UNIVERSITY OF ILLINOIS PRESS

Urbana and Chicago

Library of Congress Cataloging-in-Publication Data
Copyright information is available
from the Library of Congress.

To our husbands, Tim and Roger, and their fathers,
each of whom is part of the prostate cancer story.

Contents

Tables   ix

Figures   xi

Prologue   xiii

Chronology   xvii

Introduction   1

1. Two Activist Movements Emerge   19

2. A Typology of Grassroots Survivors' Organizations   38

3. Breast Cancer and Prostate Cancer in the Media   62

4. The Public Face of Cancer: Breast Cancer and
   Prostate Cancer in the Media and Public Perceptions of Risk   93

5. Media Advocacy Evidence   124

6. Two Cancers Go to Congress:
   Media Advocacy and the Policy Agenda   136

7. Agenda Maintenance:
   The Politics of Issue Definition and Framing   162

8. Ribbon Wars: Cause-related Marketing
   and the Selling of Breast Cancer and Prostate Cancer   184

9. Policy Dilemmas and Maturing Movements   200

Acknowledgments   225

Methodological Appendix   227

Notes   233

References   245

Index   279

Tables

Table 1. Breast Cancer and Prostate Cancer Statistics, Side by Side   2
Table 2. GSO Characteristics of Breast Cancer and Prostate Cancer   60
Table 3. Prostate Cancer and Breast Cancer News Stories by Medium and
    Story Type   73
Table 4. Prostate Cancer and Breast Cancer News Stories by Subject Matter   76
Table 5. Prostate Cancer and Breast Cancer News Stories by Story Source   78
Table 6. Prostate Cancer News Stories by Source and Year, Frequencies   80
Table 7. Prostate Cancer News Stories by Subject and Year, Frequencies   81
Table 8. Breast Cancer Stories by Source and Year, Frequencies   82
Table 9. Breast Cancer News Stories by Subject and Year, Frequencies   83
Table 10. Breast Cancer News Stories by Subject and Medium   86
Table 11. Breast Cancer News Stories by Source and Medium   87
Table 12. Breast Cancer News Stories by News Type and Medium   88
Table 13. Prostate Cancer Stories by Subject and Medium   89
Table 14. Prostate Cancer News Stories by Source and Medium   90
Table 15. Stories and Profiles by Cancer and Medium   99
Table 16. Profiles of Persons with Breast Cancer by Age, with ACS
    Comparison   101
Table 17. Profiles of Persons with Prostate Cancer by Age, with ACS
    Comparison   101
Table 18. Difference of Means Tests: Ages, Children's Ages, and Number
    of Profiles/Stories   102
Table 19. Frequencies of Mentions of Children and Prognosis by Cancer   103
Table 20. Ages of the Children of Persons with Breast Cancer   103
Table 21. Prostate Cancer and Beast Cancer: Profiles by News Story Subject Matter
    and Type of News Story   105

Table 22. Media Coverage Differences in Breast Cancer: Ages, Children's Ages, and Number of Profiles/Stories   107

Table 23. Media Coverage Differences in Prostate Cancer: Ages, Children's Ages, and Number of Profiles/Stories   107

Table 24. Profiles Mentioning Children by Medium and Cancer   108

Table 25. Profiles of Persons with Terminal Prognosis by Medium and Cancer   109

Table 26. Profiles by News Type by Medium and Cancer   110

Table 27. Health News, December 1996–October 2002   112

Table 28. Perceptions of Risk in Public Opinion Polls   117

Table 29. Comparison of Risk Perceptions over Time   118

Table 30. Television News Consumption and Perception of Risk, 1998   121

Table 31. Media Advocacy Evidence in Breast Cancer: Difference of Means Tests   129

Table 32. Media Advocacy Evidence in Prostate Cancer: Difference of Means Tests   130

Table 33. Media Coverage Differences in Prostate Cancer: Ages, Children's Ages, and Number of Profiles/Story   132

Table 34. Frequencies of Mentions of Children and Prognosis, by Cancer   133

Table 35. Prostate Cancer and Breast Cancer Research Funds, 1980–2002 (in millions of dollars)   149

Table 36. Congressional Legislation Introduced Regarding Prostate Cancer and Breast Cancer, 96th–108th Congresses   154

Table 37. Congressional Hearings on Breast Cancer and Prostate Cancer, 1980–2002   155

Table 38. Advocacy and Congressional Activity: Difference of Means Tests   156

Table 39. Changes in Breast Cancer Funding: Regression Analysis   158

Table 40. Changes in Prostate Cancer Funding: Regression Analysis   158

Table 41. Rochefort and Cobb's Characteristics Found in Problem Definition   166

Table 42. Medical Discovery Stories over Time   168

Table 43. Medical Discovery News Stories and Total Research Funding: Regression Analysis   169

Table 44. Breast Cancer Policy Agenda Items   172

Table 45. Prostate Cancer Policy Agenda Items   180

Table 46. October Breast Cancer Stories   196

Table 47. Percent of NCI Budget, by Disease and Severity Statistics   206

Table 48. Frequency Distributions: Questions Measuring Risk   230

Table 49. Correlations in Question Response   231

Figures

Figure 1. News Stories by Year, 1980–98   *74*
Figure 2. News Stories, by Month   *197*
Figure 3. National Cancer Institute Funding, by Cancer   *204*

Prologue

Spring comes reluctantly to Washington. The nation is at war in Iraq and has heightened security in government buildings and airports. Not surprisingly, the usual tourist sites are almost empty. Yet the business of running the government goes on.

Just blocks from the Capitol, three health-related organizations meet in the Renaissance Hotel. In the first-floor conference facilities, leaders from the Amyotrophic Lateral Sclerosis Foundation and the American College of Emergency Room Physicians plot congressional funding strategies. On the floor below, more than six hundred women and a few men gather this Saturday afternoon to talk about their passion and their avocation—stopping breast cancer. It's the National Breast Cancer Coalition's annual Advocacy Training Conference, and it draws breast cancer survivors from all over the world.

Armed with three-inch binders in blue tote bags, conference attendees sit through two and a half days of intensive presentations and workshops on risk assessment, the latest treatments in breast cancer, the politics of health care, and the ethics of cause marketing and fund-raising. Big-name experts from throughout the country are on the agenda. As they speak, their PowerPoint presentations appear on two large video screens flanking the speakers' platform. It's all in preparation for 8 A.M., Tuesday, when advocates will be bused to Capitol Hill for the climax of their conference, Lobby Day.

Breast cancer advocacy is serious business, and these women talk science, medicine, and politics with fervor. Representing some twenty-five state and national organizations, including young survivors, patient education groups, African Americans, Hispanics, lesbians, and a variety of other organizations, the NBCC is a powerful force in Washington politics—and everybody knows it.

Although each day's session begins with the sounds of upbeat music such as Helen Reddy's "I Am Woman," NBCC sessions are on time and on task. Seated behind rows of tables in the large convention facility, attendees begin each session listening to a brief tribute to their fallen sisters and then engage in a moment of silence before moving on to the business of advocacy. "Many organizations do the work of raising awareness," NBCC President Fran Visco tells participants. "We raise expectations and give you the power and the tools to get there."

The organization's 2003 legislative priorities are ambitious, comprehensive, and controversial. They include (1) guaranteeing quality health-care access for all; (2) seeking a $175 million appropriation for the Department of Defense peer-reviewed Breast Cancer Research Program for fiscal year 2004; (3) enacting the Breast Cancer and Environmental Research Act; (4) enacting HR 1288, the Access to Cancer Therapies Act; and (5) enacting the Genetic Nondiscrimination in Health Insurance and Employment Act. But little time is spent discussing the agenda.

Participants already know what to ask for and how to get what they want. The NBCC believes in arming members with media training and support. Many advocates are Project LEAD graduates who have taken an intensive four-day scientific training course designed to prepare them to critically evaluate scientific research. They update their knowledge at the conference and act as resource people during the Lobby Day state delegation meetings with members of Congress from forty-five states.

Although the training session is underwritten by a variety of pharmaceutical organizations and the Entertainment Industry Foundation, only the Avon Foundation will receive recognition in brief remarks during a luncheon presentation.

The advocates seem passionate but not emotional—empowered and confident. The conference theme is "Stop Breast Cancer. It's in Our Power!" and these women believe that to be true.

THREE WEEKS LATER, MAY 20

In a fourth-floor meeting room of the Loews L'Enfant Plaza Hotel, the National Prostate Cancer Coalition guides fifty people, including survivors, health-care professionals, and state advocacy leaders, through a two-day session on how to talk to members of Congress. The coalition depends on its primarily young, enthusiastic staff of men and women and its leader, Dr. Richard Atkins, to lead the training. Sessions are loosely structured, sometimes faltering, sometimes lighthearted, but always interactive.

The first activity of the training session, an ice-breaker, the "Congressional Dating Game," sets the tone for the sessions. It's part fun, part serious, and designed to make attendees comfortable talking to members of Congress.

The focus of this event is devoted to making attendees confident and compelling advocates for the coalition's two-part agenda: first, to ask for $100 million for the prostate cancer program at the Department of Defense for fiscal year 2004, and, second, to ask that Congress require the National Institutes of Health (NIH) to submit a budget for its prostate cancer research plan (for fiscal years 2004–8) within ninety days following the fiscal year 2004 appropriation. The latter request is designed to force the NIH to make an increased investment in prostate cancer research as Congress had previously required it to do.

Participants receive a training manual packaged in a one-inch binder in a white tote bag—both emblazoned with the names of pharmaceutical sponsors AstraZeneca and Pfizer. Representatives from the firms are given time on the programs. Both deliver generic presentations.

At promptly 4:45 P.M. on the first day participants are shuttled to awaiting taxis that whisk them several blocks to the Dirksen Senate Office Building. It's a Code Red security day, and the NBCC's staff is clearly nervous that delays in security clearance will affect a cocktail reception honoring the work of Senators Michael Crapo (R-ID) and Charles Schumer (D-NY) on behalf of prostate cancer. In time, each senator shows up at the reception and quickly but graciously accepts his leadership award. The purpose of the award is lost on no one.

Even though a third of the group is composed of women, advocates are urged to tell their own stories about living with prostate cancer or working with cancer patients. As Skip Lockwood, senior vice president and chief operating officer of the coalition, tells attendees, "Delivering your personal stories in an effective manner will gain leverage [with members of Congress]."

Other sessions also present opportunities to share their stories and receive constructive critiques from members of the coalition's staff and the audience of participants. After one practice presentation, an NPCC staff member advises an advocate, "Tell your story, personalize it—and ask for a commitment."

"They like us . . . [our message] is every bit as important as taxes or transportation," says another staff member. Following lunch on May 21, advocates, working in pairs, head off to visit their Capital Hill appointments.

Rain falls in Washington, but the mood is positive. It's appropriation season—again.

Chronology

Significant Events in the Breast Cancer Story

1882: William Stewart Halsted develops the radical mastectomy.

1952: Reach to Recovery of the American Cancer Society, established.

1955: The Avon Foundation founded.

1974: Betty Ford and Margaretta Fitler Murphy "Happy" Rockefeller diagnosed with breast cancer; broadcaster Betty Rollins writes *First You Cry*.

1978: Y-ME National Breast Cancer Coalition founded.

1978: Susan Sontag writes *Illness as Metaphor*.

1979: The NIH publishes consensus statement recommends the end of radical mastectomies and recognizes informed consent as a standard of practice.

1980: Audre Lorde writes *The Cancer Journals*.
Scientists conclude that hair dyes are not connected to breast cancer.
Informed consent practices debated.
Translumination, using light to detect breast tumors, approved as a breast cancer diagnostic technique.
Interferon is tested as a breast cancer treatment.
Scientists conclude that breast cancer can be inherited.

1981: Rose Kushner's *What Every Women Should Know about Breast Cancer* is published, and she crusades against the one-step procedure following diagnosis of breast cancer.
The *New England Journal of Medicine* publishes an article stating

that women may not need radical mastectomies if they also receive chemotherapy.

Rates of radical mastectomy declining.

1982: The Susan G. Komen Foundation founded.

The National Alliance of Breast Cancer Organizations (NABCO) founded, to disband in 2004.

Debate over the effectiveness of mammography for younger women (those forty to forty-nine) begins.

Alcohol consumption and breast cancer risk linked.

The antidepressant Valium found not to increase breast cancer risk.

1983: Breast self-examination touted as the key to early detection of breast cancer. The technique needs to be taught by doctors.

Caffeine thought to be linked to higher rates of breast cancer.

Consumer advocate Ralph Nader charges that the high rates of progesterone in birth control pills contribute to breast cancer risk.

Lung cancer surpasses breast cancer as the deadliest cancer among women.

The American Cancer Society begins to recommend breast x-rays.

1984: The drug DES is linked to breast cancer risk.

Actor Jill Ireland treated for breast cancer.

The character Mary Beth Cagney in the television drama series *Cagney and Lacey* develops breast cancer.

1985: Actor Brigitte Bardot and comedien Minnie Pearl are diagnosed with breast cancer.

Tamoxifen found to delay or prevent recurrence of breast cancer in postmenopausal women.

The Lancet reports that use of birth control pills does not increase or decrease risk of breast cancer in young women.

Link between caffeine use and breast cancer disputed in the *JAMA*.

"Unresolved sexual conflicts" said to increase breast cancer risk.

Effectiveness of lumpectomy plus radiation affirmed by the National Cancer Institute.

1986: DeDe Robertson, wife of 1988 presidential candidate Pat Robertson, is diagnosed with breast cancer.

The American Cancer Society recommends that women between forty and forty-nine receive mammograms every year or two and recommends annual mammograms for women fifty and over.

Researchers at the University of Pennsylvania reject attitude as key to recovery from cancer but can be important when making treatment decisions.

1987: First Lady Nancy Reagan undergoes a mastectomy, a decision criticized because her tumor may have been suitable for lumpectomy plus radiation.

Breastfeeding is linked to lower breast cancer risk.

Doctors in rural areas are found to be resistant to lumpectomy surgery.

Effectiveness of breast self-examinations called into question.

1988: The consumer group Public Citizen calls for ban of silicone breast implants.

Supreme Court Justice Sandra Day O'Connor diagnosed with breast cancer.

Actor Ann Jillian stars in a made for television special about her own breast cancer diagnosis and treatment.

Actor Jill Eikenberry discloses that she has been diagnosed with and treated for breast cancer.

1989: Look Good . . . Feel Better program established by the American Cancer Society; Cosmetic, Toiletry, and Fragrance Association; and the National Cosmetology Association.

Oral contraceptives thought to increase breast cancer risk. The FDA decides not to include warnings on package labels.

Actor Betty Davis dies of breast cancer.

Some breast cancer linked to genes on chromosome 17.

Medicare begins to cover mammograms.

1990: Breast Cancer Action founded.

Women taking estrogen after menopause may increase their risk of breast cancer.

Blue Cross Blue Shield looks at the efficacy of bone marrow transplants to treat breast cancer.

Tamoxifen thought to protect against heart disease.

Doctors are found to ignore the results of breast self-examinations among younger women.

Jill Ireland dies of breast cancer.

1991: The National Breast Cancer Coalition founded.

RU 486, the "abortion pill," seen as perhaps an effective treatment against breast cancer although the drug cannot be tested in the United States.

One percent of American women carry a gene that greatly increases their risk of developing breast cancer if they are exposed to x-rays.

Polyurethane liners used in two types of breast implants are linked to cancer.

The National Cancer Institute begins trials of tamoxifen.

Professional golfer Heather Farr dies of breast cancer.

Effectiveness of lumpectomy versus a mastectomy debated.

Breast cancer advocacy groups form and adopt many of the same tactics as AIDS groups.

The American Cancer Society changes women's lifetime risk estimate of having breast cancer to one in nine.

1992: Journalist Linda Ellerbee treated for breast cancer.

The state of New York studies breast cancer rates on Long Island.

Breast implants reportedly interfere with the detection of breast tumors using mammography.

Harvard University finds no link between dietary fat and risk of breast cancer.

The FDA calls for a moratorium on silicone breast implants.

1993: The Avon Breast Cancer Crusade, founded in the U.K. in 1992, expands to the United States.

BRCA 1, first breast cancer gene, identified.

Vitamin A linked to lower rates of breast cancer.

Tamoxifen linked to lower rates of heart disease.

1994: Sisters Network–African American women with breast cancer, founded.

President Clinton's mother, Virginia Kelley, dies of breast cancer.

The *Chicago Tribune* breaks the story about fraud in the federally funded study of the effectiveness of lumpectomy headed by Dr. Bernard Fisher of the University of Pittsburgh.

Bernard Fisher resigns his position.

The *JAMA* publishes a new study that reaffirms effectiveness of the lumpectomy.

The federal government issues mammography standards.

1995: Breast cancer surgeon Susan Love states that medical science is "close to finding a cure."

Second breast cancer gene identified. Blood test developed to detect genetic mutations.

The *New England Journal of Medicine* reports that women who take estrogen and progesterone after menopause are not at higher risk of breast cancer.

Canadian hospital charged with falsifying patient records in federal trials.

1996: Dr. Susan Love writes *The Breast Book*.

President Clinton campaigns on his support for breast cancer research.

The possible link between abortion and breast cancer is debated.

1997: The NIH recommends mammography for women aged forty to forty-nine; policy not universally accepted by some in the medical community and National Breast Cancer Coalition.

The National Cancer Institute questions efficacy of mammography in younger women (forty to forty-nine). It initially recommends against regular mammograms for that age group but later changes its position.

The American Cancer Society recommends regular mammograms for women in this age group.

Exercise found to reduce risk of breast cancer.

1998: Young Survivors' Coalition founded.

Linda McCartney, wife of former Beatle Paul McCartney, dies of breast cancer.

Tamoxifen found to prevent the development of breast cancer in healthy women at high risk of the disease.

The American Cancer Society raises women's lifetime risk estimate of having breast cancer to one in eight.

Taxol found effective as an adjuvant treatment, and Herceptin study results are promising.

The character Murphy Brown from the sit-com of the same name develops breast cancer during the show's 1997–98 season.

2001: Zillah Eisenstein writes *Manmade Breast Cancers*.

Significant Events in the Prostate Cancer Story

1980: American farmers found to have high rates of prostate cancer.

1984: Patient Advocates for Advanced Cancer Treatment (PAACT) founded.

1985: Former Georgia governor Lester Maddox receives medication contaminated with the AIDS virus to treat his prostate cancer. He announces that he does not have the virus.

Radiation exposure linked to prostate cancer in American veterans.

Supreme Court Justice Lewis Powell treated for prostate cancer.

Romanian president Nicholae Ceaucescu rumored to be ill with prostate cancer.

1986: PSA blood test developed. Controversy begins.

1987: Radioactive implants developed as a treatment for prostate cancer.

CIA director William Casey treated for prostate cancer a year before his fatal brain tumor disclosed.

Cardiologist and fitness expert George Sheehan and Supreme Court Justice Harry Blackmun treated for prostate cancer.

1988: The Prostate Cancer Educators Council (PCEC) founded.

Iranian leader Ayatollah Ruholla Khomeini dies of prostate cancer.

1989: Chinese leader Deng Zioping gives order for assault on Tiananmen Square from the hospital where he is being treated for prostate cancer.

Prostate cancer drug lupron may be effective against uterine tumors.

1990: Man to Man of the American Cancer Society founded.

US TOO! International founded.

Alan Cranston announces retirement from the U.S. Senate because of advanced prostate cancer. His illness prevents him from appearing before the Senate committee investigating his involvement in the "Keating Five" savings and loan scandal.

1991: Senators Bob Dole (R-KS) and Jesse Helms (R-NC) treated for prostate cancer.

Vasectomy thought to increase prostate cancer risk, which is later found to be untrue.

1992: French president Francois Mitterrand, financier Michael Milken, actor Robert Goulet, and Supreme Court Justice John Paul Stevens treated for prostate cancer.

Time-Warner chair Steve Ross dies of prostate cancer.

1993: Cyrosurgery attempted as a treatment for prostate cancer; later found to be ineffective.

Trials of the prostate cancer drug Proscar begin.

Musician Frank Zappa and actors Bill Bixby and Don Ameche die of prostate cancer.

CaP CURE founded; now the Prostate Cancer Foundation.

1994: Prostate Action, Inc (PROACT) founded.

The *JAMA* publishes an article questioning the effectiveness of the PSA test.

Farming linked to higher prostate cancer rates in African American men.

Norman Schwarzkopf treated for prostate cancer.

Link discovered between fatty diet and prostate cancer.

1995: Race car driver Richard Petty and the Buffalo Bills' coach Marv Levy treated for prostate cancer.

Timothy Leary dies of prostate cancer. His death is broadcast on the World-Wide Web.

1996: The National Prostate Cancer Coalition founded.

Evidence of a prostate cancer gene discovered.

French president Francois Mitterrand dies.

Former representative Dan Rostenkowski (D-IL) treated for prostate cancer.

1997: Washington, D.C., mayor Marion Berry treated for prostate cancer.

Zairean president Mobuto Sese Seko dies of prostate cancer.

Washington Post CEO Donald Graham treated for prostate cancer.

1998: The Prostate Cancer Action Network (PCAN) founded.

Link between a lack of vitamin E and trace mineral selenium and high rates of prostate cancer identified.

A character on *LAPD Blue* television series develops prostate cancer.

Golfer Arnold Palmer treated for prostate cancer.

Sales begin of impotence drug Viagra.

Kwame Ture (Stokley Carmichael) dies of prostate cancer.

Efficacy of radioactive seed treatment for prostate cancer confirmed.

Benefits of lycopene, found in cooked tomato products, publicized.

2000: 100 Black Men of America and the American Cancer Society create Let's Talk About It.

2003: Damon Harris, formerly of the Temptations, and Louis Farrakhan both start foundations to benefit prostate cancer.

Cancer Activism

Introduction

Popular and scholarly opinion holds that women have been excluded historically from the corridors of power. Male members of Congress, even if they are not overtly sexist, are accused of being inattentive or unconcerned with women's issues. Men take care of their own interests first, or so the perception holds.

Yet in the story of breast and prostate cancer advocacy that perception does not hold. Women—breast cancer survivors—wield the power. Members of Congress, male and female, moved by survivors' personal stories and reelection concerns, seek out breast cancer advocates, sponsor their legislative initiatives, and support high levels of federal research funding. Paradoxically, men—prostate cancer survivors—struggle to raise public awareness of the disease and struggle to keep it on the agenda.

Disease advocates are engaged not only in a race for a cure but also competition for media coverage, federal research dollars, corporate support, and legislative attention. In this race, breast cancer advocates are miles ahead of their prostate cancer competitors in a decades-long, billion-dollar marathon.

This book examines the reasons behind that paradox through a comprehensive study of media coverage and policy responses using both qualitative and quantitative approaches. Although the story is complex and told in detail in the following pages, it can be captured in several simple statements: Women, more than men, organize; women, more than men, make consumer decisions; and women, more than men, vote.

Why examine breast and prostate cancer instead of other gendered diseases? The epidemiology of the two diseases differs, but breast cancer and prostate cancer share at least five similarities that make them interesting to social scientists. First, the morbidity and mortality rates for the diseases are remarkably comparable. Moreover, prostate cancer is the second leading cause of cancer deaths in men, second only to lung cancer. Breast cancer is the second leading cause of cancer deaths in women, also second only to lung cancer. In addition, men and women have approximately the same lifetime risk of developing each disease. A women's lifetime risk of developing breast cancer is one in seven. A man's lifetime risk of developing prostate cancer is one in six. Both breast and prostate cancer are survivable if diagnosed early. The five-year survival rate for localized breast cancer is 97.5 percent, and the five-year survival rate for localized prostate cancer is 100 percent (American Cancer Society [ACS] 2005b) (table 1).

Second, common treatment options for both forms of cancer may result in unpleasant consequences. Mastectomy is physically disfiguring and may have side effects, such as the development of painful lymphedema (swelling) or a loss of mobility in the arm, whereas lumpectomy can leave women with scarring and asymmetrical breasts. Hormone treatment can lead to the onset of menopause or enhance its symptoms. Two common consequences of prostate treatments, impotence and incontinence, are not only embarrass-

Table 1. Breast Cancer and Prostate Cancer Statistics, Side by Side

	Breast Cancer	Prostate Cancer
Cases diagnosed, 2005	211,240	232,090
Estimated Deaths, 2005	40,870	30,350
Five-year relative survival rate, localized (%)	97.5	100
Ten-year relative survival rate, all stages (%)	77	92
Lifetime risk	1 in 7	1 in 6
Common treatments	Surgery	Surgery
	Radiation	Radiation
	Chemotherapy	Chemotherapy
	Hormone	Hormone
	treatment	treatment
Common side effects	Scarring	Impotence
	Lymphedema	Incontenence
	Loss of sexual	Bleeding in
	appeal	bladder/colon
	Hair loss	Chemical
		castration
	Menopausal	
	symptoms enhanced	

Source: American Cancer Society, "Cancer Facts and Figures, 2005."

ing but also call into question one's sexuality. In fact, hormone treatment, a common therapy, is sometimes referred to as chemical castration.

Third, the public discussion of cancer, particularly these two forms of the disease, is a relatively new development. Today, many breast cancer advocates recount how their mothers were ashamed to discuss their surgery and diagnoses because of the social stigma attached to the disease. Cancer was discussed in hushed tones in the privacy of one's home or office. Known as the "Big C," breast cancer and other female cancers were euphemistically called "female problems."

Losing a breast can be traumatic and lead some women to question their sexual attractiveness. Only in the last few years have public personalities such as Robert "Bob" Dole (R-KS) begun to discuss publicly prostate cancer and impotence. The direct-to-consumer marketing of erectile dysfunction drugs also elevated this health concern to the public's attention.

Fourth, both diseases received significant news coverage, beginning in the 1980s and into the 1990s. Such increased coverage was the result of significant medical discoveries, publicly acknowledged diagnoses of prominent personalities, and controversies surrounding various treatments.

Fifth, survivors and their families, researchers, and medical professionals created disease-specific lobbying organizations that focus on both media attention and policy change. These groups are referred to as grassroots survivors' organizations (GSOs) in this book.

This introduction provides background on the nature, causes, and treatments of both cancers; describes the theoretical background and methodology of this research; and outlines the remainder of the book.

Overview of Breast Cancer and Prostate Cancer

BREAST CANCER

For generations, women have feared the possibility of developing breast cancer. Breast cancer is a malignant growth in the breast tissue or ducts of the breast, but it often metastasizes through the bloodstream to other organs. Scientists now speculate that breast cancer is not one disease but five or six different diseases demanding different treatments and procedures (Sporn 2003).

Breast cancer is the most common form of cancer in women, and the second leading cause of cancer deaths among women.[1] After increasing steadily in the 1980s, possibly due to increased use of mammography, breast cancer incidence rates have leveled off. According to the American Cancer Society, some 211,240 cases of invasive breast cancer were diagnosed in 2005. Another

58,490 cases of noninvasive carcinoma in situ, the earliest form of the disease, also were identified. An estimated 40,870 people died of the disease (ACS 2005b). More than 90 percent were diagnosed at a local or regional stage. Because men have some breast tissue, it is possible for men to develop breast cancer. The number of breast cancer cases and deaths that occur in men, however, is less than 1 percent of the total (Giordano, Budzar, and Hortobagyi 2002).

Although experts are uncertain about what causes breast cancer, several risk factors have been identified. These risk factors include prolonged exposure to the hormone estrogen, delayed childbearing until after the age of thirty or having no children at all, and early onset of menses and late menopause. Other risk factors include having a personal or a family history of breast cancer; having a mutated form of one of the breast cancer genes, BCRA1 or BCRA2; and using alcohol and being overweight. Women who exercise regularly and who practice breastfeeding, however, are at reduced risk (ACS 2005a). Breast cancer is one of the few diseases where white women are at higher risk than African American women and where the risk of developing the disease increases with socioeconomic status (Heck and Pamuk 1997).[2]

Treatments for breast cancer are complicated, vary widely, and are individualized to the type and stage of cancer at its detection. Any discussion of treatment for breast cancer risks oversimplifying the process of excluding information. Such surgical procedures as lumpectomy, mastectomy, radiation, chemotherapy, and drug protocols, either alone or in combination, are, however, common forms of treatment.

Breast cancer detection methods and treatment options continue to be the subjects of controversy, often leaving the public confused about how to proceed with their care. Breast self examination (BSE) and mammography remain the primary means to detect breast cancer. Suspicious breast tissue is then biopsied to determine whether it is cancerous. Through the 1990s, however, the National Cancer Institute (NCI) repeatedly switched its recommendation for the use of mammography for women in their forties. In the end, the NCI left the decision in the hands of women (Shubert and Shubert 1997).

In 1994 efforts to convince the medical community and patients that a lumpectomy plus radiation was as effective as a traditional mastectomy received a major setback. The *Chicago Tribune* discovered an NCI report that revealed an agency-funded study based at the University of Pittsburgh included numerous pieces of falsified data. The results of this study, which concluded that lumpectomy and radiation were as effective as mastectomy, were called into question (Corbett and Mori 1999a; Zerbe, Young and Nagelhout 1998). Advocacy groups criticized the *Tribune* for its efforts to seek clarification of the research results and for questioning the leadership of the study (Peres interview 2003). As a result of this controversy, a renowned scientist, Dr. Bernard Fisher, was forced to resign from the study. Also in the mid-1990s, the safety of silicone breast implants, frequently used in reconstructive surgery, was called into question (Olson 2002; Palley 1995). In addition, some cancer specialists advocated the use of autologous bone marrow transplants as a treatment for advanced breast cancer. Insurance companies, however, were reluctant to cover this very expensive, experimental treatment. Several women with breast cancer, or family members of those women, sued their insurance carriers and won large settlements. Eventually, however, medical evidence determined that this treatment was ineffective (Mello and Brennan 2001).

More recently, a possible link between breast cancer and abortion was debated within scientific circles. This possible link was adopted by some pro-life advocates and resurfaced in statements promulgated by the George W. Bush administration. Early studies indicated a slightly elevated risk for women who had induced abortions and breast cancer. More than thirty more recent studies, however, including a large Danish study of 1.5 million women, found no link between the disease and abortions (Gammon, Bertin, and Terry 1996; Melbye et al. 1997; Wingo et al. 1997). Breast cancer advocacy groups such as the National Breast Cancer Coalition have argued that scientific evidence fails to support a link between the disease and abortion (NBCC 2003d).

A final controversy surrounds the questions about possible environmental causes of breast cancer. A long line of scholars, beginning in the 1960s with Rachel Carson's *Silent Spring* (1964) (Carson died of breast cancer), followed by Samuel Epstein's *Politics of Cancer* (1978) and continuing with Zillah Eisenstein's *Manmade Breast Cancers* (2001), have warned of the link between pollution and the rising rates of cancer. As Eisenstein notes, "Female bodies—especially breast tissue—absorb their environs in unique ways that need to be theorized and politicized. Women carry the polluted globe around in our bodies, especially in our breast tissue and breast milk" (61).

In the 1990s several Long Island, New York, breast cancer organizations successfully lobbied for a federal investigation into possible environmental links to the disease. Led by Senator Alphonse D'Amato (R-NY), the federal government initiated an extensive series of studies of the state's residents. The first published results of this study were largely inconclusive; consequently, advocates continue to push for further research into possible environmental carcinogens (Nugent 2003; Williamson 2002).

A similar story unfolded in Marin County, California, in the San Francisco Bay area. In 1995, Marin Breast Cancer Watch (MBCW), a grassroots advocacy organization, was founded in response to elevated breast cancer rates in the region. This organization is engaged in research to understand the causes of breast cancer, including possible environmental causes. Not only does the MBCW work with the California Breast Cancer Research Program (CBCRP) but it also worked with U.S. Representative Lynn Woolsey (D-CA) and Senator Barbara Boxer (D-CA) to persuade the NCI to investigate high rates of breast cancer in Marin County (CBCRP 2005; NCI 2003; Woolsey 2003).

Another effort is underway on Cape Cod, Massachusetts. The Silent Spring Institute, named after Rachel Carson's famous tome, is a nonprofit research institute founded by the Massachusetts Breast Cancer Coalition. Currently engaged in several collaborative efforts with scientists at Harvard University, Tufts University, and Boston University, one of its efforts is to create a geographic database of breast cancer cases and possible exposures to herbicides and pesticides (Silent Spring Institute 2005).

These local efforts are now joined by national efforts. The most prominent one underway is the Sisters Study sponsored by the National Institute of Environmental Health Sciences (NIEHS), a branch of the National Institutes of Health. This project will study fifty thousand cancer-free sisters of women with breast cancer to determine genetic and environmental links ("Clinical Trials, Sister Study" 2005).

To date, few studies have identified a link between exposure to pollution and breast cancer, and the media generally have ignored the issue (P. Brown et al. 2001). In fact, the controversy has caused something of a rift in the breast cancer movement, which concerns Susan Love, a prominent activist. "We need to be able to accept 'no relationship between breast cancer and the environment' as the right answer [if the research leads to this conclusion]," she told participants at the 2005 NBCC Annual Training Conference.

PROSTATE CANCER

For many American men prostate cancer is something they do not discuss. The prostate, a walnut-sized organ, is located at the outlet to the bladder. Its role is to provide part of the fluid that makes up semen, but the organ is not critical to reproduction and men can live without it (Walsh and Worthington 2001).

Patrick Walsh, a leading medical authority on prostate cancer, notes the delicate location of the prostate: "It lies in the midst of vulnerable structures—the bladder, the rectum, the sphincters responsible for urinary control, major arteries and veins, and a host of delicate nerves, some of them so tiny that we've only recently discovered them—that can foil any physician who ventures into the area without exquisitely precise knowledge of the terrain" (Walsh and Worthington 2001, 4).

Prostate cancer is usually a slow-growing disease, and if caught in its early stages is curable. Yet the disease is the second leading cause of cancer deaths among men. African American men have much higher chances of developing prostate cancer than white males, and their risk of dying from the disease is twice as high. According to the American Cancer Society, prostate cancer incidence rates increased dramatically in from 1989 to 1992 and then began to decline in 1993 and 1994. Incidence rates remain much higher today, however, than in the 1970s (Haas and Sakr 1997). An estimated 30,350 men died of prostate cancer in 2005, and 232,090 new cases of prostate cancer were diagnosed (ACS 2005b). Of those men who develop the disease and live fifteen years, approximately one-half will die from it (Walsh and Worthington 2001, 43). James Lewis and Roy Berger (1994) suggest several reasons for the failure of men to seek medical attention for prostate problems, including the lack of symptoms of the disease, fear of a medical examination, lack of education, lack of access to medical facilities, and fear of impotence and incontinence.

Although the cause of the disease is unknown, the incidence of prostate cancer is correlated with family history of the disease, aging, race, socioeconomic status, obesity, and a high-fat diet (Haas and Sakr 1997). A small but promising study found that prostate cancer cells significantly diminished among men who exercised for just eleven days and ate a low-fat diet (UCLA 2003). Prostate cancer is more prominent among men in western countries than in those living in the East, and some would suggest high-fat diets may be a contributing factor. The possible connection between diet and prostate cancer is now under study by the federal government. The NCI continues to test the effects of selenium and vitamin E on preventing prostate cancer; both nutrients have been linked to lower rates of cancer. The NCI also is conducting a small clinical trial on lypocopene, a product found in cooked tomatoes and watermelon, to determine whether giving the chemical to men before prostate surgery will help them stem the disease (Neergaard 2003).

Hereditary prostate cancer is linked to approximately 9 percent of those diagnosed with the disease each year. One or more of the genes HPC1 and HPX may increase the odds of developing this form of cancer. Environmental factors such as a link between herbicides and prostate cancer are not conclusive, although farmers have a higher incidence of the disease. Furthermore, the U.S. government has recognized the link between exposure to pesticides and prostate cancer in Vietnam veterans.

In fact, as men age they are very likely to develop prostate cancer or benign prostate hyperplasia (BPH), a benign enlargement of the prostate gland that exhibits many of the same symptoms as prostate cancer. This condition, however, is not necessarily a precursor of prostate cancer. The incidence of the disease is expected to rise as the population ages (Garnick 1994). Most prostate cancers are slow-growing and may be relatively symptom-free. Research has shown that older men tend to have a more aggressive form of prostate cancer than younger men and it is often diagnosed at a later stage (Walsh and Worthington 2001). Although an estimated 80 percent of men eighty and older have prostate cancer, most of these men will die of something else (Garloch 1996).

The development and widespread use of the prostate specific antigen (PSA) blood test contributed to the increase in reported prostate cancer diagnoses. Developed in 1986 to monitor the progress of prostate cancer in patients whose cancer was diagnosed by other means, the PSA test is now routinely given to men over the age of fifty. The PSA now replaces the traditional digital rectal examination (DRE) as a first test for prostate cancer. In the DRE, the physician inserts his or her finger into the rectum to feel for lumps in the prostate. Used alone, the examination could detect cancers only in their more advanced stages, when tumors were large enough to be detected by fingertips. For men with suspicious PSA test results, a DRE and a biopsy will be performed to determine if they have malignancies.

Like the mammogram, the PSA test is not without controversy. A 2004 study found that it may fail to detect many cases of prostate cancer, particularly in men with low PSA scores (Thompson 2005). The American Urological Association and the American Cancer Society recommend PSA screening for men fifty or older who have anticipated lifespan of ten years or more or who are over forty and have a family history of the disease. The Centers for Disease Control and Prevention, however, does not recommend routine screening. The PSA test detects levels of a glycoprotein called prostate specific antigen that the prostate produces in the bloodstream. Detection of this protein increases with the presence of cancer. Other factors may also cause the PSA level to rise, such as BPH or prostatitis (inflammation of the prostrate); in other cases PSA levels may be normal even though a man has prostate cancer. Thus additional tests are needed to determine the presence of cancer (Garnick 1994).

In addition, the PSA test cannot discriminate between fast-growing cancers that are likely to kill their victims and slow-growing ones that pose little or no risk or discomfort. Thus, many prostate cancer patients, faced with a diagnosis of cancer, are likely to undergo treatments they do not need for a disease that probably will not kill them. As a result of this treatment, they also endure pain and suffering at considerable expense to themselves and the health system. The PSA test will remain controversial until scientists can determine which cancers are life-threatening and which are harmless.

The treatment of prostate cancer depends upon the individual's age, PSA levels, Gleason scores (a scale pathologists use to grade the progress of the disease), and general state of health. Cultural and social factors such as race and marital status appear to be factors in treatment choice (Denberg et al. 2005). For decades, the only treatment for prostate cancer was a prostatectomy, surgical removal of the prostate gland. Surgery alone or combined with hormonal therapy are used most often in the early stages of the disease ("Prostate Cancer: What It Is and How It Is Treated" 2002). If the cancer has spread beyond the lymph nodes to the bones or other sites, the complete removal of the prostate is not usually undertaken. That surgery leaves the individual sterile and frequently impotent and incontinent.

Recent medical advances have broadened treatment options for prostrate cancer patients. Developed in the 1980s, nerve-sparing surgery preserves the tiny nerves surrounding the prostate gland that are responsible for erections. If these nerves are not severed during the surgery, patients may avoid one of the more serious complications of prostate cancer treatment (Garnick 1994). Other treatment options include radiation treatment in various forms, which often leaves patients with bladder or bowel problems, and chemotherapy for advanced-stage prostate cancer and so-called watchful waiting, where the disease is monitored but not treated. Watchful waiting is common in Europe, but that practice may change. A 2005 Scandinavian study followed men under age seventy-five for a decade after surgery. About 9.5 percent of those who received surgery, and 15 percent of those in the watchful-waiting group, died within ten years of diagnoses. But all the benefits seemed to be among the group of men under sixty-five, whereas the death rate among the watchful-waiting group was double that of those who had surgery (Bill-Axelson et al. 2005).

Another medical advance that impacts the lives of prostate cancer survivors is the development of drugs to treat impotence—or erectile dysfunction (ED)—a common side effect of prostate cancer treatment. Viagra, the first such drug, was approved by the FDA in 1998, and it became an immediate sales phenomenon (Kolata 1998). It remains popular, even with the release of other drugs that treat ED and concerns about a link to heart attacks. Although beneficial to prostate cancer patients, ED drugs are not without controversy. Several private insurance firms were under considerable pressure to cover birth control medications if they also covered ED drugs. In addition, ED drugs became an issue for public policy debate again in 2005 because, as a prescription medication, states and the federal government pay for such medications through the Medicaid program. After several states discovered that they had purchased ED medications for convicted sex offenders, other states began to ban Medicaid coverage for Viagra and all related medications (NPCC 2005a). In May 2005 Senator Charles Grassley (R-IA), chair of the Senate committee that has jurisdiction over federal health programs, introduced legislation to eliminate coverage of all such "lifestyle drugs" in the federal Medicare and Medicaid programs (Grassley 2005). In response, prostate cancer advocates argued that men with prostate cancer should not be punished or be required to "check their manhood at the door" (NPCC 2005b).

Agenda-Setting and Media Advocacy: A Framework for Research

The story of cancer politics unfolds with the assistance of a variety of actors, all of whom work to make sure policy leaders hear their stories. The saga involves attracting media attention, a component of agenda-setting. Advocates then use the media as a way to reach policymakers, a process called media advocacy. The following section presents these concepts and briefly describes the book's methodology.

AGENDA-SETTING

Since McCombs and Shaw coined the term *agenda setting* in 1972, both mass communication and public policy scholars have sought to understand what causes an issue to come onto the agenda and how it stays there (Shaw and McCombs 1977; Dearing and Rogers 1996). The agenda-setting process is "a competition among issue proponents for the attention of media professionals, the public and policy elites" (Dearing and Rogers 1996, 1–2). Scholars have noted the important role the media play in setting the public agenda and determining issue salience (e.g., Eaton 1989; Funkhouser 1973; Lang and Lang 1972). Agenda-setting theorists conceptualize three agendas, not one. The media agenda is composed of issues covered in the news media, the public agenda includes issues in the news media that have gained salience

(Shaw and McCombs 1997), and the policy agenda involves issues under consideration for government action. According to Roger Cobb and Charles Elder (1972), issues become important to public policymakers when they have captured the interest of either the attentive public (well-informed voters and grassroots members of interest groups) or the mass public.

Agenda-setting is difficult business. The clamor for attention by various issue proponents makes the policy debate noisy. Competition is fierce for a place on any of these agendas. Moreover, Deborah Stone (1989) notes that bringing an issue onto the media agenda or the public agenda is not sufficient to ensure policy change. Rather, the issue must be defined as one that is in the legitimate sphere of government action.

A few studies have applied agenda setting to health-care issues. Oscar Gandy (1982) in his critical analysis of agenda setting, argues the "war on cancer" and the proliferation of CAT scan technology were products of well-heeled individuals or corporations able to afford promoting their causes through advertising, public relations campaigns, and the like and thus influence policymakers. Reporters Haynes Johnson and David Broder maintain in their book *The System* (1996) that health care came onto the policy agenda with the surprise victory of Harris Wofford (D-PA) in the 1990 special election for the Senate seat left vacant with the death of Senator John Heinz (R-PA). Wofford campaigned on a platform of guaranteeing health care for everyone. Walsh-Childers (1994) reported how an Alabama newspaper's series on infant morality in the state positively influenced public attention and led to policy change. Another study of a Texas daily newspaper's series on children's issues reported significantly increased public funding after a year of editorial attention to the issue (Brewer and McCombs 1996)

In their study of AIDS and agenda-setting, mass communication scholars Everett Rogers, James Dearing, and S. Chang (1991) argue that the *New York Times*, a primary media agenda-setter, ignored the disease at its outset. Consequently, AIDS became salient only after it was a demonstrable public health crisis. Because the *New York Times* did not cover the disease, other media outlets, with the exception of the *San Francisco Chronicle*, ignored AIDS as a medical issue. Theodoulou, Guevara, and Minnassians (1996) later expanded this study and found statistically significant correlations between federal funding for AIDS and the media agenda.

Finally, Trumbo (1995) examined agenda-setting and global warming and found that sustained print media coverage, highlighted by bursts of television coverage, had a strong impact on public opinion polls. The polls, in turn, fueled additional media coverage.

MEDIA ADVOCACY

As Cobb and Elder point out, the first step in agenda-setting is to gain media attention. Advocacy groups, called grassroots survivors' organizations (GSOs) in this book, are instrumental in ensuring media awareness of important health policy issues. The importance of agenda-setting caught the attention of health promotion professionals who altered their perspectives on how to use media to influence health behavior.

Traditional public health communication strategies such as social marketing attempt to persuade individuals to adopt a specific innovation—essentially requiring acceptance of a new or different type of behavior (such as using sunscreen or stopping smoking) (Backer, Rogers, and Sopory 1992). Public health messages frequently use a variety of media to target those at the greatest risk for either adopting an unhealthy behavior or suffering from engaging in such behavior (Brown and Einsiedel 1990). Perhaps the longest-running traditional public health campaign is the federal government's effort to reduce the use of tobacco products. Since the publication of the first surgeon general's report in 1964, this public health campaign has included warning labels on cigarette packaging, banning tobacco advertisements on television, and other efforts (Derthick 2002). Over several decades, smoking rates declined, and the number of people who reported that they believed smoking caused cancer increased (Fritschler and Hoefler 1996). Other examples of the federal government's public health campaigns include the "Just Say No" anti-drug campaign, efforts to curb drinking and driving, and promoting sunscreen to prevent skin cancer.

But changing individual health behaviors is difficult. International health leaders who met in the late 1970s and 1980s concluded that to improve world health they needed to focus less on individual behavior and more on the environment that wasted natural and fiscal resources. In other words, public health leaders needed to be involved in the public policy process (Wallack and Dorfman 1996).

In the 1980s, grassroots organizations associated with AIDS, breast cancer, family planning, and alcohol and tobacco availability successfully developed new strategies designed to gain access to the media agenda, the public agenda, and, ultimately, the public policy agenda. Cooperation between public health professionals and grassroots groups was responsible for raising the political and social consciousness of the root causes of health problems. That blending of health issues, community action, and politics in the context of social justice is the basis of the media advocacy model.

National Breast Cancer Coalition (NBCC) President Fran Visco calls these strategies "systemic advocacy." As Visco recounted, she was first involved in breast cancer screening and follow-up care. Such "individual advocacy" is akin to traditional public health campaigns. The goal of the NBCC, however, is to change systems—whether political, governmental, medical, or research—and not focus on individual behavior (Visco 2005).

Media advocacy, therefore, applies the constructs of agenda-setting to public health campaigns and stresses the necessity for such campaigns to refocus media attention from individual behaviors to public policy. Unlike health promotion strategies that target primarily individual behavior, media advocacy has three target audiences. The primary target audience is an individual, organization, or group with the power to affect change. The secondary target is those individuals who can help influence the primary target audience, and the third target is the general public (Wallack and Dorfman 1996, 307). Thus, media advocacy strategies "exert pressure on those whose decisions influence that [public health] environment, [media advocacy is] a strategy that uses the mass media appropriately, aggressively and effectively to support the development of healthy public policies" (Wallack et al. 1993, 25). Media advocacy experts assert, for instance, that advertising campaigns such as the "Just Say No" campaign are relatively ineffective in stopping young people from drug usage. Such messages are effective in raising awareness and providing information but do not automatically result in a change of behavior (Baran and Davis 1995). Factors such as environment, self efficacy, and motivation; the differences between media; and the link between attitude change (I don't think drug usage is a safe practice) and behavior change (I will never try drugs) need to be factored into the process.

The literature suggests the media are good at raising awareness and agenda-setting but not at changing individual behaviors or opinions (McCombs and Shaw 1972).

SOCIAL MARKETING. Social marketing was first introduced by Kotler and Zaltman in 1971 and is widely practiced in the nonprofit sector. The process involves adapting the four Ps of marketing—product, price, place, and promotions—into the planning strategy. Product, in this context, becomes the actual idea or concept the organization is promoting, for example, "prostate cancer screening saves lives." Price becomes the cost of motivating the target audience to adopt this form of behavior, that is, how many lives would be saved through early detection. Place, defined in traditional marketing as the distribution channel, becomes how services are offered. The National Prostate Cancer Coalition (NPCC), for example, sends a mobile screening van to sports events to reach men in locations that are convenient to them. Finally, promotion plays its traditional role in the marketing mix, identifying the appropriate communication strategies and media vehicles to reach the target audience (Kotler, Roberto, and Lee 2002).

Those in favor of media advocacy are critical of social marketing's emphasis on individual or societal behavior change. They do acknowledge, however, that successful health campaigns use the structural components of social marketing in the planning process (Wallack and Dorfman 1996).[3] Furthermore, social marketing brought psycho-social and communication theory to the practice of health promotion.

FRAMING.   Media advocacy also incorporates the concept of framing. Robert Entman (1993) defines the process of framing as to "select some aspects of a perceived reality and make them more salient in a communicating text, in such a way as to promote a particular problem definition, causal interpretation, moral evaluation and/or treatment recommendation for the item described" (52).[4] The promotional message must be targeted to appropriate audiences and be carefully constructed or framed. This process determines whether the message is noticed, how it is remembered, and how it is acted upon. For example, the tobacco industry consistently frames smoking as an individual right, whereas anti-smoking advocates frame smoking as a public health menace, a drug delivery device, a problem among teenagers, and a pollutant (Menashe and Siegel 1998). Breast cancer advocacy groups generally frame their messages around three goals: raising awareness, providing public or private support, and funding more research (Moffett 2003). A survey of Australian women found more support for government funding of mammography if the issue was framed in terms of "relative risk reduction" (e.g., "program A will reduce the risk of dying from breast cancer by 34 percent") than other possible frames (Young, Davey, and Ward 2003).

These frames are illustrative of media advocacy that suggests that media access must be accompanied by an attempt to reframe the reporting of public health issues from individual problems to public policy. This is particularly important in the case of television, which tends to frame issues as individual problems rather than as individual consequences of larger social forces (Iyengar 1991). Consider how framing the message might play out in the case of prostate cancer—the problem of a late diagnosis is not the result of an individual's reluctance to have a PSA test but the government's refusal to cover the costs of the test. Wallack and Dorfman (1996) suggest media advocacy is organized around two framing concepts: framing for media access and framing for content. For advocacy organizations, media access requires an understanding of the nature of news and the news-gathering process. Framing for content implies an ability to provide news that has audience appeal and sustainability.

Numerous case studies point to successful media advocacy campaigns. Mothers Against Drunk Driving (MADD) provides two such examples. One is the effective use of publicized "letter grades" to rate states' drunk driving laws and then employing traditional lobbying techniques to secure tightening of state laws (Russell et al. 1995). Massachusetts MADD used media advocacy techniques to draw attention to a state senator who attempted to defeat a MADD-supported provision by using parliamentary rules (DeJong 1996). Similarly, the American Cancer Society used media advocacy techniques to generate "free media" in support of a ballot initiative to raise cigarette taxes ("Using Media Advocacy to Win Massachusetts Cigarette Tax Hike" 1994).

Sometimes "policymakers" are not elected officials but business executives targeted to effect a change in corporate policy. Examples include a media advocacy campaign to raise awareness of the connection between sexist alcohol advertising and domestic abuse (Woodruff 1996) and Philip Sokolof's efforts to call attention to high cholesterol in manufactured and fast foods and pressure food corporations to use ingredients that contribute to better health (Adams and Jennings 1993).

Few health campaigns were more systematically developed and evaluated than the Stanford Five-City Project. This ambitious undertaking was designed to build support for cardiovascular disease–related policy changes and encourage the adoption of heart-healthy behavior in five California communities. Launched in 1978, the fourteen-year study examined, among many issues, the effect of media advocacy efforts on newspaper coverage in treatment locations and how the stories were framed. In this case, was prevention emphasized over treatment? Results were mixed, and long-term media effects were weak. As the study pointed out, for media advocacy to work, "ongoing stimulation of news organizations is necessary" (Schooler, Sundar, and Flora 1996, 361).

Media advocacy works well as a framework for evaluating the efforts of grassroots survivor's organizations for several reasons. First, media advocacy was articulated by public health professionals. Because the field of public health is part of the health policy domain, that framework lends itself to this analysis. Second, media advocacy strategies allow scholars to understand how media can shape policy at numerous points in the process, including agenda-setting, problem definition, and even policy adoption. Third, the use of media strategies is not intended to replace traditional lobbying techniques. Rather, such strategies are designed to *augment* or *magnify* them, to use Christopher Foreman's (1995) terms. Fourth, media advocacy implies that both the public and the policymakers themselves are targets of media messages, which enforces scholarship on the importance of the media in the legislative process (Kedrowski 1996). Fifth, GSOs that use media advocacy techniques must continually redefine or frame the issues to sustain media and public attention.

CAUSE-RELATED MARKETING.   Cause-related marketing, a strategy that GSOs use, is easy to confuse with social marketing. Social marketing is the strategic method by which nonprofit organizations shape their health promotion or planning activities. Cause-related marketing, however, is the method some advocacy organizations use to sustain social marketing efforts or promote their visibility and economic viability

Cause-related marketing was initiated in the 1990s when industry realized that it needed to build relationships between institutions and strategic nonprofits. The relationships are characterized by an organization agreeing to contribute a designated amount of money to a cause when consumers purchase a particular product or service. These relationships by nature must be mutually beneficial to the organization and the cause it represents. Both breast and prostate cancer organizations use cause marketing to gain corporate support. Breast cancer organizations, however, particularly the Susan G. Komen Breast Cancer Foundation, have been successful in building cause marketing relationships with a variety of industries that target women consumers. As an example, Quilted Northern Ultra, a Georgia Pacific bathroom tissue, donates a portion of its profits to the foundation.

Cause-related marketing is not universally accepted by all advocacy organizations. In fact, the linking of advocacy causes with commercial products is an issue of much concern within the advocacy community.

SOCIAL CONSTRUCTION

Another concept, social construction, is used in this book to examine how various opinion leaders, groups, advocates, and the media interpret reality or events. Even disease, with its apparently irrefutable biological origins and observable response (or lack of response) to medical treatments is subject to shifting social interpretations. Cholera was once termed as the disease of the morally and physically weak (Rosenberg 1989). Tuberculosis was constructed as a disease of the virtuous and the well-to-do, whereas cancer was considered to be a shame and disgrace (Sontag 1978). AIDS has been socially constructed in various ways, including as a "gay plague," the "wrath of God upon sinners," and a tragic disease striking innocents (Donovan 2001).

Similarly, breast cancer has gone through several constructions. Initially considered untreatable, it became treatable—if not curable—with the advent of the Halsted mastectomy. The understanding of the disease has come under attack with competing interpretations of the word *cure* (Lerner 2000). The social construction of a disease may lend legitimacy to what is otherwise considered a trivial problem if not a problem at all. The American Society for Plastic and Reconstructive Surgeons, for example, defined women with small breasts as having a "disease" called micromastia. The cure was to implant silicone breast implants. Women who may be very content to be small-breasted would be surprised to learn that physical trait was considered a disease (Ferguson 2000, 70).

Methodology

This work uses a combination of qualitative and quantitative methods to study the relevant concepts of media advocacy, including media coverage, policy response, framing, social construction, and cause marketing. Media coverage is measured by news coverage of these diseases from 1980 to 1998 in five newspapers and on three television networks, omitting obituaries and letters to the editor. Among the newspapers selected for this study are two that are national in scope—the *New York Times* and the *Washington Post*—and are read by the intelligentsia, policymakers, and other journalists. The sample also includes three regional newspapers, the *Los Angeles Times,* the *Chicago Tribune,* and the *Atlanta Constitution.* These newspapers are important conduits of information in their areas of the country and are respected by reporters and policymakers in their regions. The three oldest television networks, ABC, NBC, and CBS, still are considered primary news sources in spite of shrinking ratings and the impact of cable news. Appropriate stories were identified through the newspapers' indexes, Lexis-Nexis, and the Vanderbilt Television News Abstracts. A total of 4,246 news stories were identified. Of these, 601 focused on prostate cancer. The remainder—3,645 stories—focused on breast cancer. Content analysis was used to analyze these data for a number of variables.[5]

Lexis-Nexis and the Library of Congress's THOMAS were used to identify the number of congressional hearings and pieces of legislation introduced on each disease from 1980 to 2004. Federal research funding data were collected from various public documents. These quantitative measures are augmented with qualitative data from more than thirty interviews with activists, policymakers, and reporters; a study of public documents; and participant observation.

Two Activist Movements Emerge

The National Breast Cancer Coalition is a grassroots advocacy
effort in the fight against breast cancer. In 1991, the Coalition was
formed with one mission, to eradicate breast cancer through *action*
and *advocacy.*
—Mission statement, National Breast Cancer Coalition

The National Prostate Cancer Coalition (NPCC) sets the standard for
rapidly reducing the burden of prostate cancer on American men
and their families through awareness, outreach, and advocacy.
—Mission statement, National Prostate Cancer Coalition

Organizations and activist movements are products of their histories. Experiences shape people, and people shape organizations and movements. In this case, the people who created the organizations in the breast cancer and prostate cancer movements share a common experience: cancer. Their reactions to cancer, however, are shaped by their history, personal experiences, and the gendered nature of these diseases. This chapter recounts the development of breast cancer and prostate cancer activist groups.

Breast Cancer Activism

Breast cancer activism may be relatively new, but breast cancer is not. Medical documents from Ancient Egypt include a description of what may be the earliest known case of breast cancer (Yalom 1997, 206). The historian James Olson (2002), in *Bathsheba's Breast,* paints a poignant picture of the butchery of early mastectomies and their high mortality rates (see also Leopold 1999; Yalom 1997). Olson also highlights prominent women who suffered from the disease over the centuries, including Abigail "Nabby" Adams, daughter of John and Abigail Adams; Mary Washington, mother of George Washington; and Alice Roosevelt Longworth, daughter of Theodore Roosevelt (Olson 2002).

Because of the sexualized nature of the breast in Western cultures, women who had symptoms of breast cancer were often ashamed to seek treatment and doctors were reluctant to examine women's breasts. When women did seek medical attention, they often waited until the tumors were ulcerated and the cancer had spread (Leopold 1999; Olson 2002; Yalom 1997).

In 1882 a surgeon at Johns Hopkins University Hospital, William Stewart Halsted, developed a new surgery to treat breast cancer: the "radical" or Halsted mastectomy. This procedure included removing not only the breast but also the underlying chest muscles and some of the lymph nodes under the arm. Halsted believed the cancer started in the breast tissue and then grew steadily outward to the chest muscles and the underlying bone before spreading to remote sites through the lymphatic system. Thus, he believed it was necessary to remove all affected tissue and much of the apparently healthy tissue around a tumor to be sure that the cancer was completely removed.[1] Halsted meticulously tracked his patients and published articles in which he asserted that women who had mastectomies lived longer than patients who did not (Lerner 2001). The Halsted mastectomy became the industry standard, and by the 1920s breast surgery had become the most commonly performed surgery in the world (Olson 2002, 69).

THE 1950S: REACH TO RECOVERY

A breast cancer survivor, Térèse Lasser, founded Reach to Recovery, an American Cancer Society program, in 1952. In this program, breast cancer survivors visit women hospitalized while recovering from mastectomies.[2] The volunteers provide advice on topics such as fashion and makeup, resuming sexual relations, and exercises to reduce swelling from lymphedema. Although the program was not aimed at turning breast cancer survivors into political activists, Lasser was strongly criticized by doctors, who saw her visits as interfering with the doctor-patient relationship. Despite this criticism, and despite being banned from certain hospitals, Lasser persevered (Olson 2002). Reach to Recovery still continues to be a strong outreach program.

THE 1970S: ROSE KUSHNER AND Y-ME

The Halsted mastectomy remained common medical practice for nearly a century and standard practice in the United States long after it had been abandoned in Europe. It was, however, never subjected to randomized clinical trials to document its effectiveness. In fact, its adherents opposed such trials as unnecessarily risking the lives of women.[3] The move away from the Halsted mastectomy in favor of lesser surgery is due in no small part to the efforts of Rose Kushner, a breast cancer activist first diagnosed in 1974. That year, breast cancer came into the public and media consciousness as a result of the diagnoses of First Lady Betty Ford and Margaretta Fitler Murphy "Happy" Rockefeller, wife of then-Vice President Nelson Rockefeller. Journalist Betty Rollin published *First You Cry* about the same time and became one of the first public figures to write a personal account of her battle with the disease.

Kushner was diagnosed with breast cancer when the women's health movement of the 1970s was at its peak. The movement incorporated two primary themes. The first, articulated by Barbara Ehrenriech and Deidre English (2005), documented how the medical profession systematically eliminated traditional women healers and midwives from the medical field. At the same time, the sexist medical establishment pathologized a number of women's experiences, defining women as "sick" even when well. The second theme concerned reproductive health care, including such issues as access to obstetricians and gynecologists who were not paternalistic and treated clientele with respect, access to legal abortions in the years before *Roe v. Wade,* access to birth control, protesting the use of low-income women as guinea pigs for medical residents and subjects of forced sterilizations, and calling attention to unnecessary hysterectomies and Cesarean sections (Driefus 1977; Luker 1984; Morgan 2002; Ruzek 1978). It was against this backdrop that Kushner began her crusade.

When Kushner discovered a lump in her breast she used her skills as a journalist to research the medical literature. Kushner was appalled that women would go under anesthesia and not know if they would wake up with one breast or two. As the result of her research, she decided to practice what would later be called "informed consent." In other words, Kushner wanted to separate her surgical biopsy from her treatment decision in order to have the time and opportunity to decide whether a mastectomy was appropriate. Moreover, she determined the Halsted mastectomy was out of date and unnecessarily drastic (Lerner 2001). The one-step procedure, in which a biopsy and a mastectomy were done in one surgery, without the woman regaining consciousness, did not give doctors an opportunity to stage tumors and test for metastases. A mastectomy is of no use if a woman already has terminal disease. Moreover, the one-step procedure did not provide women the opportunity to research treatment options (Olson 2002, 175–77).

After she recovered from surgery, Kushner began a campaign attacking both the one-step procedure and the Halsted mastectomy in favor of informed consent and the modified radical mastectomy. Influenced by the feminist movement (Costain 1992), Kushner rose to national prominence through publishing her books, maintaining telephone hotlines, and becoming an outspoken consumer advocate (Lerner 2001, 176–81). Kushner continued to work on breast cancer issues up until her death. Mary Rose Oakar recalls, "She called my staff person, Scott Frey, and said, 'Tell Mary Rose that I was really proud that she finally got mammography covered in the legislation. . . . But now she has to work on research.' . . . She went to Georgetown Hospital Lombardi Center and died a week later. She was still worrying about it [breast cancer], knowing that she was dying. She was so unselfish" (Oakar interview 2003).

The 1970s also marked the formation of the first national breast cancer organization. Established in 1978, Y-ME was founded by two breast cancer survivors, Ann Marcou and Mimi Kaplan, who had been introduced by a mutual acquaintance. Marcou and Kaplan recognized that they had a number of common concerns and founded a support group for women with breast cancer. According to Y-ME representatives, the organization outgrew its "kitchen table" origins and became affiliated with a local YWCA. The name does not refer to the self-pitying question, Why me? but instead was originally the YWCA and Me, then shortened to Y-ME. Today, Y-ME bills itself as the nation's foremost survivors' organization. Its national hotlines, available in both English and Spanish, are staffed by trained breast cancer survivors who provide support and information to those undergoing treatment as well as to their family members (Y-ME 2003a; Brinkman interview 2003).

THE 1980S: EARLY VICTORIES AND NEW ORGANIZATIONS

Breast cancer activism in the 1980s was characterized by the demise of the Halsted mastectomy and the establishment of new national organizations. Building upon the women's health movement, the publication of *Illness as Metaphor* by Susan Sontag and *Cancer Journals* by Audre Lorde, both of whom were feminists and breast cancer survivors, increased awareness of the issue among feminists (Kaufert 1998; Lorde 1980; Sontag 1978). Lorde, who had a mastectomy in 1978, provided one of the first feminist critiques of the Reach to Recovery program after she received a visit during her hospitalization: "The woman from Reach to Recovery, while quite admirable and even impressive in her own right, certainly did not speak to my experience or my concerns. . . . My primary concerns two days after mastectomy were hardly about what man I would capture or whether my old boyfriend would still find me attractive enough. . . . My concerns were about my chances for survival" (1980, 56).

Lorde chose not to wear a prosthesis, a decision that led to criticism. To do so, she argued, or to use breast implants, kept a woman focused on the cosmetic and forced her to "mourn the loss of her breast" in secret. Moreover, she urged other breast cancer survivors to stop wearing prostheses. "If we are to translate the silence surrounding breast cancer into language and action against this scourge," she asserted, "then the first step is that women with mastectomies must become visible to each other" (1980, 61).

In the 1980s, activists moved to promote informed consent laws at the state level. These laws specify that once a woman is diagnosed through a biopsy with breast cancer, her doctor will provide information on various treatment options and gain her consent before proceeding. That includes providing complete information about surgical options and alleviates the one-step procedure. Informed consent was part of a 1979 consensus document from the National Institutes of Health (NIH) outlining the best practices in breast cancer treatment. Rose Kushner, a consumer advocate on the panel, developed the specific language recommending informed consent (Kushner 1982; Lerner 2001). Expert recommendations aside, medical practices, especially in rural areas, changed slowly. As a result, activists turned to legislative action.

Informed consent legislation was introduced in twenty-two states and passed in sixteen. Just as Kushner's campaign against the Halsted mastectomy met with significant opposition from the medical community, state-level medical associations opposed most of this legislation. They argued that it was an assault upon doctors' professional autonomy and attacked the credibility of the women involved in the movement by making note of their emotional appeals (Berman 1994; Montini 1996, 1997). Despite this initial opposition, the use of the one-step procedure waned. Today the two-step procedure is standard practice.

The 1980s also saw the demise of the Halsted mastectomy. The same 1979 NIH document that recommended informed consent also recommended the radical mastectomy be abandoned in favor of a modified radical mastectomy that left in place most lymph nodes and the chest muscles. Some surgeons rebelled against the NIH recommendation, however, asserting that the document interfered with their professional autonomy. Others continued to believe that anything less than the Halsted mastectomy endangered women's lives. Eventually, supporters of the Halsted mastectomy retired or died, and lesser surgeries became standard practice (Lerner 2001).

Two national breast cancer organizations, the Susan G. Komen Foundation and the National Alliance of Breast Cancer Organizations (NABCO), were established in 1982. Nancy Brinker initiated the the Komen Foundation and named it in honor of her sister, Susan, who died of breast cancer. The organization is now a major source of private funds for breast cancer research. Through its Race for the Cure and other fund-raising efforts, the Komen Foundation has provided more than $180 million for breast cancer research. Komen has more than a hundred affiliates in forty-seven states and views breast cancer advocacy as a local, state, and federal crusade. The organization emphasizes the power of local activists to tell their stories to policymakers and also maintains a virtual interactive Web site with access to federal elected officials (Susan G. Komen Foundation 2005).

NABCO was co-founded by Rose Kushner and led by Amy Langer, a breast cancer survivor. The private organization was designed to provide information, resources, and referrals to persons diagnosed with the disease and to their families, the media, and medical personnel. NABCO had a searchable database of support groups nationwide as well as listings of support groups in Canada and those specifically targeted to lesbians or men with breast cancer (NABCO 2003a). The organization dissolved in 2004, largely because other breast cancer organizations subsumed its functions. Apparently, there were also fund-raising difficulties.

In 1989, the American Cancer Society created a new program for women undergoing cancer treatment: Look Good . . . Feel Better. Through it, women learn about cosmetics and skin and nail care, and those facing hair loss receive special information on wearing scarves, wigs, and turbans. Co-founded by the Cosmetic, Toiletry and Fragrance Association, Look Good . . . Feel Better seeks to "teach female cancer patients beauty techniques to help restore their appearance and self-image during chemotherapy and radiation treatments" (ACS 2003f).

THE 1990S: COALITION-BUILDING

Breast cancer activism took another turn in the 1990s, with the development of grassroots advocacy organizations. In many cases women with breast cancer joined patient support groups, which provided much-needed information about doctors, treatment options, and possible side effects as well as emotional support. Again, as a hallmark of the women's health movement, some adopted the moniker "patient advocacy groups" with the desire to empower patients to make their own treatment decisions (Laurence 1994).

Almost simultaneously, local patient support groups on the East and West Coasts became politicized. As Maureen Casamayou (2001, 65–76) recounts, their shared experiences developed into a "collective entrepreneurism." In other words, the groups became politicized as their shared experiences with breast cancer led to shared risk-taking. An unusual convergence of events led to the development of breast cancer advocacy groups. First, many of the women who began to develop breast cancer in the late 1980s and early 1990s were well-educated, politically skilled, and had been involved in the civil rights and feminist movements. They considered breast cancer as another way to move from the "personal" to the "political"—the hallmark of the American contemporary women's movement (Altman 1996; Ferraro 1993; Langer and Dow 1994). In fact, one book written by Virginia Soffa, then a Vermont-based breast cancer activist, is entitled *The Journey beyond Breast Cancer: From the Personal to the Political* (1994).

The disparate local movements coalesced into a national organization with the founding of the National Breast Cancer Coalition (NBCC) in 1991. The coalition was founded by breast cancer activists Susan Hester, director of the Mary-Helen Mautner Project for Lesbians with Cancer in Washington, D.C.; Amy Langer of NABCO; and Susan Love, a breast cancer surgeon and author of the best-seller *Dr. Susan Love's Breast Book* (Altman 1996, 315). Love's biographer writes that the surgeon came upon the idea of creating a political organization while on a 1990 book tour:

> The book tour was a revelation to her. No matter where Love went there were dozens of women waiting to talk to her, not just about their medical plight but about what they could do to get more money for medical research, to get the government to pay attention. . . . In Salt Lake City, she jokingly suggested to six hundred women, "Maybe we ought to march topless on the White House. That should get President [G. H. W.] Bush's attention." After the speech a group of women rushed to the podium to ask if there was a date set for the march. And Love thought: if the proper ladies of Salt Lake City are ready to march through the streets of the nation's capitol with their shirts off, it is time to organize. (Stabiner 1997, 58–59; see also Love and Lindsey 1995, 518)

The NBCC set three major goals for its early years: to promote research into causes and cures for breast cancer; to improve access to high-quality screening, diagnosis, and treatment; and to increase "the involvement and influence" of breast cancer patients (Langer 1992). Their timing was fortuitous. It built upon a growing awareness that women's health issues were neglected by the medical-scientific establishment and the U.S. government. By 2005 the NBCC could boast a membership of six hundred organizations and seventy thousand individual members (NBCC 2005a).

The contemporary breast cancer movement is vast. Countless local and statewide support and advocacy groups and nearly a half-dozen national organizations claim a niche within it. Y-ME is a survivors' support network and coordinates outreach to non-English-speaking women (2005). The Komen Foundation raises money for research and local research and education. The Young Survival Coalition (2003) calls attention to the special concerns of women diagnosed before age forty. The Sisters Network (2003) focuses on the particular needs of African American women. And, finally, the NBCC is the primary advocacy organization. Breast cancer advocacy is now an international movement, with the NBCC and other organizations attempting to export the notions of patient empowerment and grassroots lobbying to other countries (Batt 1994; NBCC 1997a, 1999).

ADOPTION AND ADAPTATION: MODELING THE SUCCESS OF THE AIDS MOVEMENT

Breast cancer activists across the country were influenced by AIDS activists and sought advice from them on training and tactics, navigating the bureaucracy, and understanding the drug approval process (Altman 1996; Casamayou 2001; Epstein 1996; Ferraro 1993; Kaufert 1998). In the words of NBCC President Fran Visco, "The NBCC was formed to offer breast cancer what AIDS activists had offered AIDS" (Visco 2005).

Some breast cancer groups, especially those based in northern California, where AIDS has had the greatest impact and is home to several AIDS activist organizations, have adopted some of the more confrontational, disruptive techniques of the AIDS movement. One group, for example, identified only by the pseudonym NORCAL, attempted to secure the use of a then-experimental drug on a compassionate use basis for a local woman. After the drug company denied the request, activists in NORCAL conducted "zaps"—repeated telephone calls and faxes designed to tie up the company's communication system—and staged a "die-in" at company headquarters. They also lobbied the Food and Drug Administration (FDA) to streamline the drug approval process (Anglin 1997). Similarly, Breast Cancer Action, a San Francisco–based activist group, organized a "Bay Area Women and Cancer Walk" with several other breast cancer organizations, such as those focused on the needs of Vietnamese women and Latinas with breast cancer, as an alternative to the Komen Foundation's Race for the Cure. Another event, a "toxic tour" through downtown San Francisco, was designed to call attention to industrial pollutants that might be linked to breast cancer (Klawiter 2000).

Other techniques are uniquely suited to breast cancer activists but take on a strident tone reminiscent of AIDS demonstrations. For instance, some breast cancer patients have appeared topless in gay pride parades (Yalom 1997), on calendars (Lerner 2001), or on the cover of the *New York Times Magazine* (Ferraro 1993). The latter, accompanied by the words "you can't look away anymore" by the artist Matuschka, is the most famous of several works in which she photographed her nude body after her mastectomy in an effort to raise awareness of breast cancer (Amaya 2004; Peterson and Matuschka 2004).

Others have openly disparaged the American Cancer Society's Reach to Recovery and Look Good . . . Feel Better programs. In a critique reminiscent of Audre Lorde's a decade earlier, activists decried the programs' emphases on wearing a prosthesis, wig, and makeup as an attempt to hide the effects of surgery and chemotherapy. They believe such programs encourage women to deny their disease by hiding behind props and makeup and reconstructing the image of a healthy body (Batt 1994; Read 1995). In the words of activist Ellen Hobbs, who removed her wig and breast prosthesis in a public demonstration in 1991, "I don't feel better and I won't feel better until more research is done into this horrible disease" (as quoted in Brenner 2000, 331). Similarly, the Young Survival Coalition found that material provided by Reach to Recovery did not speak to the concerns of young breast cancer survivors and worked with a Reach to Recovery program in New York City to develop brochures specifically targeted to that group (Young Survival Coalition 2002).

Breast cancer activists have adopted conventional lobbying techniques as well. The NBCC, for example, collected 2.6 million signatures in 1993 to present to executive and legislative officials. Every year the organization develops a breast cancer platform, rates legislators on their support of the NBCC's agenda, and uses grassroots and national advocates to lobby for myriad legislative initiatives (NBCC 2005b; Stabiner 1997).

The breast cancer movement has its detractors. First, many scientists thought Congress overstepped its legitimate bounds by earmarking funds for breast cancer research in response to pressure from breast cancer advocates. Some believed funds were diverted from other cancers or that the funds available exceeded what was needed for adequate support of high-quality research, leaving the government to fund poorly conceived projects simply because they dealt with breast cancer ("Activism's Toll" 1992; Anderson 1992; Langer and Dow 1994; Marshall 1993a; see also chapter 9).

Second, the breast cancer movement is primarily composed of middle-aged, middle-class, well-educated, heterosexual white women. As in the case of the women's health movement before it (Morgan 2002; Ruzek 1978), some have criticized the breast cancer movement as being insensitive to the needs of women who do not fit that paradigm. In her analysis of Boston-area breast cancer activists, Boehmer (2000) chides many of the heterosexual, white women in the movement for being insensitive to the differential impacts of the disease on women of color and lesbians.

Finally, without mentioning any particular breast cancer organization, an article in a 1997 issue of the *New England Journal of Medicine* criticized the final NIH recommendations on mammography for women aged forty to forty-nine. The author, Suzanne Fletcher of the Harvard Medical School, charged that they were contrary to current medical wisdom and that medical recommendations would be made "in the halls of Congress, and on the front page of the *New York Times,* or as the lead story on ABC World News Tonight. . . . When the discussion of medical science moves from an NIH auditorium to a hearing room in the Senate Office Building, the ground rules change. Whereas anecdotes constitute weak evidence in medical science, personal stories are powerful persuaders in a Senate hearing" (1997, 1181–82).

Prostate Cancer Activism

In some ways the prostate cancer movement is an indirect result of the development of the prostate specific antigen (PSA) blood test. Before that, prostate cancer primarily was detected at a late stage, when the prognosis was usually poor. With the PSA test, however, the number of men diagnosed with prostate cancer began to rise dramatically, as did the need for information about the disease and treatment options (Caputi interview 2003). Moreover, survival rates increased, creating a critical mass of persons who would later form the core of the prostate cancer activist community.

THE 1980S: FIRST AWARENESS EFFORTS

This decade saw the establishment of three organizations dedicated to raising awareness of prostate cancer: the American Prostate Society, Patient Advocates for Advanced Cancer Treatment (PAACT), and Prostate Cancer Education Council (PCEC). The American Prostate Society is an independent nonprofit corporation that provides information on four conditions related to the prostate: prostate cancer, prostatitis, benign prostate hyperplasia, and impotence. Its mission is strictly to raise awareness and provide information (American Prostate Society 2001). PAACT was established in 1984 by Lloyd Ney, who had been diagnosed with advanced prostate cancer in 1983 and given only six months to live. Ney, who lived until 1998, credited combined-hormonal therapy with saving his life. Believing that the American medical establishment provided poor care to men with prostate cancer, he founded PAACT to inform them about possible treatment options (PAACT 2003). The third organization, the PCEC, composed of physicians, scientists, health educators, and patients, was established in 1988 to provide free and low-cost prostate cancer screenings to men around the country during the third week in September, which the PCEC dubbed "Prostate Cancer Awareness Week." The organization maintains that these screenings have provided substantial evidence to medical researchers on the value of combining the PSA test with digital rectal examinations. The PCEC reports having screened millions of men since 1989, the first year of its effort (PCEC 2003).

THE EARLY 1990S: MOMENTUM BUILDS

In 1991 the former U.S. senator and 1996 Republican presidential nominee Bob Dole was diagnosed with prostate cancer (Abrams and Brody 1998). He became perhaps the most famous prostate cancer survivor in the United States. Not only did he go public at the time of his diagnosis, but he also remains outspoken about the disease, his treatment, and his long-term recovery.

About the same time, the men's health movement, as a counterpart to the women's health movement, gathered momentum. It is loosely organized around gender-specific diseases such as prostate and testicular cancer and concern for men's shorter life expectancy and increased susceptibility to injury and disease (Schofield et al. 2000). Men's health activists see the world of medical research far differently than women's health activists, who argue that the medical research community neglected women. Men's health advocates argue that men were, in fact, victims of their own chivalry and made guinea pigs for possibly dangerous, experimental treatments before they were given to women (Jaffee 1997). Moreover, they believe that the focus on women's health is to the detriment of men, who die younger and are more likely to be victims of violence and disease. The Men's Health Network, founded in 1992 (Men's Health Network 2002), advocates the creation of an Office of Men's Health to parallel the existing Office of Women's Health in the Department of Health and Human Services (Office of Men's Health Resource Center 2002).

Against this backdrop, two prostate cancer support organizations were founded in 1990. The first, Man to Man, is the brainchild of a prostate cancer survivor, James Mullen. Man to Man is a program of the American Cancer Society and provides information, education, and support to those with prostate cancer and their wives (ACS 2003b). The second support organization is US TOO! International. Founded in the Chicago area, its five co-founders were patients of Dr. Jerry Chodak at the University of Chicago. US TOO! International now has more than 320 chapters around the country and in several other countries as well (US TOO! 2005).

In 1993 the former junk-bond-financier-turned-philanthropist Michael Milken founded CaP CURE, now the Prostate Cancer Foundation (PCF). Milken was diagnosed with prostate cancer shortly after he was released from prison, where he had served a sentence for securities fraud (Daniels 2004). The PCF is a private foundation that raises money to fund prostate cancer research and views its mission as unique. The foundation makes grants that are only one year in duration to fund unusual, potentially pathbreaking avenues of research. Its goal is to enable researchers to gain the promising preliminary results they need to qualify for grants from the National Cancer Institute or other more mainstream sources of medical research funding (Milken 2002; Soule interview 2003).[4]

In 1994 a prostate cancer survivor and former oil company executive, William Roher, founded Prostate Action, Inc. (PROACT). Its mission is to promote awareness and provide information about prostate cancer through its newsletter *Perspectives* and its Web site (PROACT 2003a, 2003b).

THE MID-1990S: ADVOCACY BEGINS

By the mid-1990s the first prostate cancer lobbyists began to work on Capitol Hill. Ironically, both were women. Betty Gallo was the wife of Representative Dean Gallo (D-NJ), who died of prostate cancer in 1994, and Brooke Moran was from the American Foundation for Urologic Disease (AFUD) (Jaffee 1997). Although AFUD advocates for a variety of urological disorders, prostate cancer is the one with the "greatest public health impact" (Caputi interview 2003; Manne 2002).

The playing field altered in 1996 with the founding of the National Prostate Cancer Coalition (NPCC), which sought to bring together disparate organizations interested in prostate cancer to create a permanent lobbying organization. Its founding members included US TOO! International, CaP CURE, and the Men's Health Network, American Prostate Society, and American Urological Association. The NPCC is composed of organizational "partners" and corporate "sponsors" and an undisclosed number of individual supporters (NPCC 2002a). The coalition also works with a variety of state coalitions to coordinate its advocacy activities at the grassroots level even though the state coalitions are not required to support the NPCC financially. Susan Dimock (2003) calls this effort "grasstops advocacy," whereby a national organization attempts to create a grassroots movement to distinguish it from a grassroots movement that coalesces into a national force. In addition, CaP Cure and US TOO! International have their own advocacy initiatives that complement the activities of the NPCC (US TOO! International 2005).

The primary agenda item for the NPCC is to increase government funding for prostate cancer research. As men's health activists see it, nowhere is the gender gap on health issues greater than in federal support for prostate cancer research when compared to breast cancer research. Because of the NBCC's successful lobbying efforts of the early 1990s, the traditional funding gap between these two diseases increased substantially (chapter 6). In addition, the NPCC supports numerous efforts to promote screening as well as increased public awareness of the disease and access to new and more effective treatments.

In 1998 the NPCC was joined by the Prostate Cancer Action Network (PCAN), which several prostate cancer activists based in western states formed at a Phoenix, Arizona, conference. Its initial agenda item was to oppose Medicare's "least costly alternative" policy, which substituted one drug for the treatment of prostate cancer with another. PCAN now monitors a number of issues before Congress and uses its Web site as a "toolbox" to communicate with activists and organize grassroots advocacy efforts (PCAN 2003).

THE 2000S: DIVERSIFYING THE MOVEMENT

As in the breast cancer movement, most prostate cancer organizations and support groups were founded by, and largely cater to, well-educated, middle- and upper-class white men.[5] Given that African American men have increased risk of prostate cancer, however, reaching that population is particularly important. The hallmark of the first decade of twenty-first century was the development of various organizations seeking to raise awareness and mobilize the African American community and other underrepresented groups.

Two national organizations adopted prostate cancer as an agenda item: 100 Black Men of America and the Congressional Black Caucus Foundation (CBCF). In 2000, 100 Black Men of America worked with the American Cancer Society to create Let's Talk About It, a program to raise awareness of prostate cancer risk and promote screening among African American men, particularly those in the New York area (ACS 2003g). Similarly, the CBCF has co-sponsored a prostate cancer conference with the NPCC and also includes information about prostate cancer on its health Web site (CBCF 2003a). Two prominent African American prostate cancer survivors have also established foundations under their own names: a former member of the Temptations, Damon Harris, and Minister Louis Farrakhan. Both foundations are dedicated to raising awareness of prostate cancer among African American men and raising money for research or financial assistance for those undergoing treatment (Damon Harris Cancer Foundation 2003; CBCF 2003b).

Most efforts are at the local level, however. The Prostate Cancer Coalition of North Carolina, for example, initiated an effort to reduce prostate cancer deaths in the state by 50 percent in five years, and a pilot program was tested in eastern North Carolina, which has a particularly high concentration of African American residents (Botts interview 2003; "Saving Lives in North Carolina" 2003). Similarly, prostate cancer survivor Calvin Martin instituted Brother to Brother, a variant of the Man to Man program, in Harlem under the auspices of the American Cancer Society. Brother to Brother now has several chapters in the greater New York City area (ACS 2002f; personal communication July 29, 2003). Another effort to reach underserved populations was through Malecare, a New York City–based prostate cancer support group that was the first to develop programs for gay and transgendered men and women and Spanish-speaking men (Malecare 2003).

ADOPTION AND ADAPTATION:
MODELING THE SUCCESS OF THE BREAST CANCER MOVEMENT

The breast cancer movement and its success seem constantly on the minds of many prostate cancer activists.[6] Just as breast cancer activists adopted and adapted many of the techniques used by the AIDS movement, the prostate cancer movement frequently deliberately patterns itself after various components of the breast cancer movement. Consider US TOO! International. The organization's oral history states that its name is derived from the breast cancer group Y-ME, which is also headquartered in the Chicago area. Apparently, the US TOO! founders invited a director from Y-ME to attend an early meeting of the organization and discovered that they confronted many of the same problems as breast cancer survivors. Thus, they concluded, it's not just "me" but "us, too!" (Page interview 2003).

The similarities continue with the founding of the National Prostate Cancer Coalition. Not only is its name remarkably similar to that of the National Breast Cancer Coalition but its mission as primarily a lobbying organization is also much the same. Symbolically, the keynote speaker at the NPCC's organizational conference was Jane Reese-Coulburne, the former vice president of the National Breast Cancer Coalition (Men's Health Network 1998). The NPCC also compares itself to the mission of the Komen Foundation in its efforts to raise awareness of the disease through local fund-raisers. One of its national events, the Urban Challenge—a combination of urban foot race and trivia contest—used the following description: "Much like breast cancer has benefited from the Susan G. Kolman's Race for a Cure [sic], Urban Challenge aims to raise the level of prostate cancer awareness while benefiting the efforts of the National Prostate Cancer Coalition" (NPCC 2003a).

Comparisons are present in other ways as well. As Michael Korda states, "Prostate cancer is the male equivalent of breast cancer" (1996, 3). John Page notes that the tumors share much of the same biology (interview 2003); moreover, men who have a mutated form of the breast cancer gene BRCA2 are at higher risk of developing prostate cancer ("Prostate Cancer: BRCA2 Is a High Risk" 2002).

Yet prostate cancer activists have not adopted the more confrontational tactics of the AIDS or breast cancer movements. Their Web sites, with advocates' toolkits, read like textbooks for grassroots lobbying. There are tips on writing letters to the editor and courting editorial boards, exhortations to write to members of Congress and ask them to co-sponsor legislation or sign "Dear Colleague" letters, updates on the appropriations process, and lists of legislative achievements. They even may distribute a draft letter via e-mail. The NPCC published a series on the appropriations process called "Show me the money!!" in its electronic newsletter (NPCC Smartbrief 2001). In addition, they mimic breast cancer activists in uncontroversial ways. Prostate cancer activists persuaded President George W. Bush to declare September as Prostate Cancer Awareness Month, adopted the blue ribbon as a symbol of the movement (CaP CURE 2002b), supported a commemorative postage stamp and now promote a "semi-postal" stamp patterned after the breast cancer "semi-postal" stamp, and participated in the Cancer March in Washington in 1998.

Critical differences exist, however, between the two movements, the first being that the breast cancer movement developed from the ground up, where several local and statewide groups came together to form a national organization (Casamayou 2001). Although some local chapters, such as the Breast Cancer Coalition of North Carolina, formed after the creation of the NBCC (Andrews interview 2003), the NBCC is largely a product of the "collective entrepreneurism" of state and local organizations. By contrast, the NPCC's founding members were primarily national organizations; thus it is building a grassroots network from the top down. The NPCC, which has no grassroots membership of its own under its by-laws, depends upon state coalitions to provide clout at the local level. Its staff provides technical assistance to state-level advocacy groups in the form of conferences, works with local people interested in starting a coalition, and organizes periodic advocacy conference calls during which state activists discuss fund-raising and other activities (Botts interview 2003).

The second difference lies in that fact that not all prostate cancer organizations consider themselves as analogous to breast cancer organizations. For all the mimicking that NPCC and US TOO! International may do, the Prostate Cancer Foundation does not consider itself as prostate cancer's Komen Foundation, even though it appears to have a similar mission. The Komen Foundation has a reputation for taking a mainstream approach to breast cancer issues, seeking to raise awareness without becoming immersed in treatment or screening controversies and funding established avenues of research (Brenner 2000). By contrast, the PCF sees itself as unique. It uses a venture-capital mentality: fund high-risk research in the hope of producing high rewards. The PCF strives to be "anti-bureaucratic," as evidenced by its five-to-ten-page research proposals (Soule interview 2003).

A third difference between the two movements concerns the kinds of activities in which prostate cancer and breast cancer survivors are willing to participate. Certainly, as Michael Korda observed, "There are models who walk around in t-shirts with targets printed over their breasts, but there is no comparable campaign to alert men to prostate cancer" (1996, 3). The breast cancer movement, however, undertakes events that focus on physical activity of survivors and surrogates: the *Race* for the Cure, the Avon Breast Cancer *Walk,* Y-ME's annual Mother's Day *Walk* in three major U.S. cities, mountain climbing, or competitive rowing. As one prostate cancer activist said, "I can't get men to go on a walk" (interview 2003). Prostate cancer activities are more passive: a mobile screening van or watching a sports event such as major league baseball or professional golf. Notably, the Urban Challenge, which raised money for the NPCC in 2003, was not just targeted to prostate cancer survivors but to their surrogates as well. Urban Challenge literature exhorted potential participants to "do it for Dad" (NPCC 2003a). The differences even filter to lobbying efforts on Capitol Hill. As one congressional staff member familiar with both movements said, "I hear from breast cancer survivors all the time. They have a group in [member's state] . . . I don't ever recall talking to a prostate cancer survivor" (interview 2003).

Finally, another critical difference between the two movements is the asymmetric levels of awareness of each other. Certainly, breast cancer and prostate cancer are only two of a panoply of "disease groups" competing for the attention of policymakers, congressional staff, foundations and corporations, the media, and the public. Within that context, however, it was abundantly apparent that prostate cancer activists were very aware of the breast cancer movement and the essential facts surrounding the disease. The same *cannot* be said of breast cancer activists. In our interviewing process, for example, two individuals involved with breast cancer issues repeatedly maintained that prostate cancer was less serious than breast cancer, a statement belied by the facts. Many breast cancer activists were reluctant to draw comparisons between their experiences and the prostate cancer movement, citing their own ignorance. If breast cancer activists mentioned prostate cancer at all, it was in the context of a joke.[7] One health reporter even stated in 2003, "I wasn't even aware that there was a prostate cancer movement."

RELUCTANT CHAMPIONS

The prostate cancer movement developed only recently because men are reluctant to discuss their disease openly. Consequently, the movement has been shaped by this same reticence. As Michael Korda wrote of his diagnosis and treatment:

> Prostate cancer is the biggest fear of most men. It carries not only the fear of dying, like all cancer, but fears that go to the very core of masculinity—for the treatment of prostate cancer, whatever form it takes, almost invariably carries with it well-known risks of incontinence and impotence that strike directly at any man's self-image, pride and enjoyment of life, and which, by their very nature make men reticent on the subject. It is precisely this reticence which makes prostate cancer such a deadly, silent scourge. Women talk to each other about their bodies. Men do not, especially when their ability to function sexually is at risk. (1996, 4–5)

John Page, the former president and chief executive officer of US TOO! International, in a February 2003 interview agreed:

> We're in the 1985 range of where breast cancer was. It's still sort of taboo. A lot of men don't want to talk about prostate cancer, much less come out and say "I've had prostate cancer." When I was at a research conference, our booth was next to the women from [the Susan G.] Komen [Foundation]. You couldn't stop women from talking about their disease. . . . Men would walk down the aisle, and would purposely walk on the other side of the aisle, rather than walk past our booth and not even look at the booth. . . . At a heavily male-dominated conference, I had as many women stop at the booth to get information for their husbands and fathers, as I did men. And that's fairly typical.

Reluctance to discuss the disease means that men often have very little information available to them about treatment options and possible side affects.
They also may not be empowered patients who seek an active role in determining treatment. John Page again saw important differences between the
experiences of men with prostate cancer and women with breast cancer:

> Men don't even know that they could be at risk of recurrence. . . . Women go
> to an oncologist. Men go to a urologist. . . . Either doctors don't talk about it
> [side effects or recurrence] or men don't listen to it, because they don't want
> to hear it. . . . If you're diagnosed with breast cancer, you walk out of that
> initial diagnosis with probably a pink Komen bag that contains information
> about the disease, the treatment options. . . . You're supposed to look at the
> stuff in there and come back to your doctor with a list of questions to help
> determine what your best treatment is. . . . When a man walks out after his
> initial diagnosis, he'll probably have a card saying, "Come in on Tuesday and
> we'll do surgery on you."

That reluctance also means that men are less willing to engage in political
action. Prostate cancer survivor Senator Ted Stevens (R-AK) related how when
he attended a support group meeting in his home state, a friend approached
him and said, "You shouldn't be talking about this. It's a private, male thing"
(as quoted in Jaffee 1997).

One possible reason for reluctance is that prostate cancer typically strikes
men who are older than women with breast cancer. The typical man with
prostate cancer is in his mid-sixties or older, whereas breast cancer usually
strikes women in their fifties and older. As a result, men diagnosed with prostate cancer in the early part of the twenty-first century were of the Korean
War generation; women diagnosed with breast cancer came of age politically
during the women's rights/Vietnam War/civil rights era. Consequently, their
lobbying tactics, interest in a new cause, and willingness to discuss personal
issues differ. As one prostate cancer activist states, "These men have already
done all their volunteer work" (Kossover interview 2003).

The prostate cancer movement also faced some difficulties in its early
years, when there was conflict between the major prostate cancer organizations. US TOO! International joined the NPCC as a founding member but
then left the coalition in 2001, stating a desire to return to its core mission
("International Support Group, US TOO! Quits US Prostate Cancer Coalition" 2001). Although the PCF is still a member of the NPCC, some state
advocates have expressed frustration that the foundation was not an active
participant. John Page of US TOO! commented that the early leadership of

the groups sometimes seemed "to have blinders on" and worked at cross-purposes with each other. Each wanted to claim ownership of all activities, raising awareness, increasing funding, and lobbying, as evidenced in the preceding descriptions of prostate cancer groups. Moreover, they did not cooperate. Issues such as screening recommendations divided them. Changes in leadership in some organizations and clarifying each organization's niche has improved the relationships, however.

Summary

Survivors active in either the breast cancer or prostate cancer movements share one important experience: a cancer diagnosis. The way in which men and women respond politically to cancer, however, differs. The breast cancer movement draws upon a long history of activism, and most breast cancer survivors also have a different political socialization from most prostate cancer survivors. These factors lead one group to become assertive advocates while others remain reluctant champions. In the next chapter, we explore these differences in greater detail.

2

A Typology of Grassroots Survivors' Organizations

> I was living my life backwards. . . . There was a point when I was putting Post-it Notes on things I had borrowed so they would be returned to the right person after my death. I was literally waiting to die.
>
> —Robert Young

> I was diagnosed with breast cancer when I was only twenty-eight. Even after completing treatment, each day is still scary. I am involved because I could have a recurrence. There's so much we don't know and I want to make sure there are as few barriers as possible for those answers to be discovered. I might need them.
>
> —Heather Hill

Countless books and articles have been written about the influence of interest groups in American politics. Pluralist writers such as Robert Dahl (1961) see interest groups as a means through which ordinary citizens may influence the political system. Others believe interest groups stymie the political process and maintain the privileged position of elites (Olson 1982; Schattschneider 1960). Reflecting the latter, for decades health interest groups represented primarily health-care professionals and health-care industries such as hospitals and pharmaceutical companies.

A parallel force is a particular type of social movement that we label as "grassroots survivors' organizations" (GSOs). A social movement is a widespread grassroots organization or collection of organizations that focuses on a problem its activists believe is the responsibility of government to remedy. Such movements are frequently—but not always—composed of individuals outside the mainstream of politics. The activists in civil rights and women's rights movements of the 1960s often included protest and other forms of "outsider" political activity, but as they gained credibility they also partici-pated in more traditional "insider tactics" (Moffett 2003).

Perhaps the earliest disease-related social movement centered around tem-perance, which began in earnest in the 1870s and was populated by women victimized by the men in their lives who abused alcohol. Often, women were beaten by drunken husbands, or they and their children starved if the hus-bands spent the family's income at a local saloon (Bordin 1981). The current wave of disease activism began with the occupational health movements of the 1970s, which were followed by the AIDS movement of the 1980s.

The purpose of this chapter is threefold. First, we develop a typology of grassroots survivors' organizations—characteristics of apparently successful "disease groups" or GSOs. Second, we use the history described in chapter 1 to assess the degree to which these movements fit the typology of a GSO. Third, we analyze the usefulness of this typology in terms of understanding the differences between the breast cancer and prostate cancer movements in particular and speculate on its usefulness in understanding the politics of disease more generally.

Grassroots Survivor Organizations

THE POLITICS OF DISEASE

Since the early 1990s scholars have pointed to the proliferation of interest groups focused on health policy (Heinz et al. 1993; M. Peterson 1993). Among such groups are those that claim to represent consumers' interests, also known as public interest groups. Such groups "lobby for the collective good, which will not selectively benefit the membership of the organizations" (Berry 1977, 7). So-called disease groups fall into the category of public interest lobbies. Some, such as the March of Dimes, American Heart Association, and Ameri-can Cancer Society, have been active for decades. Historically, however, medi-cal professionals and philanthropists dominated the established organizations; persons who had been diagnosed with, or who survived, the disease did not play major leadership roles (Arno and Feiden 1992, 243).

OCCUPATIONAL HEALTH. Beginning in the late 1960s, a new type of dis-ease group emerged in which people with the disease were the activists. The first such groups were in the field of occupational health—the Black Lung Association and the Brown Lung Association—and composed primarily of workers and retirees who developed severe breathing problems from inhal-ing either coal dust in mines or cotton dust in textile manufacturing. Their family members also participated. Notably, however, the organizing impetus came from *outside* the workers or the unions, usually in the form of young community activists who gained experience in the poor peoples' movements of the 1960s and 1970s.

Both movements enjoyed some important successes in their day. The Black Lung Association worked with the United Mine Workers Union to coordinate strikes to pressure the West Virginia state legislature and the U.S. Congress to create black lung compensation programs. The Brown Lung Association's efforts resulted in more stringent cotton dust standards in textile mills. Both groups also worked within the Social Security Administration and with workers' compensation programs to secure disability benefits for members (Botsch 1993; Judkins 1986).

ENVIRONMENTAL HEALTH. In the 1970s a variety of unrelated health issues pointed to the growing sophistication of advocacy organizations. Similar to the brown lung and black lung movements, whose members sicken as a result of industrial exposure, were those involved in the environmental movement and focused on the health hazards accompanying fallout from nuclear testing and chemical pollution.

During the 1950s the Atomic Energy Commission conducted almost a hundred denotations of atomic devices in rural Nevada (Ball 1986). People in rural Nevada, Arizona, and Utah—downwind of the site—lived in predominately small towns inhabited by fiercely patriotic individuals who were faithful to the Morman religion. Citizens and local media were supportive of the testing and trusted the government when it said that the testing was a safe activity. But by 1953 ranchers began to experience unexplained deaths of livestock, and media reports of high radioactivity and its long-range effects aroused public sentiment against the nuclear testing. By the 1960s epidemiologists were becoming aware of the increase in the number of people in the fallout area who had leukemia. The increase in leukemia deaths spurred the formation of advocacy organizations that focused on health screening, health support from the government, and raising public awareness about the dangers of testing (Ball 1986).

The problems of toxic waste were widespread, particularly in working-class and poor communities. Civil rights organizations began to protest the location of toxic waste disposal sites, landfills, and factories in primarily minority neighborhoods. They also organized local citizens, especially those whose health was threatened due to their proximity to these polluted areas (Bullard 1990; Prindeville and Bretting 1998).

The dramatic tale of the disaster at Love Canal, a residential area of Niagara Falls, New York, began to unfold in the late 1970s. From 1942 to 1952 the Hooker Chemical Company legally disposed of twenty-one thousand tons of chemical waste in the abandoned waterway, and by 1960 modest homes and an elementary school had been built around the dump site (Levine 1982, 10). In spite of frequent problems with leachates, most of the working-class residents were unaware of the area's history and its potential impact on their health—indeed, on their lives. In 1976 the discovery of the insecticide Mirex in Lake Ontario was traced to the Love Canal site, and a series of accounts in the *Niagara Gazette* brought the story to public attention. Meanwhile, residents began to notice a growing number of birth defects and other health problems among their children, and leachates that were seeping into basements and backyards and along roadways. Led by resident Lois Marie Gibbs, the community organized into a group of more than five hundred residents: the Love Canal Homeowners Association (LCHA) (Gibbs and Levine 1982).

According to Gibbs, the original goals of the organization were to evacuate those residents who wanted to leave the area, address falling property values, force the proper repair of the canal, and complete appropriate testing of the total area surrounding the canal (1982, 41). But the residents quickly realized that complete evacuation of the area and compensation for their property were the only ways to solve the growing health problems. The crisis involved conflicts between state and federal bureaucracies. There was also evidence of poor communications skills and conflicts in role definitions of public health officials, liability issues over who was legally responsible for the public health problems, and disagreement over the nature of the problem

AIDS. By the early 1980s, the prevalence of AIDS among gay men rapidly led to the development of new activist groups. Unlike the Black Lung and Brown Lung Associations and the "environmental racism" movement, however, these groups did not depend upon outside organizers to get their start. The people affected by AIDS already had significant political resources at their disposal. The development of AIDS activist groups is important in part because they transformed health policy making and challenged fundamental assumptions about the nature of science and the role of expert knowledge.

Perhaps the most famous AIDS organization is the AIDS Coalition to Unleash Power (ACT UP). Founded in 1987 by writer and gay activist Larry Kramer, ACT UP was created in response to what AIDS patients saw as a slow federal bureaucratic response to the disease and a drug approval process that conspired to keep helpful medications out of the hands of the desperately ill. With an affluent and well-educated membership primarily composed of homosexual white males, ACT UP had significant resources that included "a motivating sense of entitlement" (Cohen 1997). Using the tactic of "disruption" popularized by social movements of the 1960s (Piven and Cloward 1977), ACT UP members staged demonstrations at such institutions as the Food and Drug Administration (FDA), the National Institutes of Health (NIH), and the drug manufacturer Burroughs Wellcome to demonstrate the need to expedite the drug approval process. ACT UP was successful in securing access to drugs under development or undergoing clinical trials, pushing the FDA to approve community-based trials, and securing a role for lay activists on various government review panels (Arno and Feiden 1992; Epstein 1996).

Despite what many AIDS activists viewed as a deplorably slow federal response to the AIDS crisis (Shilts 1987), the government did act, notably with the passage of the Ryan White CARE Act in 1990 (Donovan 1996; Levitt and Rosenthal 1999). Some scholars argue that under the Ryan White Act resources are not distributed to the neediest populations (Donovan 1996). Others maintain that AIDS activists have been successful in securing billions of dollars from the federal government (Greenberg 1992; Wachter 1996) and have seen favorable policies enacted "because of their political power" (Schroedel and Jordan 1998, 122). Furthermore, Foreman (1994) asserts that AIDS activists' confrontational tactics, although controversial, paid off in increased attention from public health officials.

Foreman has documented the development of this new type of public interest lobby, which he calls "grassroots victims' organizations." In Foreman's definition, a grassroots victims' organization "consists of persons directly affected, often quite suddenly and tragically, by a health hazard. Persons who form, join or contribute to such groups include mainly victims, their relatives or friends, and persons who fear imminent victimization of themselves or others to whom they feel a personal attachment" (1995, 36).

In this analysis we do not use the term *victims* but rather *grassroots survivors' organization* (GSO).[1] We make this distinction for two reasons. First, the word *victim* may imply that one has succumbed to a disease. Although many involved in the prostate cancer and breast cancer movements are, or have been, seriously ill, the key to activism is their lengthy survival rates. Second, some individuals we interviewed took great umbrage with the use of the word *victim*. "We are *not* victims; we are survivors," North Carolina breast cancer activists Cat Andrews and Sarah Williams told us in 2003. Moreover, the word implies a passivity that does not do justice to the commitment of the members. As writer Michael Korda was told when he attended his first prostate cancer support group meeting, "You are *NOT* a *victim*. You're a *survivor*. A victim is somebody who's helpless, who has no control over his own fate. You're not helpless. Your fate is in your hands. Got it?" (Korda 1996, 215, emphasis in original).

Third, we wish to make a distinction that Foreman does not, that between groups populated by persons who developed the disease themselves (i.e., survivors) and those populated by surrogates such as medical professionals, family members, caregivers, or philanthropists. In the first case, the activists can speak for themselves about their experiences, which is always more powerful than stories told through a third person. Moreover, the agenda of grassroots survivors' organizations may be different from those populated by surrogates. The Alzheimer's Association, populated by surrogates, is as committed to respite care for caregivers as it is to committing funds for medical research (Alzheimer's Association 2003).

The Typology of Grassroots Survivors' Organizations

Successful GSOs share most or all of seven characteristics: (1) GSOs form around long-term health hazards; (2) GSOs adopt and use the organizational structures and practices of existing activist organizations; (3) GSOs offer their own experiences as evidence; (4) GSOs depend on an empowered, educated activist base of support; (5) GSOs are dependent on the media and the courts for keeping their issues alive and in the public's agenda; (6) GSOs are heavily dependent on women as activist leaders; and (7) GSOs need financial and promotional support from traditional organizations such as business and industry for long-term viability.

THE TYPE OF DISEASE

Foreman (1995) notes that grassroots victims' organizations only form around long-term health hazards such as New York's Love Canal or Lyme disease.[2] They do not develop around outbreaks such as Legionnaires' disease (1977) or toxic shock syndrome (1980–84), which are immediately catastrophic.[3] Nor do they develop around events that are fleeting, such as a brief outbreak of an infectious disease like influenza. In the first case the disease would capture the attention of public health officials in short order; in the second there is little reason for mobilization.

AIDS fits this classification. To be diagnosed with AIDS or learning that one is HIV-positive is a searing, life-changing event. With today's drug treatments, however, experts estimate that HIV-positive individuals can enjoy good health for ten years or more before developing AIDS (Centers for Disease Control and Prevention 1998). Even after developing AIDS, a disease that certainly leads to suffering and death, it is possible to live for many months, even years, before becoming so incapacitated that participating in political action is no longer feasible.

By contrast, the former textile workers involved in the Brown Lung Association in the 1970s and 1980s were usually seriously ill, which compromised their ability to organize and participate in many political protests. Robert Botsch (1993) recounts how many could take no more than a few steps without gasping for breath. One march in Washington, D.C., took place only with the assistance of nurses, oxygen tanks, first aid stations, and wheelchairs. As a result, the movement was heavily dependent upon surrogates: professional organizers; spouses, especially the wives of former workers in textile mills; and a few union officials. One organizer told Botsch that she knew it was time to leave the organization when she had outlived the entire original executive board (1993, 175).

ANGER AND THE SEARCH FOR MEANING. Developing a serious illness can lead to anger, which can be politicizing. The anti-nuclear testing groups were angry not only because they had been needlessly exposed to the long-term effect of radiation but also because the government "had lied to them." Bernard Levy, a leader of the Nevada Test Site Workers Victims' Association, is quoted as saying, "They used these people as guinea pigs and they knew [the Atomic Energy Commission] how much they were exposed to and what has happened to them" (Ball 1986, 100).

Many AIDS activists were motivated by anger, whether at becoming seriously ill at a young age, at the way the FDA mandated the structure of drug trials that meant some people were denied treatment, or at the stigma attached to the disease (Arno and Feidan 1992; Epstein 1996; Shilts 1987). Environmental activists at Love Canal were angry at an unresponsive government (Botsch 1993; Foreman 1995). Brown lung and black lung activists were angry at the industries' repeated denials that their diseases were caused by working conditions or that their diseases even existed (Botsch 1993; Judkins 1986). Similarly, environmental activists in Dallas were angry that a lead smelter, which had a long record of releasing lead that contaminated the soil and air of surrounding neighborhoods, was not closed (Bullard 1990). Likewise, women's health activists of the 1970s were angered by the fact that unnecessary procedures were being performed on low-income women as well as by the paternalistic attitudes of medical providers (Ruzek 1978).

EXISTING ACTIVIST TRADITION

Successful disease groups can build upon existing activist traditions or networks. The temperance movement, for example, built upon the network of Protestant churches united in opposition to alcohol sales and consumption (Bordin 1981). Similarly, the most successful grassroots environmental movements in minority communities were tied closely to the black churches in these areas (Bullard 1990), and Latina and Native American women environmental activists already were active in various community organizing efforts before taking on the environmental cause (Prindeville and Bretting 1998).

The AIDS movement quickly dovetailed with the extant gay rights movement, and their agendas were sometimes indistinguishable (Epstein 1996; Shilts 1987; Siplon 2002). Although men who developed HIV/AIDS had an existing community already steeped in grassroots political involvement, other groups of people afflicted with AIDS were diffuse and unorganized, such as those who contracted AIDS through blood transfusions. It is no surprise that issues that afflicted gay men dominated the early AIDS policy agenda.

The black lung movement was able to capitalize on existing labor union organization. A national compensation program for coal workers disabled by black lung disease was enacted when the United Mine Workers Union called a general strike until legislation was passed to recognize the disease and its consequences (Judkins 1986). The brown lung movement was not successful in the same way because few textile mills were unionized and activists were unable to persuade healthy workers to strike on behalf of disabled retirees (Botsch 1993).

OFFERING ONESELF AS EVIDENCE

Sociologist Phil Brown and his colleagues (2004) argue that "embodied health movements" "introduce the biological body to social movements in central ways, especially in terms of the embodied experience of people who have the disease" (54). That practice can be seen in numerous ways. Two temperance activists, for example, Diocletan Lewis and Carry Nation, both spoke publicly of their experiences with an alcoholic father and husband respectively (Asbury 1929; Bordin 1981, 15–16).

AIDS activists also learned the power of speaking for themselves. Many, such as Kimberly Bergalis, the young woman who contracted AIDS from her dentist and advocated stricter sanctions against health professionals with HIV/AIDS, were willing to talk publicly about the impact of the disease and the degree of human suffering it entailed (Arno and Friedan 1992; Kedrowski 1996). Others appeared at medical conferences, where they used analyses of their own blood to discuss the effectiveness of various treatments (Epstein 1996).

Similarly, brown lung and black lung sufferers repeatedly testified before state legislative and congressional hearings and conducted media interviews, often gasping for breath as they spoke (Botsch 1993; Judkins 1986). One group of nonsmoking brown lung sufferers staged a demonstration at Duke University in 1980, where two researchers had published an article that concluded that brown lung disease was not caused by inhaling cotton dust but by smoking. The demonstrators carried a banner that read "we offer ourselves as evidence" (Judkins 1986, ix).

The Love Canal Homeowners Association appeared on national television talk shows, testified at dozens of state and federal hearings, and tried to get politicians and public figures to see the pollution and its problems firsthand. Guided by a university researcher, residents also conducted their own health surveys, tracing illnesses, miscarriages, and deaths in the community within the old steambeds and swampy areas along the dumping sites. Once, in order to keep the issue on the media's agenda, the group took a child's coffin to the state capital at Albany. Gibbs recalls being questioned why homeowners didn't leave the area. "I tried to explain that we lived on $150 a week take-home pay," she said. "We had sick children, house payments and other debts. Our situation was similar to that of our neighbors. People just couldn't pick up and leave" (Gibbs and Levine 1982, 97).

More recently, people with mental health problems have formed "consumer-survivor" groups to help mental health professionals and researchers define what constitutes meaningful breakthroughs in drug treatments and therapies. What makes their contribution unique, they state, is that "we are the evidence" (Kanapaux 2003).

Reluctance to discuss a personal diagnosis impedes political action, as in the case of hemophiliacs with HIV/AIDS. The National Hemophiliac Foundation (NHF) was a long-standing grassroots advocacy organization, but it did not take the lead in developing policies to ensure a safer supply of blood and blood products, even as evidence mounted that AIDS could be spread that way. The NHF membership did not want to publicize the spread of AIDS among hemophiliacs because of well-founded fears of discrimination and recrimination. Not until the establishment of the Committee of Ten Thousand (COTT) did the particular concerns of hemophiliacs come to the fore-front (Siplon 2002, 55–60). The black lung and the brown lung movements also faced barriers in this respect. Some perceive acknowledging illness as a possible sign of weakness or laziness, especially when the illness jeopardizes the ability to work in a profession. Thus, the perception of weakness due to illness impeded the organizations' abilities to recruit members (Botsch 1993, 36–37; Judkins 1986, 16–18).

AN EMPOWERED, EDUCATED ACTIVIST BASE

The long-term success of a movement depends upon having a well-edu-cated, empowered activist base. Ruth Bordin (1981, 10–13) argues that mid-dle-class women of the 1870s had unprecedented levels of education and husbands who earned enough to free them from helping support a family though some form of employment. Middle-class families also could afford to hire servants to care for children and manage households. Thus, such women had the education and means to be involved in "the crusade." Fran-ces Willard, the long-time president of the Women's Christian Temperance Union, was a former college president.

In the contemporary context, however, empowerment requires acquisi-tion of, or access to, highly specialized knowledge. In the case of the AIDS movement, activists set about educating themselves through extensive read-ing and research; some even attended medical school (Epstein 1996). Learning complex, highly technical information requires an enormous amount of time and a degree of formal education that provides the necessary skills to master complex information.[4]

Political efficacy and the ability to articulate a position to people in power are also products of higher education. The AIDS movement benefited from such a well-educated base in the gay community. Peter Cohen (1997) recounts how the well-paid, well-educated white professionals-turned-activists could easily move from being part of an oppressed minority (being gay) to a posi-tion of power (being white and male) and were accustomed to having those in the corridors of power listen to them.

The Brown Lung Association, by contrast, did not have an educated, empowered activist base. Its members had little formal education, and many were functionally illiterate. One didn't even know how to dial a telephone (Botsch 1993, 95). They had great difficulty expressing themselves verbally or in writing. Similarly, rather than recognizing their collective power, they were often paralyzed by fears of reprisal upon themselves and their children. As a result, Brown Lung Association activists were extraordinarily dependent upon professional organizers who were paid staff members. Despite their efforts to empower grassroots activists, the Brown Lung Association collapsed when its organizers were unable to maintain funding to pay their own salaries (Botsch 1993).

By the same token, African American communities affected by environmental racism were slow to organize. Handicapped by poverty and little education, such communities lacked the necessary resources to organize and were "blackmailed" by the jobs that the polluting industries provided (Bullard 1990).

Although education and social class are highly correlated, education alone is a significant asset. Botsch compares the brown lung activists to those in the Love Canal Homeowners Association. The Love Canal families were also working class, like the brown lung activists, but had more education, job skills, and political skills (1993, 181). Moreover, they had connections. Activists in Love Canal worked with environmental experts from nearby universities as well as a toxicologist whom the state hired (Foreman 1995).

But even their higher level of education and help from outside scientists did not entirely mitigate misunderstandings and communication problems over the interpretation of scientific data (Levine 1982). Levine reported that association members held a shared belief system about the nature of the problem. That belief system—a powerful force in providing cohesion to the movement—including a general feeling that the state was treating residents unfairly and they needed to stick together to effect change (177).

THE MEDIA AND THE COURTS

Foreman (1995) noted that the media and the courts are important means for grassroots victims' organizations to "magnify" other forms of political action. AIDS activists argue that there was little media coverage of AIDS in the early years of the disease, which moved onto the public agenda only when it appeared to threaten the general population (Colby and Cook 1991). Explanations vary. The *New York Times,* an agenda-setter among news organizations, paid little attention to the disease in early years (Rogers, Dearing, and, Chang 1991). Other media commentators argue the lack of attention was due to homophobia (Shaw 1987) or "media logic" that excludes the voices of drug users, gays, and other marginalized groups (Hallett and Canella 1997). Eventually, however, media coverage of AIDS grew and has since found to be associated with public funding (Theodoulou, Guevara, and Minnassians 1996) and FDA approvals of drugs (Carpenter 2002).

Media coverage also was important to the brown and the black lung movements. National media coverage helped legitimate the story for local and regional media. Activist Ralph Nader, through articles in *The New Republic* and *The Nation,* played an important role in publicizing both diseases. He even coined the term *brown lung.* A sympathetic documentary, *The Song of the Canary,* was made about the brown lung movement, and the *Charlotte Observer* published a Pulitzer Prize–winning series entitled "Brown Lung: A Case of Deadly Neglect" that helped popularize the movement (Botsch 1993; Judkins 1986).

Similarly, coal miners in Appalachia began to put words to their collective misery when Granada Television began filming a documentary about the environmental and health problems that resulted from strip mining. At the same time, other activists began videotaping interviews with local families willing to discuss their lives. The videotapes became an important means of communication between otherwise isolated mining communities. These media enabled workers to overcome their historical fear of the coal mining corporation and speak out forcefully against its practices (Gaventa 1980, 221–25).

The experience of the Love Canal Homeowners Association in getting and keeping media coverage paralleled that of other grassroots advocacy movements. As its chief organizer noted, "We had to keep the media's interest. That was the only way we got anything done. They forced New York State to answer questions. They kept Love Canal in the public consciousness. They educated the public about toxic chemical wastes" (Gibbs and Levine 1982, 96).

The courts are another important tool for health activists. Temperance activists in Ohio, for example, turned in saloon owners who sold alcohol to underage boys (Bordin 1981, 24). The government's liability and responsibility for wrongful deaths in the case of nuclear power workers in Utah and others downwind tied up federal courts for years (Ball 1986).

Brown lung and black lung activists also used adjudicative processes in the workers' compensation system and the Social Security system to gain benefits for workers disabled by their employment and to acquire additional publicity for their causes (Botsch 1993; Judkins 1986). Environmental activists throughout the South filed class-action lawsuits, at least two of which were settled out of court and resulted in payments to minority families affected by pollution. Another was dismissed but resulted in changes in Houston's zoning process.

THE ROLE OF WOMEN

Foreman (1995) observed that women compose a large proportion of the activists in grassroots victims' organizations. That is no surprise. Women have a long history of political action through social movements in general and in health movements in particular. When afforded no other means of political action they could protest and build social networks. Carol Weisman (1998) documents the history of the women's health "megamovement," which dates to the 1830s and 1840s with the Popular Health Movement. Subsequent waves include temperance, efforts to legalize birth control and concentrate on maternal and child health in the Progressive Era, and the establishment of feminist health clinics in the 1960s. Contemporary variants include groups that focus on post-partum depression (Einwohner, Hollander, and Olson 2000) and breast feeding, particularly the La Leche League (Ward 2000).

Moreover, health care is primarily the domain of women; they have long dominated professions such as nursing, occupational and physical therapy, and dental hygiene. In addition, 26 percent of doctors are female (AMA 2005). Because women bear children and live longer then men they are more likely to seek medical attention and have higher lifetime health expenditures (Mustard et al. 1998). Women also have primary responsibility for caring for children and aging parents and in doing so may incur emotional distress and expenses that perhaps jeopardize their financial security (Schoen, Duchon, and Simantov 1999). Consequently, public opinion polls show that women are more likely to support government intervention and expansion of health-care services (Conway, Steuernagel, and Ahern 1997, 37–38).

In addition, there are important gendered differences in health insurance coverage. In 2003 females (women and girls) were more likely than males (men and boys) to have health insurance; 85 percent of females are insured compared to 83 percent of males. Yet females remain vulnerable. First, those with private insurance are also more likely to be an insured dependent rather than have coverage through their own employment. Second, females are more likely than males to be covered by the publicly funded Medicaid and Medicare; approximately 24 percent of males were covered by the programs in 2003 compared to 28 percent of females (U.S. Census Bureau 2005).

Women, some of whom had been active in the women's health movement of the 1970s, also played an important role in the AIDS movement, and that led to fissures between male and female activists (Epstein 1996). The influence of women's health advocates presented itself in different ways. Male AIDS activists, for example, expected immediate results from policymakers; by contrast, female AIDS activists did not. In the following passage, Peter Cohen first quotes a female activist, and then adds his own analysis: "Women activists never imagined, 'that they were going to get anything. They just felt like they had to be a voice of dissent. . . . We would stand outside and yell because somebody had to stand outside and yell. But it never occurred to us that anyone was going to listen to us.' By contrast many of the men in ACT UP/New York came to that organization assuming that they were entitled to a response from the government and that they could force the government to produce such a response" (Epstein 1996, 96–97).

The women believed the ACT UP agenda excluded issues relevant to women, minorities, and poor people and focused primarily on "getting drugs into bodies." This emphasis presupposed that the person with AIDS had the ability to acquire and pay for these drugs, even at exorbitant prices. It also presumed that the drugs would be equally effective, and side effects equally manageable, for everyone. Moreover, the gay white males who led the AIDS movement had worked long and hard to secure seats on various scientific review panels. Then they worked long and hard to master the scientific information necessary to make a meaningful contribution. Many of the women, however, saw this as selling out. In fact, at one point a group of women AIDS activists called for a moratorium on participation on scientific panels (290–93).

Women were deeply involved in both the Love Canal Homeowners Association and the Brown Lung Association and were a majority of the organizations' leaders. In the case of the Love Canal Homeowner's Association, the women who originally became involved were mothers who did not work outside their homes and were concerned about the safety of their children. In the case of the Brown Lung Association, some of the women who became involved were afflicted with brown lung disease; others had spouses too ill to participate actively. Those who remained active were surrogates. As they lived longer, they developed leadership skills. The males married to female brown lung sufferers were unlikely to be involved in the association, thus leaving leadership opportunities to women activists (Botsch 1993, 88–89).

PROMOTION AND FINANCIAL SUPPORT

A relatively new phenomenon is the widespread use of social marketing strategy and cause-related marketing support by GSOs. Social marketing employs marketing principles to target public health messages to particular audiences, and one of its goals is to raise awareness of specific diseases. Activists also have used visual symbols to bring public awareness to their causes.

Perhaps the most visible promotional tactic of the AIDS movement was the adoption of the red ribbon to symbolize awareness of and solidarity with persons with the disease. The ribbon was designed by a New York group, Visual AIDS, in 1991, a time when those who developed the disease were stigmatized. It was inspired by yellow ribbons that symbolized awareness and support for soldiers fighting in the Persian Gulf War at about the same time (Artists About AIDS 2003; Joint United Nations Programme 2003). Ribbons in a variety of colors are now popular symbols for various worthy causes.

In some cases, social marketing has evolved into cause-related marketing, where businesses partner with a nonprofit organization. Corporations may provide services to the cause through an organization or designate a portion of the purchase price to a cause. They often employ ribbons or other symbols in their promotion efforts. Such arrangements are beneficial to both sides. The nonprofit organization is able to raise needed funds, and the corporation generates good will and stimulates sales. But such arrangements also lead to criticism from those who believe that the partnerships lessen the seriousness of the disease (chapter 8).

The Two Cancer Movements as GSOs

As Christopher Foreman admits, much of the work on grassroots victims' organizations is exploratory in nature (1995, 34). In an effort to build upon the work of Foreman and others, this section evaluates breast cancer and prostate cancer groups, using these criteria.

TYPE OF DISEASE

Both breast cancer and prostate cancers typify the kind of disease that lends itself to the development of GSOs. In the case of AIDS, people may experience a period of reasonably good health after their initial diagnosis. Breast cancer and prostate cancer reverse the pattern. Those whose cancers are found early have relatively few symptoms at the time of diagnosis (a small lump, something suspicious on a routine mammogram, an elevated PSA) and in fact may consider themselves healthy. It is the *treatments* that make people sick. Chemotherapy leaves them bald, weak, and subject to waves of nausea. Radiation leaves burns and sometimes long-term problems such as an ulcerated colon. Surgeries are disfiguring, painful, and require long periods for recovery. Recovery is characterized by drains, bandages, catheters, and sometimes painful exercises. Once the treatments are finished and recovery is complete, however, breast cancer and prostate cancer survivors have the promise of several more years of life, during which scars and long-term side-effects will be constant reminders. Persons diagnosed with localized prostate or breast cancer have high rates of survival. Thus the tragedy of diagnosis is followed by an opportunity to act. In the words of Andrew Grove, prostate cancer survivor and chair of Intel Corporation, "PSA tests are a godsend.

They give you the next best thing to not having cancer. They give you time" (NPCC 2002b, 9).

ANGER AND THE SEARCH FOR MEANING. How does experience with cancer become a politicizing event? As in the case of AIDS and environmental activism, one explanation is anger. Breast cancer activists are angry at a perceived lack of attention on the part of the medical research establishment to the human cost of breast cancer. Many are "daughters of women who died of it—who are 'getting the same chemo, the same radiation' their mothers got" (Marshall 1993b, see also Casamayou 2001). Others are angry because of the need to battle insurance companies, angry because they developed this disease when they have no known risk factors, and angry when they suffer a recurrence (Casamayou 2001, 67–68).

Anger also motivates prostate cancer survivors. As Alan Granath, president of the Georgia Prostate Cancer Coalition, stated, "My wife and I listened to my doctor talk about the surgery and its complications. Impotence. Incontinence. We left his office in tears. I am determined to do something to stop this terrible disease" (comments at NPCC conference 2003).

The second motivation is a search for meaning (Taylor 2000). One way in which activists find meaning is through political action. Another survivor of prostate cancer, Anthony Caputi, has said, "I was faced with a life-threatening disease. I now see my involvement as a calling . . . a way to make something positive out of this experience" (interview 2003). Phoenix5 founder Robert Young sought to understand how he could have "a PSA of over one thousand when 'normal' was defined as four." That led to the creation of an eight hundred–word glossary of prostate cancer terms on his Web site and publication of a booklet version of the same glossary (Shropshire 2003).

A third reason for involvement is to address emotional need. One study of men with prostate cancer and their families found that turning to advocacy organizations helped individuals make informed medical decisions and network with peers (Manne 2002). Another found survivors' sense of self-worth enhanced when they emerged as leaders in local support groups (Gray et al. 1997). One excellent example is Larry Harelik, who founded a chapter of US TOO! International in Waco, Texas, the first support group for men with prostate cancer in that city. He considers the support group to be his legacy, something that will live beyond him (Ryan 2002).

Similarly, people with cancer are the center of attention for some time. They receive considerable care and attention from doctors, family members, and other members of support groups. Once treatment is finished, however, survivors can feel lost or lonely. Thus, advocacy is a way they and their family members and friends continue to be connected (Brooks interview 2003).

Other survivor-activists agree. As Joy Simha, a cofounder of the Young Survival Coalition, recalled, "About two years later [after diagnosis], when I was done with treatment and done with breast cancer support groups, and still looking for a way to fight breast cancer, me and couple of other gals [*sic*] were having dinner in New York City. And we would meet monthly to talk about what was not available for young women and how we really needed to create something that would make it better for young women. And so was born the Young Survival Coalition" (interview 2003). Cat Andrews, a cofounder of the Breast Cancer Coalition of North Carolina, initially was recruited by her doctors at Duke University to lobby for federal funding to maintain the university's autologous bone marrow transplant program. "I was able to meet a lot of other women, a lot worse than I was," she says. "We were able to finally share some things. That encouraged me. We were so successful [lobbying] in Washington, that it just became my passion" (interview, 2003).

EXISTING ACTIVIST TRADITION

The breast cancer movement has a rich heritage of activism—an advantage over the prostate cancer movement. Breast cancer activists built upon the feminist movement of the 1960s and the women's health movement. Women's health activist Sandra Morgan (2002) has pointed out that the breast cancer movement is a significant departure from the women's health movement of the 1960s, in part because it does not emphasize well women's (i.e., reproductive) health but focuses instead upon a disease. In addition, the breast cancer movement had precedents set by Rose Kushner and the activists who fought for informed consent legislation in the early 1980s. Granted, prostate cancer activists have patient support groups upon which to draw. Heterosexual men and elderly men, however, lack the same long history of grassroots activism that characterizes women's and gay men's political involvement.

OFFERING ONESELF AS EVIDENCE

Again, breast cancer activists have an advantage over prostate cancer activists. First, many taboos surrounding public discussion of breast cancer were broken in the 1970s when Betty Ford, Happy Rockefeller, and other prominent women openly discussed their illnesses. Moreover, the women's movement demystified women's breasts and made women more likely to discuss them

(Yalom 1997). Although breast cancer activists do not refuse to wear prostheses in large numbers, as the feminist Audre Lorde envisioned in 1980, they have answered Lorde's call and "ceased to be invisible" by their willingness to speak out, participate in support groups, and engage in political action. Many men, however, are reluctant to discuss prostate cancer and its side effects. Even when they do acknowledge their diagnoses, they still say, "I've undergone surgery, but I'm fine" (Page interview 2003) without discussing the surgery's unpleasant consequences (Swift 2003).

Both the breast cancer and the prostate cancer movements use the firsthand accounts of survivors in advocacy efforts, but there are important differences of degree. Women "offer themselves as evidence" in many ways, often with dramatic results. Attend a Komen Foundation race and one sees survivors wearing pink tee shirts and visors. The event also formally recognizes those who have the survived the disease the longest. Mary Rose Oakar recounts how a breast cancer survivor riveted a congressional hearing by removing her wig as she testified (interview 2003). Cat Andrews also traveled to Washington to discuss her bone marrow transplant. The Young Survival Coalition encourages young survivors to register on its Web site to communicate the extent of the disease among young women. The NBCC has begun an effort to collect breast cancer stories from survivors and their families from across the country and will use the stories to strengthen lobbying efforts (NBCCF 2005).

Another common technique is to share narratives in a variety of forms, whether through books, plays, Web sites, journals, or, as in the case of Matuschka, artwork. Laura Potts (2000; see also DeShazer 2003) argues that such narratives provide a sense of collective identity and enable breast cancer survivors to assert themselves in the isolation of their illness. The narratives are also a powerful tool for influencing Congress (Arnold 1990; for an alternate perspective see Ehrenreich 2001).

A few breast cancer survivors have taken up Audre Lorde's call to boycott prostheses (e.g., Bricker-Jenkins 1994), but most mark their identity in a less visible way. Wearing a pink tee shirt or a pink ribbon is a far cry from collective asymmetry or marching topless. As Zillah Eisenstein, also a breast cancer survivor, writes, "I wear prostheses less frequently, but I still wear them when do not want to negotiate the world through my breast cancer" (2001, 32).

The prostate cancer movement also is populated with survivors. Although they are fewer in number than the breast cancer movement, the National Prostate Cancer Coalition (NPCC) is able to find prominent individuals to testify on its behalf at congressional hearings. At one time, CaP CURE's Web site featured photographs of famous men who had gone public with their diagnoses. But the prostate cancer movement is handicapped by the age of those who contract the disease. Men in their seventies and eighties, well into retirement, are often reluctant to discuss their personal affairs. Thus, many of the leaders in the prostate cancer movement are not survivors themselves but rather medical experts or persons with some family connection to the disease. Surrogates, although they may be quite eloquent, lack the same degree of credibility as survivors. In the words of one prostate cancer lobbyist, "[NBCC president and breast cancer survivor] Fran Visco goes up there [to Capitol Hill] and says, 'I will not have breast cancer policy dictated to me by a much of men in suits.' I can't say that for lots of reasons" (interview 2003).

AN EDUCATED, EMPOWERED ACTIVIST BASE

Both movements have at their core a desire to provide information to people diagnosed with the disease and enhance the ability to make informed treatment decisions (NBCC 2002a; NPCC 2002c; US TOO! 2002a). As such, patient empowerment remains a significant departure from the traditional physician-patient relationship and a lasting hallmark of both the women's health and the AIDS movements.

Support groups are the base from which breast cancer and prostate cancer advocacy organizations recruit activists. Participation in support groups varies significantly, however, and the variations benefit the breast cancer movement (Gray et al., 1997; Krizek et al. 1999; Manne 2002). Women, the well-educated, and white people are more likely to participate in support groups than are men, members of racial minorities, or persons of a lower socioeconomic status.

Given that breast cancer is one of the few diseases more prevalent among women of higher socioeconomic status, it is hardly surprising that its activists have high levels of education and political skills. Moreover, the women who develop breast cancer now are products of significant social change. Those in their fifties in the early twenty-first century were among the first generation of U.S. females to earn college degrees in large numbers; nearly a quarter had a college diploma, and nearly 90 percent were at least high school graduates (U.S. Census Bureau 2002). By contrast, the men of that era who developed prostate cancer were approximately ten years older and had a bi-modal pattern of educational attainment.[5] Nearly a quarter (22 percent) of men over age sixty-five held a bachelor's degree or higher, although 30 percent had less than a high school education (U.S. Census Bureau 2002). US TOO!'s primary educational packet, designed for distribution to men newly diagnosed with prostate cancer, includes items targeted to people with a sixth-grade reading level (interview 2003).

This is not to say that prostate cancer does not strike men of means and education. Numerous prostate cancer activists have both. When Jim East, the former CEO of Pulaski Bank in Little Rock, founded the Arkansas Prostate Cancer Foundation, the bank provided $250,000 in start-up funds and office space (Kossover interview 2003; NPCC 2002b). Michael Milkin and Louis Farrakhan began foundations, and Andrew Grove, chair of Intel Corporation, helped raise $10 million to fund prostate cancer research at the University of San Francisco Medical Center. The difference, however, is that these men acted as individual entrepreneurs; they did not engage in collective action. By contrast, few women have the business or economic clout to act individually and raise millions.

MEDIA AND THE COURTS

The most important way in which activists in either movement have used the media or the courts is in the case of breast cancer. Some women with breast cancer sued insurance companies to force them to pay for bone marrow transplants, or their families sued insurance companies that refused to cover those procedures for loved ones who had since died. Although medical evidence now suggests that this treatment was ineffective (Fee 2000; Mello and Brennan 2001), the effort is an excellent example of using the courts. News media coverage of both diseases is tied to the development of GSOs and to public policy changes (chapters 5 and 6). Hollywood continues to find the breast cancer cause a promising subject for movies and television episodes. Both *Cagney and Lacy* and *Murphy Brown,* for example, wove the subject into the plots of shows.

THE ROLE OF WOMEN

It is true that women compose the vast majority of breast cancer activists and were the entrepreneurs who established local and national organizations. Many activists in the prostate cancer movement are men, and they provide the leadership and sit on boards of organizations such as the Prostate Cancer Foundation and the NPCC. Women play a large role in grassroots prostate cancer activism. They are likely to attend prostate cancer support groups, even as their husbands sit in the car outside, unable to summon the courage to join the group (Gray et al. 1997). Medical studies support the idea that men with prostate cancer who are married or have partners are more likely to have a better quality of life than those not in such relationships (Gore et al. 2005). Numerous prostate cancer organizations now reach out to family members, especially wives or other female partners of prostate cancer survivors. An early slogan of the NPCC was "Families Fighting Prostate Cancer" (NPCC 1998a), and its brochures featured photographs of nearly as many smiling women as men (NPCC n.d., n.d., n.d.). The Prostate Action, Inc. (PROACT) and Phoenix5 Web sites include testimonials by women as well as information targeted exclusively to them (PROACT 2003a; Phoenix5 2003). Women are as likely as men, if not more likely, to attend Let's Talk About It sessions, and some American Cancer Society chapters host Side by Side programs. These programs are support groups for partners of men with prostate cancer and meet simultaneously with Man to Man support groups (ACS 2002f, 2003a). Malecare in New York City sponsors support groups for the partners of men who have prostate cancer (Malecare 2003). Some breast cancer organizations such as Y-ME, have support services for male partners of women with breast cancer, but they are not as ubiquitous as prostate cancer organizations' efforts to reach women (Y-ME 2003c). Women also serve in leadership roles in numerous prostate cancer state coalitions, including those in Arkansas, Virginia, and Washington.

Women founded two other prostate cancer advocacy and support organizations. One is an on-line magazine, *PSA Rising,* established by Jacqueline Strax, whose husband died in 2002.[6] *PSA Rising* includes medical stories and coverage of advocacy efforts. The other is Family to Family, initially founded in 1997 by Nikki Meloskie as Women's Suffrage for Prostate Cancer Awareness and Support. "Suffrage" is defined as "the vote for the right to have prostate cancer considered as a woman's or partner's disease as well as a man's" (Family to Family 2002a). The group is intended to provide support for wives and partners of prostate cancer survivors (and its statements appear to assume that all "partners" are also female) (Family to Family 2002b). Family to Family's advocacy statement includes the following:

> What makes us effective as advocates for health care and prostate cancer is that we are women. For a long time I have heard over and over again, that women are the people who get their husbands to take care of their own health issues. They make the doctors appointments, they harass them until they give in and go to the doctor and we are the caregivers in the family. But we are also our family's greatest advocates. We go to school with the kids and work with PTA. We call the teachers and administrators when we feel our children are not getting the education they are entitled to. We support our men by

attending functions related to their jobs and work for causes that affect our families. (Family to Family 2002c)

PROMOTION AND FINANCIAL SUPPORT

One social marketing tactic adopted by the breast cancer and prostate cancer movements is the ribbon. The breast cancer movement successfully adopted a pink ribbon as a universally recognized symbol of awareness and solidarity. The origin of the pink ribbon is unclear. Some credit the Susan G. Komen Foundation with promoting it, and others credit Evelyn Lauder of the Estee Lauder Corporation and founder of the Breast Cancer Research Foundation and Alexandra Penney, an editor of *Self* magazine, with its design and creation ("History of the Pink Ribbon" n.d.). In either case, the pink ribbon has become the preeminent symbol of the breast cancer movement and is part of the logos of scores of breast cancer organizations, including Y-Me and the Komen Foundation, or incorporated into their promotional material. It is ubiquitous in cause-related marketing efforts embraced by various corporations.

In the case of breast cancer, however, the movement has evolved beyond simply raising awareness through social marketing efforts to embarking on countless cause-related marketing relationships. Numerous breast cancer organizations, including the Komen Foundation, the Young Survivor Coalition, and Y-ME, partner with various corporate sponsors. Especially in the month of October, Breast Cancer Awareness Month, countless products and services, often adorned with the pink ribbon, are promoted and marketed as supporting the cause (chapter 8).

The prostate cancer movement adopted a light blue ribbon as a symbol. Once promoted by CaP CURE because "blue is for boys" (CaP CURE 2002c), the ribbon has been incorporated into the logos of the NPCC and several state prostate cancer coalitions. It is not a universal symbol, however, as John Page, formerly of US TOO! International points out. A blue ribbon in the same shade is also used to symbolize solidarity with the state of Israel and to promote child abuse awareness. Other prostate cancer groups have adopted, variously, a knot in a piece of rope, which resembles a prostate gland; a stylized version of the prostate cancer awareness stamp; or the logo of US TOO! International, which features a silhouette of two people holding hands (Page interview 2003).

Confusion within the prostate cancer movement does not end there. While one organization, the Prostate Cancer Education Council (PCEC), promotes one week in September as Prostate Cancer Awareness Week, the NPCC and numerous state coalitions promote the entire month of September as Prostate Cancer Awareness Month. The activities that take place in September, however, clash with other activities around Father's Day, which tend to share a "Do It for Dad" theme. The Prostate Cancer Foundation and NPCC in particular have sought relationships with major sports organizations such as the NFL, Major League Baseball, and the PGA, although the efforts are in relatively early stages (chapter 8).

Conclusion

The breast cancer movement shares all seven characteristics of a successful GSO. The prostate cancer movement, however, satisfies only three of the seven criteria and partially satisfies another two. It is the right type of disease, its activists use the media, and many women are active in the movement. In addition, prostate cancer partially fulfills the criteria of an educated, empowered activist base and uses some cause-related marketing efforts. The prostate cancer movement, however, lacks a well-developed, existing community of interest, and fewer survivors are willing to offer themselves as evidence than is the case with breast cancer (table 2).

Because of these variations, the two diseases are well suited to a study that compares the relative success of grassroots survivors' organizations. The diseases' similarities—as diseases of aging that have similar mortality, morbidity, and long-term survival rates—account for a number of important variables. The differences allow a unique opportunity to explore and understand how grassroots survivors' organizations can succeed or fail and how women's activism compares to men's.

Given the differences in their characteristics documented here, how might the strategies and tactics of these two movements differ? First, we expect

Table 2. GSO Characteristics of Breast Cancer and Prostate Cancer

Characteristic	Breast Cancer	Prostate Cancer
Type of disease	Yes	Yes
Existing activist tradition	Yes (collective)	No (individual)
Offering oneself as evidence	Yes, myriad ways	Limited
Educated, empowered activist base	Yes	Partial
Uses the media and courts	Yes, both	Yes, media
Women activists	Yes	Yes
Social and cause marketing	Yes	Partial

that both movements will have some success in generating additional media attention and public policy change. The prostate cancer movement, however, will be hampered by men's unwillingness to act collectively and discuss their experiences with disease. Both the media and Congress are receptive to entrepreneurial efforts; however, they are likely to pale in comparison to the collective efforts of the breast cancer movement. That effort will benefit from the credibility its survivors provide and the sympathetic face its activists communicate to the public and to policymakers. The breast cancer movement will garner more media attention, enjoy more public awareness, and have more policy success than its prostate cancer counterpart.

This typology should be useful to others studying social movements and interest groups in general and disease politics in particular. It may explain what type of disease groups are likely to be successful in the competition for media and public policy attention and the reasons why. Prostate cancer, breast cancer, and AIDS might be uniquely situated in this competition, but further studies of GSOs are necessary to determine the usefulness of that analysis.

3

Breast Cancer and Prostate Cancer in the Media

> We know a great deal today about the health problems of prominent people—more than some of us want to know. But we know it anyway, because they tell us. Because what used to be private has become public, in every arena of life. Savvy public figures—especially political candidates—reveal all before the rumor mill, fed by an aggressive, competitive press.
>
> —Joyce Purnick

> We are twenty years behind what women did in raising awareness for breast cancer, because men never admitted having health problems. . . . Illness is a sign of weakness. . . . Men like Gen. [Norman] Schwarzkopf, who represent the macho image of invulnerability, will help break the taboo and become a model for other men."
>
> —Robert Samuels

Disease politics is dependent upon the media to ensure that opinion and policy leaders are kept informed about the issues associated with disease. This chapter explores the first step in the agenda-setting process—moving onto the media agenda. The chapter is divided into two sections. The first summarizes and critiques the literature on breast and prostate cancer in the news media, and the second presents findings from our analyses of news coverage of these two diseases.

Breast Cancer and Prostate Coverage in the Media

THE TENSION BETWEEN SCIENTISTS AND JOURNALISTS

The media vary in their effectiveness in reaching certain populations (Roetzheim et al. 1992), and much of the public's initial information concerning disease is based on media coverage (Johnson and Meischke 1991; Nelkin, 1995; Yanovitzky and Blitz 2000). From all accounts, the public continues to place science and health information at the top of its news agenda (Readership Institute 2002). To understand the media's role in covering health issues it helps to review how reporting decisions are made and whether they may be at odds with the norms of scientists and medical professionals.

The relationship between health-care providers and the media has long been stormy. In fact, the issues of medicine and health care have been important, albeit controversial, since the publication of the first newspaper, *Publick Occurrences,* in 1690. The only issue carried two medical stories on its first page. The first concerned "epidemical fevers and Augues" growing in the country, and the second was about a smallpox epidemic in Buffalo, New York.

The issue of how to treat smallpox was to become the first American medical story to highlight the conflict between physicians and the press (Rubin and Rogers 1993). Historically, some of the division between physicians and the press stems from the early use of newspaper advertising by medical quacks to sell patent medicines. Such advertising not only tarnished the name of advertising but also threatened the growing professionalism of medicine. As a consequence, medical doctors became wary of talking to the press and in fact were prohibited by their national associations from doing so. In 1975 the Supreme Court ruled that bans against advertising by professional organizations were a violation of antitrust laws (*Virginia State Board of Pharmacy v. Virginia Citizens Consumer Council, Inc.,* 425 U.S. 748 [1976]). That action, coupled with a growing consumers' movement that demanded more information from the medical establishment, fueled public demand for medical information.

The history of media coverage of medical science is important because skepticism between journalists and medical professionals continues to shape how medical stories are reported. In political reporting, the impact of rhetoric often makes immediate news, but issues of scientific importance may not receive timely media attention due to the inherent conflict between how scientists and reporters see their roles. As one professor of journalism stated, "Journalism is an activity with no scientific methodology" (de Semir 1996). The socialization of reporters and editors links news with timeliness, proximity, conflict, human interest, unusualness, and public issues (Rich 1999). Journalists are taught to value certain conventions in delivering a news product. Because timeliness is of great value, for example, reporters tend to rely on a conventional list of sources. Consequently, they do not spend much time reflecting on the nature of news. Griswold and Packer (1991) conjecture that the epistemology of journalism, or what constitutes knowledge as viewed by journalists, is not based on a recognizable standard for knowing what they know. Instead, journalists adopt practical standards of objectivity and believability.

Medical researchers and practitioners, however, have another standard of epistemology—the scientific method—which values theorizing, testing theories by experiment, critiquing one's peers, and publishing (Griswold and Packer 1991). Scientists recognize the value of peer review and must publish to stay employed at most research institutions. Consequently, scientific discovery is often painfully slow. Scientists are reluctant to go on the record until the research can be replicated and their findings published (Griswold and Packer 1991; Nelkin 1995). This reluctance conflicts with reporters' needs for timely news, thus hindering the reporting process.

As Krieghbaum (1967) noted in his early study of science and the mass media, science consumers want the essence of the experiment, not how it was carried out. Scientists, however, want detail. Furthermore, the journalistic standard of objectivity is meaningless in the scientific community, where "standards of objectivity require not balance but empirical verification of opposing hypotheses. Simply to balance opinions gives readers little guidance about the scientific significance of different views" (Nelkin 1995, 88). Thus science reporters often defer to the peer-review system as a judge of a study's quality (Entwhistle 1995).[1] They must also acknowledge and respect the epistemology of science to maintain source credibility and evaluate scientific studies.

Susanna Hornig Priest (1999) noted in an essay on "Popular Beliefs, Media, and Biotechnology" that much emergent science—whose truth is yet to be discovered—is by its nature newsworthy. "Much of the unease of the scientific community with mass media coverage of science is likely attributable to unarticulated, perhaps only half-realized dissatisfaction with journalists' obsession with reporting 'objective' facts in cases in which the facts have yet to be established" (97).

A major complaint of medical scientists involves the lack of training of reporters in medicine or natural science. It is true that major newspapers and television were at one point highly dependent on reporters who had little background or knowledge of scientific or health issues, but now they usually employ journalists whose sole beat is health reporting (Aumente 1995). Science reporters in particular tend to form an allegiance with their sources that is unusual in the reporting business. The reporters, particularly those with scientific backgrounds, often adopt the same values as scientists and thus may have problems (Nelkin 1995). Unlike other reporters, they are rarely present at breaking news. What is reported as medical news of the day, therefore, depends less on issues of incidence than on issues that make news: personalities, fast-breaking events such as new treatments, reports from nationally recognized interest groups, or institutions such as medical universities or commercial research institutions (Colby and Cook 1991; Corbett and Mori 1999a; Freimuth et al. 1984; Theodoulou, Guevara, and Minnassians 1996).

THE ACCURACY OF BREAST CANCER MEDIA COVERAGE

The continued conflict between the press and scientists frequently plays out in scientific publications as quantitative analyses of media inaccuracy. Indeed, one evaluation of science stories conducted by scientists themselves reported that a large majority omitted information critical to the understanding of the research results (Tankard and Ryan 1974). Accounts of journalistic inaccuracy abound, including media coverage of a British study that concluded that "submissiveness" in women led to lower rates of heart attack, hyping the promise of a vaccine that did not yet exist, promoting the possibility that forty-million-year-old bacteria were returning to life, or announcing a "cancer cure" prematurely (Deary, Whiteman, and Fowkes 1998; de Semir 1995; Dresser 2001, 132–33). Errors of omission are the most frequently cited problem in studies of media coverage (Berhardt et al. 2000).

Media coverage of cancer generally is not linked to incidence (Freimuth et al. 1984). Both breast cancer and prostate cancer are among those that receive the greatest degree of news coverage in the U.S. media (Smigel 1994, 1995). Almost all academic studies of this coverage have focused on breast cancer. Consistent with other studies of media coverage of medicine, the literature evaluating breast cancer news focuses on scientific accuracy. For example, newspaper and magazine articles reporting on the association between alcohol and breast cancer were compared to articles appearing in scientific journals from January 1985 to July 1992 (Houn et al. 1995). All articles were taken from seven of the twenty-nine scientific journals reviewed; forty-seven articles were never cited. Not surprisingly, the most-quoted appeared in the *New England Journal of Medicine* and the *Journal of the American Medical Association (JAMA)*. The authors noted that "selective reporting of single studies and contradictory advice only serves to confuse and alienate the public" (Houn et al. 1995, 1082).

The Houn study, written by National Cancer Institute personnel, again points out reporters' reliance on major medical journals. It also demonstrates scientists' lack of understanding of the dynamics of reporting. From the media's perspective, the task of reporting on every single research study published is unrealistic, much less impossible; nor would all studies achieve the media's definition of newsworthiness.

A similar study compared findings of scientific articles on hormone replacement therapy (HRT) to popular media coverage from 1995 to 2000 (Whiteman et al. 2001). The authors found that the popular media were far more likely to feature scientific articles that reported a positive association between HRT and breast cancer than those that reported no association or a negative association.

Numerous studies focused on the media coverage of the continuing controversy surrounding the effectiveness of mammography for women in their forties. One reviewed 116 articles in four newspapers and four types of magazines during a two-year period for errors in reporting, whether from misleading titles or the omission of important information. The authors found that 47 percent of the articles failed to provide an adequate citation, making it difficult for scholars or readers to verify the accuracy of the information or explore a particular research finding (Moyer et al. 1995). Another study of coverage in six top-circulation U.S. newspapers from 1990 to 1997 found media coverage twice as likely to support mammography for women between forty and forty-nine as to express reservations. The support for mammography continued in spite of changes in recommendations by national organizations (Wells et al. 2001).

Schwartz and Woloshin (2002) examined media coverage in ten newspapers and on three television networks in the two weeks following each of three national events evaluating breast cancer diagnosis and treatment.[2] Their analysis considered the release of the National Institutes of Health consensus report, which did not recommend mammograms for women in their forties; the NCI's subsequent reversal of this position a month later; and the dissemination of a report from the Breast Cancer Control and Detection program recommending the prophylactic use of tamoxifen. The authors found that pro-mammography groups such as the American Cancer Society were cited widely. Schwartz and Woloshin also noted that the stories following the NCI's reversal "were also remarkable for the extent to which politicians and advocacy groups were represented and for a new focus: ensuring that mammograms were covered by insurance" (5).

An article by Michael Zerbe, Amanda Young, and Edwin Nagelhout (1998) critiqued the 1994 disclosures in two scientific journals and the *Chicago Tri-*

bune concerning fraud in federally funded breast cancer research trials. They concluded that the two journals missed a critical opportunity to discuss the ethical implications of the study and explore the "blurry boundary between 'writing up' and 'making up' results." At the same time, the *Chicago Tribune* failed to focus on the impact of these disclosures upon the women affected by the fraud (59).

A "HUMAN FACE" AND PUBLIC AWARENESS IN NEWS COVERAGE

For journalists, a newsworthy story needs to be able to captivate a reader's attention through its unusual or human-interest qualities. Some issues are, by nature of their fact-based content and immediacy, classified as hard news. Other stories, such as an interview with a young author dying of breast cancer, focus on people, places, or issues (Rich 1999, 19) and are labeled human-interest stories or soft news. Media coverage of breast cancer and prostate cancer lends itself to both hard and soft news coverage.

Breast cancer is what some have labeled a "media-friendly" disease. It is especially appealing to journalists because women can relate to profiles of persons with breast cancer and their families (Henderson and Kitzinger 1999, 569). Readers and viewers also can relate to high-profile personalities who experience a disease. Personality stories build audiences and help sustain media coverage. They also build awareness of, and encourage medical attention for, issues surrounding the disease (Corbett and Mori 1999a).

The number of stories on breast cancer doubled from 1986 to 1987, in part due to the diagnoses and treatments of then–Supreme Court justice Sandra Day O'Connor and then-First Lady Nancy Reagan. At the time, Reagan was criticized for her decision to have a modified radical mastectomy rather than a lumpectomy. As Barbara Sharf noted about such narratives, "Recipients of illness stories—be they lawmakers, policy wonks, or the public—face difficult questions. What are the criteria for making judgments about stories as a basis for generalizing public policy? How do we distinguish among competing narratives when all are compelling?" (2001, 218).

The impact of media coverage on health behavior is somewhat more complicated. Health behavior is influenced by a variety of factors, media attention being but one (Johnson and Meischke 1991). Nevertheless, the number of modified radical mastectomies over lumpectomies increased during the first four months of 1988 after Nancy Reagan's breast cancer surgery in October 1987, particularly among women of her age group (Nattinger et al. 1998). The authors found no published research or print media reports to account for that increase other than the First Lady's decision. Similarly, another study found a 12 percent increase in screening mammography in the two months following Nancy Reagan's mastectomy (Lane, Polednak, and Burg 1998).

Prostate cancer media coverage has been influenced by the attention awarded to celebrities. Coverage of prostate cancer slightly increased in 1987 with the diagnoses of several prominent men, but the disclosures, unlike the case of breast cancer, did not sustain or build coverage (Kedrowski and Sarow 2002). A medical doctor–political scientist team examined whether the media coverage of Bob Dole's 1996 presidential campaign accurately depicted Dole's risk of dying or becoming incapacitated in office, given his advanced age and related medical risks, and concluded that the media gave this topic only superficial coverage. Public opinion polls demonstrated that most voters discounted Dole's age—and by implication his potential infirmity (Abrams and Brody 1998).

Using the media to influence health behaviors is an important component of public health promotion, but it is no panacea. An American Cancer Society effort to promote low-cost mammograms to low-income and minority women generated significant interest on the part of the public but did not reach a large proportion of the target audience (Roetzheim et al. 1992). Another investigation of the utilization of breast cancer screening reinforces these findings (Yanovitzky and Blitz 2000). That effort concluded that physician advice is an important predictor of when a woman seeks mammography screening, but media coverage is more important for those who lack regular contact with or access to a physician.

MAGAZINE COVERAGE

Much of the social science research on breast cancer coverage analyzes magazines, a more targeted form of media. Breast cancer is a popular topic; more than three hundred articles on the subject appeared in high-circulation women's and general interest magazines over a four-year period (Burke et al. 2001). A similar study of three magazines targeted to African American women found that stories about breast cancer outnumbered those on cervical cancer, lung cancer, or any other tobacco-related cancers (Hoffman-Goetz et al. 1997). J. David Johnson (1997) found that women who read breast cancer–related articles in magazines report "greater fear, perceived vulnerability, general health concern, personal experience, and surveillance need" for such information (7).

Several feminist scholars have analyzed the language used in magazine coverage of breast and prostate cancer. Sociologist Juanne Clarke found that journalists used metaphors and idioms that reaffirm negative connotations of disease. Cancer, for instance, was often euphemistically portrayed as the "evil, immoral predator" (Clarke 1992, 116). According to Nelkin (1995), such metaphors shape people's thinking and allow them to create myths or beliefs about certain issues. In her analysis of Australian popular magazines and newspapers, Deborah Lupton (1994) found that the media favored medical and technological terms in reporting about breast cancer. The discourse often took on military terminology. Thus, persons with breast cancer were portrayed as "fighting battles" or "winning" or "losing wars" because of their lifestyle choices. Lupton noted contradictory beliefs about femininity. On the one hand, breast cancer was portrayed as a loss of reproductive choice; on the other, it was portrayed as a disease of women who were passive and suppressed their anger. Clarke (1999a) found a similar pattern. After studying mass-circulation women's magazines in the United States and Canada from 1974 to 1995 she observed that "breast cancer is described not as a disease that may result in human pain, suffering, even death at times but as a disease that affects 'femininity,' self-esteem and characteristically increases the emotional volatility of women" (126).[3]

Lantz and Booth (1998) applied social construction theory to interpret how popular U.S. magazines portray the increasing incidence of breast cancer. The authors noted a tendency to portray women with breast cancer as young professionals who contribute to their likelihood of developing the disease because of delayed childbirth; using oral contraceptives, tobacco, and alcohol; and considering abortion as a means of birth control. Such a portrayal in the popular press, "reflects a strong social desire to create and control a frightening epidemic" (907).

Such views were shared by Jennifer Fosket, Angela Karren, and Christine LaFia (2000), who analyzed the content of meaning and messages about breast cancer in popular women's magazines over a sixty-three-year period. Among the similar themes they found were women's responsibility for the disease, an emphasis on heroic women who overcame breast cancer, and a lack of discussion of "death, devastation, anger or political activism" (321). The authors attributed that emphasis to the need for magazines to reach the widest possible audience to increase profits, an assertion for which they provide no substantiation.

Clearly, however, not every magazine uses the same frames to report breast cancer. Julie Andsager and Angela Powers's sophisticated study (1999) analyzed 127 articles on breast cancer from three news magazines and four women's magazines from the 1990s. Frames, they found, differed between types of magazines and often within types. Both genres reported on breast cancer prevention issues. Women's magazines, however, were more likely to rely on personal stories, whereas news magazines covered economic issues such as insurance coverage of breast cancer treatment.

Two studies focused on the importance of images—pictures in magazine articles. Lisa Cartwright (1998), who argued that visual art is a powerful alternative way to promote health advocacy to communicate images of power and control, used Matuschka's self-portrait of her postmastectomy torso as an example. In a broader study of photographs and drawings accompanying articles on breast cancer, Julie Andsager, Stacy Hust, and Angela Powers (2000) suggest that images of women have become slightly less passive since the 1970s, but fashion magazines in particular portray women as submissive or somehow responsible for developing breast cancer.

Systematic studies of the portrayal of prostate cancer in the media are almost nonexistent. Juanne Clarke (1999b) studied thirty-six magazine articles from 1974 to 1995 that include all prostate cancer stories indexed in the *Readers' Guide to Periodical Literature* and the *Canadian Periodical Index*. She found similar use of war metaphors in prostate cancer coverage. In addition, sexuality issues were emphasized over the health of the whole person. Clarke mourned the lack of male celebrities to promote the early detection and screening of prostate cancer. What she did not note is probably her most significant finding—the absolute paucity of prostate cancer articles.

CRITIQUE. An extensive collection of literature provides some provocative findings, but many studies have shortcomings. First, those completed by scientists or medical doctors focus primarily on the accuracy of media coverage of scientific discoveries, yet many of these scholars do not appear to understand or appreciate journalistic practices. Second, few studies attempt to document changes over time, even when the period examined was lengthy (Clarke 1992, 1999a, 1999b; Fosket, Karran, and LaFia 2000; Houn et al. 1995; Lantz and Booth 1998). Third, many of the studies use a small sample size, analyzing fewer than a hundred items (Cartwright 1998; Clarke 1999a, 1999b; Hoffman-Goetz et al. 1997; Houn et al. 1995; Lantz and Booth 1998; Schwartz and Woloshin 2002; Zerbe, Young, and Nagelhout 1998). In others, the sample size is difficult to determine (Clarke 1992, 1999a; Lupton 1994; Whiteman et al. 2001). Similarly, coding criteria in some were vague; the coding was carried out by only one person (Clarke 1992, 1999a, 1999b; Fosket, Karran, and LaFia 2000; Lantz and Booth 1998; Lupton 1994; Whiteman et al. 2001); or the authors analyzed a very short timeframe (Burke et al. 2001).

Our analysis fills several gaps in this literature. First, we analyze a large number of news articles—more than 4,200, a number that far exceeds even the most ambitious of the previous studies (Corbett and Mori 1999a, $n = 1,999$) and is large enough to track changes over time and analyze for myriad variables. Second, our coding criteria and methods are explicit and clearly articulated, as we describe in the Methodological Appendix.

Third, we chose these specific media vehicles—major newspapers and television networks—because of their impact on the public at large and on policymakers (Hess 1984). Our analysis measures the impact of advocacy organizations on media coverage (chapter 5); ties media coverage to changes in public opinion (chapter 4); and links advocacy, media coverage, and public opinion to policy changes (chapters 6 and 7). If, for example, grassroots survivors' organizations (GSOs) use media advocacy strategies, they would likely target their efforts to media vehicles that policymakers read. Each vehicle also has a large number of viewers or a large circulation, and each plays a significant agenda-setting function within the media itself. Therefore, coverage in these outlets is likely to shape both mass opinion and elite opinion.

Areas of Exploration

DIFFERENCES IN COVERAGE, BY CANCER

We explore four issues in this chapter. The first two consider the differences in media coverage by cancer. First, we explore whether there any observable differences in the media coverage of breast cancer and prostate cancer. We expect coverage to vary by disease and that breast cancer will receive more coverage.

Second, we explore whether the *content* of the news coverage of these diseases varies. We expect the content to vary. Hard news stories, covering medical discoveries or the diagnosis of a public official, will be newsworthy regardless of disease. Given that women are more interested in health news and more likely to pay attention to messages about prevention, screening, and risk reduction, we expect breast cancer stories to include more soft news stories. Similarly, we look for variations in sources that the coverage uses. In part, the sources cited by reporters are driven logically by subject matter. A story about pending government regulations, for example, is likely to cite an official from that agency. Stories about medical discoveries will cite the journal or the experts who conducted the research.

Third, we explore whether the content of news coverage changes over time. As coverage of the two disease increases, reporting will become more complex, deal with more topics, and use a more diverse pool of sources.

Fourth, we explore whether the coverage of each cancer varies by medium. Coverage is examined in two ways. First we compare it by type of medium, whether national newspapers, regional newspapers, or television. Then we compare the *New York Times*'s coverage to that of all seven other sources. The *New York Times* is of singular importance because of the agenda-setting role it plays in national media. As such, communication and politics scholars consider its coverage as a surrogate for news coverage nationally (e.g., Baumgartner and Jones 1993; Costain 1992; Costain and Frasier 2003; Policy Agendas Project 2003).

Breast Cancer and Prostate Cancer in the News

COVERAGE COMPARED

The first issue involves a fundamental issue involving media coverage. Specifically, Were there discernable differences in the coverage of breast cancer and prostate cancer in the news media? To answer that question we tested two research questions:

RQ1: Are there more stories about breast cancer than prostate cancer in these news media sources?

RQ2: Does the gap of news coverage between these two diseases decrease over time?

OVERALL COMPARISONS. The first finding concerns the enormous disparity in media coverage between these two diseases. The dataset includes a total of 4,246 news stories in the eight media outlets studied. Almost all (85 percent, or 3,645 stories) concerned breast cancer. Only 14 percent (601 stories) addressed prostate cancer. Even if prostate cancer was the "disease of the 1990s" as some commentators have termed it, prostate cancer news coverage is entirely eclipsed by the coverage of breast cancer. Although this analysis examines differences in the nature of news coverage of these two diseases, that fact should never be forgotten. If the volume of news coverage were equated to a voice, breast cancer is a shout and prostate cancer is a whisper (table 3). Based upon that evidence, we found significantly greater coverage of breast cancer than prostate cancer.

Table 3. Prostate Cancer and Breast Cancer News Stories by Medium and Story Type

	Breast Cancer		Prostate Cancer		Wilcoxon Scores	
	%	(*n*)	%	(*n*)	Chi-Square[a]	p
Los Angeles						
Times	25.16	(917)	14.98	(90)	1.45	0.228
New York						
Times	18.22	(664)	22.63	(136)		
Atlanta						
Constitution	17.86	(651)	12.81	(77)		
Washington Post	17.23	(628)	21.30	(128)		
Chicago Tribune	9.85	(359)	14.64	(88)		
NBC	4.61	(168)	5.32	(32)		
CBS	3.73	(136)	4.66	(28)		
ABC	3.35	(122)	3.66	(22)		
Total *n*	3,645		601			
Hard news[b]	52.78	(1691)	56.89	(293)	3.02	0.082
Soft news[c]	7.22	(1513)	43.11	(222)		
Total *n*						
(newspapers)	3,204		515			

Source: Data compiled by authors.
[a]df = 1
[b] Newspaper stories only.
[c] Newspaper stories only.

News coverage of both diseases was fairly steady in the 1980s (figure 1). News outlets ran twenty to forty stories on breast cancer each year in the early part of that decade, whereas prostate cancer received essentially no coverage. In the early 1980s fewer than ten stories per year appeared in these eight outlets. Breast cancer stories increased slightly in 1985 with coverage of several scientific discoveries (eighty-eight stories).[4] It gradually increased until 1990 and then, beginning in 1991, rapidly increased. News coverage of breast cancer peaked in 1994 (465 stories) with the controversies surrounding silicone breast implants and disclosures of fraud in government-funded research trials. Coverage declined in 1995 and 1996 but peaked again in 1998 (477 stories). Prostate cancer news stories peaked briefly in 1987 (twenty-eight stories) with the diagnoses of several prominent men and then declined again until 1991, when Senators Bob Dole (R-KS) and Alan Cranston (D-CA) received considerable coverage of their diagnoses and treatments. The year 1991 proved to be pivotal because coverage did not decline again. Prostate cancer stayed on the media agenda, and coverage continued to increase, peaking again in 1998 with 132 stories (figure 1).

We expected to find more extensive coverage of breast cancer but anticipated that the gap would narrow as prostate cancer became part of the media's

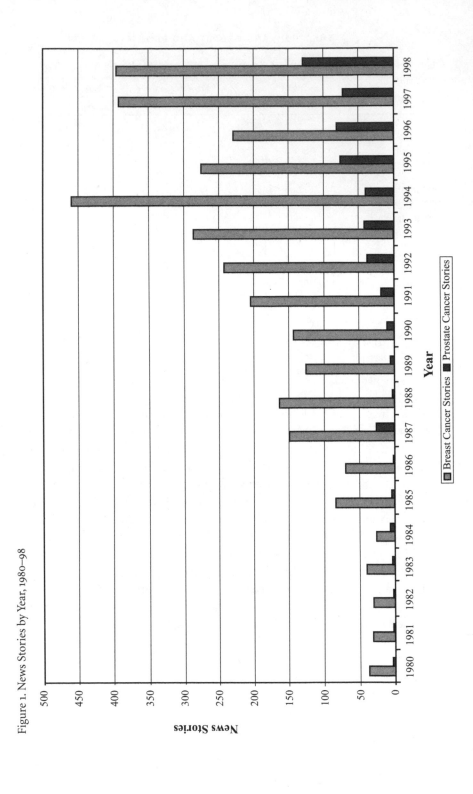

Figure 1. News Stories by Year, 1980–98

agenda. That was not the case. The number of prostate cancer stories increased in the 1990s, but breast cancer stories increased even faster. The gap did not close but widened.

What accounts for this disparity? The data do not tell us precisely, but we speculate that one major reason is the importance of women, whether as reporters, editors, or consumers of news. Women composed about 30 percent of the U.S. news reporters in the 1980s and 1990s, and over the same period more moved into managerial positions in news organizations, especially in newspaper work (Weaver 1990). The evidence is mixed on whether women reporters perceive stories about women (and issues important to them) as newsworthy even though their male counterparts, who share the same professional socialization, do not. Bernadette Barker-Plummer (2002) found that the National Organization of Women (NOW) cultivated a small group of sympathetic Washington-based reporters and supplied them with information and materials about the feminist cause. Those reporters were important in persuading editors and others that women's issues were newsworthy, and they were instrumental in getting media coverage for the cause (198).

We see some evidence of gendered reporting in the case of gender-specific cancers. In their analysis of television coverage of that topic, Corbett and Mori (1999b) found that male television reporters covered stories relating to medical discoveries or treatment. Women covered female-specific cancers when they related to health policy issues or personalities but never reported on male cancers.

Craft and Wanta (2004), however, compared issue agendas and story focus at fifteen newspapers that employed relatively high percentages of women editors with fifteen that had lower percentages of women editors. Females were more likely to cover health and environmental issues on newspapers with a higher percentage of female editors, whereas males were more likely to cover such issues on newspapers that had a low percentage of female editors.

At the same time that women made inroads into newsrooms and editorial boards, newspapers made an effort to appeal to women readers. As one former editor recalls, "I tell them [male editors] to consider women a huge suburb you don't cover well" (as quoted in Mills 1995, 53). The growing awareness that men and women are interested in different issues had an impact on story selection and placement (Mills 1995).

COMPARISONS BY CONTENT

Next we explore whether the content varied by cancer. We asked these research questions:

RQ3: Given recent medical discoveries and controversies (introduction), will there be differences in news story subject matter on the subjects of medical discoveries, ethics, support/interest groups, regulations and funding?

RQ4: Given the differences in coverage expected from the findings of RQ3, will coverage between the two cancers vary with the types of sources used?

SUBJECTS COMPARED.   The most common subjects of breast cancer stories were medical discoveries (34 percent), other (23 percent), health education (21 percent), personality profiles or narratives (19 percent), regulations (14 percent), and ethics (10 percent). All other topics appeared in fewer than 10 percent of all breast cancer stories. Prostate cancer stories followed a very different pattern. Almost half (43 percent) were personality profiles. Stories about medical discoveries (33 percent), health education (31 percent), risk (25 percent), and other (10 percent) followed. All other topics appeared in fewer than 10 percent of all prostate cancer stories (table 4).

The differences in subject matter were more than cosmetic. Statistical analyses (Wilcoxon scores) reveal that in almost every case the differences in the story content were statistically significant.[5] A higher proportion of prostate cancer stories focused on personalities, health education, risk, diagnostic discoveries, and federal funding. A higher proportion of breast cancers

Table 4. Prostate Cancer and Breast Cancer News Stories by Subject Matter

Story Subject	Breast Cancer		Prostate Cancer		Wilcoxon Scores	
	%	(n)	%	(n)	Chi-Sq[a]	p
Medical discoveries	34.43	(1,255)	33.28	(200)	0.93	0.3258
treatment	9.55	(348)	10.65	(64)	0.71	0.3980
diagnostic	8.86	(323)	12.48	(75)	7.95	0.0048
other	16.02	(584)	10.15	(61)	13.80	0.0002
Personality	19.45	(709)	42.60	(256)	157.33	<0.0001
Hearings	2.17	(79)	0.33	(2)	9.27	0.0023
Funding	2.39	(87)	3.99	(24)	5.23	0.0220
Regulations	13.94	(508)	4.99	(30)	37.30	<0.0001
Education	20.71	(755)	31.28	(755)	33.34	<0.0001
Support/Interest						
Group	8.81	(321)	3.00	(18)	23.71	<0.0001
Ethics	10.23	(373)	4.49	(27)	19.92	<0.0001
Risk	6.82	(41)	25.02	(912)	98.14	<0.0001
Other	23.29	(140)	10.01	(365)	86.82	<0.0001
Total *n*	3,645		601			

Source: Data compiled by authors.
Note: Percentages sum to more than 100 because each story could have up to three story subjects coded.
[a]df = 1

stories focused on ethics and other. In addition, breast cancer stories were proportionately more likely to cover hearings, regulations, and support/interest groups, all of which hint at more assertive advocates (table 3).

We expected to observe differences in news coverage of medical discoveries, ethics, funding, and regulations, and the coverage of support and interest groups, ethics, and regulations varied as expected. Coverage of medical discoveries and funding did not. There was no statistically significant difference in the coverage of medical discoveries, and the differences in coverage of funding were opposite that expected. These conclusions, however, are based upon comparisons of subject matter *as percentages* of the total number of news stories of each cancer. When the raw data are examined the number of breast cancer stories on any subject dwarfs the number on prostate cancer (table 4).

SOURCES COMPARED.   Did coverage vary by source? The most frequently cited sources in breast cancer stories were medical experts (43 percent), government agency/official (35 percent), persons with the disease (21 percent), medical journals (18 percent), other (16 percent), support and interest groups (12 percent), and the American Cancer Society (11 percent). All other sources were used in fewer than 10 percent of all breast cancer stories. The most frequently cited sources in prostate cancer stories were medical experts (43 percent), government agency/official (32 percent), persons with the disease (25 percent), other (24 percent), medical journals (17 percent), and the American Cancer Society (10 percent) (table 5).

As expected, breast cancer stories were more likely to cite media and support and interest groups as sources. There is no statistically significant difference in the percentage of stories that cite government agencies and officials or medical experts. Although there was no difference in the percentage of stories that cited medical journals, breast cancer stories were more likely to cite articles published in the *New England Journal of Medicine;* prostate cancer stories were more likely to cite the *Journal of the American Medical Association.* In addition, we observed some differences that were not expected: Breast cancer stories were more likely to cite private corporations, and prostate cancer stories were more likely to cite persons with the disease (table 5).

Given the importance of the *Chicago Tribune*'s investigation into fraud in breast cancer research trials and the large number of made-for-television movies and other entertainment venues that featured the topic, breast cancer stories were more likely to use the media as a source. The reasons for other differences are less clear. The prominence of personality stories in the

Table 5. Prostate Cancer and Breast Cancer News Stories by Story Source

Story Source	Breast Cancer		Prostate Cancer		Wilcoxon Scores	
	%	(*n*)	%	(*n*)	Chi-Sq[a]	p
Medical journal	17.8	(649)	16.97	(102)	0.19	0.6621
JAMA	3.29	(120)	5.82	(35)	9.39	0.0022
New England Journal of Medicine	6.01	(219)	2.3	(14)	13.46	0.0002
Government agency/ official	35.12	(1,280)	31.95	(192)	2.29	0.1304
Medical institution	8.67	(316)	9.65	(58)	0.62	0.4317
Private corporation	8.94	(326)	5.82	(35)	6.46	0.0111
Support/Interest Group	11.74	(428)	3.33	(20)	38.69	<0.0001
Media	7.38	(269)	4.33	(26)	7.45	0.0064
Medical expert	43.48	(1,585)	42.76	(257)	0.11	0.7407
Patient	20.96	(764)	24.79	(149)	4.49	0.034
American Cancer Society (ACS)	10.73	(391)	10.15	(61)	0.18	0.6708
Other	15.75	(574)	24.46	(147)	27.77	<0.0001
Total *n*	3,645		601			

Source: Data compiled by authors.
Note: Percentages sum to more than 100 because each story could have up to three story sources coded.
[a]df = 1

case of prostate cancer helps explain the use of persons with the disease as a source. Many of these stories included quotations from the person undergoing treatment. Second, government sources appeared in different types of stories. In prostate cancer stories the officials commented on the prognosis or treatment of a prominent government official, and in breast cancer stories government sources commented on regulations or controversies.

BREAST CANCER AND PROSTATE CANCER COVERAGE OVER TIME. A major drawback of many previous studies was that scholars did not look for changes in coverage over time. Given new medical discoveries and treatment options and the publicity surrounding prominent personalities and other events, we expected coverage to be dynamic—and that the content of news coverage changed over time. Thus we asked:

RQ5: Did story subjects and story sources used in the coverage of these two diseases vary over time?

The nature of prostate cancer coverage changed dramatically from 1980 to 1998. The first difference was in reporters' choice of sources. In 1980 the only story sources used were medical experts, government agencies and officials, and medical institutions. Persons with prostate cancer did not appear as sources in any article until 1983, and not in large numbers until 1991. Similarly, no article cited the American Cancer Society until 1987, and support and interest groups did not appear until 1989. The sources used most consistently over time were medical journals, medical experts, and government agencies and officials (table 6).

The second difference was in the subject matter of prostate cancer stories. In the aggregate, personality stories dominate prostate cancer news coverage, but the first personality story did not appear until 1983, and, with the exception of 1987, they did not compose a large number of stories until 1991. Stories about ethics did not appear until 1987. Those about support and interest groups did not surface until 1990, and risk was not covered until 1995. By contrast, health education and medical discoveries were the most consistent story subjects over this nineteen-year period (table 7).

What about breast cancer? All types of story sources appeared in every year, demonstrating much more diversity in sources used compared to prostate cancer coverage. Second, stories citing all types of sources increased steadily from 1980 to 1998, and those featuring medical experts, government agencies and officials, and medical journals were perennially popular. Yet there were variations. Stories featuring persons with breast cancer gradually increased over time, and support and interest groups were cited more frequently after 1990. The media became important in 1994 and peaked again in 1997. The importance of media as a source in 1994 was due to the publicity surrounding the *Chicago Tribune*'s series. Findings were reported in other news outlets, citing the *Tribune* as the source. The media became an important source in 1997 with the publicity surrounding the plot line of the sit-com *Murphy Brown*, in which the title character developed breast cancer (table 8).

The subject matter of breast cancer stories varied even more. There was little coverage of congressional hearings before 1991 and no stories concerning ethics until 1984, but stories about medical discoveries and personalities dramatically increased in the early 1990s. Coverage of several subjects peaks in 1994, among them medical discoveries, hearings, health education, regulations, ethics, and risk. Some subjects were related to the breast cancer fraud controversy, but others were not. Thus, as in the case of prostate cancer, the nature of breast cancer news coverage varied substantially over time (table 9).

DIFFERENCES BY MEDIA TYPE

Because of the agenda-setting function of the *New York Times* and the common training of journalists we did not expect significant differences in cover-

Table 6. Prostate Cancer News Stories by Source and Year, Frequencies

Year	Medical Journal	Gov.	Institution	Private Corp.	Support/ Int. Group	Media	Expert	Patient	ACS	Other	Total
1980	0	1	1	0	0	0	2	0	0	0	3
1981	0	0	0	0	0	0	2	0	0	1	2
1982	0	0	2	0	0	0	2	0	0	0	2
1983	0	2	0	2	0	0	3	2	0	0	6
1984	0	3	0	0	0	0	3	2	0	2	7
1985	1	3	1	0	0	0	0	3	0	1	6
1986	0	1	1	0	0	0	2	1	0	0	4
1987	2	9	12	1	0	7	7	3	3	2	28
1988	1	3	1	0	0	0	3	0	0	1	4
1989	1	4	0	1	0	0	4	0	2	1	7
1990	1	4	2	0	1	0	4	6	0	1	11
1991	6	8	0	3	0	0	10	4	3	6	20
1992	7	16	1	8	0	0	25	9	4	5	41
1993	13	16	7	0	0	2	22	12	6	11	47
1994	12	11	2	1	3	0	21	16	5	12	43
1995	12	12	9	3	2	0	44	29	16	21	80
1996	18	31	9	2	3	7	28	17	5	26	81
1997	4	36	3	6	2	6	14	16	2	34	77
1998	27	32	7	8	9	4	61	29	15	23	132

Source: Data compiled by authors. Each story was coded for up to three sources. Therefore, rows do not sum to the number listed in the "total" column.

Table 7. Prostate Cancer News Stories by Subject and Year, Frequencies

Year	Discovery	Personality	Hearings	Funding	Regs.	Health Ed.	Support/ Int. Group	Ethics	Risk	Other Sub.	Total n
1980	2	0	0	0	0	1	0	0	0	0	3
1981	2	0	0	0	0	0	0	0	0	0	2
1982	1	0	0	0	0	1	0	0	0	0	2
1983	5	1	0	0	0	1	0	0	0	0	6
1984	5	1	0	0	0	3	0	1	0	2	7
1985	1	4	0	0	0	3	0	0	0	1	6
1986	1	2	0	0	0	1	0	0	0	1	4
1987	8	19	0	0	1	7	0	1	0	7	28
1988	0	2	0	0	1	0	0	0	0	3	4
1989	4	2	0	1	2	3	0	1	0	2	7
1990	1	7	0	1	0	3	1	0	0	8	11
1991	7	12	0	0	0	8	0	1	0	9	20
1992	13	19	0	0	3	19	1	2	0	11	41
1993	22	13	0	2	4	20	1	4	0	11	47
1994	9	19	0	0	4	17	3	5	2	11	43
1995	18	30	0	2	2	48	3	4	2	9	80
1996	31	34	2	2	7	8	2	2	14	15	81
1997	11	50	0	6	0	7	3	5	5	35	77
1998	51	41	0	10	6	38	4	1	18	15	132

Source: Data compiled by authors. Each story was coded for up to three subjects.

Table 8. Breast Cancer News Stories by Source and Year, Frequencies

Year	Medical Journal	Gov.	Institution Corp.	Private	Support/ Int. Group	Media	Expert	Patient	ACS	Other	Total
1980	4	11	4	2	4	2	19	8	4	6	38
1981	8	5	2	1	1	1	13	6	2	2	26
1982	7	6	3	1	1	1	9	0	9	0	21
1983	6	14	2	1	6	0	21	4	9	4	36
1984	4	10	2	4	3	0	14	7	3	0	26
1985	23	31	9	2	5	9	38	15	17	10	88
1986	16	29	8	8	8	1	37	8	16	6	72
1987	34	67	10	3	7	14	64	17	30	20	153
1988	22	77	16	6	7	10	59	23	17	21	150
1989	36	60	9	7	11	4	80	20	17	25	145
1990	35	63	16	15	12	10	97	45	19	33	199
1991	20	84	14	25	29	11	97	51	28	20	193
1992	45	116	18	29	48	18	87	71	34	40	295
1993	37	114	24	22	48	19	138	73	36	48	295
1994	75	181	49	37	37	31	228	99	30	78	465
1995	65	80	24	29	39	25	115	57	22	56	287
1996	63	77	30	32	41	28	107	54	17	44	273
1997	65	126	31	43	56	53	137	82	47	72	406
1998	68	129	45	59	65	32	200	124	34	89	477

Source: Data compiled by authors. Each story was coded for up to three sources. Therefore, rows do not sum to the number listed in the "total" column.

Table 9. Breast Cancer News Stories by Subject and Year, Frequencies

Year	Discovery	Personality	Hearings	Funding	Regs.	Health Ed.	Support/ Int. Group	Ethics	Risk	Other Sub.	Total n
1980	19	4	0	0	1	11	2	0	10	1	38
1981	13	3	1	0	3	6	1	0	2	3	26
1982	10	0	0	0	3	4	0	0	9	1	21
1983	23	2	1	0	2	7	1	0	11	2	36
1984	7	3	0	0	4	12	1	1	5	2	26
1985	44	14	1	0	4	24	3	2	26	2	88
1986	34	8	0	1	6	17	3	6	23	5	72
1987	52	61	1	1	9	26	2	5	35	16	153
1988	52	49	2	2	16	30	0	5	30	14	150
1989	63	24	2	3	20	27	8	10	62	9	145
1990	78	38	6	1	17	43	11	21	52	15	199
1991	52	25	13	11	30	37	19	22	43	17	193
1992	85	44	9	14	66	54	23	22	78	28	295
1993	91	52	7	21	44	40	39	24	67	23	295
1994	144	91	22	5	79	117	48	106	106	32	465
1995	82	55	4	8	30	87	42	36	86	25	287
1996	103	47	2	6	27	39	26	38	82	53	273
1997	114	72	4	7	71	75	43	36	94	73	406
1998	173	117	4	7	76	99	49	39	91	44	477

Source: Data compiled by authors. Each story was coded for up to three subjects. Therefore, rows do not sum to the number listed in the "total" column.

age by media type. We conducted this analysis in two ways. First, we compared national newspapers (the *New York Times* and *Washington Post*), regional newspapers (the *Atlanta Constitution, Chicago Tribune,* and *Los Angeles Times*), and television (ABC, NBC, and CBS). Second, we contrasted the *New York Times* to all other media sources. Specifically, we asked:

> RQ6: Did each medium use approximately the same proportion of stories on breast cancer and prostate cancer?

> RQ7: Were the subjects of news coverage for each disease consistent across news media?

> RQ8: Were the sources used by reporters consistent across news media?

> RQ9: Was coverage in the *New York Times* similar to all other news sources with respect to subject matter and sources used?

COMPARISONS BY MEDIA TYPE. News coverage differed by type of media. Television news, given its smaller news hole, carried the fewest stories on each disease. Each network carried between 3 percent and 5 percent of all stories on either cancer (table 3).

The *Los Angeles Times* covered breast cancer more than other newspapers and published 917 stories—one-quarter (25 percent)—on that topic. The *New York Times, Washington Post,* and *Atlanta Constitution* each printed about six hundred news stories, or about 18 percent of the total. The *Chicago Tribune* printed the fewest breast cancer stories, about 10 percent of the total (359 stories) (table 3).

Several factors account for those differences. Much of the coverage in the *Los Angeles Times* featured celebrities who had the disease or who participated in various fund-raisers on behalf of breast cancer. The *Times* also published many stories about television programming on breast cancer, which is not surprising given that Los Angeles is the center of the television production and entertainment business. The smaller number of news stories in the *Chicago Tribune* may be attributable, in part, to the fact that the *Tribune* had no regular health or science section (Peres interview 2003). Therefore, stories about diseases or health competed with all others for space.

By contrast, national newspapers, the *Washington Post,* and the *New York Times* carried the largest percentage of prostate cancer stories, about 20 percent each (128 and 136 stories respectively). Regional newspapers carried slightly fewer than a hundred each, between 13 and 15 percent of the total (table 3).

BREAST CANCER VARIATIONS. Did the content of breast cancer stories differ by media type? Our analysis found significant variation between media type and content. Television news carried more stories on federal funding, hearings, ethics, and medical discoveries and fewer on personalities. Regional newspapers carried the most coverage of personalities and support and interest groups and fewer stories on funding and ethics (table 10). There was no statistically significant difference between regional and national newspapers in the proportion of hard and soft news stories (table 12).

Reporters varied in the types of sources they cited. Those for national newspapers were more likely to cite medical journals and private organizations. Regional newspaper reporters, by contrast, were more likely to cite other media and medical institutions and less likely to cite government officials and agencies. Television news reporters were more likely to cite experts and persons with the disease and less likely to cite the American Cancer Society (table 11).

Comparison of the *New York Times* to the other seven media outlets is enlightening. The *Times*'s reporters differed in the types of sources they chose to cite, which were less likely to include medical institutions, support and interest groups, other media, persons with breast cancer, and the American Cancer Society. In addition, the *Times* was more likely to quote the *New England Journal of Medicine,* government agencies and officials, private organizations, and medical experts (tables 10–12).

PROSTATE CANCER BY MEDIA TYPE. Prostate cancer coverage also showed some variation by media type. Television news, for example, carried more stories on funding, hearings, and medical discoveries. Ethics were discussed only in the *Washington Post* and *New York Times.* Television reporters were less likely to cite medical journals, and regional newspaper reporters were more likely to cite support and interest groups (tables 13–14).

Was the *New York Times* an agenda-setter in prostate cancer news? Surprisingly, no. Reporters for the *Times* were more likely to cite medical journals in general—the *Journal of the American Medical Association* and *New England Journal of Medicine* in particular—than reporters for other news outlets. They were also more likely to cite private organizations (e.g., corporations and insurance companies) than other reporters and appeared less likely to cite support and interest groups, although that relationship only approaches statistical significance (table 14). Moreover, the *Times* was likely to focus on different subjects, for example, medical discoveries, medical ethics, and other topics, in its prostate cancer coverage. Health education stories and the

Table 10. Breast Cancer News Stories by Subject and Medium

Story Subject	Medium[a]								Grouped by Type[a]		Wilcoxon Scores NYT[b]	
	NYT %	WP %	AC %	CT %	LAT %	ABC %	NBC %	CBS %	Chi-Sq	p	Chi-Sq	p
Medical discoveries	35.2	27.6	35.6	35.6	26.4	47.5	55.9	57.4	85.9	<.0001	0.6	0.452
treatment	9.6	9.9	8.0	10.3	7.7	15.6	16.1	11.8	15.9	.000	0.0	0.929
diagnostic	7.4	6.4	8.6	13.4	7.2	9.8	16.7	17.6	26.2	<.0001	2.2	0.137
other	18.4	11.6	19.5	12.8	12.0	22.1	25.0	27.9	29.8	<.0001	3.3	0.068
Personality	18.1	20.9	16.4	23.1	24.0	13.1	11.9	8.8	22.3	<.0001	1.0	0.321
Hearings	1.8	2.6	1.5	1.4	1.8	7.4	2.4	4.4	12.9	0.002	0.5	0.481
Funding	2.3	3.3	1.1	1.9	2.2	6.6	3.6	2.2	8.8	0.012	0.0	0.811
Regulations	14.2	16.7	11.1	13.1	12.4	18.0	17.9	17.6	13.2	0.001	0.0	0.857
Education	22.6	9.6	31.8	24.2	21.5	9.02	19.6	7.4	59.0	<.0001	1.7	0.187
Support/ Interest Groups	9.2	3.8	10.9	13.7	11.0	4.1	3.0	3.7	39.8	<.0001	0.1	0.702
Ethics	10.2	13.1	6.0	11.4	10.2	10.7	11.3	12.5	6.4	0.040	0.0	0.994
Risk	24.6	25.2	27.8	22.3	19.8	36.1	29.8	39.7	45.1	<.0001	0.1	0.756
Other	8.6	19.9	5.5	6.7	11.6	5.7	3.6	2.96	25.7	<.0001	1.8	0.175
Total n[c]	664	628	651	359	917	122	168	136				

Source: Data compiled by authors.
Note: NYT = New York Times; WP = Washington Post; AC = Atlanta Constitution; CT = Chicago Tribune; LAT = Los Angeles Times
[a]Grouped as national media (New York Times and Washington Post); regional media (Atlanta Constitution, Chicago Tribune and Los Angeles Times); and television (NBC, ABC, and CBS); df = 2.
[b]This analysis compares the New York Times to all other media; df = 1.
[c]Percentages sum to more than 100 because each story could have up to three story subjects coded.

Table 11. Breast Cancer News Stories by Source and Medium

Story Source	Medium								Wilcoxon Scores			
									Grouped by Type[a]		NYT[b]	
	NYT %	WP %	AC %	CT %	LAT %	ABC %	NBC %	CBS %	Chi-Sq	p	Chi-Sq	p
Medical journal	20.5	22.3	18.4	13.6	13.7	11.5	11.9	20.6	22.4	<.0001	5.5	0.019
JAMA	3.3	4.1	3.7	3.3	2.9	2.5	1.8	2.2	2.6	0.274	0.0	0.973
NEJM	8.4	6.5	5.5	4.2	3.5	8.2	6.5	13.2	22.5	<.0001	8.4	0.004
Government agency/ official	39.5	48.4	25.2	33.4	27.6	48.4	37.5	40.4	94.9	<.0001	6.7	0.009
Medical institution	5.9	11.9	8.6	10.6	9.3	4.1	3.6	8.8	6.7	0.035	8.0	0.005
Private corporation	10.8	9.7	8.0	5.8	11.1	7.4	2.4	3.7	14.6	0.0007	3.6	0.058
Support/ Interest Group	8.1	13.2	8.4	15.4	15.5	10.7	9.5	8.1	6.9	0.031	10.2	0.001
Media	3.9	10.7	7.5	8.4	9.3	3.3	2.4	2.9	16.6	0.0002	14.2	0.000
Expert	53.8	33.3	40.1	46.8	37.7	54.9	61.9	3.7	41.4	<.0001	34.9	<.0001
Patient	13.0	17.5	17.2	27.3	21.5	33.6	41.7	36.7	99.0	<.0001	31.4	<.0001
ACS	8.9	11.8	12.6	14.5	11.2	2.5	8.9	2.2	20.2	<.0001	2.9	0.090
Other	14.2	19.1	13.7	13.7	19.4	13.9	5.9	12.5	10.7	0.005	1.5	0.213
Total n[c]	664	628	651	359	917	122	168	136				

Source: Data compiled by authors.

Note: NYT = New York Times; WP = Washington Post; AC = Atlanta Constitution; CT = Chicago Tribune; LAT = Los Angeles Times

[a]Grouped as national media (New York Times and Washington Post); regional media (Atlanta Constitution, Chicago Tribune and Los Angeles Times); and television (NBC, ABC, and CBS) (df = 2).

[b]This analysis compares the New York Times to all other media (df = 1).

[c]Percentages sum to more than 100 since each story could have up to three story sources coded.

Table 12. Breast Cancer News Stories by News Type and Medium

| | Medium | | | | | | | | | | Wilcoxon Scores | | | |
| | NYT | | WP | | AC | | CT | | LAT | | Grouped by Type[a] | | NYT[b] | |
	%	(n)	%	(n)	%	(n)	%	(n)	%	(n)	Chi-Sq	p	Chi-Sq	p
Hard news	53.7	(356)	54.7	(342)	48.4	(313)	46.3	(165)	56.4	(515)	1.7	0.188	0.282	0.595
Soft news	46.3	(307)	45.3	(283)	51.6	(334)	53.6	(191)	43.6	(398)				
Total n	664		628		651		359		917					

Source: Data compiled by authors.

Note: NYT = New York Times; WP = Washington Post; AC = Atlanta Constitution; CT = Chicago Tribune; LAT = Los Angeles Times

[a]Grouped as national media (New York Times and Washington Post); regional media (Atlanta Constitution, Chicago Tribune, and Los Angeles Times); and television (NBC, ABC, and CBS). df = 2

[b]This analysis compares the New York Times to all other media (df = 1).

Table 13. Prostate Cancer Stories by Subject and Medium

| Story Subject | Medium | | | | | | | | Wilcoxon Scores | | | |
| | | | | | | | | | Grouped by Type[a] | | NYT[b] | |
	NYT %	WP %	AC %	CT %	LAT %	ABC %	NBC %	CBS %	Chi-Sq	p	Chi-Sq	p
Medical discoveries	40.4	19.5	27.3	42.0	20.0	45.4	31.2	57.1	6.2	0.044	5.8	0.016
treatment	15.4	8.9	10.4	10.2	5.6	18.2	3.1	17.9	1.9	0.387	4.2	0.040
diagnostic	14.0	8.6	10.4	19.2	6.7	9.1	18.7	21.4	1.9	0.387	0.3	0.550
other	11.7	3.9	7.8	14.8	10.0	18.1	9.4	17.9	3.4	0.184	0.5	0.479
Personality	43.4	46.1	35.1	34.1	55.6	27.3	43.7	39.3	1.3	0.526	0.0	0.833
Hearings	0	0	0	0	0	4.5	0	3.6	12.7	0.002	0.6	0.440
Funding	1.47	3.9	3.9	3.4	7.8	18.2	0	0	2.2	0.330	2.9	0.088
Regulations	5.1	5.5	6.5	4.6	3.3	4.5	9.4	0	0.1	0.951	0.0	0.924
Education	24.3	42.2	35.1	34.1	30.0	27.3	25.0	10.7	4.9	0.086	4.0	0.045
Support/ Interest Groups	1.5	7.0	1.3	2.3	2.2	4.6	3.1	0	2.3	0.321	23.9	<.0001
Ethics	8.1	7.8	1.3	4.5	1.1	0	0	0	13.9	0.001	5.2	0.021
Risk	2.9	7.0	7.8	9.1	4.4	18.2	12.5	7.1	5.2	0.073	0.6	0.444
Other	25.7	29.7	26.0	19.3	31.1	0	0	0	23.4	<.0001	4.16	0.041
Total n[c]	136	128	77	88	90	22	32	28				

Source: Data compiled by authors.

Note: NYT = New York Times; WP = Washington Post; AC = Atlanta Constitution; CT = Chicago Tribune; LAT = Los Angeles Times

[a] Grouped as national media (New York Times and Washington Post); regional media (Atlanta Constitution, Chicago Tribune and Los Angeles Times); and television (NBC, ABC, and CBS) (df = 2).

[b] This analysis compares the New York Times to all other media (df = 1).

[c] Percentages sum to more than 100 because each story could have up to three story subjects coded.

Table 14. Prostate Cancer News Stories by Source and Medium

Story Subject	Medium								Wilcoxon Scores			
									Grouped by Type[a]		NYT[b]	
	NYT %	WP %	AC %	CT %	LAT %	ABC %	NBC %	CBS %	Chi-Sq	p	Chi-Sq	p
Medical Journal	37.2	14.1	18.2	17.1	10.0	9.1	3.1	14.3	7.8	0.0205	14.1	0.0002
JAMA	10.3	4.7	7.8	5.7	2.2	0	0	7.1	3.4	0.1800	6.4	0.0114
NEJM	4.4	1.6	1.3	1.1	0	4.5	3.1	7.1	5.6	0.0615	3.4	0.0674
Government agency/ official	31.6	36.7	27.3	29.5	37.9	31.8	25.0	21.4	2.1	0.3546	0.0	0.9255
Medical institution	11.0	7.0	7.8	12.5	4.4	13.6	18.7	14.3	4.3	0.1169	0.4	0.5362
Private corporation	10.3	3.9	6.5	3.4	8.9	0	0	0	6.1	0.0482	6.4	0.0114
Support/ Interest Group	0.7	2.3	2.6	4.5	8.9	4.5	3.1	0	6.5	0.0370	3.7	0.0555
Media	4.4	3.9	3.9	7.9	3.3	4.5	3.1	0	1.1	0.5807	0.0	0.9555
Expert	48.5	43.0	36.4	55.7	31.1	54.5	28.1	35.7	2.1	0.3501	2.4	0.1225
Patient	21.3	28.9	27.3	20.4	21.1	40.9	31.2	21.4	2.0	0.3349	1.1	0.2873
ACS	11.7	11.7	15.6	11.4	5.6	4.5	3.1	3.6	4.6	0.1018	0.5	0.4787
Other	28	28.1	27.3	22.7	25.6	18.2	28.1	21.4	0.13	0.9340	1.4	0.2329
Total n[c]	136	128	77	88	90	22	32	28				

Source: Data compiled by authors.

Note: NYT = New York Times; WP = Washington Post; AC = Atlanta Constitution; CT = Chicago Tribune; LAT = Los Angeles Times

[a]Grouped as national media (New York Times and Washington Post); regional media (Atlanta Constitution, Chicago Tribune, and Los Angeles Times); and television (NBC, ABC, and CBS) (df = 2).

[b]This analysis compares the New York Times to all other media (df = 1).

[c]Percentages sum to more than 100 since each story could have up to three story sources coded.

activities of support and interest groups were less likely to receive coverage (table 14).

Although we expected to find uniformity in breast cancer and prostate cancer coverage we found more variation than consistency. Television coverage was different from print coverage, a finding that is not terribly surprising given television's time constraints and visual component. Other variations existed as well, including the coverage in regional and national newspapers, a fact that may reflect varying missions, audiences, and access to Washington news sources.

The most significant finding, however, calls into question the role of the *New York Times* as the industry standard in terms of health news. Its coverage of both diseases differed in measurable ways from that of other news outlets. These findings suggest that scholars' assumptions that the *Times* sets the agenda for all news media may no longer be true. Such assumptions tend to ignore that fact that the *Times* also has a local readership, as illustrated by its significant coverage of breast cancer on Long Island. It also suggests that *Times* reporters missed the emergence of the prostate cancer movement, key events of which occurred in Arizona, Texas, and California. By contrast, the fact that the other national newspaper, the *Washington Post*, carried more stories on the activities of support and interest groups, funding, and regulations suggests that its health reporters had a closer tie to the emerging prostate cancer movement.

Discussion

MEDIA AGENDA-SETTING

Cobb and Elder (1972) divide agenda-setting into three arenas: the media agenda, the public agenda, and the policy agenda. As Corbett and Mori (1999a) have maintained, breast cancer came onto the media agenda during the 1970s with the publicity surrounding the diagnoses of Shirley Temple Black, Betty Ford, Margaretta Fitler Murphy "Happy" Rockefeller, and Betty Rollin. If that is the case, then breast cancer would be part of the media agenda over the entire period of this study. The smallest number of breast cancer articles that appeared in our eight media sources in any given year was twenty-one (1982). By that measure, prostate cancer appeared briefly in the media agenda in 1987, when twenty-eight articles appeared in our eight sources, but that attention was not sustained. Coverage began to increase in 1991, with twenty articles in that year.

THE NATURE OF MEDIA COVERAGE

The significant differences in the coverage of both cancers, especially prostate cancer, are notable across media. Presumably, knowledge and perception of a disease varies depending upon which medium is used as an information source. This data suggest we cannot assume the *New York Times* sets the health media agenda. Rather, based upon these data, policymakers who read, for example, the *Washington Post* exclusively have a very different perception of the disease than those who read only the *Times*. People who rely exclusively on regional newspapers or television news would have still other perceptions.

Even if prostate cancer became part of the media's agenda in 1991, it is a part of a chorus and not at center stage. In the competition for media coverage, prostate cancer falls far behind breast cancer, and the gap appears to be widening. Moreover, the nature of coverage is as important as the amount of coverage. Stories that focus on prominent personalities personalize a disease—as did those on Betty Ford and Rock Hudson for breast cancer and AIDS—and communicate the potential risk to the public. By contrast, in spite of a dominance of personality stories, no single individual's diagnosis of prostate cancer led to sustained news media interest in that disease.

The change in story content about breast cancer and prostate cancer has been dramatic since the 1980s. Changes in the sources used and in the choice of subject matter coincided with important medical discoveries, public announcements of men and women who developed each disease, changes in public policy, and the emergence of support and interest groups. Reporters, who depend on national, state, and local events and activities for stories, responded to these changes. Significantly, as GSOs grew and created their own news, political and social activities related to breast cancer initially, and later prostate cancer, grew around them. Individuals were more willing to offer themselves as evidence, and so reporters had more access to sources with a personal story to tell.

The great newspaper columnist Walter Lippmann argued in *Public Opinion* (1922) that the press is a major contributor to how we see and imagine the world. Lippmann did not use the term *agenda-setting*, but his ideas set in motion much of the later research on that subject. Our perceptions of the severity of disease are related to how we frame the medical reporting of the topic in terms of our own schemas or knowledge structures (Shen 2004). This perception will be colored by the medium consumed and how and when it is used. Long-term studies that do not attempt to account for changes over time, or studies that focus on only a few weeks of media coverage, miss these important dynamics.

4

The Public Face of Cancer

BREAST CANCER AND PROSTATE CANCER
IN THE MEDIA AND PUBLIC PERCEPTIONS OF RISK

> I think the news media has largely represented breast cancer
> patients as older women, but that is changing as the YSC [Young
> Survival Coalition] works to bring awareness of the community of
> young women affected by breast cancer.
>
> —Francis Coulter
>
> We put out old, white men as the face of prostate cancer.
>
> —John Page

What occurs when an issue moves from the media agenda to the
public agenda? Certainly, in the case of a health issue, the public will begin
to internalize their perception of risk. In fact, when a disease occupies a
prominent place on the public agenda, we expect Americans to overestimate their risks of developing or contracting a disease. Such is the case in
breast cancer and prostate cancer. In spite of scientific gains since the 1980s,
Americans rank the fear of breast cancer and prostate cancer among their
greatest health concerns (Blendon et al. 2001). The bases of the public's fears
are complicated, but the nature of both diseases is no doubt a contributing
factor.

This chapter examines the "public face" of both breast cancer and prostate
cancer through an examination of newspaper coverage. A common journalistic technique is to include a human-interest angle in news coverage as a
means of personalizing a story. Such images complement the coverage and
collectively constitute the public face of an issue.

The public face of an issue has important ramifications in terms of agenda-
setting and its complement, problem definition. Political scientists David
Rochefort and Roger Cobb argue advocates must successfully define an issue's

severity, incidence, and proximity to argue it as ripe for government action (1994, 17–21). A sympathetic public face will help to do all three. It also will help move an issue from the media agenda onto public and policy agendas (Cobb and Elder 1972).

Personal profiles play a role in health promotion. Profiles communicate the extent of the disease and the personal toll that accompanies diagnosis and treatment; they also demonstrate that disease can strike people of all ages and backgrounds. As Joy Simha, cofounder of the Young Survival Coalition, recalled, seeing a made-for-television movie about Joyce Wadler, a breast cancer survivor and *People* magazine reporter, prompted her to visit a doctor. "Before I saw the movie," Simha reported, "I had no idea that I could get breast cancer. I had been feeling a lump for months. I saw the movie and decided my OB needed to feel the lump. By the time it was removed, it was 3.7 cm. Had I seen the movie sooner, perhaps it would have been smaller" (personal communication 2003).

The public face plays other roles as well. When these public faces present a distorted picture of who develops a disease, then members of the public, especially those who are heavy news media consumers, may develop an unrealistic perception of their own risk. An elevated perception of risk, in turn, adds pressure to public policymakers to take action.

Personal narratives are important to policymakers as well. R. Douglas Arnold (1990) notes that members of Congress pay attention to motivated, organized groups, and those groups may use personal experience as they argue for favorable public policies. Momentum to cover kidney dialysis for persons with end-stage renal disease (ESRD) as a covered benefit in the Medicare program, for example, grew when a person with ESRD dialyzed himself before a congressional committee (Schreiner 2000).

Risk Perception and Risk Communication

Questions of risk surround both breast cancer and prostate cancer. If a woman's chances of having breast cancer are one in seven at age eighty, what is her risk at fifty? How effective is a PSA test in diagnosing prostate cancer? Should a seventy-year-old man undergo treatment for prostate cancer or choose the alternative of "watchful waiting"? Is the risk of taking tamoxifen or raloxifene to reduce one's chances of developing breast cancer worth the possible side effects of stroke, pulmonary embolism, or endometrial cancer (ACS 2002c)?

Scientists, activists, and policymakers will debate questions of risk as long as there is uncertainty, disease, and death. As study after study has shown, issues of risk are socially constructed. An individual's perception of that risk often bears little resemblance to scientific fact. Individuals expect science to identify definitive causes of disease and provide cures for them, but in fact, scientists have not been able to accurately predict which individuals will develop breast cancer or prostate cancer (Rockhill 2003).

Perceptions of risk are based on the answers to a number of questions. Could it happen to me? What can I do to prevent the disease? What is my family history? Can I prevent a recurrence? Studies of college students, for instance, found that individuals are often unbiased about hereditary risk factors, pessimistic about environmental risk factors, but overly optimistic about the effects of their own actions or psychological attributes that might decrease their risk factors (Weinstein 1984, 452). This optimistic bias is often correlated with complacency and results in failure to adopt precautionary health behaviors (Weinstein 1984).

Experts think that crafting health intervention messages that help people understand the antecedent of a health problem and its consequences is the most effective way to communicate health risk information (Rothman and Kiviniemi 1999). For certain types of cancer, emphasis on risk assessment needs to be supplemented with an emphasis on individual self-efficacy. This belief in one's ability to execute a particular form of behavior has been found effective in preventing behavior linked to cancer, such as quitting smoking (Seydel, Taal, and Wiegman 1990). The television health reporter with a story on the six o'clock news about a new treatment for prostate cancer is unlikely to frame such information following that formula, and we know that public perception of risk is driven in part by media reports and analyses.

Understanding risk information is critical. Unrealistic perceptions of risk concerning the odds of developing prostate cancer or breast cancer not only cause unneeded stress but also may contribute to a failure to consider other medical issues of equal or more importance. Women constantly overestimate their chances of breast cancer while seriously underestimating their risk of heart disease, the number-one cause of death in women (Avon 2002a).

Developing public health policy is also dependant on understanding risk information. The assessment of science is, after all, an evaluation process that employs a variety of constituencies, from individuals to advocacy groups, politicians, government bureaucrats, and business. It becomes the job of the media to deconstruct the issues and interests of these constituencies for the public (Boffey, Rogers, and Schneider 1999).

RISKS AND BREAST CANCER AND PROSTATE CANCER

What are those risks and what do they mean? Both breast cancer and prostate cancer are strongly correlated with aging, but neither is a consequence of growing older. Prostate cancer risk increases after the age of fifty, with 70 percent of all cases identified in men over the age of sixty-five (ACS 2002d). African American men have a 70 percent higher risk than white men of developing prostate cancer and are more likely to die of the disease. One man in six will be diagnosed with the disease, but only one in thirty-two will die of prostate cancer.

Similarly, some 77 percent of all breast cancers are diagnosed in women over the age of fifty. Those in their forties compose about one-fifth of all cases (19 percent), those in their thirties compose 4 percent, and those under thirty compose less than 1 percent (ACS 2002b).

In January 1991 the American Cancer Society (ACS) modified the risks of non-Hispanic white women developing breast cancer by age eighty-six from one in ten to one in nine. The risk factor was modified again to one in eight in 1997 and to one in seven in 2005. Many women have heard these risk estimates but do not understand what they mean, nor have the media clearly explained them. The ratio represents the *absolute risk*—the average rate at which cancer occurs in the general population. It takes into consideration other causes of death over a lifespan. As an average, it overestimates the risk for women with no risk factors and underestimates it for those with more than one (Love and Lindsay 2000, 217). Another way to look at risk is to evaluate it in relative terms. *Relative risk* estimates are generally higher because they enable a user to include in the equation such factors as genetic history, family history, and menstrual and pregnancy history. It is important to know which risk figure is being used. Relative risk estimates, for example, do not include information about the absolute benefits of a form of treatment.

RISK AND SCREENING TESTS

The use of mammography in women younger than fifty is a hot topic in risk assessment.[1] Researchers at the Dartmouth-Hitchcock Medical Center asked two hundred women between forty and fifty, and who had no history of breast cancer, to estimate their probabilities of developing breast cancer and dying within ten years without screening (Black, Neese, and Tosteson 1995). As predicted, they overestimated their probability of dying of breast cancer within ten years by tenfold. They also overestimated the relative risk reduction of screening by sixfold. The respondents' assessments were made "despite the publication of articles explaining breast cancer risk in the *New York Times* and in the local papers" (724).

One of the questions troubling scientists is the relationship between the ability to interpret numbers (numeracy) and the ability to interpret risk data. Five hundred female veterans were asked to estimate their risk for death from breast cancer without mammography. In spite of adjustments for age, education, income, and framing the information, few were able to correctly describe the benefit of mammography to their individual risk for death from cancer. Problems with using and interpreting numbers affected the subjects' ability to interpret risk information correctly (Schwartz et al. 1997).

Difficulty interpreting risk information is not just a "female problem." Men frequently do not understand the risks and benefits of PSA tests. Researchers at the University of Texas-Houston Medical School studied 271 men over the age of fifty who had recently undergone routine physical examinations. Fewer than half understood that the test is sometimes inaccurate. More than 90 percent of the group believed that regular screening lowers their risk of dying from prostate cancer, and about 90 percent believed that treatment for prostate cancer prolongs life. Although their doctors urged 80 percent of the men to take the test, its efficacy was discussed in fewer than half of the cases (Chan et al. 2003).

DEPICTIONS OF RISK

The practice of health reporting involves what *Washington Post* science reporter Victor Cohn calls "the uncertainty of uncertainty" (1989, 8). This uncertainty is intensified when the nature, diagnosis, and treatment of both breast cancer and prostate cancer continue to be subjects of scientific debate (Shubert and Shubert 1997; Wells et al. 2001). Issues of risk clearly fall into this category.

Lantz and Booth (1998), who examined how magazines portrayed women with breast cancer from 1980 to 1985, found that 85 percent were under the age of fifty. Where articles contained photographs, 80 percent of the women pictured were clearly younger than fifty. "The predominant message is that breast cancer is an important disease because it strikes young, white women in the prime of their lives, often taking them away from productive careers and loving, caring families" (914). Burke and associates (2001) found similar patterns in a study of 389 articles in a variety of magazines with circulations greater than five hundred thousand. The mean age of the women in 172 profiles was forty-one (range, eighteen to sixty-six); fourteen percent featured either a woman with young children or one under fifty who was dying of breast cancer (61–62).

The image of breast cancer survivors may be changing, however. Andsager, Hust, and Powers (2000), who traced the images of women with breast cancer as portrayed in women's magazines over three decades, found that older women and those of color were more likely to be featured in the 1990s than in the previous two decades although not in relationship to their risk factors.

Issues for Exploration

We explore four issues in this chapter. First, did the public face of cancer as depicted in the news media from 1980 through 1998 resemble the "real" face of cancer? We suspect it did not in the case of breast cancer. In particular, we suspect that persons with breast cancer profiled in the news were younger than the typical person diagnosed.[2] As documented in the book *Fighting for Our Future* (Murphy 2003), young women with breast cancer face numerous issues that older women with breast cancer do not: preserving their fertility after treatment and risks associated with pregnancy. All of these factors make profiles of younger women more newsworthy, more urgent, and more tragic than those of older women. By contrast, we expect to find that the public face of prostate cancer more closely matched the typical person diagnosed.

Second, how did coverage differ between cancers? If, for example, breast cancer profiles were more likely to mention children, especially young children, then this public face would exaggerate the sense of tragedy associated with the disease. Similarly, if these profiles were more likely to mention whether a person was terminal, then that, too, would add to the sense of urgency and tragedy. Likewise, we examine the average number of persons profiled in a typical news story; including several profiles would amplify the sense of urgency and tragedy associated with the disease.[3]

Third, were there any variations in the public face of cancer? Specifically, what types of subject matter were likely to include profiles, did those profiles appear in hard news or soft news stories, and was the public face of cancer consistent across newspapers?

Fourth, what impact did the public face of cancer have upon public opinion? A previous study found that more than 92 percent of women followed news about medical developments and perceived breast cancer to be a greater health risk than heart disease (Merck 1997). We anticipate that the news media has an impact upon public opinion. To distort the public face of these diseases would in turn distort the public's perception of their risk, which impacts public policy in two ways. First, policymakers—members of Congress, their staff members, and executive branch officials—consume the same mass media as the public and are thus likely to develop the same distorted perception of the severity of the diseases. Second, the public's fear of the disease may lead to increased support for activists' policy agendas, further prompting policy-makers to act.

A total of 1,190 news stories, including more than 1,600 profiles of persons with either breast cancer or prostate cancer, were identified for this analysis. The number represents about 32 percent of all stories on breast cancer or prostate cancer that appeared in the sampled newspapers. The percentage varied by cancer. Stories with profiles composed half (51 percent) of all prostate cancer stories but fewer than a third (29 percent) of breast cancer stories. Regardless of those differences the sample remains skewed and includes more than three times as many breast cancer stories as prostate cancer stories (926 compared to 264). Breast cancer profiles outnumbered prostate cancer profiles by more than four to one (1,332 compared to 299) (table 15).[4] Because journalists may profile more than one person in a story, the unit of analysis is the person profiled unless otherwise noted.[5]

Public opinion is measured using public opinion polls. To measure changes in women's perceived risk we use three separate public opinion polls: a 1979 National Cancer Institute (NCI) study, a 1992 ABC News Women's Issues Poll, and a 1998 Harris Poll.[6] We secured copies of the datasets for the 1992 ABC Women's Issues Poll and the 1998 Harris Poll to conduct secondary analyses.[7] A similar analysis of men's perceived risk of prostate cancer was not possible because only the 1998 Harris Poll attempted such a measure.

Table 15. Stories and Profiles by Cancer and Medium

Medium	Number of Stories with Profiles				Persons Profiled			
	Breast Cancer		Prostate Cancer		Breast Cancer		Prostate Cancer	
	% of total	(*n*)	% of total	(*n*)	%	(*n*)	%	(*n*)
N. Y. Times	25.0	(166)	48.5	(66)	18.2	(243)	22.4	(67)
Washington Post	24.8	(156)	60.9	(78)	16.5	(220)	28.1	(84)
L.A. Times	34.0	(301)	62.2	(90)	29.6	(394)	20.1	(60)
Atlanta Constitution	26.0	(170)	37.7	(77)	18.8	(250)	11.4	(34)
Chicago Tribune	37.0	(133)	39.8	(88)	16.9	(225)	18.1	(54)
Total	28.8	(926)	50.8	(264)	100.0	(1,332)	100.1	(299)

Source: Data compiled by authors.

Polls from the Henry J. Kaiser Family Foundation and the Harvard School of Public Health (hereafter Kaiser/Harvard) were also examined. Those organizations regularly conduct polls to determine how closely the public follows health-care news stories. The more recent polls included questions relating to breast cancer, and a few included questions relating to prostate cancer. Results are presented to demonstrate how closely the public follows stories on the two diseases.

Finding the Public Face of Cancer

THE AGE OF THE PERSON PROFILED

We first explored whether the persons with cancer profiled by the news media are typical of those diagnosed with breast cancer and prostate cancer. Based on American Cancer Society data the typical person with breast cancer is more than fifty and the typical person with prostate cancer is more than sixty-five. We asked:

> RQ1: Did the news media accurately depict the age of the typical person diagnosed with breast cancer?

> RQ2: Did the news media accurately depict the age of the typical person diagnosed with prostate cancer?

We compared the frequencies of the ages (when reported) of persons with breast cancer, broken down by decade, with the ACS incidence data and found that the persons profiled with breast cancer are those considered to be too young to have the disease. Fewer than two-fifths (39 percent) of the persons profiled were fifty and older, the age bracket of the typical person diagnosed with breast cancer. The younger age brackets, which represent far fewer breast cancer cases, were over-represented in the media coverage. Nearly a third of the persons with breast cancer profiled were under forty, an age bracket that represents fewer than 5 percent of all breast cancer diagnoses. The youngest person profiled was seventeen (table 16).[8]

Prostate cancer profiles were more representative. A sizeable majority (59.5 percent) of those featured in media profiles were over sixty-five—still lower than the 70 percent incidence reported by the ACS, but the gap is smaller (table 17).

These findings are reinforced when we look at the average ages of persons profiled. The average age of persons with breast cancer profiled was 47.2, slightly lower than the benchmark age of fifty or more. The average age

Table 16. Profiles of Persons with Breast Cancer by Age, with ACS Comparison

Age	All Profiles		ACS Incidence Data
	%	(*n*)	% of All Cases
<30 years old	6.4	(50)	<1
30–39	23.5	(185)	4
40–49	30.6	(239)	19
50 and above	39.4	(308)	77+
Total	99.9	(781)	

Source: Data compiled by authors and taken from American Cancer Society (2002e).

Table 17. Profiles of Persons with Prostate Cancer by Age, with ACS Comparison

Age	All Profiles		ACS Incidence Data
	%	(*n*)	% of All Cases
<50	3.0	(6)	NA
50–64	37.5	(75)	NA
65 and above	59.5	(119)	70
Total	100	(200)	

Source: Data compiled by authors and taken from American Cancer Society (2002d).

of persons with prostate cancer was 65.5, almost exactly equal to the ACS benchmark of sixty-five.

In each case there is significant variation in the ages of persons profiled with either disease and a wide standard deviation (16.1 years for breast cancer and 19.8 for prostate cancer). In the case of breast cancer, however, the difference is particularly striking. Reporters were more likely to mention the ages of women in their thirties who had breast cancer than those in their seventies, even though the latter are more likely to develop the disease. In the case of prostate cancer, the wide standard deviation indicates that the media profiled as many men in their forties and fifties as they did men over seventy (table 18).

Based upon these findings, we conclude that the public face of women with breast cancer was atypical—too young. This finding contradicts the perception articulated by Francis Coulter in the opening quotation. The Young Survival Coalition's premise is that young women and physicians do not realize young women can and do get breast cancer. The same cannot be said, however,

Table 18. Difference of Means Tests: Ages, Children's Ages, and Number of Profiles/Stories

	Age/Number	(*n*)	Standard Dev.	|t|	p
Profiles' average age					
Breast cancer	47.2	(781)	16.1	19.13	<.0001
Prostate cancer	65.5	(200)	19.8		
Children's average age					
Breast cancer	17.3	(155)	12.7	2.52	0.0127
Prostate cancer	32.2	(8)	9.7		
Number of profiles/story					
Breast cancer	1.4	(926)	1.4	3.53	0.0004
Prostate cancer	1.1	(264)	0.7		

Source: Data compiled by authors.

for newspaper coverage.[9] By contrast, the public face of prostate cancer closely reflected the age of the typical man diagnosed with that disease.

THE URGENCY, SEVERITY, AND TRAGEDY OF THE DISEASE

Second, we explored how the coverage of the two cancers compared. We asked four questions to determine whether the coverage communicates the same level of severity, urgency, and tragedy:

RQ3: Were profiles of persons with breast cancer more likely to mention children than profiles of persons with prostate cancer?

RQ4: When ages of children are mentioned, were the children of persons with breast cancer younger than the children of persons with prostate cancer?

RQ5: Were profiles of persons with breast cancer more likely to feature women who were terminal than profiles of men with prostate cancer?

RQ6: Did the average breast cancer story include more profiles than the average prostate cancer story?

Again, we found significant differences in coverage by cancer. Fewer than 10 percent (7.9 percent) of prostate cancer profiles mentioned children (23 of 299) contrasted with more than a quarter (27 percent) of breast cancer profiles (360 of 1,332). These differences are highly statistically significant (table 19).

Fewer than half of the breast cancer profiles that mentioned children also cited their ages (155 profiles, or 43 percent).[10] Not only was the public face of breast cancer likely to mention women who are too young but these women were also likely to be mothers of very young children. The average age of chil-

Table 19. Frequencies of Mentions of Children and Prognosis by Cancer

Profiles	Mentions of Children				Wilcoxon Scores	
	Yes		No		Chi-Square[a]	p
	%	(n)	%	(n)		
Breast cancer	27.0	(360)	72.9	(971)	50.8	<.0001
Prostate cancer	7.9	(23)	92.3	(276)		
	Prognosis					
	Terminal		Unknown			
	%	(n)	%	(n)		
Breast cancer	17.7	(236)	82.3	(1,096)	0.0179	0.8936
Prostate cancer	17.4	(52)	82.6	(247)		

Source: Data compiled by authors. Total number of profiles: prostate cancer, 299; breast cancer, 1,331.
[a]df = 1.

Table 20. Ages of the Children of Persons with Breast Cancer

Age of Children	All Breast	Cancer Profiles
	%	(n)
Infants (<1 year)	12.3	(19)
Preschool (1–4 years)	11.0	(17)
School age (5–18 years)	41.9	(65)
Adult (19+)	34.8	(54)
Total	100.0	(155)

Source: Data compiled by authors.

dren of persons with breast cancer was seventeen, 65 percent of the children whose ages were mentioned were of school age or younger, and 12 percent were infants. The ACS does not provide data on the ages of children of persons with breast cancer, but one would expect that a person diagnosed with breast cancer in her sixties or seventies—even her fifties—would have adult children. Certainly, the typical person with breast cancer is not raising an infant (tables 18 through 20).

By contrast, only eight prostate cancer profiles that mentioned children also cited their ages. The average age of the children of men with prostate cancer was thirty-two. These differences are highly statistically significant (tables 18 and 19).

Were profiles of persons with breast cancer more likely to mention whether the person was terminal than profiles of persons with prostate cancer?[11] We found no differences in that respect. About 18 percent of all breast cancer profiles featured someone who was terminal compared to 17 percent of all prostate cancer profiles (table 19).

The number of persons profiled per story did differ. Prostate cancer news stories averaged just one profile per story (1.1) whereas breast cancer stories averaged 1.4 profiles each. In fact, more than 90 percent of all prostate cancer stories included just one profile, and another 4 percent included two. By contrast, 80 percent of breast cancer stories included only one profile, while eighty-eight (9 percent) included three or more. One featured twenty-three women with breast cancer. This difference is statistically significant (table 18).

Taken together, these findings demonstrate that the public faces of prostate cancer and breast cancer were different. Motherhood was considered more newsworthy than fatherhood, especially when young children were present. The public face of breast cancer was considerably younger than the public face of prostate cancer, and more women were profiled in breast cancer stories. These differences painted a picture of breast cancer as a more severe, urgent, and tragic disease than prostate cancer.

When presented with these findings, Joy Simha focused on the information about children. She was not surprised that the pregnancy history of young women with breast cancer was highlighted, given the onslaught of hormones that results from pregnancy (interview 2003). Indeed, one in every three thousand women who become pregnant will be diagnosed with breast cancer within one year. Approximately a third of all young women (those under forty) with breast cancer are diagnosed within a year of getting pregnant (Murphy 2003, 13). These are important associations. They were not highlighted, however, in the profiles of mothers of young children, nor did these profiles mention whether the young mothers' breast cancers were tied to pregnancies. Instead, the profiles tended to be descriptive (e.g., "the energetic mother of two").

DIFFERENCES BY MEDIA

We anticipated that profiles of persons with breast cancer and prostate cancer would be concentrated in particular story subjects, namely personalities, support and interest groups, health education, and risk. Furthermore, we anticipated that most profiles would be featured in soft news stories because longer feature stories can accommodate human-interest components. Finally, we expected the coverage would be consistent across the five newspapers. Thus we asked:

> RQ7: Did profiles of persons with breast cancer and prostate cancer appear primarily in stories about prominent personalities, support/interest groups, health education and risk?

RQ8: Were profiles of persons with breast cancer and prostate cancer more likely to appear in soft news rather than hard news stories?

RQ9: Were there any differences in the coverage by newspaper?

As expected, profiles of persons with breast cancer and prostate cancer were concentrated into a few story types. A majority containing profiles were personality stories (56 percent of all breast cancer profiles and 75 percent of all prostate cancer profiles), and profiles frequently appeared in health education stories (about 28 percent of breast cancer and prostate cancer profiles). Few prostate cancer profiles appeared in stories about risk or support and interest groups. Breast cancer profiles were, however, well-represented in these types of stories (table 21).

Second, a majority of profiles of persons with breast cancer and prostate cancer appeared in soft news stories, although the size of the majority differed. Only 56 percent of prostate cancer profiles appeared in soft news stories as opposed to 76 percent of the breast cancer profiles. The difference is statistically significant (table 21).

Table 21. Prostate Cancer and Breast Cancer: Profiles by News Story Subject Matter and Type of News Story

Story Subject[a]	Breast Cancer %	(n)	Prostate Cancer %	(n)	Wilcoxon Scores Chi-Sq[b]	p
Medical discoveries	7.7	(103)	5.0	(15)	2.6	0.1015
treatment	4.3	(58)	2.0	(6)	3.6	0.0589
diagnostic	1.6	(21)	3.0	(9)	2.8	0.0956
other	1.8	(24)	1.0	(3)	0.9	0.3283
Personality	56.5	(753)	74.6	(233)	33.1	<0.0001
Hearings	1.4	(19)	0.3	(1)	2.4	0.1211
Funding	1.3	(18)	2.3	(7)	1.58	0.2082
Regulations	5.3	(70)	1.0	(3)	10.3	0.0013
Education	27.8	(370)	28.4	(85)	0.05	0.8208
Support/Interest Group	20.6	(274)	4.0	(12)	46.3	<0.0001
Ethics	9.5	(127)	4.3	(13)	8.4	0.0038
Risk	6.9	(92)	3.0	(9)	6.4	0.0115
Other	13.4	(179)	39.1	(117)	10.4	<0.0001
Type of News Story:						
Hard news	23.7	(315)	44.0	(131)	50.2	<0.0001
Soft news	76.3	(1,014)	56.0	(167)		
Total n	1,332		299			

Source: Data compiled by authors.
[a]Percentages sum to more than 100 since each story could have up to three story subjects coded.
[b]df=1

Furthermore, significant variation existed among newspapers in the percentage of stories that included profiles. The two national newspapers and the *Atlanta Constitution* published proportionately fewer stories with profiles of persons with breast cancer, about one-quarter. The remaining two regional newspapers, the *Chicago Tribune* and *Los Angeles Times,* carried proportionately more stories with profiles, more than one-third each. More than 60 percent of the prostate cancer stories in the *Washington Post* and *Los Angeles Times* included profiles of persons with the disease. All other newspapers included profiles in fewer than half of the prostate cancer stories printed (table 15).

The public face of breast cancer varied little between regional and national newspapers. There were no differences in the average ages of persons profiled, mentions of children, the average number of persons profiled per story, or the type of news story in which the profiles appeared. Children's ages differed, however, when ages were mentioned. The children of persons with breast cancer were younger, on average, in national newspapers (13.5 years) than in regional newspapers (19.1 years), but there was considerable variation in both groups of newspapers.

More interesting, however, are the differences found between the *New York Times* and the four other newspapers. *Times* reporters were less likely to profile women with a terminal prognosis (11 percent). Futhermore, the average age of children of persons with breast cancer was 13.4 years in the *New York Times* compared to 18.1 years in the other four newspapers. Moreover, *Times* reporters appeared to mention the ages of young and teenaged children and not the ages of adult children. Thus we have further evidence that the *Times* is not a reliable surrogate for other newspapers (tables 22, 24–26).

The public face of prostate cancer varied by newspaper. Regional publications, for example, profiled more men with prostate cancer, whereas the two national newspapers tended to profile only one man at a time. More significant, however, is that the public face of prostate cancer in the *New York Times* was much different. Men profiled there were slightly older on average (sixty-seven rather than sixty-five). The *Times* published only four profiles that mentioned children, none of which included their ages; the men in its profiles were also more likely to have a terminal prognosis (37.3 percent) than any other newspaper studied (tables 23, 24, 26).

These differences may be due to the *Times*'s emphasis on prominent personalities and foreign affairs coverage. Much coverage focused on the last days of life of foreign leaders such as French president Francois Mitterrand

Table 22. Media Coverage Differences in Breast Cancer: Ages, Children's Ages, and Number of Profiles/Stories

	Age/Number	(*n*)	Standard Dev.	|t|	p
Profiles' Average Age:					
National	46.8	(493)	13.1	0.46	0.6482
Regional	47.3	(288)	12.4		
New York Times	46.2	(145)	12.9	0.90	0.3712
All other papers	47.3	(636)	12.6		
Children's Average Age:					
National	13.5	(49)	12.2	2.3	0.0230
Regional	19.1	(106)	17.4		
New York Times	13.4	(24)	11.5	1.7	0.0963
All other papers	18.1	(131)	16.8		
Number of Profiles/Story:					
National	1.43	(322)	1.2	0.13	0.9103
Regional	1.44	(604)	1.7		
New York Times	1.4	(166)	1.4	0.22	0.8222
All other papers	1.4	(760)	1.4		

Source: Data compiled by authors.

Table 23. Media Coverage Differences in Prostate Cancer: Ages, Children's Ages, and Number of Profiles/Stories

	Age/Number	(*n*)	Standard Dev.	|t|	p
Profiles' Average Age:					
National	64.7	(97)	8.7	1.2	0.2400
Regional	66.3	(103)	10.7		
New York Times	67.5	(49)	7.7	1.9	0.0547
All other papers	64.8	(151)	10.2		
Children's Average Age[a]:					
National	23.0	(3)	23.5	1.3	0.2475
Regional	37.8	(5)	7.2		
Number of Profiles/Story:					
National	1.0	(144)	0.9	2.0	0.0494
Regional	1.2	(120)	0.2		
New York Times	1.0	(66)	0.1	1.6	0.1111
All other papers	1.0	(198)	0.8		

Source: Data compiled by authors.

[a]This analysis could not be completed on *New York Times* in comparison to all other papers because the *New York Times* did not include the ages of any children of persons with prostate cancer.

or Zimbabwean president Mobutu Sese Seko. These findings suggest that the person who reads only the *New York Times* would have seen a different public face of prostate cancer: slightly older, dying men, profiled alone, their roles as father ignored. That representation contrasts with the other papers' coverage of prostate cancer and all newspaper coverage of breast cancer.

Table 24. Profiles Mentioning Children by Medium and Cancer

Medium	Profiles Mentioning Children									
		Breast Cancer					Prostate Cancer			
	% (n)	Wilcoxon Scores (National v. Regional)		Wilcoxon Scores (NYT v. Rest)		% (n)	Wilcoxon Scores (National v. Regional)		Wilcoxon Scores (NYT v. Rest)	
		Chi-Sq[a]	p	Chi-Sq[b]	p		Chi-Sq[a]	p	Chi-Sq[b]	p
NYT	23.0 (56)	1.13	0.2865	2.4	0.1205	6.0 (4)	2.4	0.1172	0.36	0.5488
WP	27.7 (61)					4.8 (4)				
LAT	29.5 (116)					2.3 (7)				
AC	29.6 (74)					17.6 (6)				
CT	23.6 (53)					3.7 (2)				
Total n	360					23				

Source: Data compiled by authors.

Note: NYT = New York Times; WP = Washington Post; LAT = Los Angeles Times; AC = Atlanta Constitution; CT = Chicago Tribune

[a] df = 4.
[b] df = 1.

Table 25. Profiles of Persons with Terminal Prognosis by Medium and Cancer

Medium	Profiles Mentioning Terminal Prognosis											
	Breast Cancer						Prostate Cancer					
	%	(n)	Wilcoxon Scores (National v. Regional)		Wilcoxon Scores (NYT v. Rest)		%	(n)	Wilcoxon Scores (National v. Regional)		Wilcoxon Scores (NYT v. Rest)	
			Chi-Sq[a]	p	Chi-Sq[b]	p			Chi-Sq[a]	p	Chi-Sq[b]	p
NYT	11.5	(28)	2.3	0.1307	7.8	0.0052	37.3	(25)	3.0	0.0804	23.8	<.0001
WP	20.0	(44)					8.3	(7)				
LAT	24.1	(95)					16.7	(10)				
AC	14.8	(37)					11.7	(4)				
CT	14.2	(32)					11.1	(6)				
Total n	17.7	(236)					17.4	(52)				

Source: Data compiled by authors.

Note: NYT = New York Times; WP = Washington Post; LAT = Los Angeles Times; AC = Atlanta Constitution; CT = Chicago Tribune

[a] df = 4
[b] df = 1

Table 26. Profiles by News Type by Medium and Cancer

	Type of News Story by Cancer															
Medium	Breast Cancer								Prostate Cancer							
	Hard News (National v. Regional)		Soft News (NYT. v. Rest)		Wilcoxon Scores		Wilcoxon Scores		Hard News (National v. Regional)		Soft News (NYT v. Rest)		Wilcoxon Scores		Wilcoxon Scores	
	%	(n)	%	(n)	Chi-Sq[a]	p	Chi-Sq[b]	p	%	(n)	%	(n)	Chi-Sq[a]	p	Chi-Sq[b]	p
NYT	27.1	(65)	72.9	(175)					53.0	(35)	47.0	(31)				
WP	24.1	(53)	75.9	(167)					40.5	(34)	59.5	(50)				
LAT	29.1	(115)	70.8	(279)					55.0	(33)	45.0	(27)				
AC	13.6	(34)	86.4	(216)					38.2	(13)	61.8	(21)				
CT	21.3	(48)	78.7	(117)					29.6	(16)	70.4	(38)				
Total n	23.7	(315)	76.3	(1,014)	1.5	0.2240	1.8	0.1737	56.0	(167)	44.0	(131)	0.5	0.4757	2.8	0.0930

Source: Data compiled by authors.
Note: NYT = New York Times; WP = Washington Post; LAT = Los Angeles Times; AC = Atlanta Constitution; CT = Chicago Tribune
[a] df = 4
[b] df = 1

The Public Perception of Risk

The fourth issue we explored is the impact of news media coverage on public opinion of breast cancer and prostate cancer. Specifically, we asked four questions:

RQ10: Did the public follow news stories about breast cancer and prostate cancer closely?

RQ11: Did levels of interest in breast cancer and prostate cancer vary by gender?

RQ12: Did women's perception of their risk of developing breast cancer increase over time?

RQ13: Did people who were high news consumers have a higher perception of their own risk?

This analysis is based upon several Kaiser/Harvard polls on health news. Although the Kaiser/Harvard studies do not correspond with the dates of news coverage analyzed (the earliest survey dates from December 1996) they nonetheless provide insight into the public's interest in breast cancer issues after the founding of the NBCC. Fourteen polls administered between December 1996 and October 2002 (table 27) included at least one question on either breast cancer and/or prostate cancer.

Health stories were not the most closely followed news story in any poll, but these studies indicate a considerable audience for stories about breast cancer and prostate cancer. In five polls a breast cancer story outranked all other health stories, and in one poll a prostate cancer story outranked all others. In three others a breast cancer story was the second most followed health story, and a prostate cancer story was the second most followed in another. Most of the time, about half of the survey respondents indicated that they "very closely" or "fairly closely" followed the breast cancer story mentioned, and in no instance did the percentage fall below 31 percent. Thus we conclude there was a significant audience for breast cancer and prostate cancer news.

Were there gender differences among the audiences for these health news stories? Because of enlightened self-interest and the fact that women are more likely to follow health news we expected more women than men to have followed breast cancer stories. Again, based upon enlightened self-interest, we expected men to have paid more attention to prostate cancer stories.

Table 27. Health News, December 1996–October 2002[a]

Question: "I am going to read a list of some stories covered by news organizations recently. As I read each item, tell me if you happened to follow this news story very closely, fairly closely, or not at all closely. How closely did you follow . . . ?"

Date	Question		% responding "very closely" "fairly closely"	Rank/total[b]	Rank/health[c]	n
12/96	New recommendations by an association of HMOs (Health Maintenance Organizations) and managed care plans about the length of hospital stays for women who have had mastectomies to treat breast cancer?					
		WOMEN	50	7/14	2/8	1,000
		MEN	54			
			44			
12/96	New guidelines recommending when women should get their first mammogram?					
		WOMEN	49	8/14	3/8	1,000
		MEN	62			
			37			
2/97	The controversy over mammograms					
		WOMEN	51	3/10	1/5	1,003
		MEN	65			
			36			
4/97	The debate whether women in their forties should get mammograms					
		WOMEN	62	3/9	2/5	1,015
		MEN	77			
			45			

Table 27. (cont.)

Question: "I am going to read a list of some stories covered by news organizations recently. As I read each item, tell me if you happened to follow this news story very closely, fairly closely, or not at all closely. How closely did you follow . . . ?"

Date	Question		% responding "very closely" "fairly closely"	Rank/total[b]	Rank/health[c]	n
6/97	News reports on health risks of breast implants		35	10/10	6/6	1,202
		WOMEN	43			
		MEN	27			
4/98	The new drug tamoxifan that may prevent breast cancer in women at high risk for the disease		56	4/12	2/9	1,201
		WOMEN	64			
		MEN	46			
4/98	A new study finding that men who use vitamin E supplements may reduce their risk of prostate cancer		44	6/12	4/9	1,201
		WOMEN	46			
		MEN	42			
10/98	The development of new treatments for breast cancer		48	4/10	1/6	1,202
		WOMEN	58			
		MEN	38			

Table 27. (cont.)

Question: "I am going to read a list of some stories covered by news organizations recently. As I read each item, tell me if you happened to follow this news story very very closely, fairly closely, or not at all closely. How closely did you follow . . . ?"

Date	Question		% responding "very closely" "fairly closely"	Rank/total[b]	Rank/health[c]	n
12/98	Reports of no linkage between breast implants and cancer		39	9/11	6/8	1,200
		WOMEN	43			
		MEN	35			
4/99	A new scientific study that found no link between a high-fat diet and breast cancer		31	7/8	5/5	1,200
		WOMEN	42			
		MEN	20			
8/99	The woman doctor stationed at the South Pole who had to perform her own breast biopsy		39	5/8	3/5	1,000
		WOMEN	41			
		MEN	38			
2/00	A medical study revealing a link between hormone replacement therapy and increased risk of breast cancer		35	6/8	3/5	1,006
		WOMEN	46			
		MEN	25			

Table 27. (cont.)

Question: "I am going to read a list of some stories covered by news organizations recently. As I read each item, tell me if you happened to follow this news story very closely, fairly closely, or not at all closely. How closely did you follow . . . ?"

Date	Question		% responding "very closely" "fairly closely"	Rank/total[b]	Rank/health[c]	n
5/00	New York Mayor (Rudy) Giuliani's announcement that he has prostate cancer and his withdrawal from the Senate race		49	3/9	1/5	1,200
		WOMEN	55			
		MEN	49			
4/02	Stories about mammograms for women		41	4/7	1/4	1,003
		WOMEN	64			
		MEN	27			
8/02	A report from the NIH on hormone replacement therapies for women		45	4/6	2/4	1,208
		WOMEN	57			
		MEN	32			
8/02	Results from an NIH study on birth control pills and breast cancer		38	5/6	6/4	1,208
		WOMEN	49			
		MEN	28			
10/02	New research findings about surgery for prostate cancer		34	8/9	5/6	1,201
		WOMEN	34			
		MEN	36			

[a]Each survey had a margin of error of +/- 3 percent.
[b]Relative rank of this question compared to all other questions in this survey.
[c]Relative rank of this question compared to all other health questions in this survey.

These polls show women were more likely to follow stories about breast cancer, and in all cases but one the differences were substantial.[12] Nine of the gender gaps were greater than 15 percentage points, and the highest was 37 percentage points. Thus we conclude that women were more interested in breast cancer stories than men (table 27).

Small gender gaps appeared in all three questions about prostate cancer, but only two exceeded the survey's margin of error. In these two cases the gender gap showed women as slightly more likely than men to follow prostate cancer stories. The small gender differences, however, demonstrate that men had more interest in prostate cancer stories than in breast cancer stories (table 27).

PERCEPTIONS OF RISK

Breast cancer and women's perceived risk of developing it have been addressed in several public opinion polls since the late 1970s. Each of the three polls on which this chapter focuses included a question that asked women to directly assess their personal risk of developing breast cancer. The questions were, however, worded differently. We tested these questions in our own poll to determine how closely responses correlated and found high positive correlations in the responses to all three questions. Therefore, the evidence suggests that the questions measured the same phenomena.[13]

What do the surveys tell us about women's perception of risk? First, it increased steadily over time. About a third of the women in the 1979 NCI poll stated that they were "very likely" or "somewhat likely" to "have breast cancer some day" (1980, 47). In the 1992 ABC News Poll, approximately 45 percent of women responded that they "worry a great deal" or "worry a good amount" about getting breast cancer. And in 1998 the Harris Poll found that 63 percent of women thought their chance of getting breast cancer was high—categorized as "very likely" or "somewhat likely" (table 28).

Second, each survey also asked respondents to assess their risk of developing breast cancer relative to other risks. As early as 1979 women appeared to overestimate their risk of breast cancer; the NCI study reported that 59 percent mentioned cancer as the "disease that worries [them] most." When prompted, 29 percent of these women cited breast cancer as their greatest worry (NCI 1980, 45). Although breast cancer was the most commonly diagnosed cancer in women in 1980, its incidence was far lower than the incidence of heart disease or diabetes for the same year (table 29).

In 1992 the ABC News Women's poll asked women whether they worried about many risks. Those most comparable to breast cancer are listed in table

Table 28. Perceptions of Risk in Public Opinion Polls

1980 NCI Survey on Breast Cancer: What do you think the chances are that you will personally have breast cancer someday?

Very likely	2%	Combined:	33%
Somewhat likely	31%		
Somewhat unlikely	32%		
Very unlikely	27%		

1992 ABC News Survey of women: We're interested in finding out what's really worrying women these days. I'm going to read you a list of things that some women are worried about, but other women are not. For each, I want you to tell me if that is something that worries you a great deal, worries you a good amount, worries you just a little or doesn't worry you at all. But please don't feel that you need to tell us that any of these things worry you just because we're asking. . . . that you will get breast cancer.

Worry a great deal	26%	Combined:	45%
Worry a good amount	19%		
Worry just a little	34%		
Worry not at all	21%		

1998 Harris Poll: I would like to ask you about various diseases and accidents. For each one, please tell me what you think are the chances of it happening to you where ten out of ten means it is certain to happen, zero out of ten means no chance at all. How many chances out of ten do you there are that you will ever . . . get breast cancer?

Very likely (8–10)	16%	Combined:	63%
Somewhat likely (4–7)	47%		
Not likely (1–3)	22%		
No chance (0)	21%		

Sources: NCI, ABC News, and Harris Poll.
Note: The Harris Poll did not use the terms *very likely, somewhat likely,* or *not likely* in its poll. These phrases are derived from the numerical responses given.

29. More than two in five women (44 percent) indicated they worried "a great deal" or a "good amount" about developing breast cancer. By contrast, fewer than 40 percent worried about any other health risk included in the survey. In 1992 an estimated 180,000 new cases of breast cancer were diagnosed. Although that is a considerable number, it is much lower than the number of women who were victims of violent crime (1.9 million) or contracted a sexually transmitted disease (275,000) in the same year. Yet women worried less about those risks than about developing breast cancer.

In 1998 significant percentages (30 percent) of women reported that they had better-than-even odds of developing breast cancer in their lifetimes, even when their actual odds of doing so were slightly more than 10 percent (Taylor 1999). The women rightly estimated that they had a lower risk of developing breast cancer than being hurt in a car accident, but they incor-

Table 29. Comparison of Risk Perceptions over Time

1980

Disease/Condition	Survey Result[a] (%)	Incidence
Cancer, all types	59	398,000[b]
Breast cancer	29 (of the 59%)	108,000[c]
Heart trouble	17	1,500,000[d]
Diabetes	8	327,000[e]

1992

Disease/Condition	Survey Result (%)[f]	Incidence
Get breast cancer	44.59	180,000[g]
Be the victim of a violent crime	39.45	1,932,270[h]
Be sexually assaulted	36.28	109,060[i]
Be sexually harassed	27.30	9,468[j]
Catch a sexually transmitted disease	19.39	275,278[k]

1998 (Women)

Disease/Condition	Survey Result (%)[l]	Incidence
Hurt in a car accident	33.27	1,660,000[m]
Breast cancer	30.07	178,000[n]
Heart attack	30.062	10,000[o]
Stroke	27.96	371,000[p]
Diabetes	27.51	540,000[q]
Lung cancer	18.33	80,100[r]
Be infected with HIV	3.29	28,742[s]

1998 (Men)

Disease/Condition	Survey Result (%)[t]	Incidence
Heart attack	28.61	200,306[u]
Prostate cancer	28.12	184,500[v]
Hurt in a car accident	27.09	1,532,000[w]
Stroke	25.31	301,000[x]
Diabetes	23.14	460,000[y]
Lung cancer	18.14	91,400[z]
Be infected with HIV	2.26	77,825[aa]

[a]The question on the NCI Survey was, "Next, please tell me which specific diseases or illnesses worry you the most?" For those who responded cancer, the following was asked, "What specific type of cancer worries you the most?"

[b]*Source:* American Cancer Society (Silverberg 1980).

[c]Breast cancer was the most common cancer diagnosed in women in 1980. *Source:* American Cancer Society (Silverberg 1980).

[d]Number of women fifteen and older hospitalized for heart disease (all types) in 1980; excludes women diagnosed with heart disease who were not hospitalized. *Source:* National Medical Expenditure Survey (McCarthy 1983).

[e]*Source:* "Prevalence, Incidence of Diabetes Mellitus—United States, 1980–1987," *Journal of the American Medical Association,* 1990.

[f]The ABC News Poll asked women about a list of items that might worry them. These are the ones

rectly estimated that their risk of breast cancer was higher than their risk of heart attack, stroke, or diabetes. Similarly, men in 1998 also overestimated their risk of developing prostate cancer, especially compared to their risk of being injured in an automobile accident, having a stroke, or developing diabetes (table 29).[14]

Based upon these findings, we conclude that women have overestimated their risk of breast cancer for decades, and their perception of this risk has increased steadily. Unfortunately, similar public opinion polls of men's attitudes toward prostate cancer do not exist, so we cannot conduct a similar analysis their perception of risk.

Cultivation theory, as developed by George Gerbner and colleagues in the

---

most comparable to developing breast cancer. The percentage reported are those who answered that they worry "a great deal" or "a good amount."

[g]*Source:* American Cancer Society (Boring et al., 1992).

[h]*Source:* U.S. Department of Justice (2003).

[i]*Source:* U.S. Department of Justice (2003).

[j]*Source:* U.S. Equal Opportunity Commission (2003). This is an approximate number of sexual harassment cases filed with the EEOC and state and local agencies by women in 1992. It is no doubt a conservative estimate because a 1999 Harris Poll found that 62 percent of those who reported being targets of sexual harassment took no action (Capstone Communications 2003).

[k]*Source:* Centers for Disease Control and Prevention (1994, 1995). This number is a conservative estimate. It includes incidence of syphilis, chlamydia, and gonorrhea among women for 1991 and an estimate of the prevalence (total number of cases) of AIDS for women for 1992.

[l]The Harris Poll asked respondents to give a numerical response between 1 and 10 representing their chance of developing a particular disease. We assume, given the question wording, that those who answered 5 or less would consider their risk to be low—less then 50 percent. Therefore, we have listed here the percentages of those who responded between 6 and 10 on this survey or those who volunteered that it had already happened.

[m]*Source:* "Traffic Safety Facts, 1998."

[n]*Source:* American Cancer Society (1998).

[o]*Source:* American Heart Association (2003).

[p]*Source:* American Heart Association (2003).

[q]*Source:* CDC (2003a). Publication of 1998 National Medical Expenditure Survey. This number is an estimate. The CDC reports that 54 percent of all diabetes cases occur in women and that a million new cases developed in 1998.

[r]*Source:* American Cancer Society (1998).

[s]*Source:* CDC (2000). The number is the total number of cases (prevalence). No incidence data were available.

[t]See note 12.

[u]*Source:* American Heart Association (2003).

[v]*Source:* American Cancer Society (1998).

[w]*Source:* "Traffic Safety Facts, 1998."

[x]*Source:* American Heart Association (2003).

[y]*Source:* CDC (1998). This number is an estimate. CDC reports that 46 percent of all diabetes cases occur in men and that a million new cases developed in 1998.

[z]*Source:* American Cancer Society (1998).

[aa]*Source:* CDC (2000). The number is the total number of cases (prevalence). No incidence data were available.

late 1960s and 1970s, argued that television is the "central cultural arm" of American society (Gerbner and Gross 1976, 178). Furthermore, the medium cultivates basic assumptions about the facts of life and how conclusions about life are made. Gerbner's early work revolved around the power of television violence, but the theory has been applied to other issues, including television's influence on health attitudes and assumptions. One study, for example, compared the psychosocial health of men and women who watched television for two hours or less a day to those who watched television more frequently. The study found that women who watched less television had a stronger psychosocial profile but men did not (Hammermeister et al. 2005) Cultivation theory might be at work in our findings.

IS RISK PERCEPTION TIED TO MEDIA CONSUMPTION?

Perhaps the final proof is our last question, Did people who were greater consumers of the media have a greater perception of their own risk? We expected that people exposed to more of the distorted public face of cancer—in addition to the hundreds or thousands of other news stories about the disease—would have an increased perception of their risk. Unfortunately, none of these three surveys asked a question that allowed us to measure that issue directly, although several indirect indicators are available.

First, the 1979 NCI poll was a sequel to a 1973 American Cancer Society poll conducted before the disclosures that several prominent women were diagnosed with breast cancer in 1974. One objective of the 1979 poll was to assess changes in women's perception of risk, given the prominence of breast cancer on the media agenda (NCI 1980, 2). A major change between the 1973 study and the 1979 study was that "cancer in general, and breast cancer in particular is more in the forefront of public thought" (NCI 1980, 40). Only 21 percent of women in the 1973 study specifically mentioned breast cancer as a major health problem facing women, compared to 58 percent in the 1979 study (NCI 1980, 40). That finding is consistent with the proposition that increased media coverage leads to increased awareness and perception of risk.

Second, the 1979 NCI poll asked respondents about sources of breast cancer information. More than half (55 percent) replied that they had seen or heard something about breast cancer recently. Television was women's primary source of information (21 percent), followed by word of mouth (15 percent), magazines (12 percent), and newspapers (8 percent) (NCI 1980, 64–68). Media consumption, especially of newspapers, is positively associated with education and income (National Newspaper Association of America 2005). Thus we can extrapolate that media consumption was positively associated with *knowledge* of the disease. Without the dataset, however, we were unable to conduct further analyses to determine how sources of information and level of knowledge impacted perceived risk.

The 1992 ABC Women's Issues poll did not ask about news media consumption in its demographic questions. Statistical analysis of this dataset revealed that higher levels of worry about breast cancer were positively associated with education.[15] Thus, assuming that levels of education are positively associated with levels of media consumption, the higher perception of risk that comes with higher levels of education may be due to increased media consumption. Based upon these surrogate measures we cautiously conclude that as media consumption increases so does the perception of breast cancer risk.

The 1998 Harris Poll provides the best data to make these comparisons. This survey asked, "Do you ever watch news shows on television, or not?" Granted, there is a small problem of mixed media. The survey asks about television news, and our sample is of newspaper stories, yet another 1998 survey found that reading a daily newspaper and watching the national television news were positively correlated.[16] We found that watching television news was positively associated with higher perception of risk in the case of prostate cancer (table 30).

Conclusions and Discussion

This chapter began with the premise that the public fears breast cancer and prostate cancer for many reasons. What role, we asked, does the media's portrayals of persons with cancer play in those fears? The results suggest the public face of breast cancer in particular was badly distorted in the 1980s and 1990s, whereas the public face of prostate cancer was less distorted during the same period. The public face of prostate cancer was, as John Page

Table 30. Television News Consumption and Perception of Risk, 1998

Disease/Condition	Average Perceived Risk[a]	Standard Dev.	n	p of t
Prostate Cancer:				
Watch news	4.7409	2.532	413	0.0106
Do not watch news	3.9091	2.384	66	
Breast Cancer:				
Watch news	4.4842	2.702	442	0.1571
Do not watch news	5.0435	3.075	69	

Source: Data compiled by authors.
[a]Scale of 0–10 where zero = no chance and 10 = certain to happen/already did happen.

stated, an "old man." By contrast, those persons with breast cancer profiled were clearly younger than the typical person with breast cancer. Furthermore, their profiles were more likely to mention their role as mothers, while the prostate cancer profiles ignored men's role as fathers. As a result, these portrayals framed breast cancer as a disease of greater urgency, severity, and tragedy than prostate cancer.

Latent sexism also appeared in the construction of profiles. Not only was parenthood treated differently, but five hundred profiles of women with breast cancer did not mention their ages. If the women were older, then why were their ages not reported? Whatever the reasons, these omissions may have distorted the public face of breast cancer as much as the inclusion of the ages of young women. In essence, the woman's age became the story.

AGENDA-SETTING

These findings matter. The explosive growth in breast cancer media coverage of itself communicates importance. A distorted public face further communicates a sense of urgency, severity, and tragedy. The shift observed in women's opinions from 1973 to 1979 suggests when breast cancer moved from the media agenda to the public agenda. As time passed and media coverage continued to increase, women's perceptions of their risk of developing the disease did so as well.

Moreover, polling data confirm that women closely follow breast cancer stories and men follow prostate cancer news stories. Thus heavy media consumers may have an elevated perception of risk, especially in the case of breast cancer where the public face of cancer was more distorted. These perceptions also influence policymakers, who are subject to the same media influences as the general public. In addition, women's inaccurate perception of their risk of developing breast cancer is a lobbying tool for breast cancer advocates, who argue that women's *fear* of the disease is one reason to maintain its current level of funding (Wood 2002).

Time constraints and concern about attracting reader interest may override issues of accuracy that reflect the demographic of a disease through choice of profiles. Nevertheless, it is an issue that needs to be brought to the attention of reporters. It is unlikely that most consider the impact of their choice of profiles on the public's perception of the diseases. Reporters often pick profiles of interesting persons—or in these cases profile cancer survivors—persons who are willing to go public with their disease.

It is critical to consider the impact of the public face of cancer on both public opinion and public policy priorities. The media's agenda-setting power, however, does not necessarily transform deeply held opinion. Similarly, we do not suggest that reporters take into account statistical averages when choosing profiles. They do need to be sensitive to how their individual choices of profiles, and the information they include in their stories, can be collectively misleading.

5

Media Advocacy Evidence

We need to own the message.
—Fran Visco

[The NPCC] garnered about 150,000,000
media impressions in 2000.
—Richard Atkins

Breast cancer and prostate cancer news coverage have evolved over the last decades in response to increasing public interest in these two diseases. Did the development of grassroots survivors' organizations influence the increase in media coverage? The purpose of this chapter is threefold. First, it reviews the literature on the impact of media strategies by interest groups to shape media coverage and public policy debate. Second, it provides qualitative evidence that breast cancer and prostate cancer advocates clearly sought to shape the debate and media coverage. Third, we look for quantitative evidence consistent with media advocacy strategies.

Interest Groups and the Media

Interest groups face intense competition for news media coverage. Consumer groups like the NBCC and the NPCC face additional challenges. They lobby on many issues in which they compete with industry and professional organizations with more resources (Bykerk and Maney 1995). Thus consumer groups often turn to "outside lobbying" or attempts to influence public opinion through shaping media coverage of an issue (Brown and Waltzer 2002; Kollman 1998; Terkildson, Schnell, and Ling 1998). Even if interest groups cannot control the message (Callaghan and Schnell 2001), they attempt to convince reporters that their perspective is one that needs to be included in balanced reporting (Terkildsen, Schnell, and Ling 1998). In this way the messages of consumer groups are repeated frequently and can shape public and elite opinion.

But influencing public opinion is not the only goal. Inducing policymakers to take action is also of consequence. Extensive media coverage of an issue will prompt policymakers to act. Furthermore, evidence suggests some presidents looked to the media for cues when determining domestic policy agendas (Edwards and Wood 1999; Wanta and Foote 1994). In these scenarios an interest group can be catapulted from the periphery to the center of the policy conversation.

Two important health policy debates of the 1990s hinged on the amount and the nature of media coverage. The Medicare Catastrophic Care Act (MCCA) and the Clinton health reform plan are two cases in point. Fan and Norem (1992) found that news media coverage of the MCCA turned increasingly negative as public opinion turned against the legislation (Himmelfarb 1995; see also Reynolds 1994). In the case of the Clinton administration's health reform plan, debate was shaped in part as a result of interest group advertising on the part of industry and consumer groups (Jamieson and Capella 1998; West, Heith, and Goodwin 1996). The *New York Times* helped the concept known as managed competition rise to national prominence through a series of editorials endorsing the approach (Liberman 1993). Studies of news media coverage found most of the coverage focused on the political aspects of reform, to the detriment of health ramifications. As the political story turned sour, public opinion began to shift away from supporting the Clinton plan. This pattern was evident in both national and local news (Dorfman et al. 1996). Moreover, interest group advertising, especially the "Harry and Louise" advertising sponsored by the Health Insurance Association of America, successfully contributed to a decline in public support of the Clinton health reform plan in 1994 (Goldsteen et al. 2001). The advertisements featured a middle-aged couple discussing the advisability of the Clinton plan and concluding that it fell short. That negative shift in public opinion resulted in changes in support among members of Congress, especially among those who were not heavily involved in crafting the legislation (Hansen et al. 1996).

Other examples abound. A study of media coverage of long-term care in 1998 found it tended toward issues related to nursing homes to the exclusion of home health-care options. Mirroring that coverage, public opinion polls from the same year found that the general public equated long-term care with nursing home care (Mebane 2001). Fay Lomax Cook and her associates found an unusual collaboration between journalists and congressional staff members that resulted in a home health-care exposé that not only raised public awareness of problems in the program but also allowed members of Congress to justify their investigation of the same program (Cook et al. 1983). Similarly, in another case, scientific evidence of the dangers of radon and asbestos alone was not sufficient to result in policy changes. These environmental threats did not become major policy priorities for Congress until there was considerable media attention (Scheberle 1994). Finally, three studies by Itzhak Yanovitzky found that media coverage of drunk driving led to an increase in the number of laws related to that issue. The laws then contributed to changes in drunk-driving behaviors—exactly the kind of effects that media advocacy strategies should produce (2002a, 2002b; Yanovitzky and Bennett 1999). These examples illustrate how media attention may support the work of GSOs in influencing changes in public policy, but is that the case with breast cancer and prostate cancer?

Media Advocacy Evidence

This chapter asks two research questions. First, Is there evidence that GSOs use media advocacy techniques in the case of breast cancer and prostate cancer? If so, we should see changes of these efforts in the behavior of the advocates in the form of media training, message development, and awareness that one can influence journalists' coverage. We also should see evidence in the media coverage itself. Second, Is there evidence that GSOs use media techniques to change the public face of these diseases to communicate more urgency and tragedy? If so, we should see evidence in newspaper profiles of persons with breast cancer and prostate cancer.

QUALITATIVE EVIDENCE

Evidence from interviews and participant observation indicates that breast cancer and prostate cancer advocates use media advocacy techniques to overcome such barriers as obscurity. Prostate cancer advocates, for example, have had to overcome the disease's anonymity and men's reluctance to discuss health and illness. Similarly, the Young Survival Coalition needed a platform to communicate to women and doctors that young women can develop breast cancer. As one told us, "We have nothing but the media" (personal communication 2003).

A method to generate media coverage, especially from television, is to involve celebrities in one's cause. If Miss America adopts prostate cancer as her cause, the disease will receive more media coverage simply because of who is discussing the issue. Celebrities have a long history of political activism, and both movements capitalized on this trend (West and Orman 2003).[1] Representative Mary Rose Oakar (D-OH) sponsored a hearing on breast cancer in the 1980s that featured humorist Erma Bombeck and Susan Ford, daughter of Betty Ford. Another featured Marilyn Quayle, spouse of then–Vice President Dan Quayle, and actress Linda Carter, who played Wonder Woman in the television series. These hearings helped put breast cancer on the policy agenda because "they [the members] all showed up for the hearings. They reacted because we put pressure on them" (Oakar interview 2003).

Prostate cancer activists agree. The prominent personalities who appeared at early congressional hearings about prostate cancer included Bob Dole and Norman Schwarzkopf. In the words of one activist, "Schwarzkopf represents our disease's Betty Ford" (Palosky 1997).

Generating news media coverage is important because it lends credibility and encourages grassroots support. If an issue receives media coverage, then convincing policy members of the urgency of one's cause is all that much easier. In the words of Susan Molinari (R-NY) (2000), "If it didn't make the front page of the newspaper, if we couldn't get it on CNN, it might not have carried the legs to get a lot of our colleagues to say, 'I want to see this issue . . . this is a politically potent issue.'"

Others agree. "Media coverage makes it real," said one prostate cancer activist. "They read the newspaper. If their local newspaper gives the disease attention, then it must be important" (interview 2003). According to a congressional staff member, "Media coverage is always helpful if a lobbyist is trying to sell their point. If it's in the news and can make that link, it's more helpful. Members can make that connection" (interview 2003). Recognizing this importance, activists and advocacy groups may claim credit for increased media attention even if they are not completely responsible for it.

Direct pressure from the grassroots is a powerful force behind legislative action. Mary Rose Oakar credits C-SPAN coverage of floor debate over Medicare coverage of mammography in 1990 as crucial to her successful efforts: "What I didn't realize is that thousands of people, women, were watching C-SPAN and seeing what we were doing to the budget. So the next day the phones were ringing off the hook and women and their families all over the country called their Congressmen and said, 'What is wrong with you, taking mammography out of the budget?!' . . . If women hadn't watched television that night, they wouldn't have called their congresspeople . . . to put it back into the budget" (interview 2003).

All media coverage is helpful, but some is more helpful than others. Specially, the most effective media advocacy efforts need to target policymakers who are in a position to affect public policy directly. The National Prostate Cancer Coalition, for example, sponsors a mobile screening unit that travels the country to provide free screening tests. The NPCC works to publicize the van's visit, but communities are not selected randomly. They are in the districts of members of Congress who serve on important committees, and the media coverage generated by the visits helps to reinforce the message that prostate cancer is a serious disease (interview 2003).

The key to a successful media effort is message development or ensuring that advocates have a consistent message that is repeated constantly. This repetition is designed to shape media attention and public opinion and define an issue (chapter 7). Both the NBCC and NPCC have extensive media relations operations and devote significant resources to message training. NBCC Advocacy Conferences included talking points to ensure that advocates communicated a consistent message to Congress. Moreover, the NBCC understands that it had to "own" the message—and that its message competes with those from other breast cancer organizations and other disease groups. Similarly, the call to the NPCC's 2003 spring training conference announced, "We are going to teach you to communicate a complex message simply to people who don't have a lot of time and don't have a scientific background. Everything we teach you can be used not only with members of Congress, but with state legislators and the media too."

MEDIA ADVOCACY IN NEWS COVERAGE

If media advocacy efforts occur, two distinct phenomena should be observable. First, media attention to the disease should increase at about the same time, or shortly after, the establishment of advocacy groups. In addition, the media should use advocacy groups as a source and/or subject in news stories. Thus we asked:

RQ1: Did media coverage increase after GSOs are established?

RQ2: Were GSOs used more frequently as a story source or as the subject of a story after they are established?

Second, because media advocacy requires advocates to define issues as problems within the legitimate scope of government intervention we expected to find more stories focusing on government action (hearings, regulations, and funding) and the work of activist organizations after their founding. We also expected support and interest groups to be cited more frequently as sources within news coverage in later years. In addition, if breast cancer and prostate cancer were defined as issues within the scope of government action, then more government officials and agencies would be used as sources. Our questions were:

RQ3: Were there more news stories on the subjects of regulations, hearings and funding after the founding of GSOs?

RQ4: Were government agencies or officials used more frequently as story sources after the founding of GSOs?

MEDIA ADVOCACY EVIDENCE

Difference of means tests were used to find evidence consistent with media advocacy efforts on the part of GSOs.[2] We found ample evidence in the case of breast cancer. The number of stories increased from an average of eighty-seven news stories per year (1980–90) to an average of 336 (1991–98), nearly a fourfold increase after the founding of the NBCC. The relationship is statistically significant, suggesting considerable media advocacy efforts on the part of breast cancer activists (table 31).

Second, we asked whether more stories discussed support and interest groups after GSOs were formed and whether these groups would be cited more frequently as sources. Again, support and interest groups appeared more frequently as both story subjects and sources, and the increases were dramatic (table 31).

Finally, more coverage about government action on breast cancer after the formation of breast cancer advocacy groups would suggest that advocates

Table 31. Media Advocacy Evidence in Breast Cancer: Difference of Means Tests

	Average Number of Stories per Year			
	1980–90	1991–98	|t|	p
All stories	86.7	336.4	6.6	<.0001
Support/interest group[a]	2.9	36.1	8.9	<.0001
Hearings[a]	1.3	8.1	3.3	0.0041
Funding[a]	0.7	9.8	5.6	<.0001
Regulations[a]	7.7	52.9	6.4	<.0001
Support/interest group[b]	5.9	45.4	10.9	<.0001
Government agency/official[b]	33.9	113.4	5.6	<.0001

Source: Data compiled by authors.
[a]As a story subject.
[b]As a story source.

had successfully reframed the topic as a policy issue. We found the number of stories about congressional hearings jumped from an average of one per year (1980–90) to an average of eight (1991–98). Stories about federal funding increased from fewer than one per year, on average (1980–90), to an average of ten (1991–98). Stories about government regulations also increased from an average of eight per year (1980–90) to more than fifty (1991–98). Similarly, government officials were cited as sources more frequently in the advocacy era, from thirty-four stories a year (1980–90) to more than a hundred (1991–98) (table 31).

Evidence consistent with successful media advocacy strategies is less clear in the case of prostate cancer. As the NPCC formed in 1996 news coverage was split into two eras, from 1980 to 1995 and from 1996 to 1998. The total number of news articles on prostate cancer increased from an average of twenty per year (1980–95) to ninety-eight (1996–98). Stories about support and interest groups increased from fewer than one per year on average (1980–95) to about five (1996–98). In addition, prostate cancer advocacy groups were cited more frequently as sources after 1995. Coverage of congressional hearings increased from zero (1980–95) to nearly one story per year on average (1996–98). News stories about prostate cancer funding increased from fewer than one per year (1980–95) to an average of six (1996–98). Similarly, stories about regulations increased from one per year (1980–95) to an average of four (1996–98). Finally, government agencies or officials were cited as sources in an average of thirty-three stories per year (1996–98) compared to six (1980–95) (table 32).

These findings, however, mask another important trend. Media coverage

Table 32. Media Advocacy Evidence in Prostate Cancer: Difference of Means Tests

	Average Number of Stories/Year							
	1980–95	1996–98	|t|	p	1980–90	1991–98	|t|	p
All stories	19.5	96.7	5.2	<.0001	7.3	65.1	5.4	<.0001
Support/Interest Group[a]	0.4	4.7	4.2	0.0379	0.1	2.1	4.9	0.0001
Hearings[a]	0	0.667	4.4	0.004	0	0.25	1.2	0.2520
Funding[a]	0.4	6.0	5.8	<.0001	0.2	2.7	2.4	0.0274
Regulations[a]	1.1	4.3	2.7	0.0142	0.4	3.2	3.6	0.0021
Support/Interest Group[b]	0.6	3.0	3.8	0.0015	0.1	2.3	2.6	0.0204
Government agency/ official[b]	5.83	3.0	8.3	<.0001	2.7	20.2	5.17	<.0001

Source: Data compiled by authors.

[a]As a story subject.

[b]As a story source.

began to increase in 1991, well before the creation of prostate cancer GSOs (figure 1). Statistical tests using the same eras as applied to breast cancer (1980–90 and 1991–98) show that media coverage of all aspects of prostate cancer coverage mirror that of breast cancer, with the exception of coverage of congressional hearings (table 32). Although prostate cancer GSOs may have begun to use media advocacy techniques in 1996, they capitalized on trends that were already underway.

A Changing Public Face?

A goal of media advocacy efforts is to communicate the human impact of a public health problem to policymakers. Therefore, we asked, Does the public face of these diseases change after the development of GSOs? If so, do these changes communicate a greater sense of urgency and tragedy? Specifically, we asked:

RQ5: Did the total number of persons profiled increase after the development of GSOs?

RQ6: Did the average number of persons profiled per story increase after the development of GSOs?

RQ7: Did the proportion of profiles mentioning children increase after the development GSOs?

THE CHANGING FACE OF BREAST CANCER

The public face of breast cancer changed after GSOs were established. The average number of profiles of persons with breast cancer, for example, increased from twenty-one per year (1980–90) to an average of eighty-six (1991–98). Similarly, the number of persons with breast cancer profiled in each story increased from an average of 1.3 (1980–90) to 1.5 (1991–98) (table 33).

In addition, after 1991 the profiles of women with breast cancer were more likely to mention children. Only 22 percent did so before 1991 and 28 percent after that date (table 34). This evidence is consistent with media advocacy efforts. The development of breast cancer advocacy groups influenced the public face of breast cancer in ways that implied a greater sense of urgency and tragedy.[3]

THE SLIGHTLY CHANGING FACE OF PROSTATE CANCER

The public face of cancer was not significantly altered after GSOs emerged. The average number of profiles increased from three per year (1980–95) to

Table 33. Media Coverage Differences in Prostate Cancer: Ages, Children's Ages, and Number of Profiles/Story

	Age/Number (n)		Standard Dev.	|t|	p
Average Number of Persons Profiled per Year					
Breast Cancer:					
1980–90	21.5		19.3	5.33	0.0002
1991–98	86.1		30.0		
Prostate Cancer:					
1980–95	2.7		11.4	6.49	0.0021
1996–98	23.6		7.0		
Prostate Cancer:					
1980–90	2.9		3.6	5.09	0.0011
1991–98	29.0		14.2		
Average Age of Person Profiled					
Breast Cancer:					
1980–90	48.7	(157)	14.4	1.57	0.1190
1991–98	46.7	(624)	12.1		
Prostate Cancer:					
1980–95	65.1	(117)	11.1	0.76	0.4454
1996–98	66.1	(83)	7.4		
Prostate Cancer:					
1980–90	67.8	(29)	15.8	0.90	0.3744
1991–98	65.1	(171)	8.2		
Children's Average Age					
Breast Cancer:					
1980–90	12.1	(23)	11.7	2.17	0.0360
1991–98	18.2	(132)	16.6		
Prostate Cancer:					
1980–95	19.0	(3)	2.0	2.17	0.0942
1996–98	40.2	(5)	21.7		
Prostate Cancer:					
1980–90	NA	(0)	NA	NA	NA
1991–98	32.2		19.8		
Average Number of Profiles per Story					
Breast Cancer:					
1980–90	1.3	(237)	1.0	2.70	0.0072
1991–98	1.5	(689)	1.5		
Prostate Cancer:					
1980–95	1.1	(141)	0.5	0.39	0.6987
1996–98	1.1	(123)	0.8		
Prostate Cancer:					
1980–90	1.1	(32)	0.4	0.05	0.9608
1991–98	1.1	(232)	0.7		

Source: Data compiled by authors.

Table 34. Frequencies of Mentions of Children and Prognosis, by Cancer

	Mentions of Children				Prognosis			
	% yes	(n)	Wilcoxon Scores		% terminal	(n)	Wilcoxon Scores	
			Chi-Sq[a]	p			Chi-Sq[a]	p
Breast Cancer:								
1980–90	22.1	(66)	4.8	0.0280	14.7	(44)	2.4	0.1228
1991–98	28.5	(294)			18.6	(192)		
Prostate Cancer:								
1980–95	7.0	(11)	0.2	0.6165	8.9	(14)	16.9	<.0001
1996–98	8.5	(12)			26.9	(38)		
Prostate Cancer:								
1980–90	2.8	(1)	1.4	0.2388	5.6	(2)	4.0	0.0461
1991–98	8.4	(22)			19.0	(50)		

Source: Data compiled by authors. Total number of profiles: prostate cancer, 299; breast cancer, 1331.
[a] df = 1.

twenty-four (1996–98), and the proportion of profiles of men with terminal prognoses slightly increased, from 9 percent (1980–95) to 27 percent (1996–98). There were no statistically significant changes, however, in mentions of children, the average age of the persons profiled, or the number of profiles per story. In addition, the average age of children cited actually increased. These findings suggest that prostate cancer GSOs either did not attempt to communicate the human impact of the disease or that these efforts were unsuccessful (tables 33 and 34).

Previously, we found that many observed differences in prostate cancer media coverage commenced in 1991. Again, we found that the public face of prostate cancer began to change at the same time as the development of breast cancer GSOs. The average number of men with prostate cancer profiled, for example, increased from three per year (1980–90) to twenty-nine (1991–98). Not a single prostate cancer profile mentioned children's ages before 1990 (table 33), and in 1991 the percentage of stories profiling men with terminal prostate cancer began to increase dramatically (table 34).

Conclusions

ASSERTIVE ADVOCATES

If there is one overriding difference between the two GSOs it is that breast cancer advocates are more assertive than prostate cancer advocates (chapter 2). These activists' claims of influencing the amount of media coverage and shaping its content are consistent with the evidence reported here. Media advocacy efforts require advocates to change the definition of cancer from the *personal* (individual focus) to the *political* (a policy problem). The evidence suggests that activists successfully defined the disease as a policy problem and promoted themselves as critical participants in the policy debate. Increased coverage of breast cancer organizations also implies that the groups have demonstrated to the media that a story is not complete or balanced without including them.

Moreover, such evidence is consistent with the proposition that breast cancer GSOs sought to change the public face of breast cancer. There are significantly more faces of breast cancer in the news media after the development of GSOs than before, and the nature of the coverage has changed as well. The public face of breast cancer in the 1990s communicated more urgency and a greater sense of tragedy than the public face of the 1980s.

This discussion would be incomplete without noting that the ability to put a local face on the disease is important to both print and broadcast media. National organizations that are supported by state and local organizations are more likely to receive media coverage. Breast cancer advocates willing to tell their stories or offer themselves as evidence support the activity of newsgathering and make reporters' jobs easier.

PIGGYBACKING ON BREAST CANCER EFFORTS

The evidence consistent with media advocacy efforts is not as clear in the case of prostate cancer GSOs. Rather, changes in prostate cancer media coverage coincide with changes in breast cancer media coverage. The reasons for this coincidence are unclear. Even current prostate cancer activists are unsure of the reasons for the increased media attention beginning in 1991 (Atkins email 2003). Given the enormous success of the breast cancer movement, however, it is logical and rational that prostate cancer advocates would link their efforts to breast cancer. Again, qualitative evidence supports these quantitative findings. For example, at its annual advocacy conference in 2003, the NPCC compared prostate cancer to breast cancer throughout the conference and trained activists to make several comparisons between the diseases when meeting with policymakers or the media. The NPCC also encouraged men (and their wives) to describe their lives with prostate cancer. They argued that increased medical research funds could be used to support clinical trials of the breast cancer drug Herceptin on some men with advanced prostate cancer. In addition, they frequently compared breast cancer's and prostate cancer's mortality and morbidity rates. One activist even characterized the prostate gland "as a breast that got lost."

Piggybacking on breast cancer activism may be all the more important given the tenuous position that prostate cancer holds on the current media agenda. Prostate cancer advocates still have much work to do to raise awareness of the disease even as they continue to frame it as a policy question.

6

Two Cancers Go to Congress

MEDIA ADVOCACY AND THE POLICY AGENDA

> I'm a breast cancer survivor. And before I was a breast cancer survivor, I didn't know or really pay much attention to it. I really didn't think it was important. . . . We finally did get legislation to cover mammograms for women age sixty-five [and over]. . . . What a fight. I think back to Bill Natcher, from Mississippi [*sic*], one of the most gracious and charming men I ever knew . . . and chairman of the Appropriations Committee. He simply couldn't understand how we could do this. We finally smartened up and included legislation for prostate cancer because we just didn't have a chance. We certainly have made progress on women's health issues.
>
> —Barbara Vucanovich (R-NV)

> You'd think the fact that 100 percent of the Alabama Senate delegation has had prostate cancer would be good [for the cause].
>
> —Prostate cancer activist

In the early 1990s there was growing awareness that both policy-makers and the medical research community had neglected women's health issues. The perception was that breast cancer was severely underfunded and other women's health issues were neglected. To demonstrate this perceived neglect, advocates frequently compared breast cancer funding to AIDS funding (Altman 1996, 9–10; Oakar interview 2003). According to Karen Stabiner, "Fran Visco believed [t]he National Institutes of Health [NIH] embarrassed itself with paltry breast cancer budgets—$90 million in fiscal 1990; $100 million the next year, and $155 million in fiscal 1992" (1997, 4). Similarly, Roberta Altman stated, "Men's diseases have consistently gotten more money for research" (1996, 9–10). Altman did not identify what "men's diseases," but certainly prostate cancer would qualify. That perception, however, was not supported by reality. As early as the 1980s and 1990s breast cancer received significantly more funding than did prostate cancer. In fact, it received more funding than any other disease except AIDS.

The disparity also came to the attention of health policy analysts. The three leading causes of death—heart disease, stroke, and cancer—have not changed in recent decades.[1] Yet the federal government spends more money on diseases that have significantly lower mortality and morbidity rates among the U.S. population than it does for the leading causes of death (Gross, Anderson, and Powe 1999).

Breast cancer and prostate cancer both experienced dramatic increases in federal funding during the 1990s. The National Cancer Institute (NCI) spent $6.4 million on prostate cancer research in 1981, but seventeen years later it spent $86.9 million on prostate cancer research, 13.5 times the 1981 amount. A similar story is true for breast cancer. In 1998 the NCI spent $384.2 million, ten times the 1981 amount (NCI 2000).

What precipitated this increase? One would expect a relationship between federal funding for research into different diseases and their incidence and mortality rates, but that is not the case. AIDS is no longer one of the leading causes of death in the United States (Anderson and Smith 2005), and its mortality rate in the United States continues to decline. Yet the federal government spends more money on AIDS research than on any other disease—some $2.8 billion in 2004 (National Institutes of Health 2005).

A study reported in the *New England Journal of Medicine* found no relationship among incidence, prevalence, or length of hospital stays and federal funding for various diseases. The same study found a weak relationship between mortality and federal funding (Gross, Anderson, and Powe 1999). These findings appear to indicate that allocating federal research dollars is arbitrary. We argue, however, it is not arbitrary but rather subject to the dynamics of agenda-setting and media advocacy, the role of policy "entrepreneurs," and concerted lobbying efforts. This chapter discusses when and how breast cancer and prostate cancer reached the policy agenda in Congress and analyzes the relationship between media coverage and the development of GSOs on public policy.

Breast Cancer Activism on Capitol Hill

Burdett Loomis (1988) points out that the contemporary Congress is amenable to the efforts of entrepreneurs, members who, acting virtually alone, adopt an issue, bring it to the agenda, and shape policy. An entrepreneurial member has at his or her disposal a personal staff of twenty or so to help engineer this effort. The member also may have access to committee or sub-committee staff and sympathetic interest groups or outside experts. Breast cancer came to the congressional agenda as a result of the entrepreneurial efforts of Mary Rose Oakar (D-OH) and Rose Kushner.

MAMMOGRAPHY COVERAGE

In the late 1980s Representative Oakar became interested in breast cancer after her sister was diagnosed with the disease. A friend told her about journalist Rose Kushner, so Oakar called Kushner to ask what she could do. Kushner suggested that Oakar promote informed consent legislation, mammography coverage in Medicare, and increased medical research funding. Oakar initially sponsored informed consent legislation, but for technical reasons that did not pass. She then turned her attention to Medicare coverage of mammography (interview 2003).

The House Energy and Commerce and Ways and Means Committees had jurisdiction over the Medicare program. Oakar was not a member of either, but she was a member of the now-defunct House Select Committee on Aging that was chaired by Claude Pepper (D-FL), who was sympathetic to the breast cancer cause. The Select Committee on Aging had no legislative authority but was an excellent platform from which to set the agenda, and Oakar organized hearings in 1984 and 1985 to call attention to the issue of breast cancer. As she recalled, "We attracted some attention. People mocked it. Oh, the breast. You can't talk about the breast" (interview 2003).

The Aging Committee was an effective platform for raising awareness, but Oakar's efforts suffered because she did not hold a seat on one of the major committees of jurisdiction. She therefore took the issue to the Congressional Caucus for Women's Issues (CCWI).[2] With its assistance she managed to have mammography screening included in the Medicare Catastrophic Care Act of 1987 (MCCA). Mammography coverage disappeared, however, when the MCCA was repealed despite efforts to save it (Casamayou 2001, 55–56). The coverage failed to be included in the budget for the next several years out of concern that it would be too expensive. A major breakthrough occurred in 1990 when Oakar was tipped off that mammography was to be deleted again from the budget. She took to the floor during the budget debate and confronted the chair of the House Budget Committee, Leon Panetta (D-CA). "So I asked Leon Panetta," she recalls, "[if they had deleted mammography coverage], and he hemmed and hawed. [Richard] Gephardt [D-MO] said, 'We are going to do it next January.' I said, 'Baloney,' and I lost it [became enraged] because we had so many women who could not afford mammography. . . . And these guys were going to kill me, except all those guys whose wives had breast cancer. They came up to me and said, 'Good for you.' They had taken it out to give some tax break to a chicken farmer" (interview 2003). Oakar was successful in ensuring that Medicare resumed mammography coverage, which began in 1991 (Casamayou 2001, 57).

The year 1990 was a critical one for another reason—the passage of the Breast and Cervical Cancer Mortality Prevention Act, which was sponsored by Representative Henry Waxman (D-CA). That legislation authorized the Centers for Disease Prevention and Control to provide free breast and cervical cancer screenings to low-income women who had no health insurance (PL 101–354; NBCC 2002b).

EXPANDING NCI FUNDING

Oakar's victory laid the groundwork for the next major initiative: expanded funding for breast cancer research. She was joined in these efforts by the newly formed NBCC. At the same time, awareness was growing among women members of Congress about federal neglect of women's health issues. Stories abounded. In 1989, for example, the NIH spent just 13 percent of its budget on women's health issues (Altman 1996, 19). Women were also omitted from the NIH-funded "Longitudinal Study on Aging" for twenty years. Thus women, a large majority of the elderly in the United States, were not a part of the study that defined the normal aging process. They were also initially excluded from the important study that documented the benefits of aspirin in preventing heart attacks (Schroeder and Snowe 1994). Unbelievably, the NIH even funded a pilot study on breast and uterine cancer that included only men as subjects (Dresser 1992; Oakar interview 2003). Oakar recalls what triggered the CCWI's involvement when the Select Committee on Aging heard testimony about the aging study. "I asked a facetious question about the demographics [of the study]. So these guys kinda elbowed themselves . . . and I said, 'How about women?' They said, 'None.' I said, 'None!' And Olympia Snowe [R-ME] on the minority side did her turn. So we took it back to the women's caucus" (interview 2003).

As a result, the CCWI commissioned a Government Accounting Office (GAO) study on the inclusion of women in clinical trials. Released in 1990, the study found that the NIH did not follow its own guidelines requiring that women be included as test subjects in NIH-funded proposals and that findings be analyzed for gender differences (Baylis, Downie, and Sherwin 1998; Dresser 1992; Nagel 1990; Schroeder and Snowe 1994). The CCWI used this opportunity to become involved in breast cancer issues as part of its general women's health agenda. The caucus was motivated further by the diagnosis of Representative Marilyn Lloyd (D-TE), who underwent a mastectomy in June 1990 and later became an important figure in the silicone breast implant debate (Lloyd 1995; "Representative Champions Legislation" 1991). That Lloyd was "one of their own" further demonstrated the threat of the disease.

The CCWI also found that breast cancer afforded an important political advantage: bipartisan, nonideological cooperation. Several observers noted that the CCWI, divided as it was (and is) ideologically and along party lines, was handicapped by members' inability to agree on such controversial issues as abortion or fetal tissue research. Mammography standards, mammography coverage in Medicare and Medicaid, and increased breast cancer research funding, however, were issues that all women in Congress, regardless of partisan or ideological bent, could rally behind (interviews 2003; see also Gertzog 1995).

The CCWI did not work alone. Breast cancer activists joined the effort to increase medical research funding. The NBCC's first lobbying effort was to organize a letter-writing campaign advocating more breast cancer research funding: "Do the Write Thing." Its goal was to generate 170,000 letters to be delivered to Congress and President George H. W. Bush, one for each person expected to be diagnosed with breast cancer in 1991. The campaign generated six hundred thousand letters (Casamayou 2001, 116–119), more than a hundred thousand of which were delivered to the White House. By all accounts their reception was frosty. The activists were not allowed into the White House, and the delivery was never acknowledged. Reception from congressional staff was equally passive (Casamayou 2001, 119; Stabiner 1997), but as NBCC co-founder Susan Love notes, the campaign helped the group establish important networks in every state and thus build its constituency (Love and Lindsay 1995, 520).

The breast cancer movement gained another prominent ally in 1991: Marilyn Quayle, whose mother died of the disease. The vice president's wife used her position as a bully pulpit to call attention to the disease and gave the Komen Foundation's Race for the Cure a boost when she and her husband participated in the Washington, D.C., race (Roberts 1991).

Beginning in 1992, the NBCC set a goal of increasing appropriations for breast cancer research by $300 million, an amount based on the outcome of conferences sponsored by the NBCC with medical researchers (Love and Lindsay 1995; Marshall 1993b). Activists were thus able to answer the question of how much money was needed.

EARMARKING

Breast cancer advocates were successful in another way as well, one not evident by numbers alone. Beginning in 1992 they lobbied Congress to earmark NIH funds for breast cancer research. Previously, the NIH received a lump-sum appropriation, and its scientists allocated funds according to what they perceived as priorities. Some members of Congress, especially then–House Appropriations Committee chair William Natcher (D-KY), did not like taking funding decisions out of the hands of experts. Breast cancer and women's health advocates, however, considered earmarking as the only way to ensure that the federal government would address the neglect they perceived (Rubin 1996). Although one scholar argues that the NBCC failed in its efforts to insert an earmark in the final legislative language of the fiscal year (FY) 1993 NIH appropriations bill (Dimock 2003), breast cancer advocates continue to assert that they succeeded. Moreover, earmarking is a common practice in Department of Defense appropriations bills. Thus, breast cancer advocates changed the nature of disease politics by putting earmarking on the agenda for all disease lobbyists.

THE DEPARTMENT OF DEFENSE

Breast cancer activists wanted yet more money dedicated to research, but it was difficult to locate funding in an era of budget deficits and firewalls that divided domestic and military spending. The temptation was to move money from one disease to another. As Oakar recalled, "The Republican leadership said . . . 'what we'll do is take some of the money out of AIDS research' . . . I said, 'No, we're not going to take money out of another research group. We need more money for all research'" (interview 2003).

Breast cancer activists and congressional advocates needed another ally in Congress. They found one in Tom Harkin (D-IA), a member of the Senate Appropriations Committee (Casamayou 2001, 147–49; Love and Lindsay 1995, 522). Harkin, who is interested in breast cancer because his two sisters died of the disease, first proposed moving some of the Department of Defense research budget into the 1992 NIH appropriations bill, which required special legislative procedures to get around budgetary firewalls. In the FY 1993 appropriations cycle, however, Representative John Murtha (D-PA), chair of the Defense Appropriations Subcommittee, sought to keep the money within the defense budget. He was joined in this effort by Alphonse D'Amato (R-NY), a member of the Senate Defense Appropriations Subcommittee, who was looking for a women's issue to embrace (Visco 2003a). The efforts of Oakar, Harkin, Murtha, and D'Amato prevailed, and the Department of Defense got into the business of medical research. The amount allocated to breast cancer, some $210 million, was chosen because it represented 1 percent of the Department of Defense's total research budget (Frey interview 2003). That amount plus the NCI appropriation made for a total of $410 million for breast cancer research in FY 1993, an amount that exceeded what breast cancer advocates had targeted (Culliton 1992). The Department of Defense program is known today as the Congressionally Directed Medical Research Programs (CDMRP) and has expanded to include diseases other than breast cancer (chapter 9).

Initially, the Pentagon was reluctant to enter a new field of medical research (Stabiner 1997, 4). In 1995, two years after the first appropriation was made, Defense Secretary William Perry announced that the department would not spend the money earmarked for AIDS and breast cancer research because the Pentagon did not consider that research to be part of its core mission. This stance led to a rebuke from President Bill Clinton, whose mother, Virginia Kelley, had died of breast cancer a year earlier. Perry was ordered to release the funds ("White House Raps Pentagon" 1995). It is uncertain whether the CDMRP, a discretionary program, will exist from one year to the next (Weitzman interview 2003a). In 2004 and 2005 it was threatened—first with outright elimination and later with cuts and a lump-sum appropriation rather than disease-specific earmarks (NPCC 2005d; Visco 2005).

CONSUMERS ON REVIEW PANELS

Another innovation in this legislation is the role of consumers on CDMRP peer review panels. This provision was added at the insistence of NBCC president Fran Visco, who wanted to ensure that the patient's perspective was represented in research funding decisions. Today, consumers (i.e., survivors) are involved at two levels of decision making. First, an integration panel decides the most relevant needs of the research, consumer, and clinical communities. Second, consumers are involved in the scientific merit review and the subsequent program review process (U.S. Department of Army 2003a).

A SEMI-POSTAL STAMP

The first efforts to use postage stamps to raise breast cancer awareness were initiated in 1994 through the efforts of breast cancer survivor Diane Sackett Nannery. Her elected representatives, Alphonse D'Amato and Representative Peter King (R-NY), also solicited support for the stamp. As a result of those efforts, the U.S. Postal Service issued its standard-priced breast cancer awareness stamp in 1996 (Peterson 1995).

This effort was merely a prelude. Reminiscent of the entrepreneurial activism that marks the men in the prostate cancer movement, in 1996 Ernie Bodai, a Sacramento-based breast cancer surgeon, began an effort to authorize the Post Office to issue a "semi-postal" stamp, one that sells for more than its face value, the extra funds being donated to charity (Bodai 2001).[3] Such stamps are common in other countries but were not used in the United States. Bodai, who reportedly learned about the legislative process from a high school civics textbook, spent thousands of dollars and countless hours traveling to Washington, D.C., to lobby on behalf of the stamp. His effort paid off in 1998 when the first breast cancer semi-postal stamp was released (King 2004).

The legislation met with some opposition from stamp collectors and the Postal Service. The former protested what they believed was an unfair tax on their hobby and argued that the stamp was unlikely to raise significant funds for breast cancer research. The latter worried such legislation would open the floodgates to myriad worthy causes and place a large and expensive administrative burden upon the Postal Service. The primary legislative sponsors, Representative Susan Molinari (R-NY) and Senators Lauch Faircloth (R-NC) and Diane Feinstein (D-CA), ridiculed these arguments. In Molinari's words, "If the Postal Service can issue stamps in honor of Bugs Bunny or Elvis Presley, surely we can ensure the lives and legacies of women who have suffered the ravaging effects of breast cancer will not go unnoticed" (as quoted in McAllister 1997).

The Postal Service's Board of Governors estimated that the semi-postal stamp would raise about $8 million for breast cancer research, far less than $60 million that Feinstein predicted in the 1997 floor debate. In 1998 the first semi-postal stamp was issued. It was priced originally at 40 cents, or 8 cents above the current rate of postage. By 2000, when the stamp was due to be reauthorized the first time, the General Accounting Office estimated that the breast cancer stamp had raised $14 million (Unger 2000). As of 2005, the semi-postal stamp had been reauthorized three times, the rate increased to 45 cents per stamp, and sales were authorized to continue through 2005. According to the Postal Service (USPS), "The stamp has raised more than $45 million for breast cancer research" (USPS 2005).

THE LONG ISLAND BREAST CANCER STUDY PROJECT

Numerous breast cancer organizations from Long Island began to lobby for a federal investigation into what they perceived as high rates of breast cancer among Long Island residents.[4] Led by D'Amato, Congress required the NIH to study residents of Long Island, New York (P.L. 103–43), an investigation that eventually included residents of Suffolk, Nassau, and Sohoharie Counties and Tolland County, Connecticut. Beginning in 1995, the Long Island Breast Cancer Study Project (LIBSCAP) explored possible links between the incidence of breast cancer and exposure to toxic chemicals, pollution, contaminated drinking water, electromagnetic fields, pesticides, municipal waste, and other determinants.

About $30 million has been invested in twelve on-going studies, including $8 million for a study entitled "Breast Cancer and the Environment on Long Island." The study focused on two pollutants—hydrocarbons and organochlorines—and their possible connections to breast cancer. It found no relationship between organochlorines and breast cancer and only a modest one between hydrocarbons and breast cancer (Nugent 2003; Williamson 2002).

The elaborate study provoked criticism from some environmentalists, among them Janette D. Sherman, who in *Life's Delicate Balance* (1999) criticized the study's procedures. Nevertheless, the issue of a link between breast cancer and the environment remains on the political agenda. The NBCC supports legislation co-sponsored by breast cancer survivor Representative Sue Myrick (R-NC) and Representative Nita Lowey (D-NY), introduced in the 106th Congress, which would fund multidisciplinary research carried out by multi-institutional consortiums across the country to study environmental factors that may be related to breast cancer.

MEDICAID EXPANSION

The NBCC was concerned that low-income, uninsured women were learning that they had breast cancer through the free screenings provided by the Centers for Disease Control (CDC) under the 1990 Breast and Cervical Cancer Mortality Prevention Act but were unable to secure any treatment. This led to another legislative initiative: the Breast and Cervical Cancer Treatment Act. Sponsored by Myrick, the law allowed (but did not mandate) states to expand their Medicaid programs to cover treatment for all low-income women diagnosed with either disease. The legislation was introduced in 1997 and became law in October 2000. The NBCC then worked with its state-level organizations to ensure that the states would participate, which all fifty and the District of Columbia eventually did (NBCC 2002d, 2003e). In 2005, an era marked by growing federal deficits and a desire on the part of the Republican majority in Congress to decrease the size of government, all optional programs under Medicaid were threatened by cuts and possible elimination. Among them was the Breast and Cervical Cancer Treatment program (Weiss 2005).

LIGHTING THE ARCH

In 2004 Congress passed a law sponsored by Senator James Talent (R-MO) that required the Department of Interior to illuminate the Gateway Arch in St. Louis with pink lights to promote breast cancer awareness during October—Breast Cancer Awareness Month (PL 108–348). Congressional action was required because the Gateway Arch is a national monument. The legislation passed both houses of Congress by unanimous voice vote.

BREAST CANCER POLITICS TODAY

Since the 1990s breast cancer has become a cause célèbre on Capitol Hill. Representative Barbara Vucanovich (2000), for example, recalls that when Nancy Brinker of the Komen Foundation approached members of Congress and their staffs about participating in a Washington, D.C., Race for the Cure, congressional offices competed to sign up participants. Harry Jaffe stated in a *Men's Health* article (1997) that members of Congress support breast cancer funding to demonstrate a commitment to women's issues. Grassroots activists recall how their participation in the NBCC Lobby Day has changed. In the early years they would meet with the staff, but now many members are anxious to meet with them personally and seek opportunities to attend NBCC events (Andrews and Williams interviews 2003). The NBCC has been named as one of the twenty-five most influential groups in health policymaking in Washington. It was the only disease-specific lobby to make the list (Heaney 2002).[5]

Breast cancer has gained political prominence for several reasons. Of course, some male members of Congress support breast cancer initiatives because of personal connections to the disease or a genuine concern about its impact on women and families. Breast cancer may also be politically charged because male members of Congress "are afraid of women" and "know women's health issues can cost them votes" (Jaffee 1997). More likely, they understand that women compose the majority of voters (Center for the American Woman and Politics 2003). Some commentators argue many male members of Congress in the 1990s wanted to appear sympathetic to women's issues in the wake of the Anita Hill–Clarence Thomas hearings. Breast cancer, one such opportunity, was less controversial than other women's issues such as reproductive rights (Love and Lindsay 1995, 520–21; Olson 2002, 202).

Breast cancer issues even have surfaced in federal campaigns. In the 1996 election cycle the NBCC identified about eleven candidates who were using their support of breast cancer research as a means to attract women voters. They included President Clinton (Wadman 1996), Senators Robert Torricelli (D-NJ) and Ted Stevens (D-AK), and Representatives Nita Lowey and Connie Morella (R-MD) (Kolata 1996). In the 1998 election cycle D'Amato touted his support for breast cancer issues in his reelection bid, a claim disputed by Democratic candidates Geraldine Ferraro and Charles Schumer (Nagourney 1998a, 1998b). Support for breast cancer legislation became an issue in the 2000 Republican presidential primary when George W. Bush attacked Senator John McCain (R-AZ) for voting against some breast cancer initiatives (Auster 2000). The issue also came to light in the 2000 New York Senate race between Representative Rick Lazio (R-NY) and Hillary Clinton. President Clinton chose not to have a public signing ceremony for the Breast and Cervical Cancer Treatment Act that year because Lazio was the bill's co-sponsor and a chief proponent of the legislation in the House ("Politics Intrudes" 2000).

In 2002 support for breast cancer initiatives became an issue as John Dingell (D-MI) faced a primary challenge from Lynn Rivers (D-MI) when the two were placed in the same district after reapportionment left Michigan with one less House seat. Dingell, a thirty-year veteran of the House of Representatives, was not known for his support of women's issues but touted his support of mammography coverage and breast cancer research funding as a way to woo women voters (Edsall 2002; Seelye 2002).

Breast cancer was also an issue in the 2004 North Carolina Senate race between the Democratic candidate, President Clinton's one-time chief of staff Erskine Bowles, and the Republican candidate, Representative Richard Burr. The dispute was characterized by dueling advertisements, news conferences, and statements by prominent breast cancer survivors such as Representative Myrick and Mary Barker, president of the North Carolina Breast Cancer Coalition. Bowles charged that Burr was exaggerating his record on breast cancer issues in the House of Representatives. Burr responded that his sister and a staff member were breast cancer survivors, and Myrick came to his defense (Gardner and Christensen 2004; Morrill 2004).[6]

Prostate Cancer Activism on Capitol Hill

QUIET ENTREPRENEURS

Prostate cancer GSOs formed later than breast cancer GSOs. In 1991, when the first breast cancer lobbyists were working Capitol Hill, prostate cancer support groups were beginning to form and did not yet have a lobbying presence. There was, however, some policy activity on the disease itself.

The policy changes were the result of the quiet entrepreneurial efforts of two well-placed senators who were also prostate cancer survivors: Bob Dole and Ted Stevens. Dole said that he became aware of the funding disparity between the two diseases after being diagnosed in 1991. Prominent surgeons at Johns Hopkins University and Walter Reed Army Medical Center, some of whom, Patrick Walsh among them, had operated upon members of Congress who had prostate cancer, called his attention to the research funding disparity between that disease and breast cancer (interview 2003).

Dole and Stevens took their cues from breast cancer entrepreneurs. As Mary Rose Oakar recalled, "The irony is that after we became successful, Bob Dole called me. He called me and he was majority leader! He said, 'You've been so successful in breast cancer advocacy . . . do you mind if we couple up with you guys?' . . . I didn't mind if they got more research money because I thought prostate cancer was underfunded. . . . We got something for prostate cancer but not as much. We [breast cancer] kept the lion's share" (interview 2003).

Initial signs of prostate cancer earmarking occurred in 1991, when the first breast cancer earmark appeared in the NCI appropriations bill. Stevens, a member of the Senate Appropriations Committee, was recovering from his bout with prostate cancer and managed to include in the appropriations bill a provision creating a "Matsunaga-Conte Prostate Cancer Research Center" in honor of Representative Silvio Conte (R-MA) and Senator Spark Matsunaga (D-HI), both of whom had died of the disease. The research center was eventually dropped from the final legislation, but a prostate cancer earmark in the NCI appropriations was included ("Future of Labor-HHS Measure Clouded" 1991).

Building upon a concern of the prostate cancer risk faced by an aging veteran population, the Department of Veterans' Affairs (VA) began to fund some prostate cancer research in 1992, although the amount remains small. The VA program is threatened, however, by increasing budget deficits and the cost of the wars against terrorism and Iraq. The FY 2006 presidential budget request called for Congress to cut $50 million from the program, which would leave little money for funding new research projects (NPCC 2005c).

More significant is the funding provided by the Department of Defense. Congress created the first of two Department of Defense programs dedicated to prostate cancer research in 1993, the Center for Prostate Disease Research (CPDR). Affiliated with a number of military health programs, its mission is to conduct basic research and clinical studies of prostate cancer, using the military population as its base (CPDR 2003). The second program was created in 1996 when Congress expanded the CDMRP to include prostate cancer research and other diseases, beginning in FY 1997 (Dole interview 2003). The status of the CDMRP is in question, however, given the opposition of prominent members of the appropriations committees, including Senator Stevens (NPCC 2005c).

As one women's health advocate reflected, "Think about who's in Congress. They didn't have to convince the powers that be, [like breast cancer advocates had to], they simply could do it" (interview 2003). Women members of Congress who championed the cause of breast cancer did not have seats on appropriations committees and sometimes had to resort to desperate measures. At one point they stormed a closed appropriations conference committee meeting to ensure that their line items remained in legislation (Oakar interview 2003).

Other legislative activity continued but at a slower pace, and the number of bills introduced concerning prostate cancer increased during the 1990s. A few committees, including the Senate Aging Committee, hosted hearings to draw attention to the disease (tables 36 and 37).[7]

SURVIVORS ORGANIZE

The activities of the NPCC and its survivor-advocates helped place prostate cancer on the policy agenda. Following the example of the NBCC, one of the NPCC's first activities was a petition drive to pressure Congress for more research funding. The goal was to obtain a million signatures by September 1997 ("Prostate Cancer Survivors" 1997), and approximately five hundred thousand were delivered to Congress in March 1998 (Atkins e-mail 2003). Prostate cancer activists frequently compared the level of funding for research into breast cancer and prostate cancer, leading some observers to call it a battle between the sexes. Breast cancer advocates were unhappy with such comparisons, arguing that "disease wars" were counterproductive (Weiss 1996). As Bob Samuels, the former president of the NPCC, said, "Certainly our lives are just as important" ("Prostate Cancer Survivors" 1997).

Prostate cancer advocates' efforts, however, have not been rewarded consistently. Congress expanded Medicare coverage to include screenings for breast, cervical and colorectal cancer, diabetes, and osteoporosis by 1998, but it delayed implementing coverage for prostate cancer screening until 2000. The coverage was omitted despite widespread support. "There was no medical or scientific reason for [the omission]," Samuels maintained. "It was a political reason" (as quoted in Gruskin 1998).

The NPCC and its grassroots activists in Alaska prevailed upon Ted Stevens to include a specific earmark in the FY 1999 NIH appropriations bill, calling upon the agency to spend $175 million on prostate cancer research. Never comfortable with the CDMRP, Stevens pushed colleagues to increase funding in the NIH, which he felt was more appropriate. The Stevens earmark was not included in the final legislation, but NCI funding for prostate cancer did reach $135 million in FY 1999 (Dimock 2003; table 35).

Table 35. Prostate Cancer and Breast Cancer Research Funds, 1980–2002 (in millions of dollars)

Year	National Cancer Institute		Defense Department		Veterans' Affairs
	Prostate Cancer	Breast Cancer	Prostate Cancer	Breast Cancer	Prostate Cancer Only
1980	—	—	0	0	0
1981	6.4	33.9	0	0	0
1982	7.5	41.1	0	0	0
1983	10.0	47.7	0	0	0
1984	10.3	53.5	0	0	0
1985	10.6	50.3	0	0	0
1986	9.5	51.5	0	0	0
1987	9.9	60.9	0	0	0
1988	9.5	70.5	0	0	0
1989	12.5	74.5	0	0	0
1990	13.2	81.0	0	0	0
1991	13.8	92.7	0	0	0
1992	31.4	145.0	2	25	1.83
1993	51.1	211.5	2	210	2.41
1994	56.1	267.6	2	25	4.08
1995	64.3	308.7	14[a]	150	4.10
1996	71.7	317.5	7.5	100	8.95
1997	82.3	332.0	45	100	11.34
1998	86.9	348.2	50	133.3	13.63
1999	135.7	387.2	50	136.8[b]	17.95
2000	203.2	438.7	75	176.3[b]	21.82
2001	258.0	475.2	100[c]	177.4[b,c]	22.92
2002	278.4	522.6	85	151.5	29.30

Sources: National Cancer Institute *Fact Book,* various years; Congressionally Directed Medical Research Program *Annual Report,* various years; Congressional Research Service; private communications with Department of Defense, Department of Veterans' Affairs and CRS.
— indicates that data are not available.
[a]Includes $10 million for DoD/VA research and $4.2 for advanced medical technology (CRS, private communication, July, 1998).
[b]Includes funds raised from the Breast Cancer semi-postal stamp: $1.8 million in 1999, $1.3 million in 2000, $2.4 million in 2001 and approximately $1.5 million in 2002.
[c]Congress appropriated the $100 million for prostate cancer research and $175 million for breast cancer research under the CDMRP for FY 2001. This amount was cut 15 percent in the wake of the September 11 terrorist attacks, and the 15 percent reduction remained for FY 2002.

MORE STAMPS

In 1999 the U.S. Post Office issued a prostate cancer awareness stamp priced at the first-class rate of 33 cents. That same year, Representative Randy "Duke" Cunningham (R-CA), a prostate cancer suvivor, introduced the first legislation to create a prostate cancer semi-postal stamp. The effort failed. Instead, the legislation that reauthorized the breast cancer semi-postal stamp through 2002 also transferred future decisions about semi-postal stamps to the U.S. Postal Service ("Prostate Cancer Research Stamp Fails in Congress" 2000). The NPCC continues to support efforts to create a prostate cancer semi-postal stamp (NPCC Advocacy Conference call March 2003; NPCC Smart-brief 2003).[8]

RELUCTANT CHAMPIONS

The NPCC now works with other national and state-level prostate cancer organizations to pressure Congress to maintain or increase its commitment to prostate cancer research. Like the NBCC, the NPCC sponsors an annual lobby day where survivors and surrogates try to influence members of Congress and their staffs. Sandra Boodman (1995) noted that the subject of prostate cancer has the attention of members of Congress, who are motivated by self-interest. "Most prostate cancer sufferers are men over fifty, a description that fits a majority of Congress." Boodman also quotes Senator Richard C. Shelby (R-AL), who said that "personal experience" compelled him to take legislative action. "'If it could happen to me, it'll happen to millions of other men.'"

Yet prostate cancer activists relate that members of Congress who are prostate cancer survivors are at best reluctant champions for their cause. The disease is common among members of Congress, but a private battle with an illness is much different from going public with one's experience. As one activist told us, "Finding a senator who will publicly act in his own self interest is very difficult. That doesn't mean that they won't work for various pork barrel additions, but that's very private. It happens within chambers" (interview 2003).

In 2005 (the 109th Congress) seven senators were known to be prostate cancer survivors: Saxby Chandliss (R-GA), Michael Crapo (R-ID), John Kerry (D-MA), Paul Sarbanes (D-MD), Jeff Sessions (R-AL), Richard Shelby, and Ted Stevens. They were joined by at least four members of the House of Representatives: Todd Akin (R-MO), Roy Blunt (R-MO), Randy "Duke" Cunningham, and Henry Hyde (R-IL). Joining them were former Senators

Ben Nighthorse Campbell, Alan Cranston, Bob Dole, Jesse Helms, Connie Mack, Spark Matsunaga, and William Roth as well as former Representatives Herb Bateman, James Clarke, Silvio Conte, Dean Gallo, Dan Rostenkowski, John Schmitz, and Gerald Solomon.[9]

Cunningham participated in several NPCC-sponsored events and was a principal sponsor of a bill to create an Office of Men's Health, analogous to the Office of Women's Health (Cunningham 2001; NPCC 2002d). Dole has participated in a number of fund-raisers for prostate cancer and sponsors a screening van at Kansas fairs. Crapo sponsors a prostate cancer screening van that visits fairs throughout the state of Idaho (Wheeler interview 2003). Stevens acknowledges his diagnosis and has promoted prostate cancer efforts through his position on the Senate Appropriations Committee. As a lobbyist for prostate cancer noted, Stevens "needs a lot of political cover, as would any one else. He needs to know that his constituents think this is important, and that prostate cancer is an important problem in Alaska. He also needs to know that the constituents of other members of the Committee care about it" (interview 2003).

As public as some men might be, many more do not discuss their diagnoses or the side effects of their illnesses. Gender differences with respect to dealing with health issues become important in this context. As one advocate put it, "You have to remember you're dealing with men" who are uncomfortable talking about their health (interview 2003). This discomfort is equally true for grassroots survivors as well as those who hold public office. As Stevens says, "Suppose you walk out of a hearing about funding medical research and there are 150 attractive young women waiting in the hall. And they're button-holing you about breast-cancer research. They'll have an impact. If you had 150 men waiting there . . . they would be older than fifty, not as aggressive, not as organized. And they wouldn't want to talk about it, anyway" (as quoted in Jaffee 1997). "This [reluctance to discuss the disease] leads one to redefine 'success' at the grassroots," one activist maintained (interview 2003).

Compounding the concern is the fact that members of Congress are elected officials concerned with their political fortunes. They may be reluctant to discuss their health histories because they do not want to be perceived as weak, either personally or politically. Some lobbyists joke that they can guess who has been diagnosed with prostate cancer because they suddenly receive telephone calls from staff members asking for information. Other legislators routinely attend hearings on prostate cancer or send staff representatives but never reveal the reason for their interest. A persistent rumor on Capitol Hill holds that a prostate cancer support group for senators meets in secret and under a pseudonym; the number of senators who attend is unknown. Even those willing to work with activists have reservations about being the "prostate cancer poster child."[10]

Prostate cancer advocates say they often have more luck with elected officials whose fathers developed prostate cancer, for example, Senator Charles Schumer (D-NY). As one activist put it, without referring to Schumer in particular, "They can say, 'this disease took my father when he was too young, but I'm just fine. I'm not weak or sick'" (interview 2003). Representative Sherrod Brown (D-OH), who sponsored the NPCC's annual "Dear Colleague" letter that articulates annual funding goals, believes prostate cancer is a worthy cause but has no apparent personal connection to the disease.

Is public acknowledgement of cancer politically risky? "Absolutely!" said Sue Myrick. "[Public officials] must think politically. It's natural to think about this" (interview 2003). Her decision reflects some of the gender dynamics at work. "When I was diagnosed [with breast cancer]," Myrick recalled, "I thought, 'I can keep this quiet.' But I have an opportunity to save lives and make it better for other people. It was the best thing I ever did, especially when I hear someone say 'You saved my life,' or 'I saw you on TV.' . . . It was well worth whatever it may have cost me. And I'm not twenty years old. If I don't get reelected, so what?" (interview 2003). Dole agreed: "My staff thought I would take a lot of heat. Some thought that I shouldn't tell anyone I had cancer. . . . There is some risk for everyone" (interview 2003).

POLITICALLY LESS POTENT

Prostate cancer advocates have a higher profile on Capitol Hill now than they did during the 1990s, but their influence pales in comparison to the clout of the breast cancer lobby. As Dole maintained, "They [prostate cancer activists] have not done a good job of exercising their constitutional right to petition the government" (interview 2003). A health staff member agrees, "When the breast cancer coalition comes, it's a big deal. These women are passionate about being a survivor. Prostate cancer groups don't have the same advocacy level" (interview 2003). Said another, "There's just no big pressure the way there is with breast cancer. . . . We just haven't heard as much about prostate cancer" (as quoted in Boodman 1995). Members of Congress do not perceive that votes for prostate cancer funding or men's health issues will help attract male voters (Kolata 1996).

Media Advocacy Evidence in Public Policy

Media advocacy efforts, if effective, should yield policy change. There is qualitative evidence that breast cancer activists had substantial impact upon policy agenda. Is there evidence of this influence in quantitative analysis? This section explores two issues. First, Are increases in media attention accompanied by increases in public policy attention, as media advocacy anticipates? These increases should occur about the same time as the development of GSOs.[11] Second, Did prostate cancer policy changes piggyback on breast cancer policy changes? Because earlier analyses of media attention found that prostate cancer media coverage appeared to piggyback upon breast cancer's media coverage for breast cancer (chapter 5), the same might be true for policy initiatives.

Public policy is measured in three ways: (1) increases in federal research spending; (2) number of bills introduced; and (3) the number of congressional hearings. All data are compiled from public records. Thus we asked:

RQ1: Did federal research funding, the number of bills introduced and the number of congressional hearings held increase after the development of GSOs?

RQ2: Were increases in federal research funding related to increases in media coverage?

RQ3: Is there evidence that prostate cancer advocates piggy backed on the efforts of breast cancer advocates?

FINDINGS

On every measure of public policy attention breast cancer received more attention from policymakers than prostate cancer. Consider, for example, NCI funding. The two diseases, which have relatively similar mortality and morbidity rates, received quite different amounts of funding. In the 1980s the NCI spent about $9.5 million on prostate cancer research each year; at the same time, it spent about $40 million a year on breast cancer research. Starting in FY 1992 (with legislation passed in 1991), funding for both prostate cancer and breast cancer started to increase exponentially. By FY 2002, prostate cancer received more generous funding from the NCI, some $291 million, and breast cancer received more than $500 million (table 35).

Other measures of policy attention show the same results. Consider legislation introduced dealing with the two cancers. From the 96th Congress (1979–80) to the 100th (1989–90), little attention was paid to either disease.

Only four bills mentioned breast cancer, and none mentioned prostate cancer. In the 101st Congress (1991–92), however, eleven bills dealt with prostate cancer and forty-five dealt with breast cancer. The pattern continued. The number of prostate cancer bills continued to rise and peaked at thirty-one in the 106th Congress (1999–2000). The number of breast cancer bills rose faster and peaked at ninety-one in the 105th Congress (1997–98). The number of bills introduced referring to either disease declined in the 107th Congress, and the number of breast cancer bills continued to outpace the number of prostate cancer bills (table 36).

Breast cancer lobbyists were also more likely to testify on a variety of topics, from appropriations to health information to biotechnology, at congressional hearings.[12] They appeared at some ninety-one hearings from 1980 to 2002. Forty percent of the hearings (thirty-eight) addressed topics directly related to breast cancer, such as its incidence on Long Island, mammography, and appropriations. Again, breast cancer activists' appearances increased dramatically in 1991 and remained high (table 37). By contrast, prostate cancer advocates or experts appeared at only ten congressional hearings between 1980 and 2002, only three of which addressed prostate cancer exclusively. The earliest was in 1993, and the remainder occurred after the founding of the NPCC.

Table 36. Congressional Legislation Introduced Regarding Prostate Cancer and Breast Cancer, 96th–108th Congresses

Congress	(Years)	Number of Bills Introduced	
		Prostate Cancer	Breast Cancer
96th	(1979–80)	0	4
97th	(1981–82)	0	1
98th	(1983–84)	0	1
99th	(1985–86)	0	5
100th	(1987–88)	0	18
101st	(1989–90)	1	45
102d	(1991–92)	11	87
103d	(1993–94)	22	59
104th	(1995–96)	20	51
105th	(1997–98)	29	91
106th	(1999–2000)	31	45
107th	(2001–2)	19	59

Source: Data complied by authors from Congressional Information Service (CIS), a Lexis-Nexis service.

Table 37. Congressional Hearings on Breast Cancer and Prostate Cancer, 1980–2002

Year	Breast Cancer		Prostate Cancer	
	All Hearings[a]	Breast Cancer Only[b]	All Hearings[a]	Prostate Cancer Only[b]
1980	1	0	0	0
1981	0	0	0	0
1982	0	0	0	0
1983	0	0	0	0
1984	1	1	0	0
1985	1	1	0	0
1986	0	0	0	0
1987	2	1	0	0
1988	5	0	0	0
1989	0	0	0	0
1990	5	3	0	0
1991	11	7	0	0
1992	9	5	0	0
1993	7	3	1	1
1994	13	7	0	0
1995	4	0	0	0
1996	4	1	0	0
1997	1	0	1	0
1998	7	2	1	0
1999	7	2	2	2
2000	3	1	2	0
2001	4	1	2	0
2002	6	3	1	0

Source: Congressional Information Service (CIS) on-line service.

[a]All hearings where breast cancer or prostate cancer was the main topic of the hearing, mentioned as one issue in a hearing on a broader topic, or where breast cancer or prostate cancer lobbyists or survivors testified.

[b]Hearings where prostate cancer, or breast cancer or mammography screening were the main topic.

Statistical analyses demonstrate that the NBCC and its allies appear to have had an impact on public policy. Federal funding for breast cancer research increased from an average of $59.8 million per year (1980–91) to an average of $468 million per year (1992–2002)—a sevenfold increase. Similarly, the number of breast cancer bills introduced jumped from an average of twelve per Congress in the 96th through 101st Congresses to an average of sixty-one in the 102nd through 107th, and the number of annual hearings jumped from an average of fewer than one (1980–90) to an average of four (1991–2002) (table 38).

Table 38. Advocacy and Congressional Activity:
Difference of Means Tests

	Mean	Standard Dev.	p
Breast Cancer Bills:			
1980–90	12.3	17.2	0.0014
1991–2002	61.0	23.3	
Breast Cancer Hearings:			
1980–90	0.07	1.9	<.0001
1991–2002	4.1	3.4	
Prostate Cancer Bills:			
1980–95	6.0	9.2	0.0520
1996–2002	19.7	8.1	
Prostate Cancer Bills:			
1980–91	0.17	0.4	0.0008
1992–2002	18.6	6.4	
Prostate Cancer Hearings:			
1980–95	0.06	0.2	0.0011
1996–2002	1.5	0.5	
Prostate Cancer Hearings:			
1980–91	0	0.0	n.a.
1992–2002	0.3	0.8	
Breast Cancer Funding ($ million):			
1980–91	59.8	18.0	<0.0001
1992–2002[a]	468.4	152.5	
Prostate Cancer Funding ($ million):			
1980–96	26.9	28.2	0.003
1997–2002[b]	263.2	115.9	
Prostate Cancer Funding ($ million):			
1980–91	8.68	2.3	0.0016
1992–2002	172.6	133.2	

Source: Data compiled by authors.

[a]1992 is used here because FY 1992 is the first year that the NBCC's advocacy efforts could have yielded increased research funding.

[b]1997 is used here because FY 1997 is the first year that the NPCC's advocacy efforts could have yielded increased research funding.

What about the case of prostate cancer? At first examination it appears that the NPCC made a mark on public policy. Federal funding for prostate cancer research grew from an average of $26.9 million a year (1980–96) to an average of $263 million (1997–2002)—a tenfold increase. The number of prostate cancer bills increased from an average of six per Congress in the 96th through 104th Congresses to an average of twenty in the 105th through

107th, and the average annual number of hearings increased from fewer than one (1980–95) to 1.5 (1996–2002) (table 38).

Prostate cancer policy activity began to increase at about the same time as breast cancer policy activity, a finding reinforced by information gathered through interviews. Thus, we analyzed the prostate cancer data to test these observations, using the founding date of the NBCC (1991–92).[13] Our quantitative findings are consistent with the interviewees' recollections. Prostate cancer policy began to change as early as 1992. Federal funding for research, for example, increased from an average of $9 million (1980–91) to an average of $173 million (1992–2002)—a nineteenfold increase. Likewise, prostate cancer legislation increased from an average of fewer than one bill per Congress in the 96th through 101st Congresses to an average of nineteen in the 102nd through 107th. Finally, no hearings addressed prostate cancer until 1993—after the founding of the NBCC but before the founding of the NPCC (table 38). Thus prostate cancer policy change began well in advance of the development of prostate cancer GSOs, probably due to the efforts of quiet entrepreneurs who piggybacked on the efforts of breast cancer entrepreneurs. These conclusions, however, to do not imply that the NPCC and its allies are inconsequential. We believe they play an important role in building upon these early policy gains.

MEDIA COVERAGE AND PUBLIC POLICY

As compelling as these results are, they do not test media advocacy itself. Media coverage and research funding do appear, however, to be correlated (figure 1; chapter 3; table 35). To test for the relationship between media and public policy we need to include media coverage in the analyses. Thus we used ordinary least squares (OLS) regression to test the relationship, duplicating an analysis used in the case of AIDS (Theodoulou, Guevara, and Minnassins 1996). We sought to determine whether annual changes in media coverage were related to annual changes in federal funding.[14]

Changes in media coverage were related to changes in federal funding of both breast cancer and prostate cancer, although the relationship is modest. Changes in media coverage predict for approximately 12 percent of the changes in breast cancer funding and 19 percent of the changes in prostate cancer funding (adjusted R^2 = 0.1251 and 0.1882, respectively). Notably, however, these relationships are stronger than that observed by Theodoulou, Guevara, and Minnassins (1996), who found that changes in media coverage accounted for only about 10 percent of the changes in federal AIDS funding in the 1980s and early 1990s (tables 39 and 40).

Table 39. Changes in Breast Cancer Funding: Regression Analysis

Independent Variable	Parameter Estimate (Standard Error)
Intercept	18.57
	(0.32)
Changes in breast cancer news stories	0.42[a]
	(0.23)
Adjusted R^2	0.1251

Source: Data compiled by authors.
[a]$p < 0.10$.

Table 40. Changes in Prostate Cancer Funding: Regression Analysis

Independent Variables	Parameter Estimate (Standard Error)
Intercept	7.73
	(3.81)
Changes in prostate cancer news stories	0.45[a]
	(0.20)
Adjusted R^2	0.1882

Source: Data compiled by authors.
[a]$p < 0.05$

Discussion

COMING ONTO THE POLICY AGENDA

Roger Cobb and Charles Elder (1972) summarized the agenda-setting process as one in which an issue is defined and expanded to a relevant public. The issue then reaches the policy agenda through one of several patterns of access, depending upon how many people it affects (i.e., the "relevant public"). When an issue affects the "mass public," policy decision making is "almost reflexive" or immediate (Cobb and Elder 1972, 157).

Policymaking, however, will be slower in all other instances. Issues that affect only a disenfranchised minority, what Cobb and Elder (1972) call "identification groups," will only reach the policy agenda when the groups threaten to disrupt the system through strikes, riots, or social protest. Issues that affect an "attention group," such as a lobby or other organization mobilized by only one political issue, will come onto the policy agenda somewhat more quickly than those affecting identification groups.

Aside from the mass public, issues come quickly onto the policy agenda when they are expanded to the "attentive public." An attentive public is "a generally informed and interested stratum of the population. Though not homogeneous, the attentive public tends to be relatively stable in composition and comes disproportionately from the more educated and higher income groups" (Cobb and Elder 1972, 107). When issues expand to include the attentive public, advocates have a strong position from which to confront policymakers and demand action.

As documented, 1991 was a crucial year for bringing breast cancer onto the policy agenda. To say, however, that breast cancer moved onto the policy agenda in 1991 gives too much credit to the NBCC and its advocates, who built upon years of activism on the part of Rose Kushner, Mary Rose Oakar, and others. Before 1991 the issue of breast cancer had expanded only to attention groups or "attention entrepreneurs"—in this case Mary Rose Oakar and Rose Kushner, and the CCWI. With formation of the NBCC and establishment of a national movement populated by thousands of articulate, educated women, breast cancer expanded onto the attentive public's agenda, which then allowed it to move onto the policy agenda. Cobb and Elder (156–57) state that issues on the attentive public's agenda are likely to become a "permanent part" of the policy agenda because legislators are keenly aware of issues that attract substantial public attention. That certainly appears to be true of breast cancer now.

By contrast, prostate cancer has reached the level of an attention group. Thus, it is important only to those who are aware of the problem— activists in prostate cancer GSOs. One primary tool available to an attention group is to threaten some type of sanction, such as withholding votes come election time, unless policymakers act on an agenda item. Unless and until prostate cancer activists are willing to block vote, such an action is unlikely. Of course, the prostate cancer attention group has one potentially powerful way of placing the disease on the policy agenda: legislative logrolling and public advocacy on the part of prostate cancer survivor-legislators. Given that prostate cancer survivors are reluctant champions, however, dramatic action remains unlikely. Thus, prostate cancer exists only on the periphery of the policy agenda, and its current position is precarious.

PIGGYBACKING ON BREAST CANCER ADVOCACY

Has there been any policy change in the case of prostate cancer? Policy activity for that disease began to increase at nearly the same time as breast cancer activity, strongly suggesting that prostate cancer benefited from the efforts of breast cancer activists. First, breast cancer advocates, including those in Congress, changed the politics of cancer research, causing Dole to ally himself with breast cancer proponents on the Hill to achieve his goals for prostate cancer. Getting one gender-specific disease on the agenda prompted some men in Congress to think about another one. Second, breast cancer proponents set the precedents of earmarking and using Department of Defense funds for medical research, initiatives that prostate cancer champions exploited. Third, women members of Congress, a small minority operating in a male-dominated institution, had to conform to the norms of that institution. As Barbara Vucanovich's quotation at the beginning of this chapter implies, women members of Congress engaged in a long-standing congressional tradition: the logroll. To get support for breast cancer initiatives, they agreed to add prostate cancer to their legislation. This link permeates subsequent legislative efforts that employ "breast and prostate cancer" as one term.[15]

THE ROLE OF SURVIVORS

Survivors are important actors in both stories. Rose Kushner single-handedly defined the breast cancer agenda in the 1980s. In the 1990s, survivors in GSOs added passion to the lobbying cause and poignantly demonstrated the human cost of disease. Survivors in Congress—Lloyd, Myrick, and Vucanovich—all sponsored breast cancer legislation and spoke out about their experiences with disease. They demonstrated how the women's health movement taught women to become informed about their bodies and take control of their health and how the feminist movement taught that the "personal is political."

Survivors play a different role in the prostate cancer story; their hands are on the levers of power but not necessarily willing to pull them. Along the same vein, they are reluctant to discuss their experiences with disease openly or use their experiences to advocate on the Hill. Male members of Congress do not have the same awareness as their female counterparts that "the personal" (experiences with disease) is "political." Aside from any electoral consequences, discussing incontinence and impotence is not easy for anyone. Often prominent personalities, and others who have had prostate cancer, will refuse to discuss the private details of their illnesses (Swift 2003).

Decades of feminist scholarly research have documented countless instances where sexism or hostility on the part of men in power has led to the neglect of issues important to women. The rhetoric of many breast cancer activists and congressional advocates reflects that premise even now. Implicit in these condemnations is that men will look out for their own interests while ignoring those of women and other disenfranchised groups. Our research, however, contradicts this assertion. In the case of prostate cancer at least, men have not looked after their best interests. This neglect ensures that prostate cancer activists will be unable to compete with breast cancer activists on the policy agenda despite the diseases' many similarities.

Agenda Maintenance

THE POLITICS OF ISSUE DEFINITION
AND FRAMING

> Women with breast cancer need to change the debate. . . .
> We need to own the message.
> —Fran Visco

> The definition of alternatives is the supreme instrument of power.
> —E. E. Schattschneider

For advocates of any stripe, getting on the agenda is only a partial success. Staying on the agenda is equally important. Here again, we find significant differences between breast cancer's assertive advocates and prostate cancer's reluctant champions. In this chapter we examine the rhetorical strategies that both groups use.

The first of this chapter's four sections reviews the relevant academic literature on agenda-setting, problem definition, and the uses of language in politics. The second analyzes the language that breast cancer advocates employ to maintain high levels of funding for research and expand the policy agenda. The third considers the rhetorical strategies of prostate cancer activists and compares them to breast cancer activists' efforts, and, finally, we discuss the implications of these practices.

Agenda Maintenance

Securing a place on the policy agenda is difficult, but it also is challenging to remain there. In the early 1970s Anthony Downs (1972) defined the "issue attention cycle," where initial excitement about a problem is followed by realization of the costs of addressing the problem and then a gradual decline in public interest. Eventually, other problems move onto the agenda. The issue attention cycle has been addressed in the field of media advocacy as well. Lawrence Wallack and his colleagues (1993) cite one case study concerning the placement of billboards advertising alcoholic beverages. Advocates successfully used the media to draw attention to the problem of billboards' proximity to schools and frame the problem as a policy issue. The issue, however, did not receive sustained attention, and eventually all policy gains were lost.

Policies fade from the policy agenda for a myriad of reasons. John Kingdon (1984, 108–10) provided several possible explanations for this phenomenon. One is that policymakers believe that problems are solved or addressed through legislation (see also Cobb and Elder 1972, 158). A second reason is that action at another level of government (i.e., state or local) solves the problem. A third is that growth is self-limiting. Exponential rates of growth in spending for one policy area cannot be sustained indefinitely; eventually such spending would crowd out funding for all other programs. Similarly, zealous enforcement of new regulations may lead to a backlash. In addition, failure to solve a problem may lead to its demise. Policymaking takes time and energy on the part of lobbyists, congressional staff, and members. If an effort appears futile, then supporters will move on to other issues. The repeated failures to enact comprehensive health-care reform are one example. Finally, policy issues are faddish. As Kingdon observed, "a subject gets attention when it is novel" (1984, 110).

Part of this phenomenon has to do with the nature of the policy process. Baumgartner and Jones (1993) argued the policy agenda is best characterized as "punctuated equilibrium." In this system, most policy arenas are marked by long periods of equilibrium where policymaking is incremental. As new issues come onto the agenda they result in institutional changes that may stay in place for decades—what Cobb and Elder called "durability" (1972, 158)—and become part of a new equilibrium. This accurately describes the case of AIDS. Various government health agencies continue to devote large sums to AIDS research and public health efforts, but the perceived urgency of the AIDS epidemic has waned. It has become part of the new policy equilibrium.

THE IMPORTANCE OF PROBLEM DEFINITION

Maintaining a new equilibrium may not be enough for some advocates, however. Some breast cancer activists believe AIDS has lost its primacy on the agenda and fear the same might happen to breast cancer (Brinkman interview

2003). By continuously *redefining* the breast cancer problem in new ways they can keep the issue on the public agenda and expand it (Kingdon 1984).

How does problem redefinition occur? As Kingdon (1984) vividly described, policy solutions and policy problems exist in a "primeval soup." As a result, countless policy problems interact and collide with countless policy solutions. When new issues come onto the media's and public's agendas, advocates attempt to redefine their cause so that it "fits" with the issue of the day and remains relevant. An example of this is the National Prostate Cancer Coalition (NPCC)'s "Protect our Protectors" campaign, which commemorated the first anniversary of the September 11, 2001, terrorist attack. The campaign was designed to raise awareness of prostate cancer by providing cancer screening for firefighters and emergency response personnel nationwide (NPCC 2002e). Problem definition at the policy level does not occur in a vacuum, of course. Advocates' efforts to define and redefine a problem will be successful only if these definitions resonate with the dominant social construction (introduction).

USE OF LANGUAGE IN THE POLICY PROCESS

An important component of the process of issue definition and continuous redefinition is, of course, the use of language. Murray Edelman described many of these dynamics in his classic work *The Symbolic Uses of Politics* (1964). The use of language is central to politics since it is "the key to the universe of speaker and audience." Naming an issue, or in our use *defining* an issue, places it into a "class of objects, thereby suggest[ing] with what it is to be judged and compared, and defin[ing] the perspective from which it will be viewed and evaluated" (131).

Edelman also argued that language is used to keep issues on the agenda, what he called "persistence" and what others call "framing" or "issue redefinition." Edelman maintained, for example, that when issues such as increasing medical research funding by a particular amount have been defined in quantifiable terms, advocates will continue to ask for more even when their initial demands have been satisfied. Their success will lead to similar claims by other advocates whose causes "lie upon a common latent value continuum" (154–55).

We can see such phenomena in the case of breast cancer, where advocates' successful efforts to increase medical research funding resulted in continued pressure for more funding and the institution of the first semi-postal stamp. Advocates for a myriad of health conditions now urge the adoption of their own semi-postal stamps (Unger 2000) and compete for opportunities to plead for additional funding from the National Institutes of Health (Dresser 2001, 73).

Finally, Edelmen noted that using symbolic language in politics appeals to a mass audience. The masses are not interested in the particular details of policy or appeals to reason; rather, they respond to emotion. Language that appeals to the "moral codes" embedded in our understanding has the greatest resonance (1964, 172). Congressional supporters of the breast cancer semi-postal stamp, for example, made symbolic appeals to Americans' generosity and spirit of volunteerism (King 2004) rather than the precedent this stamp might create or the relatively small sum of money its sales might generate.

Deborah Stone (1989) developed the notion of causal stories to help explain problem definition, a concept closely related to the concept of framing (introduction). She observed that political actors compose causal stories that provide support for their side. Thus the causal story that poverty is due to poor education and few economic opportunities is different from the causal story that poverty is the result of personal failure or a character flaw such as laziness.

Building upon these works, David Rochefort and Roger Cobb (1994) argue that the rhetoric of problem definition involves several characteristics that help communicate the urgency of an issue. The first is causality, or a claim about the origins of a particular problem. Considered one of the most important components of problem definition, it lies at the heart of media advocacy efforts. If individual behavior causes diseases, then there is no legitimate role for the government. If some outside agent like pollution or a failure to immunize causes them, then a role for government exists. The second characteristic is severity. Unless a problem is defined as severe it will be consigned to the bottom of the policy agenda. The third characteristic is incidence, or the use of statistics to quantify a problem. Of course, such may be fraught with difficulty because advocates on both sides will use competing measures to quantify a problem in a way that benefits their positions. They may even use the same statistics to reach vastly different conclusions. The fourth characteristic is novelty; as Kingdon noted, new issues receive more attention. The fifth is proximity. Unless a problem is likely to affect you or someone you know it fails to capture attention. Witness the importance of personal narratives and of prominent personalities who go public with their diagnoses (Sharf 2001; chapter 4). The final characteristic is the ability to define a problem as a crisis, which "denotes a condition of severity where corrective action is long overdue and dire circumstances exist" (Rochefort and Cobb 1994, 21) (table 41).

Table 41. Rochefort and Cobb's Characteristics
Found in Problem Definition

>Causality
>Severity
>Incidence
>Novelty
>Proximity
>A "Crisis"

The quotation in this chapter's epigraph from E. E. Schattschneider, author
of the classic *Semi-Sovereign People: A Realist's View of Democracy in America,*
is a reminder of the importance of selecting policy alternatives. This discussion of agenda-setting literature is a reminder that the alternatives under consideration depend on efforts to define and redefine problems. An alternative
that does not speak to the dominant definition will not be adopted. Thus, the
definitions of the problem limit the available alternatives. Expanding an issue
also expands the possible alternative solutions. Given that we are creatures
who communicate with words—either written or oral—the use of language,
and the symbols embedded therein, also cannot be ignored.

ISSUES FOR EXPLORATION

Breast cancer and prostate cancer advocates all use language to frame the
policy debate and nature of science. The two are related, of course, because
one of the major policy questions surrounding both diseases concerns funding medical research.

We first explore how activists have been successful at keeping breast cancer on the policy agenda and avoided the boredom and waning of attention
predicted by the issue attention cycle. Specifically, the activists continued
to redefine and expand breast cancer as a policy issue. They have defined
breast cancer as not one but three problems: underfunded research, lack of
access to health-care services, and civil rights. As Congress has solved each
problem as originally defined, the activists have expanded the definition
of the problem to stay on the policy agenda. They have framed science as
neglect, which communicates a sense of urgency to activists, the public, and
policymakers.

Second, we explore how activists defined prostate cancer to keep it on
the policy agenda and communicate a sense of urgency, given the disease's
tenuous position on the policy and media agendas. Although the activists
defined prostate cancer in several ways, one definition overrides all others: a

lack of adequate medical research funding. We then document how prostate cancer advocates have not framed science as neglect but as salvation.

Framing Breast Cancer as a Policy Problem

DEFINING BREAST CANCER AS A PROBLEM OF FUNDING

VARIATION ONE: BREAST CANCER IS NEGLECTED AND NEEDS MORE MONEY. In the early 1990s breast cancer advocates and their allies in Congress defined the disease as one that was neglected by the federal government. Although women's health issues in general had not received the attention they were due according to the National Institutes of Health's guidelines, funding breast cancer research became synonymous with supporting "women's health." To justify their definition of breast cancer as a neglected disease, activists compared its funding with the funding for AIDS (chapter 6; Altman 1996; Oakar interview 2003). AIDS received, and still receives, more federal research funding than breast cancer, but that is only half the story. Even in the 1980s, breast cancer was relatively generously funded compared to all other cancers in the National Cancer Institute (NCI) budget (chapters 6 and 9). AIDS was the only disease that received *more* NCI funding than breast cancer. Granted, some promising research on breast cancer may have gone unfunded. Arguably, that might be a result of insufficient investment in research and development generally, but it is not necessarily a product of systematic neglect of women's health issues in general or breast cancer in particular.

If breast cancer is defined as a problem of neglect, then how much money is needed to alleviate this neglect? Advocates had to quantify the problem. Their conference with breast cancer scientists resulted in an amount of $433 million (Love and Lindsay 1995, 520–21), a level that funding approached by 1993. What Love failed to mention is, Needed for what? Was the money needed to fund all the unfunded research that breast cancer researchers want to undertake, to find the causes of breast cancer, to find new and better treatments, or to find a cure? Love also did not answer the question, For how long? Did scientists need the funds for one year? Five years? Ten years?

These questions remain unanswered. The continued appeals to sustain levels of funding demonstrate the phenomenon Edelman described: When an issue is defined in quantifiable terms and these terms have been met, advocates will continue to ask for more (1964, 154–55). Every year during the appropriations cycle, breast cancer activists work to ensure that something approximating this level of funding is sustained or increased.

VARIATION TWO: "LET'S BUILD ON OUR SUCCESS."   One way to justify continued and increasing amounts of funding is to highlight medical discoveries funded by federal programs. In this arena breast cancer activists have assistance from the news media. Discoveries or "breakthroughs" make news (Nelkin 1995). Although many medical researchers charge that reporters and editors are prone to exaggerate the potential importance of medical discoveries, science reporters express a collective sense of concern with overstating the implications of a particular discovery (Cooper and Yukimura 2002). Assuming that science reporters' intentions are reflected in their choices and framing of stories, then medical discovery news stories should approximate, or even underestimate, the number of important medical discoveries. Stories about medical discoveries compose about a third of all breast cancer stories in our sample from 1980 to 1998 (chapter 3). An acceleration in medical discovery stories after funding increases were implemented in 1992 would lend credence to the arguments of breast cancer activists that federal investment has not been for naught.[1]

Stories about medical discoveries compose a smaller percentage—29 percent—of all breast cancer news stories in the advocacy period (1991–98) than in the preadvocacy period (1980–90) (41 percent). The number of stories about medical discoveries increased over the same period, from 395 stories (1980–90) to 795 (1991–98) (table 42).

The increase in coverage was due in part to important medical discoveries during the 1990s: the role of tamoxifen in preventing cancer, the discovery of two breast cancer genes, and the development of the drugs Herceptin and raloxifene. Alternatively, the increase also may have been because reporters

Table 42. Medical Discovery Stories over Time

Cancer, Years	% of total	(*n*)	Wilcoxon Scores Chi-Square[a]	p
Breast cancer, 1980–90	41.0	(395)	31.64	<.0001
Breast cancer, 1991–98	29.0	(844)		
Total breast cancer discovery stories	34.0	(1,239)		
Prostate cancer, 1980–95	31.8	(99)	0.0038	0.9508
Prostate cancer 1996–98	32.0	(93)		
Prostate cancer, 1980–90	37.5	(80)	1.31	0.2530
Prostate cancer, 1991–98	31.2	(162)		
Total prostate cancer discovery stories	31.9	(192)		

Source: Data compiled by authors.
[a]df = 1.

and editors were aware of the popularity of breast cancer news and decided to run stories about less significant discoveries. A third possibility is that there were more medical discoveries to report in later years because of the increased investment in breast cancer research since 1992.

Regression analysis demonstrates that changes in the number of stories about breast cancer medical discoveries were associated with changes in levels of federal funding and predicted about 23 percent of the changes in funding (adjusted R^2 = 0.2290; table 43). This measure is certainly crude.[2] It does, however, demonstrate something of the relationship between media coverage of medical discoveries and policy outcomes.

It is important to recognize that breast cancer activists use these discoveries in their testimony to justify additional funding. Consider a statement by Fran Visco before a House Appropriations subcommittee, subtitled "Continued Funding for Breast Cancer Research is Critical": "The Coalition would like to emphasize the advancements in breast cancer research that have come about as a result of your longstanding support for this issue. Developments in the past few years have begun to offer breast cancer researchers fascinat-

Table 43. Medical Discovery News Stories and Total
Research Funding: Regression Analysis

Independent Variables	Parameter Estimate (Standard Error)
Model 1 Breast Cancer Intercept:	7.72
	(18.2)
Changes in breast cancer	1.48[a]
Discovery stories	(0.60)
Adjusted R^2	0.2290
Model 2 Prostate Cancer Intercept:	7.12[a]
	(3.14)
Changes in prostate cancer	1.01[b]
discovery stories	(0.27)
Adjusted R^2	0.4221
Model 3 Prostate Cancer Intercept:	4.64
	(2.95)
Changes in prostate cancer	1.08[c]
discovery stories	(0.24)
Changes in breast cancer funding	0.081
	(0.03)
Adjusted R^2	0.5546

Source: Data compiled by authors.
[a]$p < 0.05$
[b]$p < 0.01$
[c]$p < 0.001$

ing insights into the biology of breast cancer and have brought into sharp focus the areas of research *that hold promise and will build on the knowledge we've gained. . . . Now is precisely the time to continue your support for this important research*" (2002a, emphasis added).

The same themes resonate in Visco's 2003 statement before the Senate Defense Appropriations subcommitte: "The DOD BCRP [breast cancer research program]'s decade of progress in the fight against breast cancer was made possible by this Committee's investment in breast cancer research. To continue this unprecedented progress, we ask that you support a $175 million appropriation for the next fiscal year" (2003b).

Similarly, the National Breast Cancer Coalition (NBCC) is proud of Herceptin, which is effective against certain types of metastatic (stage IV) breast cancer.[3] Herceptin was developed using funds from the Congressionally Directed Medical Research Program (CDMRP), the Department of Defense's research effort. Not only was the NBCC instrumental in the creation of the CDMRP but it was also involved heavily in recruiting women into the clinical trials for the drug. NBCC advocates repeatedly use Herception to justify the program and demonstrate that it is "federal money well spent." Visco (2002b) also highlighted basic research funded by the Department of Defense into the role of estrogen in developing breast cancer, stating that "it is anticipated that work from this funding effort will yield insights into the effects of estrogen process on breast cancer risk."

VARIATION THREE: THERE IS STILL MUCH UNKNOWN. Given these promising results, the temptation might be to reduce breast cancer funding, thinking that the "problem" has been "solved." In fact, some scientists, policymakers, and advocates for other diseases question the definition that breast cancer is neglected and point out the enormous federal investment in research for it and AIDS. Often they compare the funding for these diseases to funding levels for heart disease, stroke, and lung cancer, which also have high mortality and morbidity rates. Breast cancer activists frame their responses in two ways: They chronicle how much is still unknown about the disease and make symbolic appeals to unrelated issues.

Susan Love defends the level of spending by making a comparison to lung cancer that uses a twist on the "cause" definition outlined by Rochefort and Cobb. Love argues that breast cancer is not a problem because it is caused by some agent or event that can be regulated, controlled, or banned by the government. Rather, it is an important problem because its causes are unknown. "The other argument is that the amount of money per case of cancer should be equal across cancers. X amount of money per case of breast cancer, X amount for lung cancer. But that's too simplistic a way to measure it. The important measure is what we know about the disease. We know what causes lung cancer. But we don't know what to do about breast cancer yet" (Love and Lindsey 1995, 524).

Other advocates make similar arguments about the unknown origins of the disease. The NBCC (2003f) supports legislation to research into possible environmental causes of breast cancer, an effort also supported by groups such as Breast Cancer Action in San Francisco.[4] Another area of neglect is the causes of breast cancer in younger women, as defined by the Young Survival Coalition (2003).

Love also made a symbolic argument that evades the larger question. The level of spending for breast cancer research, she maintains, is small—about the cost of one B-1 bomber (as quoted in Rosser 2000, 254; Altman 1996, 323). This is an example of using symbolic language. Such an appeal only deals with funding priorities in a most general way and fails to engage in a discussion about how research funds should be allocated among diseases.

DEFINING BREAST CANCER AS A PROBLEM
OF HEALTH-CARE ACCESS

Another way in which breast cancer activists keep the disease on the policy agenda is to define the problem as a lack of access to necessary health-care services. Consider the policy efforts supported by various advocates (table 44).

Not every item listed in table 44 has been enacted into policy, and not every breast cancer GSO agrees with these agenda items. It is evident, though, that breast cancer advocates gradually expanded the health-care access issue. The breast cancer problem was defined first as access to high-quality *screening* mechanisms.[5] Once the issue of screening access was solved, advocates defined the problem as the ability to pay for health-care *treatments*. These first addressed issues most relevant to the privately insured: minimum hospital stays for mastectomy, coverage for breast reconstruction, and bone marrow transplants. As these issues were resolved the problem of access to treatments was expanded to public programs: ensuring Medicare payment for services (clinical trials and outpatient anticancer drugs) and Medicaid coverage for indigent women.

The last agenda items—expanding Medicare to cover outpatient anticancer drugs and all outpatient drugs and granting universal health insurance—

Table 44. Breast Cancer Policy Agenda Items

Access to Screening:
>Providing mammography screening for women under the Medicare and Medicaid programs
 and by the CDC for low-income women who otherwise have no health coverage for this
 service.
>Establishing mammography standards, including for design of equipment, radiation exposure,
 and training for medical personnel.
>Ensuring availability of mammography services for women with disabilities, pursuant to the
 Americans with Disabilities Act (Rhode Island Breast Cancer Coalition 2003).

Access to Health Care for Women with Breast Cancer:
>Keeping silicone breast implants on the market and available for women who choose them
 (Lloyd 1995; Volpe interview 2003).
>Expanding Medicare coverage to include expenses related to participating in clinical trials
 (NBCC 2000).
>Mandating that private insurance pay for minimum hospital stays for mastectomies and lymph
 node dissection, reconstructive surgery, and routine medical expenses related to participation in clinical trials (NBCC 1997b, 2000).
>Mandating that private insurance companies pay for autologous bone marrow transplants for
 women with certain types of breast cancer.
>Providing coverage for treatment of breast cancer and cervical cancer under Medicaid for
 women under sixty-five who are medically indigent.

Beyond Breast Cancer:
>Expanding Medicare Part B to cover outpatient, oral, anticancer drugs.
>Expanding Medicare Part B to cover all outpatient prescription drugs.
>Supporting universal health insurance.

signal an expansion of the breast cancer agenda to issues that characterize the
health-care system as a whole. The NBCC, Y-ME, and others supported the
Access to Cancer Therapies Act that would cover prescription drugs under
Medicare Part B for cancer patients, but only as a temporary measure until
Congress passed comprehensive prescription drug coverage (Volpe interview
2003). Similarly, the passage of the Breast and Cervical Cancer Treatment
Act expands health-care coverage for these diseases. Now the NBCC and
its allies are promoting health-care coverage for people with diseases *other*
than breast cancer.

DEFINING BREAST CANCER AS A CIVIL RIGHTS PROBLEM

The third way that breast cancer activists have defined the disease is by focusing on potential discrimination. Two items on the agenda are enactment of
legislation that would prohibit employers and insurers from using genetic
information as the basis to deny insurance coverage or employment and legislation for a "patient's bill of rights" for those currently enrolled in managed-

care plans (NBCC 2002c, 2003f).[6] Such agenda items go beyond eradicating breast cancer and keep the disease at the forefront of the policy agenda.

Framing Science as Neglect

THE BREAST CANCER "EPIDEMIC"

The most ubiquitous way that breast cancer activists have framed science as neglect is by characterizing breast cancer as an epidemic. This effort is a variant of the "crisis" definition that Rochefort and Cobb (1994) mention as being key. In so doing they engage in a form of symbolic politics: appealing to emotion and a mass audience (Edelman 1964).

The women who founded the NBCC adopted this use of the term, a decision Fran Visco recalls was controversial and unpopular (2003a). Their goal was to communicate a sense of urgency to their cause. As Karen Stabiner has described a 1993 White House meeting with the Clintons, "She [Visco] knew what she wanted President Clinton to say to them. More than anything, Visco wanted him to refer to breast cancer as an epidemic. An epidemic required a solution, however long that took" (1997, 5).

What is an epidemic? Among public health professionals and epidemiologists, it is any unusually high number of cases of a disease in a particular geographic location. That does not necessarily mean hundreds or thousands or millions of cases. Indeed, an epidemic could be an outbreak of ten cases of a rare disease when one expects to find none (Fisher and Worth 1995). In addition, the term is generally used in reference to contagious diseases. In spite of its increasing incidence rate, breast cancer is not an epidemic.

In common usage, however, an epidemic is defined in *Webster's Dictionary* as "affecting or tending to affect many individuals within a population, community or region at the same time; excessively prevalent." Given that definition, breast cancer activists are not incorrect when they refer to an "epidemic," but they are less accurate in the public health sense. *Webster's* second definition, "contagious," does not apply to breast cancer, but the concern that this connotation raises among the public may add to the sense of urgency. A more accurate term, "endemic," meaning "common" or "native," is also bound by geographic location (Gorner 1994). Decrying the "breast cancer endemic," however, does not have the same emotional appeal or urgency.

Visco did not escape criticism for calling breast cancer an epidemic. As Stabiner described it, "Visco had debated the linguistic point on countless radio talk shows with scientists who preferred the formal definition of the term. Breast cancer was not a true epidemic like AIDS. It had not exploded out of nowhere, nor did it spread from one person to another, nor was there as dramatic a rise in incidence. *Epidemic* was a literal distinction, they reminded her, not an emotional state" (1997, 5).

Visco is not the only advocate who uses the term *epidemic.* Virginia Soffa, an author and breast cancer activist, wrote that "we were focused on getting a 'comprehensive strategy to end the epidemic'" (1994, 205). Similarly, Web sites for numerous state and local breast cancer organizations also refer to

---

THE BREAST CANCER EPIDEMIC IN SCHOLARLY WORK

The use of term *breast cancer epidemic* has found its way into work by medical doctors and academics, apparently without regard for its public health definition. American and British authors, for example, have used the term. Among them are Cathy Read (*Preventing Breast Cancer: The Politics of an Epidemic* [1995]); Jeanette Sherman ("The Breast Cancer Epidemic on Long Island" in *Life's Delicate Balance: A Guide to Causes and Prevention of Breast Cancer* [1999]); Anne S. Kasper and Susan J. Ferguson (editors of *Breast Cancer: Society Shapes an Epidemic* [2002]); and Sandra Goodman ("Breast Cancer: The Epidemic That Won't Go Away" [2003]).

Sherman's use of the term *epidemic* to refer to Long Island "may refer to the fact that Long Island has higher rates of breast cancer than the national average. However, they are not the highest rates in the country and are comparable to rates in other affluent suburban areas" (Fagin 2002a). Therefore, to use the term in that way remains problematic and misleading.

Similarly, Read uses the term in her title and text in a broad sense. "This book is about breast cancer," she informs readers, "a disease which was comparatively rare only two hundred years ago.

Since then the incidence has increased everywhere, and in the industrialized world, breast cancer has achieved the proportions of an epidemic" (1). She later observes, "Like the absence of the right to vote, or a life of household drudgery, they see the breast cancer epidemic as a gross injustice (3).

Kasper and Ferguson also refer to breast cancer's "epidemic proportions" (2002, 1). Goodman uses the term to describe breast cancer in the United Kingdom but does not explain it in the body of the short item. In neither case do the writers acknowledge completing definitions. Nor do they discuss how some might object to the use of the term *epidemic* in reference to breast cancer.

The distortion easily can be compounded. As Stanford University professor Marilyn Yalom wrote in *A History of the Breast,* "And among these cancers, breast cancer alone 'has achieved the proportions of an epidemic.'" She cites Read as her source (1997, 227). She appears to assume that the use of the term is appropriate, but adding the word *alone* makes the statement untrue. If breast cancer is an epidemic, then prostate cancer must be an epidemic as well.

breast cancer as an epidemic. Among them are the Connecticut Breast Cancer Coalition, Georgia Breast Cancer Coalition, Florida Breast Cancer Coalition, Ithaca Breast Cancer Alliance, Massachusetts Breast Cancer Coalition, and Marin County Breast Cancer Watch.[7] To their credit, however, breast cancer activists have been successful in linking the terms *breast cancer* and *epidemic*. The term *breast cancer epidemic* is prevalent in casual conversations, media coverage, and on the Internet.[8] Witnessing its adoption in common parlance by individuals who lack an epidemiological background is understandable although the difficulty of that achievement should not be overlooked.

SCREENING, PREVENTION, AND EARLY DETECTION

Advocates further framed science as neglect through criticism of early detection and screening techniques. The American Cancer Society (ACS)and its precursor the American Society for the Control of Cancer has been a proponent of early detection since the 1920s (Leopold 1999, 161). Since the 1980s the American Cancer Society has touted mammography and self-examination (BSE) as primary tools in surviving breast cancer. They assert that early detection, discovering breast cancer while the tumor is small and contained in the breast, vastly increases chances for survival (ACS 2003b, 2003c).

In response, some advocates charge that the ACS's reassuring language dupes women into thinking that these screening tools prevent breast cancer. Instead, advocates correctly argue, these measures detect cancer only after it has developed and becomes visible on an x-ray or palpable by fingertip (e.g., Batt 1994; Read 1995; Soffa 1994). Invoking the mantra "early detection is not early detection," breast cancers for many women are years old before they become detectable by either tool.[9] What is the difference here? The American Cancer Society uses the term *early detection* in the precise medical sense. "Early" refers to the stage of the cancer, not its age in years. Because most breast cancers are slow-growing, they can be years old before they are detectable using current technology. Breast cancer advocates use these facts to further condemn the medical establishment by asserting that inadequate screening tools (BSE and mammography) and the lack of effective preventive measures are further evidence of scientific neglect.

EQUATING RISK WITH BLAMING PATIENTS

Breast cancer activists also framed science as neglect by equating risk factors with patient-blaming. In so doing they imply that risk factors *cause* breast cancer. Thus, to apply Deborah Stone's (1989) concept, they reject this causal story about the origin of breast cancer and attempt to redefine it as something other than lifestyle choices.

Although the precise cause of breast cancer is unknown, what is known are the many risk factors connected with the disease: being female, aging, obesity, higher socioeconomic status, early onset of menarche, late menopause, late childbearing or remaining childless, not breastfeeding, lack of exercise, a family history of breast cancer, having a mutated version of the breast cancer gene, lesbianism, and alcohol consumption.

Some breast cancer activists interpret these scientific findings as blaming women for their illness. Such risk factors, they assert, imply that women are responsible for their own disease because they grew old, ate the wrong foods, delayed childbearing, got fat, went to college, prospered, did not breastfeed, or inherited mutated genes. As Ellen Leopold, a breast cancer survivor and feminist writer, has noted, "Women were conditioned to accept responsibility for whatever calamities befell them. A woman's role as household manager put her in charge of everything within her domain, herself included. . . . Anything that threatened to disturb the integrity of either would be her failure and put her at risk. This was as true of a burned casserole as it was of disease" (1999, 160).

Breast cancer advocates argue that listing risk factors detracts from other potential causes of breast cancer. One New York State Department of Health study led Long Island activists to push for the federal study: "When the [health] department announced its results in 1988, demographics got the blame. . . . The tone was set for what would become a pattern for ever-deepening mistrust and misunderstanding between the cancer activists and government health agencies. The activists, many of whom were cancer survivors, were incensed that the government seemed to be blaming them for their disease. The agencies, meanwhile, became convinced that the only answer activists would be willing to accept was that something other than their own lifestyle was to blame" (Fagin 2002a).

Similarly, Cathy Read has argued that the focus on lifestyle choices constitutes "blaming women for breast cancer." "Simply translated," she wrote, "the lifestyle explanation says one thing—you have brought breast cancer on yourself because of something you have done" (1995, 6–7). Virginia Soffa agrees:

> A punishing attitude blames women who are childless, overweight, over fifty, depressed or who openly share the consequences of their disease. I remember watching a network television news report on magnetic resonance imaging (MRI) technology for detection of breast cancer, in which the anchorman

participated in the blaming of women with this statement: "Women die every day because they did not get a mammogram soon enough." . . . Guilt occurs because society tells a woman she is less of a woman without perfect breasts, that she is a personal failure for getting breast cancer. (1994, 182–83)

Yet another critique of media coverage discussed the issue of risk this way:

The most persistent risk factor for breast cancer at present . . . is reproduction. Women are told that it is within their control to protect themselves against breast cancer by fulfilling the culturally prescribed roles of reproduction and motherhood. For example, in a 1982 *Glamour* [magazine], readers were told that an important factor in the reduction of risk of breast cancer, "is whether or not you had children and your age when you gave birth to them. The more children you've had by the time you reach thirty, the more protected you appear to be against developing breast cancer." (Fosket, Karran, and LaFia 2000, 311–12)

To properly understand risk one needs to remember the old saw about statistics: Correlation is not causation. In scientific jargon, however, risk factors *correlate* with the incidence of disease. Some may in fact *cause* disease, but correlation does not necessarily prove that to be the case. The causal factor may be some unidentified variable that is unobserved or immeasurable and correlates with both the risk factor and development of breast cancer.

Similarly, stating that lifestyle factors "blame" a person for developing disease is to misread a great deal of the thrust of public health campaigns and the nature of science. Some individual behaviors do have a dramatic and measurable impact on public health (e.g., smoking or driving while intoxicated). Moreover, risk factors related to lifestyle are fairly easy to identify, which is why they have been cataloged for decades. Such exogenous factors as possible environmental exposures are more difficult to document and study. Dismissing this list of risk factors as "blaming the women" ignores the fact that the information can, in fact, empower them. Exercising regularly, maintaining a healthy body weight, consuming alcohol in moderation, and following a low-fat diet are healthy behaviors for many reasons. They will not eliminate a woman's chance of breast cancer, heart disease, or stroke, but they will lower her risk.

Defining Prostate Cancer as a Policy Problem

Prostate cancer activists mimic most of the problem definition strategies of breast cancer activists. As in the case of breast cancer, they define prostate cancer as a problem of inadequate funding (the overriding policy definition), a lack of health-care access, and an issue of civil rights.

DEFINING PROSTATE CANCER AS AN ISSUE OF FUNDING

VARIATION ONE: PROSTATE CANCER IS NEGLECTED AND NEEDS MORE MONEY. A favorite tactic of prostate cancer advocates is compare funding for prostate cancer to that of breast cancer and AIDS—the only two diseases that receive more NCI funding. These comparisons take several forms. One is to compare the amount of funding per death, an amount that, given the increases in prostate cancer research funding, has varied from $8 to $14,000 per death (Houser 1998; AFUD n.d.). The latter figure compares to $18,000 per breast cancer death and $275,000 per AIDS death. As the *St. Petersburg Times* stated, "We spend fifteen times more per fatality on AIDS research than on prostate cancer research" ("A Fight Worth Funding" 1998). Of course, these advocates do not mention that prostate cancer funding is neglected only in comparison to breast cancer and AIDS.

Neglect also is defined as the percentage of cancer funding compared to the percentage of cancer cases. In 1998 the NPCC stated that 20 percent of all non-skin cancers were prostate cancer although prostate cancer received only 3.6 percent of all cancer research funds (NPCC 1998b). In 2003 the numbers were adjusted to 17 percent of all non-skin cancers and 6 to 7 percent of all cancer funding (Atkins 2003a).[10] These frames provide data for one year only. They mention neither increases in funding nor decreases in the mortality rate.

Neglect also is framed in terms of unfunded promising research. In a move reminiscent of the NBCC's early days, in 1996 the NPCC and the M.D. Anderson Cancer Center in Houston cosponsored a conference attended by some seventy prostate cancer researchers. Participants concluded that $500 million was needed for full funding of prostate cancer research. Similarly, in 1997, the NPCC identified some $250 million in unfunded prostate cancer research (NPCC 1997, 2002b). As in the case of breast cancer, prostate cancer advocates did not address the length of time such funding would need to be sustained or what kinds of projects went unfunded. Military comparisons also are present. Craig Palosky of the *Tampa Tribune* compared the level of prostate cancer funding to the cost of an F-22 fighter jet (Palosky 1997).

VARIATION TWO: "LET'S BUILD ON OUR SUCCESS." Just as in the case of breast cancer, prostate cancer activists justify additional funding in terms of building on past successes. The details of their arguments are similar.

Take this statement by Richard Atkins, president of the NPCC: "Since its inception in FY 1997, the PCRP has been the most efficient federally directed prostate cancer research program because it's building sound accountability mechanisms into its fundamental operation. The PCRP strives 'to offer awards to fill gaps in ongoing research and complement initiatives sponsored by other agencies.' Among other achievements, the . . . DoD program has helped determine the effectiveness of the prostate specific antigen (PSA) screening exam" (2003b).

Broadly speaking, NPCC advocates point to the falling death rates for AIDS, breast cancer, and prostate cancer. Those for AIDS dropped from nearly fifty thousand per year in the early 1990s to fewer than ten thousand in 2002. Similarly, prostate cancer deaths declined from about forty-two thousand in 1997 (NPCC 1998b) to approximately twenty-nine thousand in 2002 (ACS 2003f). As Atkins (2003a) said, "Either someone invented a cure for prostate cancer and didn't tell anyone, or federal investment in medical research works."

As in the case of breast cancer, prostate cancer activists have support from the news media. Stories about medical discoveries composed about a third of all prostate cancer news stories in the pre-advocacy period (1980–95) and in the advocacy period (1996–98). Thus, the number of news stories about prostate cancer discoveries increased at the same rate as all news coverage. Moreover, regression analysis demonstrates that changes in news coverage of medical discoveries were related to changes in the level of federal funding for prostate cancer (adjusted $R^2 = 0.4221$). The model is even more predictive when controlling for changes in levels of breast cancer funding, predicting over half of the changes in funding from 1981 to 1998 (adjusted $R^2 = 0.5546$; table 43).[11]

DEFINING PROSTATE CANCER AS A PROBLEM OF HEALTH-CARE ACCESS

As in the case of breast cancer, various advocates define the problem of prostate cancer as one of a lack of access to health care; the list of issues is, however, shorter (table 45).

Of course, not all prostate cancer organizations have supported these efforts. The list in table 45 mentions the PSA blood test twice, a reflection of the on-going controversy about its efficacy. Prostate cancer activists are frustrated by fact that the Centers for Disease Control does not recognize the PSA test as prostate cancer's equivalent to the mammogram—as the primary screening tool for the disease—and cites "insufficient evidence to

Table 45. Prostate Cancer Policy Agenda Items

Screening:
>Expanding Medicare to cover the PSA test.
>Pressuring the CDC to recommend widespread use of the PSA test.
New Hope:
>Accelerating drug development and streamlining the drug approval process at the FDA.
>Improving patient access to clinical trials.
Insurance Issues:
>Expanding Medicare Part B to cover oral, outpatient anti-cancer drugs.
>Opposing Least Costly Alternatives[a] policies under Medicare and private insurance.

[a]Least Costly Alternatives are when private insurance companies and managed-care firms only will pay for the "least costly" drug to treat a certain condition, which may not be the drug the doctor wishes to prescribe. Opponents of these policies argue that the least costly alternatives may not be as effective as the drugs the doctors wish to prescribe or may cause avoidable, adverse side effects.

recommend for or against" (CDC 2002). Given that lukewarm endorsement, advocates must work to ensure insurance coverage for this screening tool.

Prostate cancer activists want to ensure that they have access to improved medical treatments through new prescription drugs and access to existing drugs and clinical trials. What is missing, however, is attention to the larger issue: the uninsured. Medicare covers the vast majority of men with prostate cancer and many others are eligible for VA benefits. Thus there is little need for advocates to be concerned with private insurance coverage and less need for worry about Medicaid coverage.

DEFINING PROSTATE CANCER AS A CIVIL RIGHTS PROBLEM

Activists define prostate cancer as a civil rights problem but do so only through their support of a "patient's bill of rights" for persons enrolled in managed-care plans. Even though men may be at risk because of having a mutated prostate cancer gene, no prostate cancer group to date has taken up the issue of genetic discrimination.

THE PRIMACY OF THE FUNDING DEFINITION

Although prostate cancer activists have a broader agenda than increasing federal research funding, their energies are concentrated primarily upon maintaining and securing government research dollars. In so doing they primarily focus on "neglect." At the 2003 NPCC advocacy conference, for example, attendees received training in a two-point message strategy, called the "ask," and both points focused on funding issues.[12] The other NPCC agenda items were discussed only peripherally.

Framing Science as Salvation

The most striking difference between the two movements is that prostate cancer activists have framed the language of science as salvation.[13] They do not frame science as neglect even though they conceivably could construct such a frame. The screening tools available for prostate cancer, the PSA and the digital rectal examination (DRE), do not, for example, prevent the disease's development. Just like mammography and BSE, PSAs and DREs detect prostate cancer *after* it has developed and has been in the body for some time. Prostate cancer advocates do not declare that "early detection is not early detection" or assert that promoting the prodigious use of screening tools dupes men into thinking that their prostate cancer can be prevented. Instead, they consistently argue for expanded access to both screening tests, especially the PSA test, as life-saving. They do not call attention to their limitations or inability to prevent cancer.

Similarly, the list of risk factors for prostate cancer is remarkably similar to that for breast cancer: aging, diet, weight, being male, family history, race, socioeconomic status, or having a mutated version of the prostate cancer gene (introduction). Yet prostate cancer advocates do not argue that these risk factors imply a lack of interest on the part of the medical establishment or that men are somehow to blame for their own cancers. In fact, advocates regularly publicize findings related to diet and lifestyle, and at least one has noted the difficulty in getting men with prostate cancer to understand the importance of lifestyle changes (Caputi interview, May 2003).

By contrast, prostate cancer activists place enormous faith in science, which they consider to symbolize hope and empowerment. Examples abound. The Prostate Cancer Foundation sponsors an annual three-day conference that brings together physicians and scientists. The invitation-only event is designed to facilitate communication among scientists working in the field "to solve problems" (Soule interview 2003). Because science is framed as salvation and not neglect, Richard Atkins's quip that "medical research works" resonates with grassroots activists. Finally, because science is framed as salvation, one sees the importance of access to prescription drugs in the health-care access frame (table 45). Howard Soule of the Prostate Cancer Foundation noted that the primary challenge facing the movement was expediting the federal drug approval process. The goal of the movement is to "cure [prostate cancer] or to turn it into a chronic, treatable disease" (Soule interview 2003).

Implications

Prostate cancer and breast cancer occupy different places on the policy agenda. Breast cancer sits comfortably at the apex of the issue-attention cycle. Therefore, its advocates' primary challenge is agenda maintenance. Thus they must continually redefine and expand the breast cancer problem. Prostate cancer has a presence on the policy agenda, but its position is tenuous. Its advocates face the challenge of keeping it on the agenda and not being replaced by a new issue.

In spite of their different positions on the public agenda, breast cancer and prostate cancer advocates define their diseases in similar ways, whether as a problem of historical neglect and a desire to build upon successes or a problem of access to health-care services and civil rights. Why these parallels? First, prostate cancer advocates continue to piggyback on breast cancer advocates' successes. Second, disease advocacy shares common elements. Yet the breast cancer movement, possibility because of its longer history and its higher profile, has adopted a more ambitious policy agenda that includes items that go far beyond serving only persons with breast cancer. Prostate cancer advocates support a less ambitious policy agenda and concentrate exclusively on issues of importance to persons with the disease.

In addition, each movement bemoans a lack of federal funding when in fact the NCI's funding for both breast cancer and prostate cancer is relatively generous. Such characterizations are misleading at best. At worst, they can become misconceptions that are perpetuated. Certainly we do not condemn breast cancer and prostate cancer lobbyists for doing what lobbyists do, telling the truth in such a way that benefits their cause. But for many other issues there are lobbyists on all sides who can refute the claims of one group, and policymakers can construct a complete picture from the disparate pieces. There is no "anti-breast cancer" or "un-prostate cancer" lobby, however, to refute these claims. And they continue to be perpetuated.

One major difference, of course, is that prostate cancer advocates frame science as salvation whereas breast cancer advocates frame science as neglect. What benefits do breast cancer advocates accrue when they frame science as neglect? First, terms such as epidemic and patient-blaming are provocative and capture the attention of reporters and the public. Second, their stridency motivates grassroots activists and keeps them from becoming complacent or dropping out of the movement. Third, patient-blaming appeals to feminists who are accustomed to discerning patterns of neglect and oppression on the part of men and male-dominated institutions. Finally, they continue to frame breast cancer as an urgent problem and call attention to gaps in public policy. Such terminology has negative consequences, of course. It may alienate members of the scientific community unaccustomed to the stridency of advocacy who may resent what they see as a distortion of precise scientific concepts.

Prostate cancer advocates, even those inclined to frame science as neglect, are unlikely to be successful. Imagine a group of men arguing that a paternalistic medical establishment blames them for being male, growing old, or being African American. Imagine a group of older men arguing that the insensitive and sexist medical establishment uses lifestyle explanations as a means to avoid looking for exogenous causes for their cancers. Feminism has created a social construction of society that finds women placed at a disadvantage to men.[14] According to that construction, women's issues and needs are neglected and overlooked. It is within this social construction that framing science as neglect works.

By contrast, given the weight of history, men's health advocates cannot argue convincingly that their needs have been neglected or overlooked in favor of women's health issues because of women's dominance. Rather, framing science as salvation resonates because it accords with a social construction that calls upon (mostly male) elites to act independently. Collective action is not required. Advocates who frame science as salvation are not motivated by stridency or anger. They can act individually; they are supplicants. Their job is to persuade one set of (mostly male) elites (members of Congress) to generously fund the professional activities of another set of (mostly male) elites (medical researchers).

Ribbon Wars

CAUSE-RELATED MARKETING AND THE SELLING
OF BREAST CANCER AND PROSTATE CANCER

> Like beauty, ethical problems regarding fund raising are often in
> the eyes of the beholder. One organization's much needed dona-
> tions may be seen by other organizations as crass and commercial.
> —Ronald Johnson

> I think there are a lot of women out there who really like to support
> the cause by buying the product. They don't want to go out there
> and run. They want to go into the market and buy a product that
> has a pink ribbon [on it]. By doing this, they are showing their
> support. And that is something that is important to them.
> —Elizabeth Woolfe

Nothing is more controversial among advocacy organizations today
than the issue of corporate participation in fund-raising. This participation
takes many forms—foundations, sponsorships, donations, and cause-related
marketing. Some would say the pink ribbon, the rallying cry and symbol
of the breast cancer movement, is fraying. Breast Cancer Action (BCA), a
California-based watchdog organization with eleven thousand members,
has initiated several campaigns, among them "think before you pink" and
"think twice before you walk," to question the involvement of corporate
America in the fight against breast cancer. In the fall of 2002 the National
Breast Cancer Coalition (NBCC) launched a media-identity campaign, "Not
Just Ribbons," to refocus public attention to what it believed were the real
issues behind attempts to eliminate the disease. And while organizations in
the breast cancer movement debate the issues surrounding corporate involvement, prostate cancer advocacy groups are openly envious of the success
breast cancer organizations have had in forging such relationships.

Most advocates agree that external support is necessary if an organization is to thrive and accomplish its goals. As Diane Balma, senior counsel and director of public policy for the Komen Foundation, noted, "It's going to take private-public partnerships to raise much needed dollars and awareness [to support advocacy initiatives]" (Balma interview 2002). But without exception, advocacy organizations concur that aligning an organization with outside money, whether corporate or from major donors or government, may be fraught with ethical dilemmas. Likewise, strategic business partnerships with advocacy organizations create problems if either institution is accused of breaching ethical standards or the relationships do not accomplish their goals.

Promotion and financial support are key ingredients to the success of grassroots survivors' organizations. Breast cancer and prostate cancer GSOs occupy different places on the policy agenda (chapter 7). Organizations may display aspects of our typology but lack specific cause-related marketing support that helps ensure sustained education, lobbying, and promotional efforts, thus hampering their effectiveness. Breast cancer organizations are clearly more successful at using cause-related marketing.

This chapter examines the changing face of corporate giving and promotion and its impact on the breast cancer and prostate cancer movements. A central question in this discussion is, Why did partnering with breast cancer organizations become so popular? Advocates in each movement are confronted by different issues. Over time, breast cancer's assertive advocates developed extensive corporate relationships, but now the movement is fractured over their prevalence and propriety. Prostate cancer's reluctant champions, however, have had less time and opportunity to forge extensive relationships. Thus there is no debate, only envy.

The Growth of Corporate Support in the United States

American public institutions have depended on corporate philanthropy since the seventeenth century. Libraries, hospitals, and institutions of higher learning were early beneficiaries of large gifts from wealthy individuals, not the companies those individuals owned or represented. Throughout most of U.S. history, legal and unwritten codes were barriers to business involvement in social affairs. Not until 1954 did the Supreme Court remove the final obstacles (Smith 1994). By the 1960s most U.S. companies—Levi-Strauss and Dayton Hudson (now Target) among them—had established their own foundations in order to demonstrate social responsibility by giving away up to 5 percent of pre-taxed income.

As Smith (1994) describes it, the "unspoken ethic" among business, non-profits, and government was a version of "don't tread on me." Each sector prided itself on independent decision making. As a consequence, corporations stayed away from causes that could be associated with their lines of business and chose to contribute to umbrella organizations like the United Way, which was trusted to be knowledgeable and fair in its distribution of goods and services. That philosophy fell apart with the Exxon Valdez oil spill in 1989. Exxon, which had steered away from building ties with environmental groups, had no relationships upon which to fall back. By contrast, Arco, one of its chief competitors, had formed alliances with environmental groups and understood the need to respond immediately to crisis (Smith 1994, 108). When Arco had an oil spill the incident received little media attention and, as a result, little public criticism.

Corporations such as Coca Cola, IBM, and the former AT&T, among others, initiated a new form of philanthropy in which the practice was considered to be an integral part of business. Businesses began to reshape giving patterns to serve communities and build relationships between institutions and strategic nonprofits. Such reciprocal relationships or strategic partnerships include not only financial investments but also investments in expertise and personnel.

Cause-related marketing became a popular tactic in building relationships. With roots in the ideas of enlightened self-interest of French philosopher Jean-Jacques Rousseau, the first cause-marketing relationship is believed to be a physical fitness campaign based on the benefits of walking that Cone, Inc. developed for Rockport Shoes in 1983, although American Express's Campaign to Support the Restoration of the Statute of Liberty Fund is widely mentioned in the literature as the first time the term *cause-related* was used. P. Rajan Varadarajan and Anvil Menon (1998) define cause-related marketing as "the process of formulating and implementing marketing activities that are characterized by an offer from the firm to contribute a specified amount to a designated cause when customers engage in revenue—providing exchanges that satisfy organizational and individual objectives" (60).

In a typical cause-related marketing campaign a percentage of sales from a pre-designated item is donated to a nonprofit organization. Luna Bars, a 180–calorie bar with soy protein and other healthy ingredients, for example, donates $1.50 per bar to the Breast Cancer Fund. Such campaigns are built on channeling money to nonprofit organizations, but some corporations choose to support educational or awareness-building activities through the use of their considerable resources. Ben and Jerry's Homemade Ice Cream promotes peace through its Web site's link "Fifty Ways to Support Peace"

(Ben and Jerry's 2005). United Colors of Benetton, an international retailer of clothing and a member of the Benetton Group, promotes the need to preserve the world's apes, improve race relations, and address AIDS and other issues through its often controversial advertising (Benetton 2005). Both corporations engage in cause-related marketing without tying it to a particular organization.

There is another important trend inherent in the involvement in cause-related marketing. Businesses have become painfully aware since 9/11 that corporate social responsibility is a paramount issue among consumers. A Cone national survey on consumer attitudes toward corporate behavior found that consumers "are willing to use their individual power to punish those companies that do not share their values" (as quoted in the Cause Marketing Forum 2003). Carol Cone notes that cause-related marketing is especially important for global companies whose activities are more transparent in today's Web-connected society (Cause Marketing Forum 2003).

BUILDING EFFECTIVE CAUSE-RELATED MARKETING RELATIONSHIPS

Effective cause-related marketing relationships involve a business, the organization or cause it agrees to support, and the consumer. American Express raised $2.3 million from 1988 to 2003 to support the Komen Foundation and Lauder Foundation (Orenstein 2003a). The company had to be assured that women would use its credit card when shopping at one of the ninety-five participating stores during Breast Cancer Awareness Month. Likewise, the foundations had to be assured that American Express was serious about its pledge and would promote the organizations in the most positive light. Finally, consumers needed to believe that the organizations they patronized were serious about their commitments, that American Express believed in the cause, and that the foundations would use the money wisely. The commitment had a time limit, a social benefit, and an expectation that American Express would not be compensated for its participation (Andreasen and Drumwright 2001, 100).

In addition to the issues of mutual trust and respect, such cause-related marketing relationships must reflect the core missions of the nonprofit organization and its for-profit partner (Lorange and Roos 1992). In 1995 the Ford Motor Company entered into a relationship with the Komen Foundation because the company wanted to build credibility with women consumers who not only purchase cars but also have significant input in family auto purchasing decisions (Rosenhaus 2003).

Successful cause-marketing relationships take time to cultivate and often do not produce initial results (Aschermann 2002). Both organizations have to buy into the relationship over a period of time, which makes evaluation and assessment difficult to measure (Aschermann 2002; Pringle and Thompson 1999, 145–46). Varadarajan and Menon (1988) suggest other factors need to be taken into consideration before a business chooses a cause, including the characteristics of its product offering. New Balance Athletic Shoe, Inc. was a 2005 National Sponsor of Komen's Race for the Cure (Susan G. Komen Foundation 2005), which is a logical extension of a product to a cause-marketing activity.

As a practical issue, a business needs to "walk the talk" as well. If a corporation provides support for a cause that promotes screening for either breast cancer or prostate cancer, then it needs to cover such screening for its own employees. If the cause is breast cancer, then women need to be represented on corporate boards and in top management. Similarly, neither cause-related marketing partner should align itself with organizations that produce products or services that may conflict with its goals or those of its partner or jeopardize either partner's independence. GSOs need to be careful in aligning themselves with pharmaceutical companies least they be seen as advocating one particular drug or another; likewise, pharmaceutical companies cannot support advocacy groups that take negative stands against their products.

WHAT'S IN IT FOR BUSINESS?

North American companies spent an estimated $1.08 billion on sponsorships related to cause-related marketing in 2005 because such marketing works when business are aligned with appropriate issues (Cause Marketing Forum 2005). It also increases corporate profits. "National surveys indicate that the majority of consumers would be influenced to buy, or even switch and pay more for brands, when the product supports a cause, especially when product features and quality are equal" (Kotler, Roberto, and Lee 2002, 354).[1]

The Ford Motor Company found in a consumer survey in 2000 that "75 percent of those surveyed felt better about Ford, while 29 percent were more likely to purchase Ford products as a result of its [breast cancer] involvement" (Marconi 2002, 177). The experience of BMW was similar. It donated $1 to the Komen Foundation for every test mile driven during a particular timeframe; the campaign aligned the brand with a popular women's cause and reportedly resulted in the sales of four hundred new cars for the automaker (Pringle and Thompson 1999). From a business standpoint, one of

DEFINING CORPORATE SUPPORT

Corporate support takes various forms, including foundations, sponsorship, and cause-related marketing alliances. Each form has specific strategic advantages, rules of engagement, and tax benefits, although the public neither cares about nor understands the differences.

Corporate foundations are tax-exempt organizations that operate with a percentage of corporate profits as well as outside donations. Avon, for example, manages its extensive involvement in breast cancer through a foundation. Foundation gifts may be given directly to nonprofit organizations with little media fanfare and little expectation of extensive institutional involvement. The amount of money that corporations can give away and still receive tax credits for is limited, however.

Sponsorships come from marketing or promotional dollars and involve institutional commitments, primarily to single events or activities. Drug companies, for example, were underwriters of both the 2005 NBCC and 2005 National Prostate Cancer (NPCC) advocacy training conferences.

Cause-related marketing involves a more direct relationship between an institution and its cause. A percentage or predetermined amount of corporate profits on the sales of a particular product is contributed to the cause. Publicity promoting the involvement not only links the product with the cause but also raises awareness.

the greatest benefits of cause-related marketing is accountability, "the better the sales, the greater the contribution" (Ptacek and Salazar 1997).

Finally, a cause may be an opportunity to build company morale. Avon uses its considerable international sales force—estimated to be 4.9 million persons worldwide—to help generate funds for its foundation through its pink enameled-ribbon products. The sales force educates customers about early detection and access to care. In 2005 Avon celebrated its fiftieth anniversary with a series of events around the world and raised a portion of its support through the "Walk around the World Pin," which was designed to show commitment to the breast cancer cause (Avon Foundation 2005). Komen's races bond survivors with other survivors, their families, and their communities. As the executive director of one affiliate noted, "The race is so emotional that women come back year after year. We have growth every year—in the last five years by 20 to 25 percent. Why? Because you can see the survivors" (Wilson interview 2003).

BREAST CANCER AND CAUSE-RELATED MARKETING

The discovery of the power of cause-related marketing in the late 1980s and the early 1990s coincides with development of breast cancer advocacy groups and their expanding agendas. At the same time, corporate America, looking for causes that recognized the importance of women in consumer decision making, built community linkages between customers and employees and promoted causes that resonated with their interests and concerns. Breast cancer was just such a cause. It was simple, uncontroversial, and of primary concern to women consumers.

Andreasen and Drumwright (2001) attribute the attraction of the breast cancer cause to a variety of factors, among them the high interest in the disease among affluent women, its morbidity but low mortality rate, and its lack of association with any "'sins' or with disreputable socioeconomic classes" (106). They failed to mention, however, the powerful forces behind breast cancer advocacy organizations.

The cosmetic industry has been particularly drawn to the cause. In 2005 consumers could choose among sixteen products from Estee Lauder brands, twelve from Avon, eight from Revlon, and five from Sephora (Singer 2005). By 2004 the Avon Foundation had donated more than $350 million to fund access to care, education, screening, and research. Amy Langer, former executive director of NABCO, credited its partnership with the foundation for transforming its organization from one serving primarily "'the haves,' educated white women, to a broader mission of serving medically underserved women" (as quoted in Andreason and Drumwright 2001, 101). From 1982 to 2004 the Komen Foundation and its more than one hundred U.S. affiliates and three international affiliates raised more than $180 million for breast cancer research alone (Komen 2005). Three-quarters of the funds that affiliates raised through more than one hundred races, 5K runs/fitness walks, and cause-related marketing relationships supported local breast cancer education and research initiatives.

Races have proven successful ways to raise money for many other breast cancer organizations. Y-Me holds a race each Mother's Day in Chicago, Houston, and San Diego, and Revlon holds the Revlon Run/Walk for Women each year in New York and Los Angeles in conjunction with the Entertainment Industry Foundation. The *New York Times* also co-sponsors the New York race. The American Cancer Society, among other cancer-related organizations, has found walks a valuable way of raising funds while generating publicity for the cause.

The fashion industry, including Ralph Lauren and Saks, takes a special interest in breast cancer. As a company executive told *Women's World Daily,* breast cancer is particularly relevant to Saks, whose primary customers and employees are women (Feitelberg and Moin 2002). Saks Fifth Avenue operates through its sixty-five nationwide locations to raise money for cancer at a local level. The company donates 2 percent of sales over a four-day shopping weekend, and its vendors often match the amount. From 1998 to 2002 the chain donated $6 million to the cause (Feitelberg and Moin 2002).

Publicity for the cause may be, in some cases, just as important as financial support. The Ford Motor Company, for instance, underwrote the famous *Murphy Brown* episode by donating three minutes of advertising to breast cancer public service announcements (PSAs), which reportedly resulted in increased traffic to a toll-free telephone line and Web site (Marconi 2002).

Thus, a health awareness message may touch segments of the population who are ordinarily hard to reach. As a spokesperson for NABCO noted, "Our partnership with Lifetime Television enabled us to disseminate our breast health message to forty-four million households. We might not be able to get that kind of reach on our own. And our partnership with the Women's Basketball Association enables us to reach a different kind of audience in terms of race, age, geography. That kind of relationship can be incredibly valuable" (Woolfe interview 2003). But Susan Orenstein (2003a) noted in one of the first public examinations of the impact of the relationship between corporate America and breast cancer that companies provide unaudited numbers and measure their contributions in different ways. It is thus difficult to determine how much has been spent on breast cancer. The impact on the corporate bottom line must be significant, however, because corporations spend from their marketing budgets rather than their philanthropic budgets.

PROSTATE CANCER AND CORPORATE SUPPORT

Prostate cancer organizations have a shorter fund-raising history than that of breast cancer organizations and are likely to develop associations with sports-related organizations. The Prostate Cancer Foundation (formerly CaP CURE) and the NPCC have ongoing relationships with Major League Baseball. In 2001 CaP CURE received almost $6 million from its annual Home Run Challenge. During the 2003 season a national campaign called "Take a Swing against Prostate Cancer" involved a variety of awareness activities during the season, including distribution of blue ribbons and baseball cards with a prostate cancer checklist. There were also money-raising efforts through online contests. The Gillette Company is one of the largest corporate supporters of the prostate cancer movement. In its innovative efforts to raise awareness of the disease and funds for the NPCC, Gillette has partnered with drivers on the NASCAR Nextel Cup circuit and Discovery Channel's popular show *American Chopper.* In every case the

---

BREAST CANCER MARKETING 24/7

Large companies are not the only partners in the breast cancer business. The number of products and services that align themselves with the disease are considerable. Consider this possible scenario. Today, you wear your Champion pink sports bra, a Michael Simon-designed "Hope 1" pink sweater, Lee denim jeans, and Wright double-layer crew socks. Your makeup includes Courageous Coral Avon lipstick or Pink Ribbon lip gloss by Revlon and Estee Lauder powder in a pink compact, and you tweeze your eyebrows using light-pink Anastasia tweezers. Caswell-Massey rosewater and glycerin hand cream protects your hands.

You put Polaner All Natural Fruit Spread on your breakfast toast, drink Silk Soymilk, and later snack on Keebler's Wheatables. During your day you shop for shoes at Shoe Carnival—both Keds and Hushpuppies make special pink shoes—order flowers for your mother through Proflowers.com/, and catch the latest movie at the local Loews Cineplex. And a percentage of each purchase will go to fight breast cancer. The percentage of a company's donations for the cause varies widely. Some may lose money but are likely to profit from the publicity and goodwill.

The danger in this scenario is, of course, that some consumers may believe that in purchasing a product they have fulfilled their responsibility. They are, in fact, making a purchasing decision rather than a direct contribution to a cause. As business writer Susan Ornstein asked the audience at the 2003 NBCC Advocacy Training Conference, "If you buy a vacuum cleaner [that contributes to the cause] will you really be taking care of breast cancer?"

---

activities involved some aspect of interaction, often with a form of gaming or Internet activity. Gillette, which also has programs to address breast and gynecological cancers, reaches a broad general audience vital to the message of the NPCC (Gillette 2005).

In spite of these partnerships, prostate cancer organizations have not been as successful with cause-related marketing as breast cancer organizations. Debra Goldman (1997) has commented in *Adweek* on why corporate support has not been greater: "This seems wise. If you want a man to bond with your brand, reminding him that his penis may be a ticking time bomb is not the way to go about it" (2).

Jim Miller, CEO of Real *e* Marketing in San Francisco, is a prostate cancer survivor and activist and coauthor with his wife, Julia, of *Our Journey through Prostate Cancer*. He believes that the prostate cancer advocacy movement has "a lot to learn from the breast cancer movement" (interview 2003). Businesses are willing to form strategic partnerships with breast cancer organizations because they knew that women make the majority of purchase decisions in the home. Miller also observes that men are reluctant to talk about prostate cancer, which has been a strong deterrent to mobilizing more male involvement. "We don't talk about our cancer. It isn't a natural thing to do; we don't routinely talk about impotency and incontinence." He suggests that prostate cancer organizations must align themselves with organizations that appeal to both men and women in order to attract cause-related marketing dollars. "Women are the customers," he says. "Women will bring along their men." He also believes that successful strategic partnerships require alignment with products that are exciting and "have flair." The partnership with Major League Baseball has been successful because women are baseball fans, too. He maintains that activities involving the whole family—"the do it for Dad" concept—may have more appeal in the prostate cancer movement.

By contrast, BCA executive director Barbara Brenner believes prostate cancer organizations may have a difficult time eliciting corporate support. "It is so easy for companies to do breast cancer," she says. "You can look like you care about women without doing very much at all. Prostates, are not as sexy. Women are easier to target. It will be harder to sell a car to a guy because Ford supports prostate cancer" (interview 2003).

The disparity in corporate support between breast cancer and prostate cancer remains an issue, primarily for prostate cancer organizations. As John Page, former president of US TOO International! remarked, "Breast cancer has been highly successful in getting partners. Ford Motor Company and Gillette have done little for prostate cancer" (interview 2003).

Ethical Concerns of Cause-related Marketing

Cause-related marketing presents ethical challenges for both causes and their supporters. Partnerships like marriages tend to have problems when there are differences in expertise and expectations, clashes in culture, and lack of agreement on goals and objectives. Businesses may see advocacy organizations as only going after money. Nonprofit organizations may see some businesses as seeking an enhanced image without contributing to the cause. It may be difficult for some organizations to realize that cause-related marketing is not philanthropy. Andreasen and Drumwright point out (2001, 104) that there may be an imbalance in the emotional stakes that each put upon the relationship: "For the corporation, the alliance is often just one of a great many corporate marketing activities whereas the nonprofit partner may have much more invested in the venture. Among other things, such an imbalance can lead to differences in the perceived magnitude of ethical lapses or conflicts and for the nonprofit, possibly raise the 'heat' of the reaction." Such issues as the size and source of the donations may cause disagreement. A company may pledge a percentage of profits without stipulating a limit or publicizing how much of each purchase price will be donated. Some companies insist on market exclusivity with a particular organization, thus ruling out financial relationships with other potential corporate sponsors.

From a public policy perspective, cause-related marketing has been criticized for exploiting causes rather than contributing to them, especially because corporations receive tax deductions for contributions and promotional activities (Varadarajan and Menon 1998). An important criticism, often levied at the breast cancer movement, is the overselling of one cause at the expense of others. This practice ("cherry picking") implies that a cause, in this case breast cancer, receives a disproportional amount of support over other causes that are perceived as more controversial or having less caché. Cherry picking can occur within a movement when certain important activities are perceived as less interesting to outside funders and consequently receive less monetary support (Andreason and Drumwright 2001).

Orenstein, who has called breast cancer "the queen of good causes," notes that the "jockeying by so many companies to lash their images to breast cancer drains resources away from many other worthy causes, including other diseases that kill far more women" (2003, 89). She worries that the packaging of the disease may undermine the seriousness of its treatment and consequences.

Some businesses are beginning to view the breast cancer cause as being overcrowded. Packaging inserts from a major manufacturer of women's hosiery, for example, now feature facts about cholesterol and heart disease, the number-one killer of women. The inserts previously educated women on breast self-examination.

A BACKLASH IN THE BREAST CANCER MOVEMENT

As GSOs mature and are successful in cause recognition, cracks in the movement are inevitable. So it is with breast cancer. The 2003 publicity campaign by the NBCC, "Not Just Ribbons," used the color pink in three print advertisements featuring various symbols of power and strength—a tool belt, a hard hat, and a bulldozer—to communicate its message that stopping breast cancer takes hard work as well as races and special events. Some breast cancer organizations criticize the Komen Foundation for "getting all the money," and Avon has been the subject of intense public scrutiny by BCA. As Brenner said, "We have never been pink ribbon people. There is nothing pretty or soft or comfy about breast cancer" (interview 2003). BCA has been particularly critical of cause-related marketing relationships and disparaged Yoplait's support of the Komen Foundation. Yoplait, which widely promoted its relationship, promised 10 cents from every label mailed into the company. As the BCA saw it, a woman would have to eat three containers of the product a day for the duration of the four-month campaign to raise $36.

BCA's complaints generated quick responses from cause marketers and the Komen Foundation. Carol Cone, a nationally known expert in cause-related marketing, noted that "the criticism showed a lack of understanding of the activity. It's not about eating that many containers to raise $36. It's the fact that millions of people can come together to raise money by doing activities they do every day" (Cause Marketing Forum 2003). Her sentiments are similar to those of Cindy Schneible, vice president for national programs for the Komen Foundation, who said, "I think that their message—that consumers need to be fully informed of company's programs—is right on target. But I think the piece that is missing is that it's not just about fund raising. It's about the ability to raise awareness" (as quoted in "Brand Names" 2003, 39).

Although acknowledging that Komen is "pretty public about how they get their money" (Brenner interview 2003), the BCA has been more critical of the practices of the Avon Foundation and since 2000 has leveraged a publicity and stockholders' campaign against it. The campaign "Think Before You Walk" was organized to protest what BCA believed were the high costs of Avon's successful Walks for Cancer and distribution of funds to cancer centers that were already heavily supported by the federal government or pharmaceutical companies. In 2001 BCA joined with other breast cancer and women's health organizations to challenge the accountability of Avon's fund-raising practices (Brenner interview 2003).

The coalition's technique mimicked a long tradition of using disruptive tactics to influence the structure and philosophy of advocacy movements. Postcards, e-mail messages, and advertising in newspapers in cities where races were held were used to influence Avon. Later the coalition attempted to influence company shareholders. As Brenner notes, "Avon can't say it both ways ... on one hand we care about breast cancer and at the same time do things that contribute to the problem. We are perfectly happy to talk about that in a very public and a very proactive way" (interview 2003).

The business of breast cancer also has been under attack by others. Breast cancer survivor Barbara Ehrenreich, writing in *Harper's Magazine* (2001), characterized the breast cancer "marketplace" as emotional and sometimes infantile. A tote bag that the Libby Ross Foundation distributed to breast

AWARENESS MONTHS

A traditional promotional tactic designed to build awareness of a cause or an idea is to commemorate a cause by designating days, a week, or a month. This tactic is more likely to attract media attention and as a result build public support. International Breast Cancer Awareness Month was created in 1985 by a British-owned corporation, Imperial Chemical Industries, which later became AstraZeneca. The company manufactures tamoxifen among other drugs and was responsible for the designation of September as Prostate Cancer Awareness Month. The events of the September and October commemoration are no longer solely in the hands of the pharmaceutical company. National, state, and local elected officials now recognize each month's designation through proclamations or legislation, and September and October have become rallying points for advocacy efforts and the corporate sponsorship of events.

Because this study focused on media advocacy, we asked whether Breast Cancer Awareness Month had an observable impact on news coverage of breast cancer. We also asked whether Prostate Cancer Awareness Month had an observable impact on news coverage of prostate cancer.

Because AstraZeneca Pharmaceuticals began Breast Cancer Awareness Month in 1985 there has been an observable shift in news coverage of breast cancer. If news stories about breast cancer were randomly distributed over the course of the year, one would expect 8 percent of all news stories to appear in any given month, especially over a period of years. There is a spike of news coverage in October (figure 2); 16 percent of all news coverage about breast cancer appeared in that month, fully twice the percentage expected. The proportion of news stories that appeared in October from 1985 to 1998 is six points higher than the percentage of news stories that appeared in October from 1980 to 1984. The difference is statistically significant (table 46).

By contrast, Prostate Cancer Awareness Month has not had a measurable impact on news coverage of the disease. There is no spike of news coverage of prostate cancer in September. In fact, the fifty-eight stories that appeared in September from 1980 to 1998 represent fewer than 10 percent of prostate cancer news stories, fewer than the percentages in May, June, and November (figure 2).

Table 46. October Breast Cancer Stories

Year	%	(n)	Wilcoxon Scores	
			Chi-Sq.[a]	p
1980–84	10.9	(16)	3.00	0.0831
1985–98	16.2	(568)		
1980–98 combined	16.03	(584)		

Source: Data compiled by authors.
[a]df = 1.

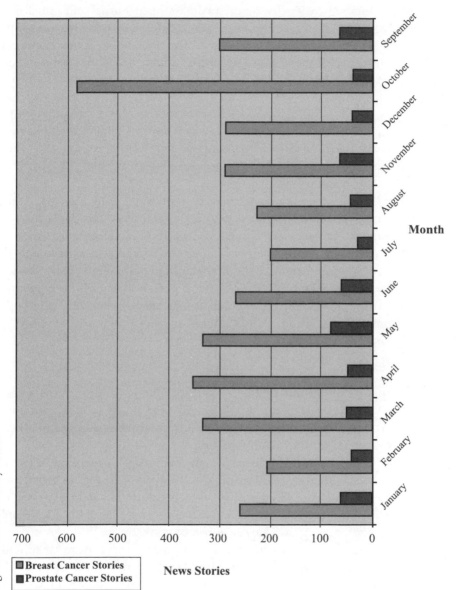

Figure 2. News Stories by Month

cancer patients through hospitals included perfume, a hot-pink satin pil-lowcase, inexpensive jewelry, candies, a pink-striped journal, and a small box of crayons, which were, Ehrenreich was told, for expressing her thoughts. "Possibly the idea is that regression to a state of childlike dependency puts one in the best frame of mind which to endure the prolonged and toxic treatments," she commented. "Or it may be that, in some version of the prevailing gender ideology, femininity is by its nature incompatible with full adulthood—a state of arrested development. Certainly men diagnosed with prostate cancer do not receive gifts of Matchbox toys." Ehrenreich cites the use of teddy bears by various organizations as a fund-raising tool as further evidence of infantile behavior: "I have identified four distinct lines, or species of these creatures" (6, 5).

The trivialization of the movement has not been lost on activists. Wearing a pink ribbon for breast cancer or a blue ribbon for prostate cancer is easy. Supporting the causes through contributions and legislative action is not. The NBCC released a poll in October 2002 that reported "although 50 percent of the population believes that wearing a pink ribbon is a somewhat effective tool to fight breast cancer and 32 percent has worn a ribbon as a symbol of support, only six percent has contacted an elected official to push for Congressional action" (NBCC 2002e).

Conclusion

This chapter points out another important difference between the breast cancer and the prostate cancer movements: the ability to raise corporate support. Just as politicians are dependent on fund-raising to stay in office, GSOs also need outside funding to survive.

The chapter leaves many questions unanswered. Who, for example, owns the breast cancer message? Some in the movement believe it has been compromised by the cause's relationships to corporate dollars and that its popularity with corporate America undermines the seriousness of the disease and the urgency for its cure. Or, has cause-related marketing perhaps elevated the level of awareness and support that breast cancer receives from media and politicians? Is it possible that the prostate cancer movement will receive the same criticism? The data on Prostate Cancer Awareness Month suggest that marketing efforts have miles to go before they rival that of breast cancer. The prostate cancer movement appears to be a quick study, however, and may avoid overselling the disease.

Certainly, cause marketing has elevated support for both causes. Ronald Johnson's cautionary note in the first epigraph of this chapter is worth repeating, "One organization's much needed donations may be seen by other organizations as crass and commercial." And so we arrive at the final question, What happens if both the public and corporate America tire of hearing about breast cancer or prostate cancer? What then? Cause-related marketing relationships depend on the investment of marketing dollars. If consumers tire of a cause and do not invest in a product or service, then corporations will have to find new causes. Perhaps the answer is that other health-related causes will capture the attention of corporate America.

Policy Dilemmas and Maturing Movements

> We have worked to get a bigger slice of a bigger pie.
> —National Breast Cancer Coalition employee

> We don't ask for a bigger slice of the pie. . . .
> We are looking for a bigger pie.
> —Robert Samuels

The preceding chapters compared the effectiveness of breast cancer's assertive advocates and prostate cancer's reluctant champions and analyzed their ability to climb onto the media and policy agendas and stay there. By every measure, breast cancer grassroots survivors' organizations (GSOs) have been more successful than those for prostate cancer. Prostate cancer's reluctant champions were even able to piggyback on some of the breast cancer advocates' successes. This paradox is due to women's history of activism and collective action; their political efficacy; breast cancer's higher profile in the media; breast cancer's younger, more urgent, and more tragic "public face"; survivors' willingness to tell their stories publicly; and advocates' ability to raise corporate dollars.

So what can be learned from studying breast cancer and prostate cancer activism? This chapter first considers policymaking dilemmas resulting from the breast cancer and prostate cancer advocacy movements. Second, we reflect upon what insights these movements bring to media advocacy and GSOs. Third, we explore the challenges the movements may face as they mature.

Policymaking Dilemmas

GSOs can communicate powerfully the human cost of a disease to policymakers (Dresser 1998). In this respect and in all others, breast cancer advocacy especially has been successful. Yet the successes of breast cancer and prostate cancer activism bring to light several important ethical dilemmas that are not a critique of these movements but rather of the American political system in which they operate.[1] The following section examines several dilemmas that arise from GSOs: directing science through legislation, allocating medical research dollars, and including consumers effectively in determining research priorities.

THE FIRST DILEMMA: LEGISLATING SCIENCE

One of the achievements of the breast cancer movement was the congressional mandate to undertake the Long Island Breast Cancer Study (introduction; chapter 6). Although the efforts of One-in-Nine and Alphonse D'Amato are noteworthy, they raise the question of the appropriateness of legislating a specific study, down to the details of research design. The fact that such a study was passed through legislation harkens to the continuing perception that policymakers neglect breast cancer and women's health issues, specifically that environmental pathogens are neglected within the discipline of epidemiology (Fagin 2002b). Congress is within its rights to determine broad spending priorities and direct scientific agencies to invest in research geared to specific policy goals (Macilwain 1994), but Congress remains a collection of laypersons. The bureaucracy is intended to be the source of expertise within government. Thus, mandating the details of research design and the scope of a project as Congress did in this case is best left in the hands of the bureaucracy and subject to congressional oversight.

The issue of the possible link of breast cancer to the environment remains on the agenda in the form of legislation sponsored by Representatives Sue Myrick and Nita Lowey (D-NY). This legislation is a model of an appropriate and effective means for Congress to direct scientific research. It mandates the subject of research (environment), sets broad parameters for this research (through multidisciplinary and multi-institutional collaboration), and ensures it is broadly applicable through nationwide involvement.[2] Yet the particulars of research design and evaluation are left to the scientists and bureaucrats.

THE SECOND DILEMMA:
HOW TO ALLOCATE MEDICAL RESEARCH RESOURCES

The debate over allocation of medical research dollars primarily focuses on whether policymakers should respond to organized "disease groups" when making funding decisions. Disease groups advocate either for direct earmarks or pressure Congress to suggest priorities within the legislative histories of appropriations laws.

Earmarks tend to come in two guises. Specific earmarks for projects at particular medical institutions clearly subvert the peer review process. What is at issue in this discussion, however, is primarily the second type of earmark, one that directs a specific amount of spending for one disease over another. These earmarks have not escaped criticism from the medical and scientific community. In 1997, for example, Dr. Harold Varmus, then-director of the National Institutes of Health (NIH), testified before Congress in opposition to such earmarking. He stated that much of the NIH budget in any given year was committed to support long-term projects through multiyear awards. If substantial funds were earmarked for certain avenues of research, then fewer were available for promising projects in those fields that did not have earmarks. Varmus urged Congress to trust scientists to make such judgments (Dresser 1998).

Earmarking, however is critical to advocates. As Amy Langer, former executive director of the National Alliance of Breast Cancer Organizations (NABCO) and cofounder of the National Breast Cancer Coalition (NBCC), reflected:

> Is earmarking funding wrong? Demanding funds for breast cancer research, as opposed to cancer research or even biomedical research, seemingly overlooks the historical fact that discoveries benefiting breast cancer can arise from other fields of investigations, such as retinoblastoma. And in an era of a stable, or more likely, shrinking funding pie, is there a parallel implication that other types of cancer or disease should *not* be funded?
>
> On this issue, cancer advocates working at national organizations may be open to these subtleties, but the grassroots community advocate's viewpoint is very clear. Typically breast cancer has transformed her life and that of her family to the extent that it has become both her currency and her measuring stick. Nothing matters as much, so the actions of politicians are judged by how they contribute to or detract from the cause (Langer 1997, 502, emphasis in original).

Short of earmarking, Congress also exercises its constitutional authority to direct spending by citing particularly worthy endeavors in official committee documents that accompany appropriations bills. Such language provides advocates with a powerful tool when confronting the bureaucracy in its efforts to see grant funds awarded. Both have a measurable impact on how research funds are allocated to particular diseases. Elsewhere we have documented advocates' success in substantially increasing research funds for both breast cancer and prostate cancer under the National Cancer Institute (NCI) and Department of Defense (chapter 6). However, these data were not placed into a larger context. We now compare breast cancer and prostate cancer with other cancers.

THE ALLOCATION OF NCI FUNDS OVER TIME. The NCI budget increased from $900 million in 1981 to $3.740 billion in 2001, a 400 percent increase over twenty years.[3] Increases were largest in the last three or four years due to Congress's commitment to double the NIH research budget, of which the NCI is a beneficiary.

Changes in the percentage of NCI research funds, by cancer for up to eighteen different cancers, over the same twenty-year period is given in figure 3.[4] Figure 3 tells a dramatic story. First, the benefits of GSOs were evident. The three diseases that received the most NCI research funds are those that have the best-established GSOs: AIDS, breast cancer, and prostate cancer. Two of these diseases have experienced dramatic increases in funding. Breast cancer increased from just 3 percent of the NCI research budget in 1981 ($32 million) to 13 percent in 2001 ($475.2 million), down from a high of 14 percent in 1995–98. In terms of unadjusted dollars, the 2001 funding level was nearly 150 times greater than the 1981 funding level. The NBCC is indeed getting a "bigger slice of a bigger pie." Given these funding patterns and the enviable position that breast cancer holds as the most generously funded cancer, it is no surprise that Fran Visco states that she "never talks about other diseases when she's lobbying for more breast cancer money" ("Prostate Cancer Survivors" 1997). To do so would only call attention to the momentarily privileged position of breast cancer.

The National Prostate Cancer Coalition (NPCC) has also experienced considerable success in its short history. Prostate cancer research funding increased from less than 1 percent of the NCI budget in 1981 ($7.6 million) to 7 percent in 2001 ($258 million), a nineteenfold increase. Large increases were not noticeable until FY 1998, which roughly coincides with the establishment of the NPCC. Thus NPCC too is getting "a bigger slice of a bigger pie."

Common cancers with high five-year relative survival rates also lend further insight into the development of GSOs (table 47).[5] Effective GSOs need large numbers of activists who can be active for many years, and both breast cancer and prostate cancer are common and have five-year survival rates in excess of 85 percent. Compare their survival rates to those for the third-most-common, and deadliest cancer, lung cancer. Its five-year relative survival rate is only 14 percent. Three other cancers have five-year relative survival rates over 70 percent—melanoma, Hodgkin's Disease, and cervical cancer—but they are much less common than either prostate or breast cancer. Melanoma, which

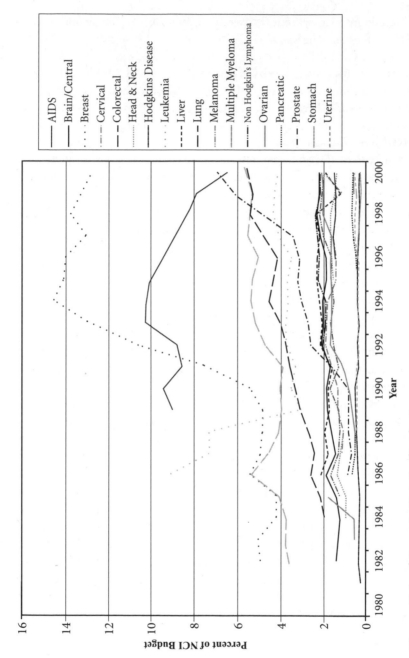

Figure 3. National Cancer Institute Funding, by Cancer

has the highest incidence rate of the three, constitutes fewer than 25 percent of the number of breast cancer or prostate cancer cases in any given year. The others are fewer than 10 percent. At the same time, prostate cancer and breast cancer have witnessed the largest increase in the percentage of the NCI research budget—6 percent and nearly 8 percent, respectively (table 47).

There is also some evidence that flat funding levels are associated with cancers with low survival rates (table 47). Those with the lowest five-year relative survival rates—pancreatic, liver, lung, stomach, multiple myeloma (bone marrow), and brain—have funding curves that are relatively flat. The largest percentage changes were in the cases of lung cancer and ovarian cancer, which increased approximately 2 percent over the decade. Thus, table 47 implies that cancers not likely to develop GSOs do not necessarily see research funding levels compromised in the face of competition from GSOs. They are not punished in the race for funds, but neither are they rewarded. As a representative from the Alliance for Lung Cancer Advocacy, Support and Education told Cox News Service, "The fact is that lung cancer cannot pressure Congress from the grass roots up. The people who get it are dying" (Evans 2003).

WHO FUNDS THE INCREASE? Where has the additional funding for breast cancer and prostate cancer come from? There are several possible explanations. The first is that the increases are new funds. If so, the advocates' efforts to "raise the tide" have lifted some boats more than others. Another is that NCI overhead costs, and other initiatives not reported here, such as cancer education and clinical trials, may receive smaller percentages of a growing total NCI budget without receiving cuts in terms of real dollars. Yet figure 3 indicates that there are two "losers" in the race for funds in the 1980s and 1990s: leukemia and AIDS. Leukemia is the most common form of cancer found in children, although the disease also strikes adults (ACS 2003e). Its funding dropped from 9 percent of the NCI budget in 1987 to just 3 percent of the NCI budget in 1990; leukemia received about 4 percent of the NCI budget in 2001. The reasons for the smaller commitment to leukemia research are unclear. It may be a due to earlier strides, or, as an NCI spokesperson stated in an e-mail, "In developing its budget, the NCI plans for research that can address critical unanswered questions covering the many types of cancer and the various populations that experience them" (Pearson, personal correspondence 2003).

Alternatively, it may be because leukemia advocates were unsuccessful in competing for funds. In the latter case, leukemia is unlikely to develop a large,

Table 47. Percent of NCI Budget by Disease and Severity Statistics

Type of Cancer	NCI Funding Data			Cancer Statistics, 2001	
	%in 1990	% in 2001	% change	Number of cases	5–year relative survival rates (%)
Prostate	0.8	6.9	6.1	98,100	94
Breast	4.9	12.7	7.8	93,000	86
Lung	3.9	5.5	1.6	169,000	14
Colorectal	3.1	5.5	2.4	98,200	63
Non-Hodgkin's lymphoma[a]	n.a.	2.1	0.4	56,200	53
Melanoma	1.3	1.9	0.6	51,400	89
AIDS	8.9	6.4	−2.5	41,311	n.a.
Uterine	0.4	0.5	0.1	38,300	86
Leukemia	3.0	4.1	1.1	31,500	45
Pancreatic[a]	n.a.	0.6	0.2	29,200	4
Ovarian[a]	0.6	2.0	1.9	23,400	50
Stomach[a]	n.a.	0.2	−0.1	21,700	20
Brain and central nervous system	1.8	2.1	0.3	17,200	30
Liver	1.7	1.4	−0.3	16,200	6
Multiple myeloma[a]	n.a.	0.5	0.0	14,400	28
Cervical	1.3	1.9	0.6	12,900	72
Hodgkin's disease	0.5	0.3	−0.2	7,400	83
Head and neck	1.0[b]	1.3	−0.2	n.a.	n.a.

Source: The National Cancer Institute *Fact Book,* various years; the American Cancer Society. Funding dollars may be counted for more than one cancer. Relative survival rates represents persons who are living five years after diagnosis, adjusted for normal life expectancy.

[a]The National Cancer Institute did not record the research dollars awarded for these cancers in 1991. The percentage change reported uses the earliest available data for each cancer. These are: head and neck, 1996; multiple myeloma, 2000; Non-Hodgkin's lymphoma, 1992; pancreatic, 1996; stomach, 1996.

[b]Data from FY 1989; 1990 data are unavailable.

powerful GSO for several reasons. First, far fewer people develop leukemia in a given year than develop breast cancer, prostate cancer, or many other cancers. Second, the five-year relative survival rate (45 percent) is lower for leukemia than it is for other cancers (table 47). Third, leukemia is common among children, a group that by definition lacks access to the political system and cannot form a significant voting block. Their parents, who could potentially form a group of surrogate-activists, may be too exhausted from caring for their seriously ill children to organize and become politically active.

The finding with respect to AIDS is something of a surprise. The fact that a disease supported by a highly successful GSO is now receiving a relatively smaller share of funds is startling. Granted, the NCI research funds constitute only a portion of the federal government's entire investment in

AIDS research; the NIH still spends about $2.4 billion (NIH 2005). Perhaps a growing AIDS backlash is a reason. Several policymakers and opinion leaders have criticized AIDS in particular for benefiting from a research commitment that is disproportionate to the actual number of cases in the United States (Dresser 1998; Murphy 1991). Another possible explanation is that the efficacy of drug treatments and the declining death rate have undermined advocates' sense of urgency.

A third possible explanation, however, also is plausible. As GSOs mature they develop some problems that are products of their successes. They become a target of criticism by other disease groups. Or, they become institutionalized, behave more like traditional lobbies, cultivate long-term relationships with agency personnel and members of Congress, and advocate incremental rather than comprehensive policy changes. Finally, dramatic success eventually leads to another policy priority: maintaining one's gains, especially in light of additional competition for resources. In this case, there has been an increase in the NCI budget for AIDS—from $106.9 million in 1990 to $239.1 million in 2001. That 220 percent increase was comparable to the overall increase in the NCI budget for the same period.

Clearly, lobbying by disease groups is most effective for those diseases that affect legions of people and stand a good chance of enjoying relatively good health for several years after diagnosis, an advantage that one breast cancer lobbyist acknowledged (interview Jan. 2003). This unfairly disadvantages diseases that affect many people but are also extremely deadly, such as lung cancer. Diseases that may have long-term survival rates but affect few people, such as ovarian cancer, are similarly disadvantaged. Success appears to lie in striking legions of people who can then be transformed into legions of activists. Of course, the best grassroots activists are voters. Cancers that strike large portions of nonvoters—childhood cancers like leukemia, for example—are also not likely to succeed in the competition for funds.

The importance of lobbying for specific priorities is evident in the evolution of GSOs as well. First, before the 1980s and 1990s, disease groups shared a tacit understanding that they would not promote funding for one particular disease over another; rather, they all would advocate for increased funding for medical research generally. But that changed when AIDS activists broke the traditional mold. Their monumental successes changed the science policy landscape. Normally quiescent disease groups are more militant in demanding funds (Marshall 1998; Nethercutt 1999). New groups continue to form, primarily as a defensive measure, even though, inevitably, there are diminishing returns for this kind of advocacy.

Second, in 1998 Congress enacted a law calling for the doubling of the NIH's budget within five years. This was a significant acceleration; the NIH's funding had been doubling every decade. According to one congressional staff member, the effort was predicated on the hope that this policy would eliminate some of the intense competition for funds among advocates for particular diseases (interview, Jan. 2003). Third, numerous cancer advocacy groups have come together to create the umbrella coalition "One Voice Against Cancer," which includes some thirty-six public health and cancer organizations and advocates for increased spending on cancer without specifying any particular earmarks. Notably, the NBCC and the NPCC are not members, although the Komen Foundation and Y-ME are ("One Voice against Cancer" 2000). The NPCC and NBCC regularly request earmarks, so joining the coalition would run counter to their lobbying strategies.

Should funding decisions be left in the hands of experts in government, medicine, and the academy? Not necessarily. Their track records are hardly unblemished. Robert Proctor (1996) argues that the federal government ignored a large body of medical evidence documenting the lung cancer risk associated with uranium mining yet was willing to sacrifice the lives of thousands of miners, many of whom were Native Americans. From 1932 to 1972 the federal government sponsored the Tuskegee syphilis experiment in order to document the course of the disease, and African American men were denied treatment even after the discovery of penicillin ("Bad Blood" n.d.; Clinton 1997). In the 1980s AIDS activists asserted that government response to the AIDS epidemic was slow, in no small part because the disease disproportionately affected homosexuals and drug users rather than "mainstream Americans" (Shilts 1987). It was also asserted that the traditional means to test drug effectiveness were unresponsive to the devastating toll of the disease (Arno and Feiden 1992; Epstein 1996). Thus, activism—often strident, confrontational activism at that—was necessary to gain the attention of the media, government, scientists, and the medical community.

As described earlier in chapter 6, breast cancer activists came upon the scene at a time of growing criticism of the NIH for funding medical research studies using only men and neglecting diseases of particular importance to women. Directing funds to breast cancer research as part of a larger women's health initiative was one way that women's health advocates would be assured that medical research funds would be directed to long-neglected women's health issues. In response to scientists' objections to disease-specific earmarks, Fran Visco said, "The scientific community is telling us 'fight for more money, but don't tell us how to spend it,' that politics don't belong in breast cancer. But there's politics in the scientific community, and those politics have worked in the past to the expense of breast cancer and the expense of women's lives" (as quoted in Olson 2002, 247).

The question of research priorities is all the more important when one considers the state of medical research funding worldwide. Much of the world's medical research funds come from American sources. According to the Global Forum for Health Research (GFHR), about $73.5 billion was spent on medical research and development (R&D) worldwide in 1998. Of this amount, nearly half (46 percent), or $34.2 billion, came from public sources from industrialized nations with developed market economies. The U.S. government provided about $19.5 billion, or about one-quarter of the world's total spending; only 6 percent ($2.5 billion) was provided through government expenditures by low- and middle-income countries (GFHR 2002).

Pharmaceutical companies are the next-largest source of medical R&D funds. Collectively, the pharmaceutical industry spent about $30.5 billion in 1998, about 42 percent of the total. U.S.-based companies spent approximately two-thirds of that amount. Private industry funding, however, is problematic. Several studies found an association between pharmaceutical company sponsorship and the reporting of favorable outcomes in drug trials (e.g., Warlow et al. 1999; Yaphe et al. 2000). In other cases industry sponsorship has led to patent disputes and charges of conflicts of interest on the part of academicians who work at universities (Chopyak and Levesque 2002; Orlans 2002; Woliver 2002). Thus, landing an NIH grant is important to one's success at many major academic research centers (Rajan and Clive 2000), and government funding becomes even more critical given that it may produce the most dependable results.

Considering the importance of American medical research funds (both public and private), one might assert that the medical research priorities of the United States become the medical research priorities of the world. The diseases that afflict people in the industrialized world, however, are quite different from those that afflict persons in developing nations. Understandably, countries in the developed world prioritize the diseases that afflict their populations. That leads to what the GFHR has called the "10/90 gap," defined as "less than 10 percent of global health research spending is devoted to diseases or conditions that account for 90 percent of the global disease burden" (2002, ix). The 10/90 gap would be even larger if the U.S. government spent less on AIDS research or more on breast cancer and prostate cancer.

Certainly, GSOs should not be blamed solely for these inequalities. Rather they effectively used their skills, exercised their First Amendment rights and changed policy. They would hardly tolerate such criticisms at any rate. In the words of Amy Langer, formerly of NABCO, "Grassroots activists refuse to accept arguments that penalize them for having been so effective in getting research funds appropriated. A Capitol Hill swarming with breast and prostate and lung cancer patients, each making his or her case, would seem to be the American way" (1997, 502).

Proving once again that organized interests with well-educated and well-heeled grassroots activists have an impact on public policy is no surprise. Indeed, pluralist critiques that state the American polity is hyper-responsive to organized interests and unresponsive to unorganized interests come to mind. In other contexts the solution proposed to hyper-pluralism is to organize the unorganized, such as the poor. Here, however, there may be little ability to organize GSOs in some diseases. Some cancers are too rare. Others are too deadly. There are not enough survivors—and enough survivors healthy enough—to create their own GSOs. Thus they are dependent upon surrogates to make their cases, and surrogates are unlikely to have the impact of legions of survivors although they can be effective in their own right. Contrary to Langer's assertion, Capitol Hill is not swarming with either prostate cancer or lung cancer survivors. The prostate cancer movement may in time mimic the political clout of the breast cancer movement, but there is little likelihood that lung cancer survivors will be able to create GSOs like those of breast cancer.

THE THIRD DILEMMA:
CONSUMER INPUT INTO RESEARCH PRIORITIES

Breast cancer advocacy, however, does provide a successful example of addressing another policy dilemma: how to include consumer (lay) perspectives into technical government decisions. Beginning with the consumer movement of the 1970s, a wide variety of government boards, commissions, and bureaucracies sought to include some sort of lay or consumer perspective. Medical licensure boards, institutional review boards (IRBs), peer review panels, and federal bureaucracies such as the NIH have consumer representatives in the field of health policy. Policy evaluations of these efforts, however, generally found the consumer members to be ineffective. One problem was that of definition: Who represents the public? Academics have defined "the public" variously as interest group advocates (Dresser 1998; 2001; Fitzgerald 1996; Gormley 1981a; Marshall 1998); ordinary citizens with no specialized knowledge ("Missed Opportunity" 1997; Litzelfelner 2001); proxies such as elected officials, be they members of Congress or state Attorneys General; or a separate bureaucracy, such as a consumer affairs agency (Gormley 1981b). All of these definitions lead to different interpretations of who represents the public. To the degree that interest groups may indeed do so, as in the case of utility rate increases, the interest groups can have a beneficial impact on policy outcomes (Gormley 1981c).

A related problem is that lay or consumer members generally have an ill-defined constituency. Many are unsure of exactly whom they represent: the public writ large or a smaller group, such as persons with a disease or their caregivers (Dresser 2001). This problem is broader than the medical field. Even self-styled public interest or consumer groups have adopted agenda items most beneficial to the middle class rather than policies more advantageous to the poor (Gormley 1981a). Thus it is difficult to conceive of many interest groups that represent all members of the public. In some cases (e.g., proxies) the problem is avoided by picking elected officials directly accountable to all people via elections. Elected officials, however, may be subject to pressures such as reelection. By contrast, urban fiscal control boards are composed of ordinary citizens, not politicians, to ensure that board members are free of political pressure when making tough decisions in times of fiscal crisis ("Missed Opportunity" 1997).

Another question is, What is input? Again, the type of input varies. It may include full membership on a body with decision-making ability that replaces or overrides the bureaucracy (Litzelfelner 2001; "Missed Opportunity" 1997); service as a voting member of a board or commission that is otherwise comprised of experts (Chesney 1984; Fitzgerald 1996; Gormley 1981b, 1986; Hiller, Landenburger, and Natowicz 1997); participation in a public hearing (Gormley 1981c, 1986); or simply signing a consent form for a medical procedure (Hiller, Landenburger, and Natowicz 1997). Obviously, the potential to influence bureaucratic decision making varies widely by one's definition of "input." When signing a consent form, a person hardly makes an impact upon public policy, even if that gains autonomy over his or her own medical care. Citizens rarely participate in public hearings. To the degree that any members of the public appear, it is in the form of interest groups (Gormley 1986). The actual sway that any public testimony has over the bureaucracy is questionable.

Also problematic is the role of citizens on boards and commissions. Several studies have demonstrated that citizen members on myriad boards and commissions are perceived as ineffective because they lack expertise on an issue. Without that expertise, or even a background in advocacy, consumer members may be co-opted by the industrial or professional members of the board (Chesney 1984; Gormley 1986). A 1984 study of lay members of IRBs found they often did not play a role significantly different from the scientists on the board (Porter 1987). Moreover, the presence of nonscientist members on peer review boards has been criticized because they are ill-equipped to understand the quality of the science or the potential ramifications of the findings (Schwarcz et al. 1981). AIDS activists, Love Canal activists, and breast cancer advocate Rose Kushner reported that when they sought a voice on various review boards, scientists often treated them with hostility (Epstein 1996; Gibbs and Levine 1982; Kushner 1982).

The NBCC was instrumental in creating the Congressionally Directed Medical Research Programs (CDMRP) and including consumers on the peer review panels. Such review panels currently exist for all fields of research covered by the CDMRP, including prostate cancer. "Consumer" in this case is defined as a survivor of the disease in question or, in the case of neuro-fibromatosis or tuberous sclerosis, a family member (U.S. Dept. of Army 2003a).[6] The role of the consumer is carefully defined. It is not so much to evaluate the quality of the science involved as to "bring [the] perspective as a patient, survivor or other affected individual to the review of research and study proposals" (U.S. Dept. of Army 2003b). The consumers are full voting members of the research panels.

The qualifications necessary to become a consumer peer reviewer are broad. An applicant must have a minimum of a high school education, although most hold a bachelor's degree or higher (Andejeski et al. 2002b; U.S. Dept. of Army 2003a). Persons with science backgrounds review proposals outside their areas of expertise to preserve their roles as consumer advocates. Applicants must have a background in advocacy and write a personal statement articulating the role they would play if selected for a peer review panel. Consumer reviewer positions are publicized through local support and advocacy groups. CDMRP personnel report that the breast cancer and prostate cancer panels are among the most popular. More applicants apply to participate on peer review panels than can be accommodated in any one year (Weitzman interview 2003).

The CDMRP appears to have avoided many of the problems that plagued earlier efforts to incorporate consumers on such boards and commissions. First, the NBCC took another cue from AIDS activists and began to train its advocates in the scientific issues related to the disease. In 1995 the NBCC instituted a training program, Project LEAD (Leadership, Education and Advocacy Development). The four-day process provides training in the basic science behind breast cancer research, rudimentary statistics, current avenues of research, the medical research review process, and advocacy training. Persons accepted to Project LEAD must have a history of involvement in breast cancer advocacy and are expected to use the knowledge to participate in the CDMRP or on peer review panels for the state-level programs, the Komen Foundation, on institutional review boards, or with other organizations (NBCC 2003h). The Project LEAD curriculum changes with advances in breast cancer research and in response to student evaluations of the program (Dickersin et al. 2001). Project LEAD is unique to breast cancer; no analogous project exists for prostate cancer or any other CDMRP program. The NBCC reports training more than nine hundred advocates through Project LEAD.

Second, the CDMRP has carefully defined a number of historical ambiguities that have plagued previous efforts at consumer involvement. "Input" is clearly defined as being a full voting member. The role of the consumer member is clearly articulated, and the constituency is clearly defined. A portion of the Project LEAD training is devoted to the appropriate role of the advocate. The CDMRP staff also provide orientation before the peer review panels begin and are available during peer review panel meetings to help consumers clarify their role. In addition, the CDMRP appoints an experienced consumer member as a mentor to each first-time reviewer (U.S. Dept. of Army 2003b; Weitzman interview 2003).

Translating the technical information into digestible form for consumer members is more difficult. In one study, consumer reviewers and scientists alike expressed concern that a lack of scientific preparation would be a drawback to consumer participation (Andejeski et al. 2002a). Grant applications must include a lay abstract. "We're told to assume the science is correct" one advocate told us (interview 2003). All advocates interviewed who participated on such panels, however, reported that they attempted to evaluate the technical scientific information as well. Breast cancer advocates also universally agreed that Project LEAD training had prepared them well and had eliminated a great deal of mystery about the science. Project LEAD graduates keep up with scientific advances through a journal club, a listserv hosted by the NBCC, and by attending additional panels at the annual advocacy conference.

A prostate cancer consumer peer reviewer related that he believed that lay abstracts were not well written or very accessible. The CDMRP and/or university grant officers, he said, needed to communicate better to scientists the important role consumers play on the review panel to ensure they justify the importance of their study from a consumer standpoint. Instead, "some read just like the technical abstract, with maybe a word or two changed." Although the reviewer spent hours on proposals in an effort to understand the science involved, he believed other consumer peer reviewers were completely overwhelmed. He believed the CDMRP orientation was helpful but thought training such as Project LEAD would have been beneficial (Caputi interview 2003).

Initially, including consumers on the peer review panels met with some resistance from scientists (Rich et al. 1998). Before the 1995 Department of Defense panel meeting, for example, more than half of the scientists anticipated some drawbacks to consumer participation. They were uncomfortable over the consumers' advocacy role and concerned that the consumers' inadequate background in science might unnecessarily lengthen the discussions. They maintained as well that consumers would be too "emotional" because of personal experience with disease, would emphasize treatment proposals, or would not see the benefit of basic science. In addition, some worried that the consumers' voting rights could result in funding proposals of questionable quality. After the panel, however, nearly three-quarters of the scientists agreed that there were no drawbacks to consumer participation on the panel (Andejeski et al. 2002a).

The scientists' fears may have been unfounded, but there is some question about the adequacy of the Project LEAD preparation. One evaluation found graduates who were not confident in their abilities to explain statistical concepts such as a "p" value or an odds ratio, and more than one-fifth confused correlation with causation (Dickersin et al. 2001).

What has been the impact of consumer reviewers on these panels? One major study found researchers' concerns that consumers would vote for "bad science" because they lacked the appropriate medical background was unfounded. Rather, the voting patterns of consumers and the scientists were much the same (Andejeski et al. 2002b). Although comforting to scientists who are worried about funding inferior proposals, the finding may point to cooptation on the part of consumer review panelists, a problem cited in earlier evaluations of consumer participation. As one person close to the process commented, "It's impossible to know what was going on in their [the consumers] heads when they voted" (interview 2003).

A variety of qualitative evidence mitigates against that conclusion. Qualitative studies found that medical researchers believed having a consumer on a panel provided a human face to the disease, especially important to researchers who work primarily in a laboratory setting. In addition, interaction between scientists and consumers provided researchers with new avenues of investigation (Andejeski et al. 2002a; Platner et al. 2002). Advocates interviewed for this research enthusiastically agreed that scientists took their opinions seriously, a finding consistent with other studies (Andejeski et al. 2002a). As Kenneth Bertram, director of the CDMRP, has stated, "Consumers, whose courage and commitment led to the creation of these programs, continue to infuse the CDMRP with passion, inspiration and vision" (U.S. Dept. of Army 2002).

Moreover, all consumer panelists interviewed provided anecdotes to illustrate their unique contributions. A prostate cancer survivor related that he gave a proposal that dealt with BPH a low score because there appears to be no connection between BPH and the development of prostate cancer, "Maybe I'm naive, but I was told to use the whole scoring range. The scientists tended to be conservative, putting everything in the middle. When it came to be my turn, and I gave the study a 1, jaws just hit the table. They had been reading the science, but I kept thinking 'this is no big deal. It doesn't make any difference.' The others [scientists] followed suit" (Caputi interview 2003).

Similarly, a breast cancer advocate interested in alternative medicines inspired one researcher to propose a study of the efficacy of those treatment options (Platner et al. 2002). An observer recalled a peer review panel considering a study of anti-nausea drugs using animal subjects. The consumer panelist raised an important ethical point by asking, "Why would we sicken these animals when there are thousands of women who are already sick from chemotherapy who might be willing to try these medications?" (Weitzman interview 2003). Her question changed the entire tenor of the conversation. A third breast cancer advocate stated that in one instance she would not vote in favor of a proposal to use gene therapy to treat ductal carcinoma in situ, a proposal that was very popular among the scientists on the panel, because she was concerned about the potential impact of the treatment on healthy tissues in the breast (Volpe interview 2003).

Most emblematic of the difference in perspective between scientists and consumer advocates is an anecdote from Sara Williams, who recounted a scientist on her panel saying "these are great when a woman fails chemotherapy" when discussing new treatments he was developing for those with advanced breast cancer. Williams corrected him by saying, "The woman doesn't fail chemotherapy. Chemotherapy fails the woman" (interview 2003).

All the consumer panelists found the experience rewarding. Some had served on as many as a half-dozen different panels—both in the CDMRP and elsewhere. In the words of prostate cancer activist Anthony Caputi, "I [can't] think of anything in my life that was more rewarding or meaningful. It was really, really remarkable. I can't wait to do it again" (interview 2003).

Are there any limits to the effectiveness of consumers on the panel? This remains unclear. Evidence does point to the significant contributions of advocates on the CDMRP peer review panels, but evaluations have focused on the role of breast cancer advocates. The consumers who review the CDMRP proposals for other diseases have not been subject to the same scrutiny. Because consumers on the breast cancer panels have the advantage of training through Project LEAD, their participation may be qualitatively different from those who do not have the same preparation. Without a program analogous to Project LEAD, the CDMRP selection process, which attempts to ensure that consumer reviewers have an advocacy background and personal experience with a disease and its orientation and mentoring programs, are the only ways to ensure the effectiveness of consumer advocates on other review panels.

One strength of the CDMRP program may also be a weakness. The CDMRP's definition of the constituency of the consumer reviewer as persons who have a disease is a narrow definition of public interest. The interest of persons with the disease is certainly important and should be represented, but it may be different from that of family members caring for persons with the disease. The general public may have yet another interest. Nonetheless, the CDMRP program appears to be a shining example of successful consumer involvement.

Reconsidering GSOs

Elsewhere (chapter 1) we developed a typology of grassroots survivors' organizations. Among their characteristics are having a particular type of disease, an existing activist tradition, access to an empowered, activist base, a symbol to represent the movement, and access to cause-marketing funds; offering oneself as evidence; using the media and/or the courts; and providing a prominent role for women. We concluded that the breast cancer movement has all eight characteristics of a successful GSO. By contrast, the prostate cancer movement fits only three criteria well: type of disease, using the media and/or courts, and prominent women as activists. The movement partially met three others: having an empowered and educated activist base, willingness to offer oneself as evidence, and access to cause marketing resources. It did not meet two criteria: a ubiquitous symbol or an existing activist tradition.

The typology developed in chapter 2, however, did not provide insight into the relative importance of these various characteristics. Are all of them equally important to a successful GSO? Are some necessary but not sufficient elements? One of the characteristics, symbol ambiguity in the prostate cancer movement, can be rectified with enough time and promotion. The blue ribbon and Prostate Cancer Awareness Month can become as familiar as the pink ribbon and Breast Cancer Awareness Month, especially if they are tied to future cause-related marketing relationships. Similarly, prostate cancer activists are working to create new, more creative, cause-related marketing relationships. The blue ribbon may not be as ubiquitous in September as the pink ribbon is in October, but we do expect prostate cancer awareness to grow.

In addition, the prostate cancer movement lacks an empowered, well-educated activist base. Breast cancer groups have access to well-educated, articulate members because the disease is one of few that is more prevalent among persons of higher socioeconomic status. Because prostate cancer is more likely to strike men of lower socioeconomic status, advocates have a smaller pool of well-educated, articulate, efficacious survivors from which to draw. Yet the disease does strike men of means, status, and power. They tend, however, to engage in individual, entrepreneurial action rather than collective action.

The gendered nature of these diseases also explains some of the differences between these GSOs. Ironically, a long history of sexism works to the benefit of women in this case. One major difference between disenfranchised, traditionally unempowered groups and white males, the dominant subpopulation, is that disenfranchised groups are forced to organize to effect change. Thus the breast cancer movement draws upon decades of grassroots organizing experience and the political skills wrought by the feminist and women's health movements. By contrast, white males do not have a strong set of analogous grassroots health or political organizations. The default mode, however, is in favor of white males, whose dominance in institutions such as Congress (85 percent) explains how even reluctant champions can change policy.

To engage in collective action, the prostate cancer movement must look to existing organizations. Some exist within the African American community, such as 100 Black Men of America, black churches, and the national organizations of traditionally African American fraternities. These organizations may be effective at mobilizing African American men but will be less effective at organizing white men. Similarly, white men can look to medical professional associations such as the American Urological Association, but those groups have broader agendas and may be ill-suited to grassroots political action.

Prostate cancer survivors are reluctant to offer themselves as evidence. Both movements include surrogates and survivors, but the presence of breast cancer survivors in that movement is unmistakable. They're everywhere. They speak forcefully for themselves. Without question, they are assertive advocates. The prostate cancer movement also has survivors as active participants, but their proportion within the larger movement is smaller. Surrogates—wives and widows, children, medical professionals, and community organizers—are more visible and more outspoken. Legions of prostate cancer survivors remain silent and uninvolved, unwilling to offer themselves as evidence. Consequently, the personal impact of the disease is not communicated as forcefully.

One reason for this difference offered over and over again by activists is that men are unwilling to discuss their experience with illness; American culture equates illness with weakness. Men in their sixties and seventies are products of a generation that is unaccustomed to discussing personal problems.[7]

That critique is not to understate the effectiveness of surrogates as political actors. On the contrary, the prostate cancer movement—survivors and surrogates together—has achieved measurable success in increasing awareness of the disease, increasing the federal investment in medical research, and garnering media attention. Yet those efforts pale in comparison to those of breast cancer activists. The prostate cancer movement may eventually see more of its reluctant champions become assertive advocates as men presently in their forties and fifties develop prostate cancer. These men are products of the enormous social changes since the 1960s, have higher rates of education than their forbears, and may be more willing to speak out about their diagnoses and disease experiences.

Reconsidering Media Advocacy and the Role of the *New York Times*

Most previous studies of media advocacy have been case studies, often accompanied by exhortations to public health professionals to use media advocacy tactics to promote public health goals with little analysis of these tactics over the long-term. Our analysis uses media advocacy differently. Using quantitative methods, a significant departure from the methodology of previous studies allowed us to test the efficacy of media advocacy over the long term. We found evidence consistent with sustained media advocacy efforts, especially on the part of breast cancer.

Media advocacy is useful because it reflects how interest groups today combine traditional "inside" lobbying strategies with "outside" strategies to garner favorable media attention. Separating the two and discerning the independent effectiveness of each tactic is less important than understanding that lobbyists operate under the assumption that media coverage for their cause enhances their credibility and communicates the cause's importance when they go knocking on the doors of policymakers.

In addition, this study calls into question the common practice of using the *New York Times* as a surrogate for all media coverage. We found that the

Times's coverage—especially of prostate cancer—was measurably different than in the other media studied. This finding suggests that the *Times* is less of a national agenda-setter than previously believed. Moreover, our findings are a reminder that media coverage continues to have a local focus. In spite of the diagnoses of prominent persons, newspapers continue to cover local notables, local industries, and local activists.

Maturing Movements

[When NPCC was founded] every other prostate cancer group thought this group would usurp their power. US TOO! wanted to be the whole enchilada. That's not true now. The problems were driven by personalities. Now we have a great relationship. We're not intimate, but we have mutual respect.

—NPCC staff member, 2003

Just try to find a picture of Nancy Brinker [founder of the Komen Foundation] and [NBCC president] Fran Visco together. You simply won't find one.

—Breast cancer activist at the NBCC Advocacy Conference, May 2003

PROSTATE CANCER AS A MATURING MOVEMENT

Both the breast cancer movement and the prostate cancer movement have had difficulties coordinating their efforts. The myriad groups involved have, at various times, competed and cooperated with each other. In the case of the prostate cancer movement, the competition happened in the early years as each national organization worked to define a niche. The most notable dispute came when US TOO! left the NPCC board in 2001. Several activists we interviewed offered a gendered explanation for these problems. "Men are used to being in charge," observed one, "to having their own way. So [they thought], 'my group will do everything—advocacy, support, awareness, you name it.' As those personalities have been replaced, the groups now get along much better" (interview 2003).

To a person, however, representatives of the national organizations asserted that the relationships among organizations have matured and competition has waned. The prostate cancer movement appears to have fought its internal battles and settled into a period of cooperation. Yet the movement is still young and faces a number of challenges that the breast cancer movement does not. The first is to raise awareness of a disease that despite its incidence, prevalence, and mortality rates is not nearly as well known as breast cancer. Symptoms of the problem are found in the public opinion polls, media coverage, the movement's nascent cause-related marketing relationships, its less ambitious lobbying efforts, and the small number of state coalitions. The second problem that it faces is overcoming the many challenges to organizing thousands of prostate cancer survivors into a potent political force. Even with these difficulties, the prostate cancer movement has achieved much.

The movement also remains fairly monolithic. Most prostate cancer support groups and state coalitions are umbrella groups designed to serve all men with the disease as well as their families. Few groups target gay men or men of color, and none that do boast national memberships (chapter 2). Several national organizations serving the African American community are involved in prostate cancer issues, but the illness remains only one of many items on their agendas. As the prostate cancer movement matures we expect to witness the development of organizations that target specific populations, like those that exist in the breast cancer community.

As time passes and new issues arise, disagreements may emerge within the prostate cancer movement. Most national prostate cancer groups, for example, now promote the use of the PSA test as a means of detection. As such, they disagree with the federal government's current recommendation. Should the Centers for Disease Control endorse the PSA test, as it does mammography in the case of breast cancer, consensus may erode, because the major prostate cancer organizations differ in their recommendations for the age at which screening should begin and the frequency of the test.

BREAST CANCER AS A MATURING MOVEMENT

Although the breast cancer movement is older than the prostate cancer movement, Barbara Brenner rightly notes that it is still new, little more than a decade old (interview 2003). As this movement matures it may be threatened by several developments.

The first is the issue-attention cycle. At some point the media and the public may tire of breast cancer. Compounding the possibility of boredom could be frustration, especially if death rates do not drop dramatically, incidence rates continue to rise as the population ages, promising treatments are slow to appear, and prevention is elusive. One breast cancer activist worried that "we [breast cancer] would be like AIDS—we don't hear about it any more" (interview 2003).

Given the current popularity of breast cancer among the media, policymakers and marketers alike, reminders are not likely to disappear from our refrigerators or televisions any time soon. More threatening, instead, are the fractures developing within the breast cancer movement itself. Currently, there is some competition for volunteers and dissention among groups. As

Susan Love commented, "The breast cancer advocacy movement has been so successful in increasing awareness and funding that it has become a victim of its success. There are rival national groups (NABCO, Komen, NBCC, Y-ME) competing for local breast cancer survivors' loyalty and national corporations' public relations dollars. And advocacy has become institutionalized" (2000, xii). Not only is there competition among the various breast cancer groups but there is also significant confusion on the part of consumers and corporate sponsors. As one activist put it, "It's just one big pink ribbon to them" (interview 2003).

The split between the NBCC and Komen Foundation is well known within breast cancer circles and may have its basis in the differing political ideologies of their founders. None of the breast cancer organizations are overtly affiliated with one political party or another. Visco, however, has roots in the anti-Vietman War movement and later became a women's rights attorney (Stabiner 1997, 9). Nancy Brinker, founder of the Susan G. Komen Foundation, is a "lifelong friend" of Laura Bush and was appointed by George W. Bush as U.S. ambassador to Hungary ("A Taste of Budapest" 2002; U.S. Department of State, 2001). Similarly, Barbara Brenner characterizes Breast Cancer Action (BCA) as "on the left" of the breast cancer movement and named the Komen Foundation as "on the right." She also noted that BCA's position on the far left allowed the NBCC to move farther to the left than it would have otherwise.

Another dispute, also ideologically driven in part, divided breast cancer activists on Long Island and compromised their ability to be involved with the Long Island Breast Cancer Study (Fagin 2002a). On a national level, the NBCC has taken positions against the widespread use of both breast self-examinations (BSE) and mammography (NBCC 2003g, 2003h), a position at odds with the American Cancer Society, Komen Foundation, NABCO, Young Survival Coalition, and Y-ME (Susan G. Komen 2003b; Murphy 2003, 29; NABCO 2003b; Stolberg 2003; Y-ME 2003b). While, as one advocate states, Fran Visco seems to speak with a louder voice on Capitol Hill than do other breast cancer advocates (Volpe interview 2003), such disputes may compromise the political power of the entire breast cancer movement. As one congressional aide noted, when breast cancer groups splinter on an issue such as the efficacy of mammography, politicians have a more difficult time because they do not want to offend any one group. "We then turn to the federal government for correct information," she noted (interview 2003).[8]

Another disagreement is over the appropriateness of cause-related marketing (chapter 8) and the role of pharmaceutical companies in supporting the activities of local and national breast cancer organizations. Some argue that these efforts merely "pink wash" breast cancer or try to "make breast cancer pretty" instead of communicating the real human toll of the disease. Others worry that pharmaceutical company sponsorship will undermine the groups' abilities to advocate or criticize the companies' practices (Brenner interview 2003; NBCC 2003c). "Which leads me," Susan Love said, "to contemplate whether we can afford to cure breast cancer? I worry that there are too many companies, organizations, researchers and universities depending on the breast cancer dollar" (Love 2000, xii). Another activist agreed: "Sometimes I get concerned that the consumer is going to see a divide in the breast cancer community. There are a lot of different conversations going on. We may not look very united. We may not be very united. . . . What concerns me about that is that if the consumer has that perception . . . they may take their dollars outside the cause altogether and go somewhere else" (interview 2003).

The future may see even more splinters within the breast cancer movement. The movement is already a "big tent" that includes not only a myriad of local organizations but also support and advocacy organizations for lesbians, African American women, Latinas, younger women, men with breast cancer, persons with metastatic breast cancer, women with inflammatory breast cancer, and people suffering from lymphedema.[9] The development of these targeted groups that articulate the needs and provide support to people of particular populations is not in and of itself problematic. On the contrary, they provide many important services to constituents and the movement at large.

Consider, however, that the science of breast cancer is moving away from considering it as one disease to conceptualizing it as several different diseases.[10] In time, researchers hope to individualize breast cancer treatments to the particular type of breast cancer a person has. Some cancers probably affect relatively few people—few enough so drugs developed to treat them may qualify for orphan drug status (Sledge 2003). Yet one of the reasons the breast cancer movement has hung together so far is that so much about the disease remains unknown. As medical discoveries untangle the Gordian knot of breast cancer, they may further fracture the movement. Women with "Breast Cancer One" may be pitted against women with "Breast Cancer Six" in the competition for resources and the attention of policymakers and medical researchers. Similarly, women with relatively rare forms of breast cancer may feel oppressed or ignored by those who have more common forms. At the same time, women with a more common form of breast cancer may believe that resources should be invested in their disease because it would benefit the largest number of people. In an interview about her experience as a consumer reviewer on a medical research panel, one activist said that she had to be convinced to support a project on inflammatory breast cancer, which fewer than 10 percent of women with breast cancer have. Her objection was that inflammatory breast cancer affected very few women. In the end, however, she was convinced that science held out the promise of improving the lives of women with that particular form of breast cancer (interview 2003). Will new scientific developments endanger the power of the breast cancer movement? Only time will tell.

Final Thoughts

This book is a story of contrasts and paradoxes. It is a story of influencing media coverage and public policy. It is a story of assertive advocates engaging in collective action and reluctant champions working individually. It is a story of women's power and men's weakness. This direct comparison of men's and women's activism may be able to explain much about how men and women collaborate and influence the media and American political system on other issues as well.

Yet we cannot ignore the ethical and policy consequences of breast cancer and prostate cancer activism. We admire the women in the breast cancer movement and applaud their successes. We congratulate the survivors and surrogates in the prostate cancer movement for their achievements. Indeed, we have been touched by both diseases, and as women we risk developing breast cancer one day. Yet as persons concerned with justice and equity we also realize that media attention and financial investment imply that breast cancer and prostate cancer are more important than all other cancers and nearly all other diseases. As horrific and deadly as these diseases are, we also think of the human toll of lung cancer, stroke, leukemia, malaria, and the many other diseases whose public face is not prominently displayed in the media and whose advocates cannot walk the corridors on Capital Hill. We ask policymakers, journalists, and readers to remember them, too.

Acknowledgments

An oncologist once asked one of us, "What can a social scientist know about cancer?" It is a valid question. While on this journey we learned a lot about breast cancer and prostate cancer science and risk and the atrocious side effects of treatment; yet we learned far more about activists' passion, intelligence, and devotion to their cause.

Why did two social scientists write this book? We believe the world of cancer goes far beyond the laboratory, clinic, and hospital. It is a comprehensive enterprise, encompassing policy and politics, regulation, philanthropy, media coverage, marketing, and what some have called the "cancer industry"—drug and medical equipment manufacturers who provide goods and services to thousands of people undergoing treatment. As such, the world of cancer moves into the world of social scientists, who as scholars seek to understand human behavior.

This book had modest beginnings. We intended to write a short article about prostate cancer media coverage, see it published in some journal somewhere, and move on. More than eight years later, we find ourselves writing a much longer manuscript about a compelling story that needs to be told and asking important ethical questions that need to be considered.

Once underway, we realized the prostate cancer story could not be told without also telling the breast cancer story. "Breast and prostate cancer" were linked in media coverage and legislation alike. Funding increases appeared to be linked. Prostate cancer activists adopted the advocacy strategies of the breast cancer movement.

While on our journey, we were personally touched by both diseases. For a number of reasons, one of us is at high risk of developing breast cancer. Our fathers-in-law, one of whom is no longer alive, both battled prostate cancer. One of our mothers developed breast cancer in her waning days. And we have watched colleagues undergo treatment for both diseases.

We are indebted to many who assisted us over the years. Margaret Conway planted the seed for this book by saying to Karen over breakfast at a conference, "Why don't you just write a book?" Augie Grant and Laura Woliver reviewed two versions of the manuscript and provided insightful comments. Winthrop University generously supported this effort through Research Council grants and sabbatical leaves. Portions of this manuscript were presented at several professional conferences in political science and mass communication, and we received many helpful comments from the reviewers and discussants. Our research assistants, Gisela DeSantiago, Patrick Jebaily, and Carolyn Barringer, did an enormous amount of coding for the "public face" analysis in chapters 4 and 5. Joy Simha of the Young Survival Coalition reviewed and critiqued portions of the manuscript and provided thoughtful commentary. Of course, this project would not exist without the assistance of all the individuals we interviewed (listed in the bibliography) who shared their thoughts and reviewed portions of the manuscript. Dr. Laura Glasscock of Winthrop University and Dr. Beverly Rockhill of University of North Carolina, Chapel Hill, vetted the portions of the manuscript in which we discuss science and epidemiology. The research staff at the Kaiser Family Foundation provided additional analysis of their media surveys; the Roper Center and the Odum Center provided original data sets for secondary analysis; Dr. Scott Huffmon gave time and advice generously on questions of statistical analysis; Winthrop University's Social and Behavioral Research Laboratory included questions supporting this research in one of its surveys; and the staff at Winthrop University's Dacus Library cheerfully secured countless articles and books through interlibrary loan and helped us locate countless pieces of obscure information. Our friends at Pure Creative helped us with the figures. We are grateful to April Lovegrove, the political science department's administrative specialist, for her able assistance with manuscript preparation and willingness to run countless errands and to our long-suffering spouses and other family members who provided unwavering support in all phases of this project.

Finally, we are grateful to the staff and editorial board of the University of Illinois Press for publishing this book. Kerry Callahan, our acquisitions editor, was perpetually cheerful and encouraging throughout the review process, and Mary Giles did a great job of copyediting and also provided constructive comments.

Methodological Appendix

This book uses both qualitative and quantitative methods of analysis. News stories are analyzed using content analysis. Eight media sources were used in this study: three television networks (ABC, NBC, and CBS); two national newspapers known for their coverage of policy issues (the *Washington Post* and *New York Times*); and three regional newspapers (the *Atlanta Constitution, Chicago Tribune*, and *Los Angeles Times*). Relevant newspaper stories were identified through the Lexis-Nexis database and the newspaper's indexes for those years not included in Lexis-Nexis. Newspaper stories were further classified as hard news or soft news.

Television news stories were identified through the Vanderbilt Television News Abstracts. We traveled to Vanderbilt University to watch and code the newspaper stories. Every story was coded for the following variables: medium, year of publication, month of publication, first three sources cited in the story, first three subjects covered in the story, and which cancer the story addressed. When in a few instances a story mentioned both cancers the story was analyzed twice, once as a breast cancer story and once as a prostate cancer story.

Several possible sources were identified based upon previous studies of medical news coverage (e.g., Friemuth et al. 1984; Nelkin 1995; Theodoulou, Guevara, and Minnassians 1996). The story sources included medical journals, with particular note taken when the *Journal of the American Medical Association* (*JAMA*) or the *New England Journal of Medicine* were used. Any government official or agency was coded as "government." One example is a statement released by the office of Representative Y that he was diagnosed with prostate cancer; another would cite the Food and Drug Administration in a story about the approval of a new drug treatment. Items coded as "medical institution" include hospitals or university medical research centers. Stories that used this code usually cited "researchers at Harvard" or elsewhere.

Individual doctors or researchers quoted were coded as "medical experts." "Private industry" includes insurance companies, pharmaceutical companies, or medical equipment manufacturers. Media was considered a source when the story stated something like "the *Chicago Tribune* disclosed today." Such stories were common in 1994 during the scandal surrounding fraud in the federally funded breast cancer studies. "Patient support groups" and "interest groups" were considered as the same type of source, which is appropriate given this historical development of breast cancer and prostate cancer advocacy organizations (chapter 1). Patients featured had to speak for themselves to be counted as a source. Family members, friends, attorneys, or other surrogates (other than medical experts or government officials) were coded as "other." Any other sources were also coded as "other."

Similarly, subject matter was broken down into several broad categories. Medical discoveries were divided into treatment discoveries such as the success of tamoxifen or the nerve-sparing surgery pioneered at Johns Hopkins University; diagnostic discoveries such as more accurate mammography machines or the development of the PSA test; and other discoveries, which could include the discovery of a new risk factor. Personality stories focused on the diagnosis, treatment, or death of a person, including prominent persons such as Stokley Carmichael, Bob Dole, or Ann Jillian; they also might have included the personal account of a survivor who is not famous. Stories dealing with government action were coded as "hearings," "funding," or "regulations," as appropriate. Stories about patient support groups or advocacy organizations were coded as such. Stories about insurance coverage, treatment dilemmas, fraud in medical research trials, or similar issues were coded as "ethics." Anything else was coded as "other." A common coding as "other" might be a story about the death of former French President Francois Mitterrand (coded as a personality story), and what his passing might mean for French politics ("other").

Two coders working independently coded the data. They both coded a sample of six hundred news stories to determine intercoder reliability. The intercoder reliability rate for the variables averaged 83 percent. For areas of disagreement, the two coders discussed the article and reached an agreement.

Further coding was conducted to classify stories as "hard news" or "soft news." Hard news stories were classified as "timely" if they were about events, discoveries, or conflicts that have happened or are about to happen. Soft news stories were defined as those with an emphasis on the human interest or novelty or were of less immediacy than hard news. They also included feature stories that focused on people, places, or issues in someone's life, according to definitions adapted from C. Rich (1998). Stories were coded for this variable after the initial coding was completed and television stories were no longer available. On this item, three coders working independently coded the stories and achieved an intercoder reliability rate of 93 percent ($n = 264$ stories).

For chapters 4 and 5, the public face of cancer was measured by first examining newspaper stories to determine whether they included a profile. We included only newspaper stories because television included few if any direct mentions of a person's age, and estimating someone's age from television footage would be highly subjective. Newspaper stories including profiles were coded along the following criteria: person's age if known, prognosis (coded as "terminal" or "unknown"), mentions of children, ages of children if known, and number of persons profiled per story. Infants were coded as age 0. Persons with ages listed by decade (e.g., "a woman in her fifties") were coded using the midpoint (i.e., fifty-five). The dataset also included the codes for the medium, year, and the story subject. The unit of analysis was the person profiled rather than the story, which allowed for multiple data points per story. Two coders working independently coded the dataset. Based upon a sample of 124 stories, which included 180 individual profiles, the coders achieved an intercoder reliability of 90.4 percent.

Because a large majority of the stories that included a patient profile featured a prominent personality (60 percent of breast cancer stories and 78 percent of prostate cancer stories), we conducted each analysis on the entire sample of profile stories and on those where personality was *not* a story subject. In the latter, a profile would be used to highlight some other story subject such as a risk factor, treatment discoveries, or ethical issue. The results of this analysis were in the same direction as the analyses including prominent personalities.

Polling Question Convergence

In chapter 4 we assess women's perception of their risk of developing breast cancer by using three different public opinion polls, one from the National Cancer Institute, one from ABC News, and one from Louis Harris and Associates. Given that these three surveys used very different question wordings, we sought to determine how closely responses to the questions correlate with each other. In October 2002 the Winthrop University Social and Behavioral Research Laboratory (SBRL) conducted a telephone survey of residents of Rock Hill, South Carolina, in which the three questions were tested to determine how closely the answers tracked ($n = 494$; margin of error +/- 4.4 percent). In this survey, women ($n = 322$) were asked about breast cancer; men ($n = 171$) were asked the same questions with the word *prostate* inserted in place of the word *breast*. To emulate the ABC News and Harris Polls as closely as possible the cancer questions were included in a longer list of health risks (table 48).

The responses from the National Cancer Institute (NCI) and the Harris Polls are substantially the same. The question from the ABC News poll, which specifically asks about "worry," yields a much lower perception of risk in the 2002 SBRL survey. Therefore, the 1992 ABC News Poll may very well *underestimate* women's perception of their risk of developing breast cancer. We cannot state this definitively because details about the 2002 SBRL survey, such as the question order and the fact that this survey asked *three* questions about risk, could have affected the responses. We are confident, however, that the 1992 ABC News Poll does not appear to *overestimate* women's perception of their risk of developing breast cancer. Therefore, we are reasonably confident that

Table 48. Frequency Distributions: Questions Measuring Risk

Question	Women		Men	
	%	n	%	n
NCI[a]	55.2	175	60.6	100
ABC[b]	24.9	80	10.5	18
Harris[c] (4–10)	63.6	171	59.7	83
Harris[c] (5–10)	54.3	146	49.6	69

Source: SBRL; analysis by authors.

[a]The question was, "What do you think the chances are that you will have breast (prostate) cancer someday? Do you think it's very likely, somewhat likely, somewhat unlikely or very unlikely?" The data reported are those answering "very likely" or "somewhat likely."

[b]The question was, "We're interested in finding out what's really worrying women (men) these days. . . . For each I want you to tell me if it's something that worries you a great deal, a good amount, worries you just a little or doesn't worry you at all." The data reported are those answering "a great deal" or "a good amount."

[c]The question was, "I would like to ask you about various diseases and accidents. For each one, please tell me what you think are the chances of it happening to you, where ten out of ten means that it is certain to happen and zero out of ten means no chance at all." The data reported are those responding with numbers between 4–10, inclusive, or 5–10 as indicated above.

the trend that appears from these disparate surveys with different question wording captures some increase in perceived risk (table 49).

Statistical analysis was conducted using the SAS statistical package. Statistics used include correlations; chi-square statistics; frequency distributions; Wilcoxon scores, a nonparametric test that emulates chi-square statistics for highly-skewed, categorical level data; and difference of means tests and regression for interval level data. Regression analyses that compare levels of funding and media coverage in chapters 6 and 7 use change variables. These variables were calculated by subtracting the previous year's value from the current year's value.

Public Policy

This analysis identified relevant policy data through various public sources. Legislation was found through searching the Lexis-Nexis Congressional database and the Library of Congress site, THOMAS. The NCI and Department of Defense funding levels were found in printed and electronic versions of their annual reports, and some additional information was provided by the NCI through a Freedom of Information Act request.

Qualitative Methods

The primary qualitative component is interviews with activists, members of Congress and congressional staff, agency staff, and selected health reporters. National breast

Table 49. Correlations in Question Responses

Questions	Correlations			
	Women		Men	
	Pearson's R	p	Pearson's R	p
NCI and ABC	0.4246	<.0001	0.3911	<.0001
NCI and Harris	0.5442	<.0001	0.4985	<.0001
Harris and ABC	0.5897	<.0001	0.5159	<.0001

Source: SBRL; analysis by authors.

cancer and prostate cancer organizations were contacted for interviews. All agreed to participate, and each organization identified the individual(s) most appropriate to speak for the organization. Some interviews were conducted in person, others by telephone conference call. In some cases, clarification or follow-up was conducted by e-mail.

Selected local and state level activists were interviewed to provide a grassroots perspective. Particular organizations were chosen due to their proximity to the authors or when their organizations or experience were somehow unique.

Relevant current and former members of Congress and congressional staff were identified through public records such as bill sponsorships, news coverage, or referrals from activists. Officials were identified through contacts and requests with the agencies involved. Often interviews resulted from referrals or suggestions from activists or other interview subjects. In addition, we attended the National Breast Cancer Coalition Advocacy Conference in 2003 and 2005 and the National Prostate Cancer Coalition Spring Training in 2003.

Notes

Introduction

1. Skin cancer is more common, but records are not kept on all skin cancers, including basal and squamous cell cancers (ACS 2005b).

2. African American women are more likely to be diagnosed at a later stage than white women and more likely to die from the disease.

3. Social marketing and media advocacy sometimes are viewed as competitive concepts. Others have attempted to meld the two approaches. The Division of HIV/ AIDS Prevention at the Centers for Disease Control and Prevention (CDC) has done such through an approach called prevention marketing, which is intended to reach individuals, social networks, communities, and institutions to prevent the transmission of AIDS (Shepherd 1997).

4. See also Benford (1993) and Gamson and Modigliani (1989).

5. Further information on specific coding criteria appears in the Methodological Appendix.

Chapter 1: Two Activist Movements Emerge

The first epigraph is from the National Breast Cancer Coalition's mission statement (2003b), emphasis in the original; the second epigraph is from the mission statement of the National Prosate Cancer Coalition (2005e).

1. Current medical wisdom holds a different theory for the spread of breast cancer. Evidence indicates that breast cancer spreads through the body via the lymphatic system (Lerner 2001).

2. A precursor to this program began in the 1930s, when the American Society for the Control of Cancer (ASCC), now the American Cancer Society, encouraged

women to tell other women that early detection saves lives. The ASCC campaign was specifically targeted to white, upper- and middle-class women (Moffett 2003).

3. Halsted's studies were based upon observations of his own patients; they were not randomly assigned to various treatment groups. Most certainly, those who survived the longest were likely to have had the least serious cases of cancer. Surgical removal of the cancer probably helped them, but they might have received the same benefit from a less disfiguring procedure (Lerner 2001).

4. For events, policies and statements that predate 2003, the term *CaP CURE* is used.

5. Robert Samuels, the first president of the NPCC, is African American.

6. Over the course of our interviews we informed subjects that we were conducting a comparison of these two disease movements. Although it is possible that some parallels we observed may have been prompted by the nature of our questions and research agenda, we believe these observations are real, not manufactured, phenomena. Comparisons were often made by the interview subjects themselves, even when we did not ask them to make comparisons. In addition, the level of awareness of each disease is asymmetrical.

7. At the 2003 NBCC conference, for example, the opening tribute was to the late Jean Powers. Apparently outraged that the breast cancer awareness stamp issued by the U.S. Post Office featured a profile of a naked woman, she photographed some men and developed a mock-up of her "prostate cancer awareness stamp." The anecdote drew a chuckle from the audience.

Chapter 2: A Typology of Grassroots Survivors' Organizations

Robert Young (first epigraph) is a prostate cancer activist and founder of Phoenix5, a prostate cancer Web site and on-line support group (Shropshire 2003); Heather Hill (second epigraph) is a Young Survival Coalition (2003) activist.

1. We use the term *grassroots survivors' organization* when referring to our insights and analysis. When referring to Foreman's work, however, we will continue to use his term: *grassroots victims' organization*.

2. Lyme disease is a tick-borne illness that causes chronic pain and other ailments. Approximately seventeen thousand people are diagnosed with the disease each year in the United States (American Lyme Disease Foundation 2005).

3. Legionnaires' Disease was first identified in 1977 after thirty-four delegates to an American Legion convention in Philadelphia became terminally ill. The Centers for Disease Control (CDC) traced the outbreak to bacterium in the air-conditioning system cooling tower. The organism is named *Legionella pneumophilia* (acute bacterial pneumonia) and now consistently ranks as a top cause of community-acquired pneumonia. Officials estimate it affects some twenty-five thousand persons a year and results in more than four thousand deaths. The CDC indicates that 95 percent of the cases are undetected (Lane, Ferrari, and Dreher 2004).

Toxic shock syndrome is caused by blood poisoning from a streptococcus infection in the lungs, throat, or bones or on the skin. More than fifteen thousand women were stricken with the disease between 1980 and 1984, and 15 percent of them died. The cause of the disease was traced to the use of super-absorbent tampons (Turkington and Odle 2003).

4. This was possible even when an activist did not have a scientific background. As one remarked to Steven Epstein, "Now every day, the phone rings ten times, and there's a physician on the other end wanting advice. [From] me! I'm trained as an opera singer!" (1996, 229).

5. According to the American Cancer Society, 70 percent of all prostate cancer cases are diagnosed in men over age sixty-five (chapter 4).

6. Note the play on words. A high result (over 4.0) on the PSA blood test is an indication of possible prostate cancer.

Chapter 3: Breast Cancer and Prostate Cancer in the Media

The first epigraph is from Joyce Purnick (2000, 2); Robert Samuels (second epigraph) is the former chair of the National Prostate Cancer Coalition (Steimle 1997).

1. Peer review does not necessarily guarantee that a study is accurate. One of the most glaring examples is a *JAMA* study published in January 1996 by a National Center for Infectious Diseases (NCID) official. Using NCID data, the author claimed that the death rate from infectious diseases in the United States increased 20 percent between 1980 and 1992. Murray and Schwartz (1997) review how methodology decisions skewed these results.

2. Note here that CNN was classified as a major network—ABC was left out of the analysis.

3. For additional studies on magazine coverage of breast cancer in Australia, see McKay and Bonner (1999, 2004).

4. These discoveries included the recommendation of lumpectomy for women with small tumors, the discovery that chemotherapy was an effective adjuvant therapy for women whose visible tumors had been removed, and scientific evidence that birth control pills were not linked to breast cancer.

5. The exceptions were all medical discoveries and medical discoveries related to treatment.

Chapter 4: The Public Face of Cancer: Breast Cancer and Prostate Cancer in the Media and Public Perceptions of Risk

Francis Coulter (first epigraph) is a public relations co-chair (Young Survival Coalition 2003); John Page (second epigraph) is the former president of US TOO! International (Page interview 2003).

1. Gigerenzer (2002) presents five central points about screening: (1) the purpose of screening is early detection; (2) screening does not reduce the incidence of a disease; (3) early detection can but does not necessarily lead to mortality reduction; (4)

screening, as in the case of mammography and the PSA test, may identify cancers that are unlikely to progress; and (5) early detection is not always beneficial. For these reasons, among others, the NBCC does not endorse mammography as a screening tool for women of any age.

2. Although elsewhere in this book we use the term *survivor,* here we use the term *persons with.* Because some of the people profiled in the news media died of these diseases, we determined that using the term *survivor* was inappropriate in this context. Our sample of profiles of persons with breast cancer did include a minute number of males—fewer than a dozen. That number was insufficient to run separate analyses. Thus, given the overwhelmingly large number of women profiled, we will refer to persons with breast cancer as "she" and "her" even though the disease strikes both men and women.

3. We were not able to analyze the racial and ethnic composition of the profiles because the vast majority of profiles did not mention the person's race or ethnicity. We used news stories downloaded from Lexis-Nexis and did not have access to any accompanying photographs.

4. For more information about the methodology, see the Methodological Appendix.

5. We were concerned that findings might be skewed because a large majority of the stories included profiles of prominent persons with the disease. Therefore, we conducted separate analyses of those stories that were not coded as personality stories. These analyses did not yield any different results and thus are not reported here.

6. These polls were identified through a search of a health public opinion database maintained by the Kaiser Family Foundation and the Roper Center.

7. We tried repeatedly and unsuccessfully to secure the 1979 NCI dataset as well.

8. When the age of the person profiled was listed by decade (e.g., "mid-fifties"), the mid-point was used (fifty-five).

9. This trend predated the Young Survival Coalition, which was founded in 1998, the last year included in the dataset. Thus the YSC's media relations efforts are not reflected in this analysis.

10. Ages of children were coded by year. The ages of up to three children were included but only when an exact age was listed. Mentions such as "two school aged children" were not included. Infants were coded as zero years.

11. The person was coded as a 1 if the story mentioned that the person was terminal or had died. If the story made no mention of the person's prognosis or if the prognosis was good, then the item was coded as 0.

12. The differences by gender exceed the study's margin of error in all cases but one.

13. See the Methodological Appendix for more details on this survey and its results.

14. This trend appears to continue. A 2002 poll conducted for the Avon Founda-

tion found that more than half (56 percent) of women surveyed believed that breast cancer was "one of the most critical health problems facing women at the present time." Breast cancer was mentioned more frequently than any other health condition or disease, including heart disease (34 percent), ovarian cancer (25 percent), and smoking (19 percent). The same survey found that more women believe they are "very likely" to develop breast cancer than to experience any other disease or injury, including heart disease. Not surprisingly, women who perceived that they were at highest risk of breast cancer also believed that breast cancer was one of the most critical health issues facing women (Avon Foundation 2002a, 2002b).

15. Chi-square analysis was used here ($r = 0.37$. $p = 0.0530$).

16. The second study is the 1998 National Election Study. Interviewers asked, "How many days in the past week did you read a daily newspaper?" and "How many days in the past week did you watch the national news on TV?" Respondents' answers varied from zero to seven. The correlation between these two questions is positive and fairly strong ($r = 0.25$; $p < 0.00$). The results did not change when the data were recoded as a dichotomous variable to approximate the wording of the Harris poll question, which asked simply whether or not respondents "watch television news."

Chapter 5: Media Advocacy Evidence

The first epigraph is from Fran Visco, president, National Breast Cancer Coalition, May 6, 2003; the second is from Richard Atkins, president, National Prostate Cancer Coalition, May 26, 2003. The number in the second epigraph is probably generated using a technique common in public relations—adding the circulations of all publications, or audience as defined by ratings, where one's organization is mentioned. Such calculations uniformly overestimate the impact of these mentions because they assume that everyone paid attention to the news coverage.

1. By contrast, one long-time health reporter for print and radio noted that she rarely covered congressional hearings featuring celebrities, considering them rather gimmicky. She did note that such events would be particularly attractive to television reporters because of their compelling visuals (Rovner interview 2003).

2. We use "consistent with" rather than "caused by" because we cannot definitively conclude that the observed changes in media coverage result from advocates' media advocacy efforts. In fact, increasing numbers of support and interest groups, and changes in media coverage and public policy, may be due to some unidentified, exogenous variable

3. Two more findings are in the expected direction but do not achieve statistical significance. First, there is a slight increase in the proportion of persons profiled with breast cancer who are terminal (1991–98) (table 34). Second, the average age of the persons with breast cancer dropped modestly (table 33). In addition, children's ages were mentioned, the average increasing from twelve years (1980–90) to eighteen (1991–98), a statistically significant difference (table 34). At first blush, this finding

appears contradictory, but two factors contradict that conclusion. First, there was wider variation in ages since 1991, demonstrating that many young children were included in both eras. Second, the nature of the data is highly skewed. Mentions of children of any age were phenomena of the advocacy era. These findings also indicate that the public face of breast cancer in the advocacy era communicated more urgency and tragedy.

Chapter 6: Two Cancers Go to Congress: Media Advocacy and the Policy Agenda

The first epigraph, from Barbara Vucanovich, is from 2000; the second epigraph is from 2003. An earlier version of this chapter appeared as "Gendering Cancer Policy" in *Women Transforming Congress,* edited by Cindy Simon Rosenthal (Norman: University of Oklahoma Press, 2002). This revision is published with permission of the University of Oklahoma Press.

1. Lung cancer is the leading cause of cancer deaths for both men and women.

2. The Congressional Caucus for Women's Issues (CCWI) was founded in 1977 as a bipartisan legislative service organization for women members of the House of Representatives. Its purpose is to advance legislation on issues important to women. In 1981 it expanded to include male members of Congress. It now exists as an informal caucus supported by the private nonprofit corporation, the Women's Policy Institute (Gertzog 1995; Hall interview 2003).

3. Bodai was diagnosed with prostate cancer in June 2000. He then pledged that his next effort would be to lobby for a prostate cancer semi-postal stamp (Bodai 2001).

4. As described in the introduction, other federal government initiatives explore the possible relationship between environmental pollution and breast cancer—particularly NCI studies of Marin County, California, and the Sisters Study that is underway at the NIH. These efforts are not analyzed here because they were not the result of congressional mandates.

5. The American Cancer Society also made the list, however it lobbies on behalf of all variety of cancers (Heaney 2003).

6. Breast cancer is a political issue at the state level as well. Most states have at least one grassroots advocacy organization that monitors state and federal legislation; some states have several such coalitions. State legislatures across the country have grappled with how to implement and fund the Breast and Cervical Cancer Treatment Act. In Arkansas, $4 million was appropriated initially from general purpose revenue and tobacco tax money (now only the latter) to provide diagnosis, travel, and follow-up care to uninsured women in the state (McDaniel interview, 2003). Both Illinois and California have state-funded breast cancer research programs, and protecting those has become an issue for activists (Brooks interview 2003). In 1998 support for breast cancer issues became an issue in the Colorado gubernatorial race, and in 2000 the Democratic candidate for governor of North Dakota was treated for breast cancer

during the campaign, which catapulted both health issues, breast cancer in particular, onto the agenda (Crowder 1998; Haga 2000).

7. There was also some administrative activity within federal agencies. In 1996, the year the NPCC was founded, the Veterans' Administration published its final rule stating that prostate cancer was a "presumptive" service-connected illness for those exposed to Agent Orange in the Vietnam War and, later, for those exposed to ionizing radiation in World War II. These administrative actions, however, did not appear to be promoted by prostate cancer advocates (United States Department of Veterans' Affairs 1996, 1997).

8. Prostate cancer has made some modest inroads in state legislatures. The Arkansas state legislature, for example, allocated a half million dollars in general improvement funds for prostate cancer and testicular cancer screening and education in 2001, considerably less than the $4 million allocated to breast cancer. The Arkansas Prostate Cancer Foundation administers the funds. About fourteen states have grassroots prostate cancer organizations, but most of them are small and staffed only by volunteers. Arkansas and Florida are the only two that have paid administrators for state-level prostate cancer organizations (Kossover interview 2003).

9. This list is compiled from newspaper articles, news releases, interviews, members' Web sites, and the Political Graveyard Web site (http://www.politicalgraveyard.com). It is almost certainly incomplete. Some of these individuals died.

10. When one of us contacted the office of one senator who is a prostate cancer survivor, and whose Web site featured a button dedicated solely to the senator's disease history and awareness efforts, the person who answered the telephone immediately said, "Well, you know Senator Y doesn't want to be known as the prostate cancer poster child."

11. The direct influence of the media on public policy change is hotly contested within the field of political science. Some scholars argue that the point of using the media—"going public" or using "outsider strategies"—is to shape public opinion. The public, in turn, will pressure policymakers to institute changes. Such a direct link is difficult at best to determine because, of course, media coverage is not the only factor that shapes public or elite opinion.

Media advocacy, however, expects advocates to court media attention and use traditional lobbying techniques simultaneously. The purpose is not only to raise public awareness but also to raise elites' awareness. Thus the advocate's message in a face-to-face meeting (insider strategy) will have more credibility. Because we looked for evidence that breast cancer and prostate cancer advocates used media advocacy strategies, determining whether increased media attention causes increased policy attention is not important. We merely need to look for the correlation between the two phenomena.

12. Offering testimony at congressional hearings is critical to disease politics. A mention in a report is an important signal to the Institutes of Health when it comes time for the allocation of funds (Stolberg 2002).

13. We use 1992 in the analysis of federal funding because FY 1992 was the first year in which we would see evidence of the NBCC's lobbying efforts. All other analyses use 1991.

14. The independent variable was the changes in the number of breast cancer stories from the previous year; the dependent variable was the changes in federal funding for the next fiscal year. This model is, of course, grossly oversimplified given the complexity involved in news reporting and the federal budget processes. Therefore, it is remarkable if the model is even modestly predictive and the independent variables reach or approach statistical significance.

15. We noticed the same linkage in media coverage as well. Journalists and medical experts alike frequently compared prostate cancer to breast cancer.

Chapter 7: Agenda Maintenance: The Politics of Issue Definition and Framing

Fran Visco (first epigraph) is president of the National Breast Cancer Coalition (May 6, 2003); the second epigraph is from E. E. Schattschneider (1960).

1. We recognize that the federal government is only one source for research funds for breast cancer. Private foundations, notably the Susan G. Komen Foundation and the Avon Foundation, also provide considerable resources. Private industries such as pharmaceutical companies also are major investors in medical research and development. Most news stories do not include references to the source of research funds in their coverage.

2. We used ordinary least squares regression analysis to make this point. This measure is inadequate for a couple of reasons. First, it does not account for the fact that medical research may take years to complete. Second, the media coverage usually did not disclose the source(s) of funding for the various medical discoveries reported.

3. The Komen Foundation also claims Herceptin as a success through its grant support to researchers who helped develop the drug (Balma interview 2003).

4. The NBCC is critical of the Long Island Breast Cancer Study Project, which it believes was too narrowly focused.

5. Access to screening remains on the agenda for some groups today.

6. Breast cancer organizations supported different versions of the bill. Reportedly, the Komen Foundation supported the George W. Bush administration's version, which included a cap on potential damages and blocked class-action lawsuits. The NBCC supported the Democratic alternative, which included neither provision (Swissler 2002).

7. The URLs for these organizations are the Connecticut Breast Cancer Coalition at http://www.cbccf.org/about.htm; the Florida Breast Cancer Coalition at http://www.fbccoalition.org/BreastCancerTag.asp; the Georgia Breast Cancer Coalition at http://www.gabcc.org/Accomplishments.htm; Ithaca Breast Cancer Alliance at http://www.ibca.net/ibc_about.html; Marin Breast Cancer Watch at http://www

.breastcancerwatch.org; and the Massachusetts Breast Cancer Coalition at http://www
.mbcc.org/. (All retrieved June 13, 2003).

8. One Internet search using the Altavista search engine and the keywords *breast
cancer epidemic* yielded twenty-five thousand hits. The conservative media critic
Michael Fumento states that a Nexis search of the words *breast cancer* within fifteen
words of the word *epidemic* yielded some 681 articles (Fumento n.d.)

9. This phrase was repeated by advocates attending the 2003 NBCC advocacy
conference.

10. According to American Cancer Society data, prostate cancer composes 16.5
percent of all cancers, including skin cancer. By comparison, breast cancer accounts
for 15.9 percent of all cancers, including skin cancer (ACS 2003d).

11. This measure is crude and does not account for multiyear projects and private
sources of funds.

12. The two points were to increase funding under the CDMRP to $100 million
and ask the NIH/NCI to produce a professional judgment budget to accompany its
prostate cancer research plan.

13. This phrase is adapted from the title of the book by Rebecca Dresser: *When
Science Offers Salvation* (2001). She uses the term, however, in a somewhat different
context.

14. As noted in the introduction, social constructions are tools for interpreting and
understanding empirical reality. Social constructions do not resonate if they do not,
in some way, reflect individuals' experiences. Feminism does call attention to real,
systematic discrimination against women.

Chapter 8: Ribbon Wars: Cause-related Marketing and the Selling of Breast Cancer and Prostate Cancer

Ronald Johnson (first epigraph), the associate director of the Gay Men's Health Clinic,
spoke at the National Breast Coalition's Annual Advocacy Conference, Washington,
D.C., on May 2, 2003; Elizabeth Woolfe (second epigraph) is from the National Alliance of Breast Cancer Organizations (interview Feb. 22, 2003).

1. Research has been inconclusive about the power of cause-related advertising
appeals and their impact on the behavior of subjects (Mizerski, Mizerski, and Sadler
2001; Sandler and Shani 1989).

Chapter 9: Policy Dilemmas and Maturing Movements

The first epigraph is from a National Breast Cancer Coalition employee (Jan. 2003);
Robert Samuels (second epigraph) is the former president of the National Prostate
Cancer Coalition (Steimle 1997).

1. One might wonder whether these dilemmas also derive from the American
health-care system that leaves millions uninsured. As one anonymous reviewer asked

us, "Do breast cancer/prostate cancer survivors in Canada have to do all of this: mark, bike, wear ribbons, have a dance marathon, whatever? Canada has a national health care system." The answer is, yes, they do. Advocates in Canada and in many countries of Western Europe, where universal health care exists, also raise money for medical research through various means, including walks and races; raise awareness of the disease; push for access to screening; and provide community support.

2. One criticism of the Long Island Breast Cancer Study is that it does not compare the pollution levels on Long Island to those found in other suburban areas around the country.

3. These dollars are not inflation-adjusted. We understand that the NCI is only one of several institutes within the larger NIH and that other institutes also devote resources to breast cancer and prostate cancer research. We also recognize that the NIH is only one of several agencies providing medical research funds. The NCI, however, is the premier federal cancer research agency, its grants are highly competitive and prestigious, and its mission is to fund cancer research for all types of cancer. Thus comparisons are possible using these data that are not possible elsewhere. It is also important to note that the NCI may apply funds from a single grant to several cancers if the potential discoveries have broad applications. Thus the percentages provided for each cancer are not mutually exclusive. Any changes observed will be muted because of this practice.

4. The funding data for the 1980s was provided by the National Cancer Institute through a Freedom of Information Act request. Because the NCI did not track the funding for all eighteen cancers through the entire twenty-year period, this graph includes some gaps.

5. This table includes NCI data for the 1990s because the data provided by the NCI from 1981 to 1989 are very sparse and do not include most cancers for these years. The 1990 data are more complete and include the entire advocacy period for both breast cancer and prostate cancer.

6. According to an official of the CDMRP, these diseases affect primarily children, which explains the inclusion of family members (interview 2003).

7. In addition, one advocate asserts men with prostate cancer who are undergoing hormonal treatment feel tired and unwell and have difficulty concentrating (Caputi interview 2003). That also mitigates their desire and ability to become active.

8. Some members of Congress even doubt the reliability of the information from the federal government, noting that some government Web sites prominently displayed what some view as flawed science touting the alleged link between breast cancer and abortion.

9. NABCO's Web site listed nineteen different support groups for lesbians with breast cancer (http://www.nabco.org). Among those for African American women are the Sisters Network (http://www.sistersnetworkinc.org/index.htm) and the African American Breast Cancer Alliance, based in Minneapolis (http://www.omhrc.gov). Those for Latinas include Nueva Vida (http://www.nueva-vida.org), and the most

notable among those for younger women is the Young Survival Coalition (http://www.youngsurvival.org/). NABCO's Web site provided information for five different support groups for men with breast cancer. A well-known group for persons with metastatic breast cancer is Club Mets-BC, an online support group (http://listserv.acor.org); the Metastatic Breast Cancer Web site is at http://www.bcmets.org. For women with inflammatory breast cancer, there is IBC Support at http://www.ibcsupport.org/ and the Inflammatory Breast Cancer Research Foundation (http://www.ibcresearch.org/). The National Lymphedema Network has listings for lymphedema support groups nationwide (http://www.lymphnet.org/support.html). Lymphedema is a complication of cancer surgery not limited to persons with breast cancer.

10. Medical professionals have long known, for example, that some breast cancers are estrogen-receptive whereas others are not (Olson 2002). Some are HER-2/neu–positive, and others are not (NBCCF 2003). Some are a result of a genetic mutation, and others are not. Some respond to chemotherapy, and others do not. Some women with breast cancer confined to the milk ducts, known as ductal carcinoma in situ (DCIS), will see their cancers spread outside the ducts. Others will not. In addition, inflammatory breast cancer and Paget's Disease of the Breast do not develop as tumors. They develop as rashes, mimic the symptoms of mastitis, develop as a crust on the surface of the breast, or result in a nipple discharge.

References

Abrams, Herbert L., and Richard Brody. 1998. "Bob Dole's Age and Health in the 1996 Election: Did the Media Let Us Down?" *Political Science Quarterly* 113(3): 471–91.

"Activism's Toll: The US Congress Must Reverse Its Growing Tendency to Play the Role of Peer Reviewer." 1992. *Nature* 360(6399): 2.

Adams, Ronald J., and Kenneth M. Jennings. 1993. "Media Advocacy: A Case Study of Philip Sokolof's Cholesterol Awareness Campaigns." *Journal of Consumer Affairs* 27(1): 145–65.

Altman, Roberta. 1996. *Waking Up, Fighting Back: The Politics of Breast Cancer.* Boston: Little Brown.

Alzheimer's Association. 2003. "Federal Legislative Priorities." http://www.alz.org/GetInvolved/Advocate/fed.html (retrieved March 17, 2003).

Amaya, Hector. 2004. "Photography as Technology of the Self: Matuschka's Art and Breast Cancer." *International Journal of Qualitative Studies in Education* 17(4): 557–73.

American Cancer Society (ACS). 1998. "Cancer Facts and Figures 1998." http://www.cancer.org/downloads/STT/F&F98.pdf (retrieved July 24, 2003).

———. 2002a. "Cancer Facts and Figures 2001." http://www.cancer.org/downloads/STT/F&F2001.pdf (retrieved Nov. 14, 2002).

———. 2002b. "What Are the Risk Factors for Breast Cancer?" http://www.cancer.org (retrieved Nov. 14, 2002).

———. 2002c. "Tamoxifen and Raloxifene to Reduce Breast Cancer Risk: Questions and Answers." http://www.cancer.org (retrieved Nov. 14, 2002).

———. 2002d. "How Many Men Get Prostate Cancer?" http://www.cancer.org (retrieved Oct. 8, 2002).

———. 2002e. "What are the Risk Factors for Breast Cancer?" http://www.cancer.org (retrieved Oct. 8, 2002).

———. 2002f. "Best Father's Day Gift: Have the Men in Your Life Get a Checkup, Get Screened." ACS News release (June 14). http://www.cancer.org. (retrieved July 20, 2003).

———. 2003a. "ACS Man to Man Program Background." http://www.cancer.org (retrieved April 8, 2003).

———. 2003b. "Can Breast Cancer Be Found Early?" http://www.cancer.org (retrieved June 13, 2003).

———. 2003c. "Value of Mammography Questioned; Experts Support Screening." http://www.cancer.org (retrieved June 13, 2003).

———. 2003d. "Cancer Facts and Figures 2003." http://www.cancer.org (retrieved June 17, 2003).

———. 2003e. "Overview: Leukemia—Children's. How Many Children Get Leukemia?" http://www.cancer.org/docroot/CRI/content/CRI_2_2_1X_What_is _leukemia_24.asp?sitearea= (retrieved June 25, 2003).

———. 2003f. "Look Good . . . Feel Better." http://www.cancer.org (retrieved July 28, 2003).

———. 2003g. "Let's Talk About It." http://www.cancer.org/docroot/M2M/ content/M2M_2_7_1x_Lets_Talk_About_It_2002_01.asp?sitearea= (retrieved July 28, 2003).

———. 2005a. "What Are the Risk Factors for Breast Cancer?" http://www.cancer .org/docroot/CRI/content/CRI_2_4_2X_What_are_the_risk_factors_for_breast _cancer_5.asp (retrieved Aug. 11, 2005).

———. 2005b. "Cancer Facts & Figures, 2005." http://www.cancer.org/docroot/STT/ content/STT_1x_Cancer_Facts__Figures_2005.asp (retrieved Aug. 11, 2005).

American Foundation for Urologic Disease (AFUD). n.d. "For Immediate Release." www.afud.org (retrieved April 7,2003).

———. 2003. "Comparison of Prostate Cancer, Breast Cancer and AIDS." http:// www.afud.org (retrieved April 7, 2003).

American Heart Association. 2003. "Heart Disease and Stroke Statistics 2003 Update." http://www.americanheart.org/downloadable/heart/10461207852142003 HDSStatsBook.pdf (retrieved July 18, 2003).

American Lyme Disease Foundation. 2005. "What Is Lyme Disease?" http://www .aldf.com/Lyme.asp (retrieved July 14, 2005).

American Medical Association (AMA). 2005. "Physicians by Gender." www.ama-assn .org/ama/pub/category/print/12912.html (retrieved June 6, 2005).

American Prostate Society. 2001. "Home Page." http://www.ameripros.org/index .html (retrieved July 27, 2003).

Andejeski, Yvonne, Erica S. Breslau, Elizabeth Hart, Ngina Lythcott, Linda Alexander, Irene Rich, Isabelle Bisceglio, Helene S. Smith, Fran M. Visco, and the U.S. Army Medical Research and Materiel Command Fiscal Year 1995 Breast Cancer Research Program Integration Panel. 2002a. "Benefits and Drawbacks of Including

Consumer Reviewers in the Scientific Merit Review of Breast Cancer Research." *Journal of Women's Health and Gender-Based Medicine* 11(2): 119–36.

———, Isabelle T. Bisceglio, Kay Dickersin, Jean E. Johnson, Sabina I. Robinson, Helene S. Smith, Frances M. Visco, and Irene M. Rich. 2002b. "Quantitative Impact of Including Consumers in the Scientific Review of Breast Cancer Research Proposals." *Journal of Women's Health and Gender-Based Medicine* 11(4): 379–88.

Anderson, Christopher. 1992. "Opponents of US Earmarks Propose Reviews to Temper Worst Elements of Growing Practice." *Nature* 360(6399): 4.

Anderson, Robert N., and Betty L. Smith. 2005. "Deaths: Leading Causes: 2002." *National Vital Statistics Reports* 53(17): 1–90.

Andreason, Alan R., and Minette E. Drumwright. 2001. "Alliances and Ethics in Social Marketing." In *Ethics in Social Marketing,* edited by Alan R. Andreason, 95–124. Washington, D.C.: Georgetown University Press.

Anglin, Mary K. 1997. "Working from the Inside Out: Implications of Breast Cancer Activism for Biomedical Policies and Practices." *Social Science and Medicine* 44(9): 1403–15.

Andsager, Julie, and Angela Powers. 1999. "Social or Economic Concerns: How News and Women's Magazines Framed Breast Cancer in the 1990s." *Journalism and Mass Communication Quarterly* 76(3): 531–50.

———, Stacey J. T. Hust, and Angela Powers. 2000. "Patient-Blaming and Representation of Risk Factors in Breast Cancer Images." *Women and Health* 31(2–3): 57–77.

Arno, Peter S., and Karyn L. Feidan. 1992. *Against the Odds: The Story of AIDS.* New York: Harpers Perennial.

Arnold, R. Douglas. 1990. *The Logic of Congressional Action.* New Haven: Yale University Press.

Artists About AIDS. 2003. "Red Ribbon: The History." http://www.artists-about-aids .com/en/rrhistory.htm (retrieved March 17, 2003).

Asbury, Herbert. 1929. *Carrie Nation.* New York: Alfred A. Knopf.

Aschermann, Kurt. 2002. "The Ten Commandments of Cause-Related Marketing." Cause Marketing Forum. www.causemarketingforum.com/page.asp?ID=103 (retrieved May 6, 2003).

Atkins, Richard N. 2003a. "The Importance of Rese-arch Dollars." Presentation before the NPCC Spring Training Advocacy Conference. May 21.

———. 2003b. "Statement of Richard N. Atkins, MD, before the Defense Appropriations Subcommittee." May 7.

Aumente, Jerome. "A Medical Breakthrough." *American Journalism Review* 17(10) (1995): 27–32.

Auster, Elizabeth. 2000. "With Super Tuesday behind Them, Gore and Bush Gird for Single Combat; Misleading McCain Ad Should Haunt Bush." *Cleveland Plain Dealer,* March 9, 11B.

Avon Foundation. 2002a. "Avon Women's Health Index." http://www.avoncompany
.com/women/survey/finaldecklogo.PDF (retrieved May 12, 2003).

———. 2002b. "Breast Cancer a 'Critical' Health Issue for More than Half of U.S. Women According to Avon Survey." http://www.avoncompany.com/women/ avoncrusade/news/press20021017.htm (retrieved Jan. 28, 2003).

———. 2003. "Avon Breast Cancer Crusade." www.avoncompany.com/women/ avoncrusade/background/;overview.shtml (retrieved Jan. 31, 2003).

———. 2005. "Walk Around the World." www.avonfoundation.org (retrieved Dec. 19, 2006).

Backer, Thomas E., Everett M. Rogers, and Pradeep Sopory. 1992. *Designing Health Communication Campaigns: What Works?* Beverly Hills: Sage Publications.

"Bad Blood: The Troubling Legacy of the Tuskegee Syphilis Study." n.d. University of Virginia Health System. http://www.med.virginia.edu/hs- library/historical/ apology.index.html (retrieved Feb. 11, 2003).

Ball, Howard. 1986. *Justice Downwind: America's Atomic Testing Program in the 1950s.* New York: Oxford University Press.

Baran, Stanley J., and Dennis K. Davis. 1995. *Mass Communication Theory: Foundations, Ferment and Future.* Belmont, Calif.: Wadsworth.

Barker-Plummer, Bernadette. 2002. "Producing Public Voice: Resource Mobilization and Media Access in the National Organization for Women." *Journalism and Mass Communication Quarterly* 79(1): 188–205.

Batt, Sharon. 1994. *Patient No More: The Politics of Breast Cancer.* Charlottetown, P.E.I., Canada: Gynergy Books.

Baumgartner, Frank R., and Bryan D. Jones. 1993. *Agendas and Instability in American Politics.* Chicago: University of Chicago Press.

Bayliss, Francoise, Jocelyn Downie, and Susan Sherwin. 1998. "Reframing Research Involving Humans." In *The Politics of Women's Health: Exploring Agency and Autonomy,* edited by Susan Sherwin, 234–60. Philadelphia: Temple University Press.

Ben and Jerry's. 2005. "Fifty Ways to Support Peace." http:www.benjerry.com/our_ company (retrieved Aug. 30, 2005).

Benetton. 2005. "Our Communication: Last Campaigns." http://www.benettongroup .com/en/whatwesa/ (retrieved July 30, 2005).

Benford, Robert D. 1993. "Frame Disputes with the Nuclear Disarmament Movement." *Social Forces* 71(3): 677–701.

Berman, Maxine. 1994. "The Politics of Breast Cancer: A State Representative Takes Aim at Her Colleagues." *Detroit Monthly* 17(7): 50–51.

Bernhardt. B. A., G. Geller, E. Tambor, E. Mountcastle-Shah, J. G. Mulle, and N. A. Holtzman. 2000. "Analysis of Media Reports of Breast and Prostate Cancer Susceptibility Genes." *American Journal of Human Genetics* 67 (4): 62.

Berry, Jeffrey M. 1997. *Lobbying for the People: The Public Behavior of Interest Groups.* Princeton: Princeton University Press.

Bill-Axelson, Anna, Lars Holmberg, Mirja Ruutu, Micheal Haggman, Swen-Olof Anderson, Stefan Bratell, Anders Spanberg, Christer Bush, Stig Nordling, Hans Garmo, Juni Palmgren, Hans-Olov Adami, Bo Johan Norlen, and Jan-Erik Johansson. 2005. "Radical Prostatectomy versus Watchful Waiting in Early Prostate Cancer." *New England Journal of Medicine,* May 12, 1977–85.

Black, William C., Robert F. Nease Jr., and Anna N. A. Tosteson. 1995. "Perceptions of Breast Cancer Risk and Screening Effectiveness in Women Younger Than Fifty Years of Age." *Journal of the National Cancer Institute* 87(10): 720–31.

Blendon, Robert J., Kimberly Scoles, Catherine DesRoches, John T. Young, Melissa J. Herrmann, Jennifer L. Schmidt, and Minah Kim. 2001. "Americans' Health Priorities: Curing Cancer and Controlling Costs." *Health Affairs* 20(6): 222–32.

Bodai, Ernie. 2001. "In Their Own Words: One Man's Mission Against Cancer." *Bulletin of the American College of Surgeons* 86(2): 28–30.

Boehmer, Ulrike. 2000. *The Personal and the Political: Women's Activism in Response to the Breast Cancer and AIDS Epidemics.* Albany: State University of New York Press.

Boffey, Phillip M., Joann Ellison Rogers, and Stephen H. Schneider. 1999. "Interpreting Uncertainty: A Panel Discussion." In *Communicating Uncertainty,* edited by Sharon M. Friedman, Sharon Dunwoody, and Carol L. Rogers, 81–95. Mahwah, N.J.: Lawrence Erlbaum.

Boodman, Sandra G. 1995. "Self-Interest Yields High Profile on Hill." *Washington Post,* May 23, Z20.

Bordin, Ruth. 1981. *Women and Temperance: The Quest for Power and Liberty, 1873–1900.* Philadelphia: Temple University Press.

Boring, Catherine C., Teresa S. Squires, and Tony Tong. 1992. "Cancer Statistics, 1992." *Ca: A Cancer Journal for Clinicians* 42(1): 19–38.

Boston Health Collective. 1994. *The New Our Bodies Our Selves.* New York: Simon and Schuster.

Botsch, Robert E. 1993. *Organizing the Breathless: Cotton Dust, Southern Politics and the Brown Lung Association.* Lexington: University Press of Kentucky.

"Brand Names: The Folks behind the Best Work of 2002." 2003. www.promomagazine.com 16(2): 28–39.

Brenner, Barbara A. 2000. "Sister Support: Women Create a Breast Cancer Movement." In *Breast Cancer: Society Shapes an Epidemic,* edited by Anne S. Kasper and Susan J. Ferguson, 325–53. New York: St. Martin's Press.

Brewer, M., and B. McCombs. 1996. "Setting the Community Agenda." *Journalism and Mass Communication Quarterly* 73(1): 7–16.

Bricker-Jenkins, Mary. 1994. "Feminist Practice and Breast Cancer: 'The Patriarchy Has Claimed My Right Breast.'" *Social Work in Health Care* 19(3–4): 17–42.

Brown, Clyde, and Herbert Waltzer. 2002. "Lobbying the Press: 'Talk to the People to Talk to America.'" In *Interest Group Politics,* 3d ed., edited by Allen J. Cigler and Burdett A. Loomis, 249–74. Washington, D.C.: CQ Press.

Brown, Jane D., and Edna F. Einsiedel. 1990. "Public Health Campaigns: Mass Media Strategies." In *Communication and Health: Systems and Applications,* edited by Eileen B. Ray and Lewis Donohoew, 153–70. Hillsdale, N.J.: Lawrence Erlbaum Associates, 1990.

Brown, Phil, Stephen M. Zavestoski, Sabrina McCormick, Joshua Mandelbaum, and Theo Luebke. 2001. "Print Media Coverage of Environmental Causation of Breast Cancer." *Sociology of Health and Illness* 12(6): 747–75.

———, ———, ———, Brian Mayer, Rachel Morello-Frosch, and Rebecca Gasior Altman. 2004. "Embodied Social Movements: New Approaches to Social Movements in Health." *Sociology of Health and Illness* 26(1): 50–80.

Bullard, Robert D. 1990. *Dumping in Dixie: Race, Class and Environmental Quality.* Boulder: Westview Press.

Burke, Wylie, Amy H. Olsen, Linda E. Pinsky, Susan E. Reynolds, and Nancy A. Press. 2001. "Misleading Presentation of Breast Cancer in Popular Magazines." *Effective Clinical Practice* 4(2): 58–64.

Bykerk, Loree, and Ardith Maney. 1995. "Consumer Groups and Coalition Practices on Capitol Hill." In *Interest Group Politics,* 4th ed., edited by Allen J. Ciger and Burdett Loomis, 259–79. Washington, D.C.: CQ Press.

California Breast Cancer Research Program. 2005. "Marin County Breast Cancer Study of Adolescent Risk Factors." http://www.cbcrp.org/research/PageGrant .asp?grant_id=1709 (retrieved Aug. 11, 2005).

Callaghan, K., and F. Schnell. 2001. "Assessing the Democratic Debate: How the News Media Frame Elite Policy Discourse." *Political Communication* 18(2): 183–214.

CaPCure. 2002a. "About Us." http://www.capcure.org/aboutus/aboutus .asp?param=aboutus (retrieved Nov. 21, 2002).

———. 2002b. "Our Achievements." http://www.capcure.org/aboutus/OurAchieve- ments.asp?mainid=1&subid=3&param=aboutus (retrieved Nov. 22, 2002).

———. 2002c. "Wear the Blue Ribbon." http://www.capcure.org/GetInvolved/index2 .html (retrieved Nov. 22, 2002).

Capstone Communications. 2003. "Statistics on Sexual Harassment." http://www .capstn.com/stats.html (retrieved July 24, 2003).

Carpenter, Daniel P. 2002. "Groups, the Media, Agency Waiting Costs, and FDA Drug Approval." *American Journal of Political Science* 46(3): 490–505.

Carson, Rachel. 1964. *Silent Spring.* Boston: Houghton Mifflin.

Cartwright, Lisa. 1998. "Community and the Public Body in Breast Cancer Media Activism." *Cultural Studies* 12(2): 117–38.

Casamayou, Maureen Hogan. 2001. *The Politics of Breast Cancer.* Washington, D.C.: Georgetown University Press.

Cause Marketing Forum. 2003. "Conversations with Cause Marketers: Carol Cone." http://www.causemarketingforum.com/page.asp?ID=177 (retrieved May 6, 2003).

———. 2005. "The Growth of Cause Marketing." www.causemarketingforum.com/ page.asp?iD=188 (retrieved July 30, 2005).

Center for the American Woman and Politics. 2003. "Fact Sheet: Sex Differences in Voter Turn Out." http://www.rci.rutgers.edu/~cawp/pdf/sexdiff.pdf (retrieved March 21, 2003).

Centers for Disease Control and Prevention. 1994. "Summary of Notifiable Diseases, United States 1993." *Morbidity and Mortality Weekly Report* 42(43): 1–73.

———. 1995. "Summary of Notifiable Diseases, United States 1994." *Morbidity and Mortality Weekly Report* 43(53): 3–80.

———. 1998. "How Long Does It Take for HIV to Cause AIDS?" http://www.cdc .gov/hiv/pubs/faq/faq4.htm (retrieved Jan. 8, 2003).

———. 2000. "HIV Infection Cases by Sex, Age at Diagnosis and Race/Ethnicity, Reported through December 1998, from Thirty-three Areas with Confidential HIV Infection Reporting." *Surveillence Report* 10(2). http://www.cdc.gov/hiv/stats/ hasr1002/table8.htm (retrieved June 9, 2003).

———. 2002. "Screening. Prostate Cancer: U.S. Preventive Services Task Force Update, 2002 Release." http://www.cdc.gov (retrieved June 2003).

———. 2003a. "National Diabetes Fact Sheet." http://www.cdd.gov/diabetes/pubs/ estimates.htm (retrieved June 24, 2003).

———. 2003b. *Morbidity and Mortality Weekly Report: Special Focus Surveillance for Sexually Transmitted Diseases.* Aug. 13.

Center for Prostate Disease Research. 2003. "The History of CPDR." http://www .cpdr.org/pop_up/history.html (retrieved July 31, 2003).

Chan, Evelyn C. Y., Sally W. Vernon, Frederick T. O'Donnell, Chul Ahn, Anthony Greisinger, and Donnie W. Aga. 2003. "Informed Consent for Cancer Screening with Prostate-Specific Antigen: How Well Are Men Getting the Message?" *American Journal of Public Health* 93(5): 779–85.

Chesney, James D. 1984. "Citizen Participation on Regulatory Boards." *Journal of Health Politics, Policy and Law* 9(1): 125–35.

Chopyak, Jill, and Peter Levesque. 2002. "Public Participation in Science and Technology Decision Making: Trends for the Future." *Technology in Society* 24: 155–66.

Clarke, Juanne N. 1992. "Cancer, Heart Disease and AIDS: What Do the Media Tell Us About These Diseases?" *Health Communication* 4(2): 105–20.

———. 1999a. "Breast Cancer in Mass Circulating Magazines in the U.S.A and Canada, 1974–1995." *Women and Health* 28(4): 113–30.

———. 1999b. "Prostate Cancer's Hegemonic Masculinity in Select Print Mass Media Depictions, 1974–1995." *Health Communication* 11(1): 59–74.

Clinton, William Jefferson. 1997. "Remarks by the President in Apology for Study Done in Tuskegee." May 16. http://clinton4.nara.gov/textonly/New/Remarks/ Fri/19970516–898.html (retrieved Feb. 11, 2003).

Cobb, Roger W., and Charles D. Elder. 1972. *Participation in American Politics: The Dynamics of Agenda Building.* Baltimore: Johns Hopkins University Press.

Cohen, Peter F. 1997. "'All They Needed': AIDS, Consumption and the Politics of Class." *Journal of the History of Sexuality* 8(1): 86–115.

Cohn, Victor. 1989. *News and Numbers: A Guide to Reporting Statistical Claims and Controversies in Health and Other Fields.* Ames: Iowa State University Press.

Colby, David C., and Timothy E. Cook. 1991. "Epidemics and Agendas: The Politics of Nightly News Coverage of AIDS." *Journal of Health Politics, Policy and Law* 16(2): 215–49.

Congressional Black Caucus Foundation. 2003a. "CBCF Health." http://www.cbcfhealth.org/content/catContentID354 (retrieved July 29, 2003).

———. 2003b. "Farrakhan Launches Prostate Cancer Foundation." http://www.cbchealth.org/content/contentID/1845 (retrieved July 20, 2003).

Conway, Margaret M., Gertrude A. Steuernagel, and David Ahern. 1997. *Women and Political Participation: Cultural Change in the Political Arena.* Washington, D.C.: CQ Press.

Cook, Fay Lomax, Tom R. Tyler, Edward G. Goetz, Margaret T. Gordon, David Protess, Donna R. Leff, and Harvey L. Molotch. 1983. "Media and Agenda Setting: Effects on the Public, Interest Group Leaders, Policy Makers and Policy." *Public Opinion Quarterly* 47: 16–35.

Cooper, Crystale Purvis, and Darcie Yukimura. 2002. "Science Writers' Reactions to a Medical 'Breakthrough' Story." *Social Science and Medicine* 54: 1887–96.

Corbett, Julia B., and Motomi Mori. 1999a. "Medicine, Media and Celebrities: News Coverage of Breast Cancer, 1960–1995." *Journalism and Mass Communication Quarterly* 76(2): 229–49.

———. 1999b. "Gender-Specific Cancers, Gender-Specific Reporters?: Twenty-four Years of Network TV Coverage." *Science Communication* 20(4): 395–408.

Costain, Anne N. 1992. *Inviting Women's Rebellion: A Political Process Interpretation of the Women's Movement.* Baltimore: Johns Hopkins University Press.

Costain, Anne N., and Heather Frazier. 2003. "Congress and the Transformation of the Woman's Movement." In *Women Transforming Congress,* edited by Cindy Simon Rosenthal, 69–94. Norman: University of Oklahoma Press.

Craft, Stephanie, and Wayne Wanta. 2004. "Women in the Newsroom: Influences of Female Editors and Reporters on the News Agenda." *Journalism and Mass Communication Quarterly* 81(1): 124–38.

Crowder, Carla. 1998. "Candidates' Old Votes Return to Confront Them: Owens, Schoettler Dig Deep into Past to Expose Health Care, Bond Issues." *Denver Rocky Mountain News,* Oct. 14, 7A.

Culliton, Barbara J. 1992. "Disease-of-the-Month Alive and Well." *Nature,* Nov. 5, 13.

Cunningham, Randy "Duke." 2001. "Cunningham Submits Testimony in Support of Men's Health." Press release, June 27. http://www.house.gov/cunningham (retrieved Jan. 30, 2003).

Dahl, Robert A. 1961. *Who Governs? Democracy and Power in an American City.* New Haven: Yale University Press.

Damon Harris Cancer Foundation. 2003. "Mission Statement." http://www .dhcancerfoundation.com/mission.htm (retrieved July 29, 2003).

Daniels, Cora. 2004. "The Man Who Changed Medicine." *Fortune,* Nov. 29, 90–112.

de Semir, Vladimir. 1996. "What Is Newsworthy?" *The Lancet* 347(9009): 1163–66.

Dearing, James W., and Everett M. Rogers. 1996. *Agenda-Setting.* Thousand Oaks, Calif.: Sage Publications.

Deary, Ian J., Martha C. Whiteman, and F. G. R. Fowkes. 1998. "Medical Research and the Popular Media." *The Lancet* 351(9117): 1726–27.

DeJong, William. 1996. "MADD Massachusetts versus Senator Burke: A Media Advocacy Case Study." *Health Education Quarterly* 23(3): 318–29.

Denberg, Thomas D., Brenda L. Beaty, Fernando J. Kim, and John F. Steiner. 2005. "Marriage and Ethnicity Predict Treatment in Localized Prostate Cancer." *Cancer.* Published Online: March 28. DOIU:10.1002/cncr.20982 (retrieved June 19, 2005).

Derthick, Martha A. 2002. *Up in Smoke: From Legislation to Litigation in Tobacco Politics.* Washington, D.C.: CQ Press.

DeShazer, Mary K. 2003. "Fractured Borders: Women's Cancer and Feminist Theatre." *NWSA Journal* 15(2): 1–26.

Dickersin, Kay, Lundy Braun, Margaret Mead, Robert Millikan, Anna W. Wu, Jennifer Pietenpol, Susan Troyan, Benjamin Anderson, and Frances Visco. 2001. "Development and Implementation of a Science Training Course for Breast Cancer Activists: Project LEAD (Leadership, Education, Advocacy, and Development)." *Health Expectations* 4: 213–20.

Dimock, Susan Halebsky. 2003. "Demanding Disease Dollars: How Activism and Institutions Shape Medical Research Funding for Breast and Prostate Cancer." Ph.D. diss., University of California, San Diego.

Donovan, Mark C. 1996. "The Politics of Deservedness: The Ryan White Care Act and the Social Constructions of People with AIDS." In *AIDS: The Politics and Policy of Disease,* edited by Stella Z. Theodoulou, 68–87. Upper Saddle River, N.J.: Prentice-Hall.

———. 2001. *Taking Aim: Target Populations and the Wars on AIDS and Drugs.* Washington, D.C.: Georgetown University Press.

Dorfman, Lori, Helen Helpin Schauffler, John Wilkerson, and Judith Feinson. 1996. "Local Television Coverage of President Clinton's Introduction of the Health Security Act." *JAMA: Journal of the American Medical Association* 275(15): 1201–5.

Downs, Anthony. 1972. "Up and Down with Ecology: The 'Issue Attention Cycle.'" *Public Interest* 28(2): 38–50.

Dreifus, Claudia, ed. 1997. *Seizing Our Bodies: The Politics of Women's Health.* New York: Vintage Books.

Dresser, Rebecca. 1992. "Wanted: Single, White Male for Medical Research." *Hastings Center Report* 22(1): 24–30.

———. 1998. "Setting Priorities for Science Support." *Hastings Center Report* 28(3): 21–23.

———. 2001. *When Science Offers Salvation: Patient Advocacy and Research Ethics.* New York: Oxford University Press.

Eaton, Howard, Jr. 1989. "Agenda-Setting with Biweekly Data on Content of Three National Media." *Journalism Quarterly* 66: 942–59.

Edelman, Murray. 1964. *The Symbolic Uses of Politics.* Urbana: University of Illinois Press.

Edsall, Thomas B. 2002. "EMILY'S List Makes a Name for Itself: Pro-Choice Democratic Women's Lobby Is Proving a Powerful Opponent." *Washington Post,* April 21, 5A.

Edwards, George C. III, and B. Dan Wood. 1999. "Who Influences Whom? The President, Congress and the Media." *American Political Science Review* 93(2): 327–44.

Ehrenrich, Barbara. 2001. "Welcome to Cancerland." *Harper's Magazine* 303 (Nov): 1818.

———, and Deirdre English. 2005. *For Her Own Good: Two Centuries of Experts' Advice to Women.* Rev. ed. New York: Anchor Books.

Einwohner, Rachel, Jocelyn A. Hollander, and Toska Olson. 2000. "Engendering Social Movements: Cultural Images and Movement Dynamics." *Gender & Society* 14(5): 679–99.

Eisenstein, Zillah. 2001. *Manmade Breast Cancers.* Ithaca: Cornell University Press.

Entman, Robert M. 1993. "Framing Toward Clarification of a Fractured Paradigm." *Journal of Communication* 42(4).

Entwhistle, Vikki. 1995. "Reporting Research in Medical Journals and Newspapers." *British Medical Journal* 310: 920–23.

Epstein, Samuel S. 1978. *The Politics of Cancer.* San Francisco: Sierra Club Books.

Epstein, Steven. 1996. *Impure Science: AIDS, Activism and the Politics of Knowledge.* Berkley: University of California Press.

Evans, Becky. 2003. "Lung Cancer War Seeks Money, Respect." *Arizona Republic,* Nov. 12, A16.

Fagin, Dan. 2002a. "Tattered Hopes: A $30 million Federal Study of Breast Cancer and Pollution on LI Has Disappointed Activists and Scientists." *Newsday,* July 28. http://www.newsday.com/news/local/longisland/ny-licanc0728.story (retrieved June 6, 2003).

———. 2002b. "So Many Things Went Wrong: Costly Search for Links Between Pollution and Breast Cancer Was Hobbled from the Start, Critics Say." *Newsday,* July 2. http://www.newsday.com/news/local/longisland/ny-licanc0729.story (retrieved June 6, 2003).

Family to Family. 2002a. "WSPCa Home Page." http://www.pcafamily.org/default .html (retrieved Nov. 22, 2002).

———. "History." 2002b. http://www.pcafamily.org/Family_to_Family_history.htm (retrived Nov. 22, 2002).

———. 2002c. "Get Involved in Prostate Cancer Advocacy and Be Thankful for the

Lives You Will Change . . ." http://www.pcafamily.org/Family_to_Family_advocacy .htm (retrieved Nov. 22, 2002).

Fan, David P., and Lois Norem. 1992. "The Media and the Fate of the Medicare Catastrophic Extension Act." *Journal of Health Politics, Policy and Law* 17(1): 39–70.

Fee, Kevin. 2000. "No Place for Politics: Breast Cancer Treatment Debacle Shows What Happens When Politics Interferes with Science." *Modern Healthcare,* May 22, 48.

Feitelberg, Rosemary, and David Moin. 2002. "Shopping for a Cause." *WWD* [online edition], Sept. 20, 20.

Ferguson, Susan J. 2000. "Deformities and Diseased: Medicalization of Women's Breasts." In *Breast Cancer: Society Shapes an Epidemic,* edited by Anne S. Kasper and Susan J. Ferguson, 51–88. New York: St. Martin's Press.

Ferraro, Susan. 1993. "The Anguished Politics of Breast Cancer." *New York Times Magazine,* Aug. 15, 24–27, 58, 61–62.

"A Fight Worth Funding." 1998. *St. Petersburg Times,* Sept. 4, 20A.

Fisher, Alan C., and Wendy Worth. 1995. *Update: Is There a Cancer Epidemic in the United States?* Report published by the American Council on Science and Health.

Fitzgerald, Amy. 1996. "Oak Ridge Community Shapes DOE's Future." *Forum for Applied Research and Public Policy* 11(4): 125–28.

Fletcher, Suzanne W. 1997. "Whither Scientific Deliberation in Health Policy Recommendations? Alice in the Wonderland of Breast Cancer Screening." *New England Journal of Medicine* 336(16): 1180–83.

Foreman, Christopher H. Jr. 1994. *Plagues, Products and Politics: Emergent Public Health Hazards and National Policy Making.* Washington, D.C.: Brookings Institution.

———. 1995. "Grassroots Victim Organizations: Mobilizing for Personal and Public Health. In *Interest Group Politics,* 4th ed, edited by Allan J. Cigler, and Burdett A. Loomis, 33–53. Washington, D.C.: CQ Press.

Fosket, Jennifer R., Angela Karran, and Christine LaFia. 2000. "Breast Cancer in Popular Women's Magazines from 1913–1996." In *Breast Cancer: Society Shapes an Epidemic,* edited by Anne S. Kasper, and Susan J. Ferguson, 202–323. New York: St. Martin's Press.

Freimuth, Vicki S., Rachel Greenberg, Jean DeWitt, and Rose Mary Romano. 1984. "Covering Cancer: Newspapers and the Public Interest." *Journal of Communication* 34(Winter): 62–73.

Fristschler, Barbara, and James M. Hoefler. 1996. *Smoking and Politics: Policy Making and the Federal Bureaucracy.* 5th ed. New York: Anchor Books.

Fumento, Michael. n.d. "Who's Stirring Up Breast Cancer Fear?" http://www .consumeralert.org/fumento/breast2.htm (retrieved June 13, 2003).

Funkhouser, G. Ray. 1973. "Trends in Media Coverage of the Issues of the Sixties." *Journalism Quarterly* 50(3): 533–38.

"Future of Labor-HHS Measure Clouded by Veto Threat." 1991. *Congressional Quarterly Weekly Report,* Sept. 14, 2624–27.

Gammon, Marillie D., Joan E. Bertin, and Mary Beth Terry. 1996. "Abortion and the Risk of Breast Cancer: Is There a Believable Association?" *Journal of the American Medical Association* 275(4): 321–23.

Gamson, William A., and Andre Modigliani. 1989. "Media Discourse and Public Opinion on Nuclear Power: A Constructionist Approach." *American Journal of Sociology* 95(1): 1–37.

Gandy, Oscar. 1982. *Beyond Agenda Setting: Information Subsidies and Public Policy.* Norwood, N.J.: Abex Publishing.

Gardner, Amy, and Rob Christensen. 2004. "Election Board Rules Easley Ad Legal." *Raleigh* (N.C.) *News Observer,* Oct. 12, B5.

Garloch, Karen. 1996. "Facing Prostate Cancer." *Charlotte Observer,* Sept. 16, 1E, 8E.

Garnick, Mark. 1994. "The Dilemmas of Prostate Cancer." *Scientific American* 270(4): 72–81.

Gaventa, John. 1980. *Power and Powerlessness: Quiescence and Rebellion in an Appalachian Valley.* Urbana: University of Illinois Press.

Gerbner, George and Larry Gross. 1976. "Living with Television: The Violence Profile." *Journal of Communication* 26(2): 172–94.

Gertzog, Irwin. 1995. *Congressional Women: Their Recruitment, Integration and Behavior.* Rev. ed. Westport: Praeger Publishers.

Gibb, Fiona. 1994. "Avon: Cause Marketing." *Sales and Marketing Management* [electronic version] 146(10): 85.

Gibbs, Lois M., and Murray Levine. 1982. *Love Canal: My Story.* Albany: State University of New York Press.

Gigerenzer, Gerd. 2002. *Calculated Risks: How to Know When Numbers Deceive You.* New York: Simon and Schuster.

Gillette Company. 2005. "Cancer Programs." www.gillette.com/community/womenscancersprog_connection.asp (retrieved Sept. 6, 2005).

Giordano, Sharon H., Aman U. Budzar, and Gabriel N. Hortobagyi. 2002. "Breast Cancer in Men." *Annals of Internal Medicine* 137(8): 678–87.

Global Forum for Health Research (GFHR). 2002. *The 10/90 Report on Health Research, 2001–2002.* Geneva. www.globalforumhealth.org (retrieved Jan. 27, 2003).

Goldberg, Marvin E., Martin Fishbein, and Susan E. Middlestadt, eds. 1997. *Social Marketing: Theoretical and Practical Perspectives.* Mahwah, N.J.: Lawrence Erlbaum Associates.

Goldman, Debra. 1997. "Illness as Metaphor: From the Marketer's Point of View, Breast Cancer Is a Dream Cause: It's a Feminist Issue without Politics." [electronic version] *Adweek,* Nov. 3, 70–71.

Goldsteen, R. L., K. Goldsteen, J. H. Swan, and W. Clemena. 2001. "Harry and Louise and Health Care Reform: Romancing Public Opinion." *Journal of Health Politics, Policy and Law* 26(6): 1325–53.

Goodman, Sandra. 2003. "Breast Cancer: The Epidemic That Won't Go Away." *Positive Health Magazine*. www.positivehealth.com (retrieved June 13, 2003).

Gore, John L., Tracey Krupski, Lorna Kwan, Sally Maliski, and Mark S. Litwin. 2005. "Partnership Status Influences Quality of Life in Low-Income, Uninsured Men with Prostate Cancer." *Cancer,* July 1, 191–98.

Gormley, William T. 1981a. "Public Advocacy in Public Utility Commission Hearings." *Journal of Applied Behavioral Sciences* 17(4): 446–62.

———. 1981b. "Nonelectoral Representation as a Response to Issue-Specific Conditions: The Case of Public Utility Regulation." *Social Science Quarterly* 62(3): 527–39.

———. 1981c. "Statewide Remedies for Public Underrepresentation in Regulatory Proceedings." *Public Administration Review* 41(4): 454–62.

———. 1986. "The Representation Revolution: Reforming State Regulation Through Public Representation." *Administration and Society* 18(2): 179–96.

Gorner, Peter. 1994. "Statistics Give Confusing, Alarming View." *Chicago Tribune,* April 10, 1, 15.

Granath, Alan. 2003. Remarks before the National Prostate Cancer Coalition Advocacy Conference. Washington, D.C. May 21.

Grassley, Charles. 2005. "Grassley Calls on Congress to Eliminate Federal Payment for Lifestyle Drugs." Press release, May 24. http://grassley.senate.gov/index.cfm?FuseAction=PressReleases_id=4922 (retrieved June 23, 2005).

Gray, Ross E., Margaret Fitch, Christine David, and Catherine Phillips. 1997. "Interviews with Men with Prostate Cancer About Their Self-Help Group Experience." *Journal of Palliative Care* 13(1): 15–21.

Greenberg, Daniel S. 1992. "Washington Perspective: The New Politics of AIDS." *The Lancet* 340(8811): 105–6.

Griswold, William F., and Cathy Packer. 1991. "The Interplay of Journalistic and Scientific Conventions in Mass Communication about AIDS." *Mass Communication Review* 18(3): 9–20.

Gross, Cary P., Gerald F. Anderson, and Neil R. Powe. 1999. "The Relation between Funding by the National Institutes of Health and Burden of Disease." *New England Journal of Medicine* 320(24): 1881–87.

Gruskin, Shana. 1998. "Screened Out, Again; Men Fight Two-Year Wait for Medicare Coverage of Prostate Exams." *Chicago Sun-Times,* May 15, 58.

Haas, Gabriel P, and Wael A. Sakr. 1997. "Epidemiology of Prostate Cancer." *Ca: A Cancer Journal for Clinicians* 47(5): 273–88.

Haga, Chuck. 2000. "Raising Campaign Spirits in ND: Supporters Rally for Ailing Gubernatorial Candidate." *Minneapolis Star Tribune,* Sept. 25, 1A.

Hallett, Michael A., and David Cannella. 1997. "Gatekeeping Through the Media Format: Strategies for Voice for the HIV-Positive via Human Interest News Formats and Organizations." *Journal of Homosexuality* 32(3/4): 17–36.

Hammermeister, Jon, Barbara Brock, David Winterstein, and Randy Page. 2005.

"Life without TV? Cultivation Theory and Psychosocial Health Characteristics of Television-Free Individuals and Their Television-Viewing Counterparts." *Health Communication* 17(3): 253–64.

Hansen, Orval, Robert J. Blendon, Mollyann Brodie, Jonathan Ortmans, Matt James, Christopher Norton, and Tana Rosenblatt. 1996. "Lawmakers' Views on the Failure of Health Reform: A Survey of Members of Congress and Staff." *Journal of Health Politics, Policy and Law* 21(1): 137–51.

Heaney, Michael T. 2003. "Money is Important, but So Is Work at the Grassroots with Seniors, Patients: Survey." *The Hill,* Oct. 1, http://www.thehill.com/news/100103/ss_heaney.aspx (retrieved Nov. 25, 2003).

Heck, Katherine E., and Elsie R. Pamuk. 1997. "Explaining the Relation between Education and Postmenopausal Breast Cancer." *American Journal of Epidemiology* 145(4): 366–72.

Heinz, John P., Edward O. Laumann, Robert L. Nelson, and Robert H. Salisbury. 1993. *The Hollow Core: Private Interests in National Policy Making.* Cambridge: Harvard University Press.

Henderson, Lesley, and Jenny Kitzinger. 1999. "The Human Drama of Genetics: 'Hard' and 'Soft' Media Representations of Inherited Breast Cancer." *Sociology of Health and Illness* 21(5): 560–78.

Hess, Stephen. 1984. *The Government/Press Connection: Press Officers and Their Offices.* Washington, D.C.: Brookings Institution.

Hiller, Elaine H., Gretchen Landenburger, and Marvin R. Natowicz. 1997. "Public Participation in Medical Policy-Making and the Status of Consumer Autonomy." *American Journal of Public Health* 87(8): 1280–89.

Himmelfarb, Richard. 1995. *Catastrophic Politics: The Rise and Fall of the Medicare Catastrophic Coverage Act of 1988.* State College: Pennsylvania State University Press.

"History of the Pink Ribbon." n.d. http://www.pinkribbon.com/ (retrieved March 18, 2003).

Hoffman-Goetz, Laurie, Karen K. Gerlach, Christina Marino, and Sherry L. Mills. 1997. "Cancer Coverage and Tobacco Advertising in African-American Women's Popular Magazines." *Journal of Community Health* 22(4): 261–70.

Houn, Florence, Mary A. Bober, Elmer E. Huerta, Stephen G. Husting, Stephen Lemon, and Douglas L. Weed. 1995. "The Association between Alcohol and Breast Cancer: Popular Press Coverage of Research." *American Journal of Public Health* 85(8): 1082–86.

"House Approves Second Continuing Resolution through Nov. 7." 2003. *The Source on Women's Issues in Congress* 9(35). http://www.womenspolicyinc.org (retrieved Dec. 1, 2003).

Houser, Sara. 1998. "Seeking a Cure: Couple Helps Fight Prostate Cancer." *Desert Trail,* June 19, A4.

"International Support Group, US TOO! Quits US Prostate Cancer Coalition." 2001. *PSA Rising,* April 3. http://www.psa-rising.com/grassroots/us-too-npcc030401 .htm (retrieved Nov. 22, 2002).

Iyengar, Shanto. 1991. *Is Anyone Responsible? How Television Frames Political Issues.* Chicago: University of Chicago Press.

Jaffe, Harry. 1997. "Dying for Dollars." *Men's Health.* Sept. 12, 132–39.

Jamieson, Kathleen Hall, and Joseph N. Capella. 1998. "The Role of the Press in the Health Care Reform Debate of 1993–1994." In *The Politics of News, the News of Politics,* edited by Doris Graber, Denis McQuail, and Pippa Norris, 110–31. Washington, D.C.: CQ Press.

Johnson, Haynes, and David S. Broder. 1996. *The System: The American Way of Politics at the Breaking Point.* Boston: Little Brown.

Johnson, J. David. 1997. "Factors Distinguishing Regular Readers of Breast Cancer Information in Magazines." *Women and Health* 26(1): 7–27.

———, and Hendrika Meischke. 1991. "Cancer Information: Women's Source and Content Preferences." *Journal of Health Care Marketing* 11(1): 37–44.

Johnson, Judith. 1996. "Cancer Research: Selected Federal Spending and Morbidity and Mortality Statistics." *CRS Report for Congress* 96–253 SPR. March 3.

Johnson, Ronald. 2003. "Not Just Ribbons: Accountability and Ethics in Fundraising." Panel discussion at the National Breast Cancer Advocacy Conference, Washington, D.C., May 2.

Joint United Nations Programme on HIV/AIDS (UNAIDS). 2003. "What Is the Red Ribbon?" http://www.unaids.org/hivaidsinfo/faq/ribbon.html (retrieved March 17, 2003).

Judkins, Bennett M. 1986. *We Offer Ourselves as Evidence: Toward Workers' Control of Occupational Health.* Westport: Greenwood Press.

Kanapaux, William. 2003. "We Are the Evidence: Consumers Seek Shift in Research Focus." *Behavioral Healthcare Tomorrow* 12(1): SR25–27.

Kasper, Anne S., and Susan J. Ferguson, eds. 2000. *Breast Cancer: Society Shapes an Epidemic.* New York: St. Martin's Press.

Kaufert, Patricia A. 1998. "Women, Resistance and the Breast Cancer Movement." In *Pragmatic Women and Body Politics,* edited by Margaret Lock and Patricia A. Kaufert, 287–309. New York: Cambridge University Press.

Kedrowski, Karen M. 1996. *Media Entrepreneurs and the Media Enterprise in the U.S. Congress.* Cresskill, N.J.: Hampton Press.

———, and Marilyn Stine Sarow. 2002. "The Gendering of Cancer Policy: Media Advocacy and Congressional Policy Attention." In *Women Transforming Congress,* edited by Cindy Simon Rosenthal, 240–59. Norman: University of Oklahoma Press.

King, Samantha. 2004. "Pink Ribbons Inc.: Breast Cancer Activism and the Politics of Philanthropy." *International Journal of Qualitative Studies in Education* 17(4): 473–92.

Kingdon, John. 1984. *Agendas, Alternatives and Public Policies.* Boston: Little Brown.

Klawiter, Maren. 2000. "Racing for the Cure, Walking Women and Toxic Touring: Mapping Cultures of Action within the Bay Area Terrain of Breast Cancer." In *Ideologies of Breast Cancer: Feminist Perspectives,* edited by Laura K. Potts, 63–97. New York: St. Martin's Press.

Kolata, Gina. 1996. "Vying for the Breast Vote." *New York Times,* Nov. 3, pp. 4, 5.

———. 1998. "Ideas and Trends: Drugs That Deliver More Than Originally Promised." *New York Times.* April 1, p. 3.

Kollman, Ken. 1998. *Outside Lobbying: Public Opinion and Interest Group Strategies.* Princeton: Princeton University Press.

Korda, Michael. 1996. *Man to Man: Surviving Prostate Cancer.* New York: Random House.

Kotler, Philip, Ned Roberto, and Nancy Lee. 2002. *Social Marketing: Improving the Quality of Life.* 2d ed. Thousand Oaks: Sage Publications.

Krieghbaum, Hillier. 1967. *Science and the Mass Media.* New York: New York University Press.

Krizek, Claudette, Cleora Roberts, Robin Ragan, Jeffrey J. Ferrara, and Beth Lord. 1999. "Gender and Support Group Participation." *Cancer Practice* 7(2): 86–92.

Kushner, Rose. 1982. *Why Me? What Every Woman Should Know about Breast Cancer to Save Her Life.* Philadelphia: W. B. Saunders.

Lane, Dorothy S., Anthony P. Polednak, and Mary Ann Burg. 1998. "The Impact of Media Coverage of Nancy Reagan's Experience on Breast Cancer Screening." *American Journal of Public Health* 79(11): 1551–52.

Lane, George, Anne Ferrari, and H. Michael Dreher. 2004. "Legionnaire's Disease: A Current Update." *MedSurg Nursing* 13(6): 409–15.

Lang, Kenneth, and Gladys Lang. 1972. "The Mass Media and Voting." In *The Process and Effects of Mass Communication.* Rev. ed., edited by W. Schramm, and D. Roberts, 678–700. Urbana: University of Illinois Press.

Langer, Amy S. 1992. "The Politics of Breast Cancer." *Journal of the American Medical Women's Association* 47(5): 207–9.

———. 1997. "The Role of Advocacy in Cancer Research: Not a Monster." *Cancer Investigation* 15(5): 500–502.

———, and Karen Hassey Dow. 1994. "The Breast Cancer Advocacy Movement and Nursing." *Oncology Nursing* 1(3): 1–13.

Lantz, Paula M., and Karen M. Booth. 1998. "The Social Construction of the Breast Cancer Epidemic." *Social Science and Medicine* 46(7): 907–18.

Laurence, Leslie. 1994. "The Proactive Patient." *Town and Country* 143(5173): 126.

Leopold, Ellen. 1999. *A Darker Ribbon: A Twentieth-Century Story of Breast Cancer, Women and Their Doctors.* Boston: Beacon Press.

Lerner, Barron H. 2000. "Inventing a Curable Disease: Historical Perspectives on Breast Cancer." In *Breast Cancer: Society Shapes an Epidemic,* edited by Anne S. Kasper and Susan J. Ferguson, 25–49. New York: St. Martin's Press.

———. 2001. *The Breast Cancer Wars: Hope, Fear and the Pursuit of a Cure in Twentieth-Century America*. New York: Oxford University Press.

Levine, Adeline Gordon. 1982. *Love Canal: Science, Politics, and People*. Lexington, Mass.: Lexington Books.

Levitt, Miriam, and Donald B. Rosenthal. 1999. "The Third-Wave: A Symposium on AIDS Politics and Policy in the United States in the 1990s." *Policy Studies Journal* 27(4): 783–95.

Lewis, James, and Roy Berger. 1994. *How I Survived Prostate Cancer, and So Can You: A Guide to Diagnosing and Treating Prostate Cancer*. Westbury, Conn.: Health Education Literary Publisher.

Liberman, Trudy. 1993. "Covering Health Care Reform: Round One, How One Paper Stole the Debate." *Columbia Journalism Review* (Sept.–Oct.), www.cjr.org/year/93/5/health.asp (retrieved Nov. 18, 2002).

Lippmann, Walter. 1922. *Public Opinion*. New York: Macmillan.

Litzenfelner, Pat. 2001. "The Use of Citizen Review Boards with Juvenile Offender Cases: The Evaluation of the Effectiveness of a Pilot Program." *Juvenile and Family Court Journal* 52(1): 1–9.

Lloyd, Marilyn. 1995. "The Real Tragedy behind Silicone Breasts." *Chicago Tribune*, Nov. 9, 31.

Loomis, Burdett. 1988. *The New American Politician: Ambition, Entrepreneurship, and the Changing Face of Political Life*. New York: Basic Books.

Lorange, Peter, and Johan Roos. 1992. *Strategic Alliances: Formation, Implementation, and Evolution*. Cambridge, Mass.: Blackwell Publishers.

Lorde, Audre. 1980. *Cancer Journals*. San Francisco: Spinsters/Aunt Lute Book Co.

Love, Susan. 2000. "Foreword." In *Breast Cancer: Society Shapes an Epidemic,* edited by Anne S. Kasper and Susan J. Ferguson, viii–xii. New York: St. Martin's Press.

———. 2005. "Breast Cancer and the Environment: Do We Have What It Takes to Find the Link?" Speech presented before the National Breast Cancer Coalition Advocacy Conference, Washington, D.C., May 22.

———, and Karen Lindsay. 1995. *Dr. Susan Love's Breast Book*. 2d ed. Cambridge, Mass.: Perseus Publishing.

———, and ———. 2000. *Dr. Susan Love's Breast Book*. 3d ed. Cambridge, Mass.: Perseus Publishing.

Luker, Kristen. 1984. *Abortion and the Politics of Motherhood*. Berkeley: University of California Press, 1984.

Lupton, Deborah. 1994. "Femininity, Responsibility and the Technological Imperative: Discourses on Breast Cancer in the Australian Press." *International Journal of Health Services* 24(1): 73–89.

Macilwain, Colin. 1994. "Congress and Administration Differ over Views of Threats to Science." *Nature* 370(6489): 401.

Malecare. 2003. "About Malecare." http://www.malecare.com/about_malecare/about_malecare.html (retrieved July 20, 2003).

Manne, Sharon L. 2002. "Prostate Cancer Support and Advocacy Groups: Their Role for Patients and Family Members." *Seminars in Urologic Oncology* 20(1): 45–54.

Marconi, Joe. 2002. *Cause Marketing: Build Your Image and Bottomline Through Socially Responsible Partnerships, Programs and Events.* Chicago: Dearborn Trade Publications.

Marshall, Eliot. 1993a. "The Politics of Breast Cancer." *Science* 259(29): 616–17.

———. 1993b. "Lobbyists Seek to Reslice NIH's Pie." *Science* 276(5311): 344–46.

———. 1998. "NIH Urged to Involve the Public in Policy-making." *Science* 281(5374): 152.

McAllister, Bill. 1997. "Congress Offers New Way to Raise Money by Mail." *Washington Post,* July 23, A21.

McCarthy, Eileen. 1983. "Inpatient Utilization of Short-Stay Hospitals, by Diagnosis, United States 1980." *Vital and Health Statistics* 13(74): 4, 5, 11, 15.

McCombs, Maxwell E., and D. L. Shaw. 1972. "The Agenda-Setting Function of the Mass Media." *Public Opinion Quarterly* 26 (Summer): 167–87.

McKay, Susan, and Frances Bonner. 1999. "Telling Stories: Breast Cancer Pathologies in Australian Women's Magazines." *Women's Studies International Forum* 22(5): 563–72.

———, and ———. 2004. "Educating Readers: Breast Cancer in Australian Women's Magazines." *International Journal of Qualitative Studies in Education* 17(4): 517–35.

Mebane, Felicia. 2001. "Want to Understand How Americans Viewed Long Term Care in 1998? Start with Media Coverage." *The Gerontologist* 41(1): 24–33.

Melbye, Mads, Jorgen Wolhlfahrt, Jorgen H. Olson, Morten Frish, Tine Westergaard, Karin Helwing-Larsen, and Anderson Per Keragh. 1997. "Induced Abortion and the Risk of Breast Cancer." *New England Journal of Medicine* 336(2): 81–85.

Mello, Michelle M., and Troyen A. Brennan. 2001. "The Controversy over High-Dose Chemotherapy with Autologous Bone Marrow Transplant for Breast Cancer." *Health Affairs* 20(5): 101–15.

Menashe, Claudia L., and Michael Siegel. 1998. "The Power of a Frame: An Analysis of Newspaper Coverage of Tobacco Issues—United States, 1985–1996." *Journal of Health Communication* 3(4): 307–25.

Men's Health Network. 1998. "National Prostate Cancer Coalition based on the National Breast Cancer Coalition Model." Press release, July 26. http://www.fathermag.com/htmlmodcules/sep96/xnpcc.html (retrieved Aug. 28, 1998).

———. 2002. "About MHN." http://www.menshealthnetwork.org/about.html (retrieved Nov. 21, 2002).

Merck Media Minutes. 1997. "Majority of Women Control Health-Care Decisions." (Summer newsletter).

Milken, Michael. 2002. "Message from Our Founder and Chairman." http://www.capcure.org/aboutus/MessageChairman.asp?mainid=1&subid=4&param=aboutus (retrieved Nov. 21, 2002).

Mills, Kay. 1995. "What Difference Do Women Journalists Make?" In *Women, Media and Politics,* edited by Pippa Norris, 41–55. New York: Oxford University Press.

Miller, Jim, and Julia Miller. 2003. *Our Journey Through Prostate Cancer.* San Francisco: JJM Publishing.

"Missed Opportunity: Urban Fiscal Crises and Financial Control Boards." 1997. *Harvard Law Review* 110(3): 733–50.

Mizerski, Dick, Katherine Mizerski, and Orin Sadler. 2001. "A Field Experiment Comparing the Effectiveness of 'Ambush' and Cause Related as Appeals for Social Marketing Causes." In *Social Marketing,* edited by Michael T. Ewing, 25–45. Binghamton: Haworth Press.

Moffett, Jill. 2003. "Moving beyond the Ribbon: An Examination of Breast Cancer Advocacy and Activism in the US and Canada." *Cultural Dynamics* 15(3): 287–306.

Molinari, Susan. 2000. *Roundtable: Women and Reflections on Congressional Life.* C-SPAN, April 20.

Montgomery, Kathryn. 1989. *Target: Prime Time.* New York: Oxford University Press.

Montini, Theresa. 1996. "Gender and Emotion in the Advocacy for Breast Cancer Informed Consent Legislation." *Gender and Society* 10(1): 9–23.

———. 1997. "Resist and Redirect: Physicians Respond to Breast Cancer Informed Consent Legislation." *Women and Health* 26(1): 85–105.

Morgan, Sandra. 2002. *Into Our Own Hands: The Women's Health Movement in the United States, 1969–1990.* New Brunswick: Rutgers University Press.

Morrill, Jim. 2004. "Breast Cancer Simmers as Issue." *Charlotte Observer,* Oct. 29. [Online edition] retrieved Oct. 29, 2004.

Moyer, Anne, Susan Greener, John Beauvais, and Peter Solovey. 1995. "Accuracy of Health Research Reported in the Popular Press: Breast Cancer and Mammography." *Health Communication* 7(2): 147–61.

Murphy, Beth. 2003. *Fighting for Our Future: How Young Women Find Strength, Hope and Courage while Taking Control of Breast Cancer.* New York: McGraw Hill.

Murphy, Timothy F. 1991. "No Time for AIDS Backlash." *Hastings Center Report* 21(2): 7–11.

Murray, David, and Joel Schwartz. 1997. "Alarmism Is an Infectious Disease." *Society* 34(4): 35–41.

Mustard, Cameron A., Patricia Kaufert, Anita Kozyrskyj, and Teresa Mayer. 1998. "Sex Difference in the Use of Health Care Services." *New England Journal of Medicine* 338(23): 1678–83.

Nagel, Mark V. 1990. "National Institutes of Health: Problems in Implementing Policy on Women in Study Populations." Testimony before the Subcommittee on Housing and Consumer Interest, Select Committee on Aging. U.S. House of Representatives, July 24. GAO-T-HRD-90-50.

Nagourney, Adam. 1998a. "Ferraro Assails D'Amato over Breast Cancer Effort." *New York Times,* May 19, B4.

———. 1998b. "Tense Debate for D'Amato and Schumer." *New York Times,* Oct. 25, A1.

National Alliance of Breast Cancer Organizations (NABCO). 2003a. "Welcome to NABCO." http://www.nabco.org/ (retrieved March 17, 2003).

———. 2003b. "Early Detection of Breast Cancer." http://www.nabco.org/index .php/3 (retrieved June 24, 2003).

National Breast Cancer Coalition (NBCC). 1997a. First World Conference on Breast Cancer Advocacy: Influencing Change. http://www.natlbcc.org (retrieved July 9, 2002).

———. 1997b. "Legislative Update." Document provided by the NBCC.

———. 1999. Second World Conference on Breast Cancer Advocacy: Influencing Change. http://www.natlbcc.org (retrieved July 9, 2002).

———. 2000. "NBCC Legislative Priorities List for 2000." Document provided by the NBCC.

———. 2002a. "Home Page." http://www.natlbcc.org (retrieved Nov. 19, 2002).

———. 2002b. "Legislative Priorities." http://www.natlbcc.org/bin/index.asp?strid =20&depid=3&btnid=2 (retrieved Nov. 22, 2002).

———. 2002c. "Guide to Quality Breast Care." http://www.natlbcc.org/nbccf/index .html (retrieved Nov. 22, 2002).

———. 2002d. "The National Breast Cancer Coalition's (NBCC) Score Card on State Participation in the Breast and Cervical Cancer Treatment Program." http://www .stopbreastcancer.org/pdf/Complete_State_CDC_Scorecard.pdf (retrieved June 8, 2003).

———. 2002e. "National Breast Cancer Coalition Asserts Advocacy, 'Not Just Ribbons' Will End Breast Cancer." News release, Oct. 2.

———. 2003a. "History, Goals and Accomplishments." http://www.stopbreastcancer .org (retrieved Jan. 8, 2003).

———. 2003b. "Conference Agenda." Document included in NBCC Advocacy Conference packet.

———. 2003c. "Position Statement on Abortion and Breast Cancer Risk." Document included in NBCC Advocacy Conference packet.

———. 2003d. "Status of the Breast and Cervical Cancer Treatment Program in the United States (as of Jan. 10, 2003)." http://www.stopbreastcancer.org/bin/index .asp?strid=480&depid=3&btnid=2 (retrieved June 8, 2003).

———. 2003e. "NBCC Legislative Priorities for 2003." Document included in NBCC Advocacy Conference packet.

———. 2003f. "Position Statement on Breast Self Exam, April 2003." Document included in NBCC Advocacy Conference packet.

———. 2003g. "Position Statement on Screening Mammography, April 2003." Document included in NBCC Advocacy packet.

———. 2003h. "Project LEAD." http://www.stopbreastcancer.org/bin/index.asp ?Strid=483&btnid=4&depid=7#cost (retrieved June 28, 2003).

———. 2005a. "Grassroots Advocacy." http://www.stopbreastcancer.org/bin/index .asp?strid=546&depid=5&btnid=0 (retrieved Aug. 11, 2005).

———. 2005b. "Public Policy Activities." http://www.stopbreastcancer.org/bin/ index.asp?strid=8&depid=3&btnid=0 (retrieved Aug. 11, 2005).

National Breast Cancer Coalition Fund (NBCCF). 2003. "Questions and Answers about HER-2/neu." Document included in NBCC Advocacy packet.

———. 2005. *Stop Breast Cancer: Personal Stories, Public Action.* Brochure.

National Cancer Institute (NCI). 1980. *Breast Cancer: A Measure of Progress in Public Understanding.* Technical Report. NIH Publication 81–2291. Princeton: Opinion Research Corporation.

———. 1996. *Fact Book.* Washington, D.C.: Government Printing Office.

———. 1997. *Fact Book.* Washington, D.C.: Government Printing Office.

———. 2000. "Research Dollars by Various Cancers." http://www.nic.nih.gov/ public/factbook98/varican.htm (retrieved July 11, 2000).

———. 2001. *Fact Book.* Washington, D.C.: Government Printing Office. http:// www3.cancer.gov/admin/fmb/2001factbook.pdf (retrieved Sept. 9, 2005).

———. 2003. "Progress in Addressing Breast Cancer Rates in Marin County." News release, March 28. http://www.nci.gov/newscenter/pressreleases/marin (retrieved June 6, 2005).

———/DEA (Division of Extramural Activites). 2001. *Division of Extramural Activities, Annual Report 2001.* Washington, D.C.: Government Printing Office. http:// deainfo.nci.nih.gov/DEArpfy2001.pdf (retrieved June 30, 2003).

National Institute of Environmental Health Services. 2005. "Clinical Trials: Sister Study." http://www.clinicaltrials.gov (retrieved June 24, 2005).

National Institutes of Health. 2005. "Estimates of Funding for Various Disease, Conditions and Research Areas." March 5. http://www.nih.gov/news/funding-researchareas.htm (retrieved July 17, 2005).

National Newspaper Association of America. 2005. "Daily Newspaper Readership Trends-Education (1998–2004)." http://www.naa.org/artpage.com?AID=1468&SID=2113 (retrieved Aug. 12, 2005).

National Prostate Cancer Coalition (NPCC). n.d. *Prostate Cancer . . . It Shouldn't Be His Future.* Informational brochure.

———. n.d. *Prostate Cancer. Forty Thousand Dead. In America. Every Year. We Can Stop It.* Recruitment brochure.

———. n.d. *Prostate Cancer. Kills Forty Thousand Fathers, Husbands, Sons, Friends, Every Year. We Can Stop It.* Recruitment brochure.

———. *Urgent Action Alert.* 1997. NPCC brochure.

———. 1998a. *NPCC Official Merchandise Available Now.* Flyer for ordering tee-shirts. March.

———. 1998b. "By the Numbers: Prostate Cancer in America."

———. 2002a. "Teammates Home Page." http://www.4npcc.org/Teammates/teammates.htm (retrieved Nov. 21, 2002).

———. 2002b. "Advocates Toolkit." http://www.4npcc.org/Advocates_advocates_toolbox/advocates_advocates_toolbox.html (retrieved Nov. 22, 2002).

———. 2002c. "PCA Community." http://www.4npcc.org/Pca_community_resources/pca_community_resources.html (retrieved Nov. 22, 2002).

———.2002d. "Congressional Prostate Cancer Briefing." April 25, 2002, http://www.4npcc.org/Legislative_Affairs/Legislative_Activities/AZbriefing/azbriefing.html (retrieved Jan. 7, 2003).

———. 2002e. "Protecting Our Protectors: Prostate Cancer Awareness Month." Sept. 2002, http://www.4npcc.org (retrieved Sept. 2002).

———. 2003a. "Urban Challenge." http://www.pcacoalition.org/programs/urbanchallenge.php

———. 2003b. "Public Policy Platform for 2003." Document distributed at the NPCC Spring Training Advocacy Conference.

———. 2003c. "Idea for Prostate Treatment Based on Breast Cancer Discovery." *Aware: Newsletter of the National Prostate Cancer Coalition.* March 14. http://www.pcacoalition.org/archives/aware031403.htm. (retrieved March 18, 2003).

———. 2004. "Public Policy Platform for 2004." http://www.pcacoaltion.org/site/Pageserver?pagename=advocacy_platformhome (retrieved July 17, 2005).

———. 2005a. "Battle over Funding ED Drugs." *Aware: Newsletter of the National Prostate Cancer Coalition.* May 31. http://pcscoaltion.org/archives/aware2005_05_31.htm (retrieved June 6, 2005).

———. 2005b. "Prostate Cancer Research Dollars in Jeopardy: Advocates Coming as Far as Alaska to Demand Federal Research Funds." News release, May 6. http://www.pcacoalition.org/site/News2?page=NewsArticle&id=5297 (retrieved June 24, 2005).

———. 2005c. "Response to Issue of State Funding of Erectile Dysfunction Drugs." May 31, http://www.pcacoaltion.org/pressroom.2005_ed.php (retrieved June 6, 2005).

———. 2005d. "About NPCC." http://www.pcscoalition.org/site/PageServer?pagename=npcc_home (retrieved Aug. 11, 2005).

Nattinger, Ann Butler, Raymond G. Hoffmann, Alicia Howell-Petz, and James S. Goodwin. 1998. "Effect of Nancy Reagan's Mastectomy on Choice of Surgery for Breast Cancer by U.S. Women." *Journal of the American Medical Association* 279(10): 762–66.

Neergaard, Lauran. 2003. "Nutrients Are Key to Preventing Cancer." *US TOO! International Prostate Cancer Hotsheet,* 7.

Nelkin, Dorothy. 1995. *Selling Science: How the Press Covers Science and Technology.* Rev ed. New York: W. H. Freeman.

Nethercutt, George R. Jr. 1999. "Increasing Diabetes Awareness and Promoting

Research Funding in the House of Representatives: A Letter from the Chairman of the Congressional Diabetes Caucus." *Diabetes Spectrum* 12(4): 236.

NPCC Smartbrief [email advocacy newsletter]. 2000. "Prostate Cancer Research: Pork Barrel Spending?" March 3.

———. 2001. "Show Me the Money!—the Series." Jan. 26, Jan. 30, Feb. 2, Feb. 6.

———. 2003. "Semipostal Bill Reauthorized without Prostate Cancer Stamp." July 31.

Nugent, Alfred. 2003. "The Long Island Breast Cancer Study: Where Do We Go From Here?" Presentation before the National Breast Cancer Coalition Advocacy Conference, Washington D.C., May 5–6.

Office of Men's Health Resource Center. 2002. http://www.menshealthoffice.info/ (retrieved Nov. 21, 2002).

Olson, James S. 2002. *Bathsheba's Breast: Women, Cancer and History.* Baltimore: Johns Hopkins University Press.

Olson, Mancur. 1982. *The Rise and Decline of Nations: Economic Growth, Stagflation and Social Rigidities.* New Haven: Yale University Press.

"One Voice against Cancer Speaks Loud and Clear." 2000. *Charity Wire,* June 20.

Orenstein, Susan. 2003a. "The Selling of Breast Cancer." *Business 2.0,* Feb., 88–94.

———. 2003b. "Not Just Ribbons: Accountability and Ethics in Fundraising." Panel discussion at the National Breast Cancer Coalition Annual Advocacy Conference, Washington, D.C.

Orlans, Harold. 2002. "Institutional Conflicts of Interest." *Change* 34(3): 10–11.

Palley, Howard A. 1995. "The Evolution of FDA Policy on Silicone Breast Implants: A Case Study of Politics, Bureaucracy and Business in the Process of Decision-Making." *International Journal of Health Services* 25(4): 573–61.

Palosky, Craig S. 1997. "Coalition Targets Prostate Cancer." *Tampa Tribune,* Jan. 2, 1.

Patient Advocates for Advanced Cancer Treatments, Inc. (PAACT). 2003. "PAACT Biography." http://www.paactusa.org/pgs/biography.html (retrieved July 28, 2003).

Peterson, Helen. 1995. "Fight to Stamp Out Breast Cancer." *Daily News,* July 28, 11.

Peterson, Jennifer, and Matuschka. 2004. "Interviews with Matuschka: Breast Cancer, Art, Sexuality and Activism." *International Journal of Qualitative Studies in Education* 17(4): 493–516.

Peterson, Mark. 1993. "Political Influence in the 1990s: From Iron Triangles to Policy Networks." *Journal of Health Politics, Policy and Law* 18(2): 395–438.

Phoenix5. Main Menu. 2003. http://www.phoenix5.org/menumain.html (retrieved July 20, 2003).

Piven, Frances Fox, and Richard A. Cloward. 1997. *Poor People's Movements: Why They Succeed, How They Fail.* New York: Pantheon Books.

Platner, Janice H., L. Michelle Bennett, Robert Millikan, and May D. G. Barker. 2002. "The Partnership between Breast Cancer Advocates and Scientists." *Environmental and Molecular Mutagenesis* 39(2–3): 102–7.

Policy Agendas Project. 2003. http://www.policyagendas.org/PAOVerview.html (retrieved July 26, 2003).

"Politics Intrudes on Clinton's Signing Breast Cancer Bill."2000. *Cleveland Plain Dealer,* Oct. 24, 11A.

"Post 9/11 Consumer Attitudes." 2002. Cause Marketing Forum. http://www.coneinc .com/Pages/research.html (retrieved May 6, 2003).

Porter, Joan P. 1987. "How Unaffiliated/Nonscientist Members of Institutional Review Boards See Their Roles." *IRB: A Review of Human Subjects Research* 9(6): 1–6.

Potts, Laura K. 2000. "Publishing the Personal: Autobiographical Narratives of Breast Cancer and the Self." In *Ideologies of Breast Cancer: Feminist Perspectives,* edited by Laura K. Potts, 99–127. New York: St. Martin's Press.

"Prevalence, Incidence of Diabetes Mellitus—United States, 1980–1987." 1990. *JAMA: Journal of the American Medical Association* 264(24): 3126.

Priest, Susanna Hornig. 1999. "Popular Beliefs, Media and Biotechnology." In *Communicating Uncertainty: Media Coverage of New and Controversial Science,* edited by Sharon M. Friedman, Sharon Dunwoody, and Carol L. Rogers, 95–112. Mahwah, N.J.: Lawrence Erlbaum.

Prindeville, Diane-Michele, and John G. Bretting. 1998. "Indigenous Women Activists and Political Participation: The Case of Environmental Justice." *Women and Politics* 19(1): 39–58.

Pringle, Hamish, and Marjorie Thompson. 1999. *Brand Spirit: How Cause Marketing Builds Brands.* Chichester, U.K.: Wiley.

PROACT (Prostate Action, Inc.). 2003a. "About Prostate Action Inc." http://www .prostateaction.org/about (retrieved July 20, 2003).

———. 2003b. "William C. Roher." http://www.prostateaction.org/about.billr.html (retrieved July 29, 2003).

Proctor, Robert. 1996. *Cancer Wars: How Politics Shape What We Know.* New York: Basic Books.

Prostate Cancer Action Network (PCAN). 2003. "Welcome to the Prostate Cancer Action Network." http://www.prostatepointers.org/pcan/ (retrieved June 10, 2003).

"Prostate Cancer: BRCA2 is a High-Risk Susceptibility Gene, Has Potential Implication for Management." 2003. *Genomics and Genetics Weekly,* March 14, 31.

Prostate Cancer Education Council (PCEC). 2003. "About the PCEC." http://www .dentalwebdesign.com/about.index.asp (retrieved July 27, 2003).

"Prostate Cancer Research Stamp Fails in Congress." 2000. Men's Health Network. http://www.menshealthnetwork.org/prostate.html#fails (retrieved April 4, 2003).

"Prostate Cancer Survivors Take Their Cause to Congress." 1997. *Tampa Tribune,* May 20, 1.

"Prostate Cancer: What It Is and How It's Treated." 2002. Brochure. AstraZeneca Pharmaceuticals.

Ptacek, Joseph J., and Gina Salazar. 1997. "Enlightened Self-Interest: Selling Business on the Benefits of Cause-Related Marketing." *Nonprofit World* (July-Aug.): 9–12.

Purnick, Joyce. 2000. "First Call a Doctor, Then a News Conference: Politicians Open Up upon What Ails Them." *New York Times,* April 30, 35.

Rajan, T. V., and Jonathan Clive. 2000. "NIH Research Grants: Funding and Re-funding." *JAMA: Journal of the American Medical Association* 283(15): 1963.

Read, Cathy. 1995. *Preventing Breast Cancer: The Politics of an Epidemic.* New York: HarperCollins Publishers.

Readership Institute. 2002. *Consumers, Media and U.S. Newspapers: Results from the Impact Study.* http://www.readership.org (retrieved July 25, 2003).

"Representative Champions Legislation for Breast Cancer." 1991. *Cancer Weekly,* Nov. 18, 12.

Reynolds, Sandra L. 1994. "The Print Media and Aging Policy: How Differential Coverage of Medicare Catastrophic Led Congress Astray." *Journal of Aging and Social Policy* 6(4): 53–71.

Rhode Island Breast Cancer Coalition. 2003. "Mammography for Women with Disabilities." Poster presented at the 2003 NBCC advocacy conference, Washington, D.C.

Rich, Carole. 1999. *Writing and Reporting News.* 3d ed. Belmont, Calif.: Wadsworth Publishing.

Rich, Ilene M., Yvonne Adejeski, Marianne H. Alciati, Isabelle Crawford Bisceglio, Erica S. Breslau, Lisa McCall, and Alex Valadez. 1998. "Perspective from the Department of Defense Breast Cancer Research Program." *Breast Disease* 10(5–6): 33–45.

Roberts, Roxanne. 1991. "Nancy Brinker's Race to Save the Women; The Activist, Fulfilling Her Sister's Last Wish." *Washington Post,* June 12, F1.

Rochefort, David A., and Roger W. Cobb. 1994. "Problem Definition: An Emerging Perspective." In *The Politics of Problem Definition: Shaping the Policy Agenda,* edited by David A. Rochefort and Roger W. Cobb, 1–31. Lawrence: University of Kansas Press.

Rockhill, Beverly. 2003. "The Problem with Individual Risk." Speech delivered to the National Breast Cancer Coalition Advocacy Training Conference, Washington, D.C., May 3.

Roetzheim, Richard G., Daniel J. Vandurme, Harrison J. Brownlee, Arthur H. Herold, Rubens J. Panies, Laurie Woodard, and Clifford Blair. 1992. "Reverse Targeting in a Media-Promoted Breast Cancer Screening Project." *Cancer* 70(5): 1152–58.

Rogers, Everett M., James Dearing, and S. Chang. 1991. "AIDS in the 1990's: The Agenda-Setting Process for a Public Issue." *Journalism Monographs* 126. Columbia, S.C.: Association for Education in Journalism and Mass Communication.

Rollin, Betty. 1976. *First You Cry.* New York: HarperCollins.

Rosenberg, Charles E. 1989. "Disease in History: Frames and Framers." *Milbank Quarterly* 67 (suppl. 1): 1–15.

Rosenhaus, Janice. 2003. "Not Just Ribbons: Accounting and Ethics in Fundraising." Panel discussion at the National Breast Cancer Coalition Foundation Annual Advocacy Training Conference, May 4.

Rosser, Sue V. 2000. "Controversies in Breast Cancer Research." In *Breast Cancer: Society Shapes an Epidemic,* edited by Anne S. Kasper, and Susan J. Ferguson, 245–70. New York: St. Martin's Press.

Rothman, Alexander J., and Marc T. Kiviniemi. 1999. "Treating People with Information: An Analysis and Review of Approaches to Communication Health Risk Information." *Journal of the National Cancer Institute Monographs* 25: 44–51.

Rubin, Alissa J. 1996. "New Breast Cancer Research Funding Raises Old Questions about Priorities." *Congressional Quarterly Weekly Report,* May 29, 1364–65.

Rubin, Rita, and Harrison L. Rogers Jr. 1993. *Under the Microscope: The Relationship between Physicians and the News Media.* Arlington: Freedom Forum.

Russell, Anne, Robert B. Voas, William DeJong, and Marla Chaloupka. 1995. "MADD Rates the States: A Media Advocacy Event to Advance the Agenda against Alcohol-impaired Driving." *Public Health Reports* 110(3): 240–46.

Ruzek, Sheryl Burt. 1978. *The Women's Health Movement: Feminist Alternatives to Medical Control.* New York: Praeger Publishers.

Ryan, Terry Jo. 2002. "Prostate Cancer Victim Hopes Legacy Can Be Local Support Group." *Waco Tribune,* Oct. 20. http://www.wacotrib.com (retrieved July 18, 2003).

Sandler, Dennis M., and David Shani. 1989. "Olympic Sponsorship vs. 'Ambush': Marketing: Who Gets the Gold?" *Journal of Advertising Research* 24 (Aug.–Sept.): 9–14.

"Saving Lives in North Carolina." 2003. *Health and Healing,* June 19. http://nc.healthandhealing.info/artman/publish/printer_122.shtml (retrieved July 23, 2003).

Schattschnieder, Elmer E. 1960. *The Semi-Sovereign People: A Realist's View of Democracy in America.* New York: Holt, Reinhardt and Winston.

Scheberle, Denise. 1994. "Radon and Asbestos: A Study of Agenda Setting and Casual Stories." *Policy Studies Journal* 22(1): 74–86.

Schoen, Cathy, Lisa Duchon, and Elisabeth Simantov. 1999. "Issue Brief: The Link between Health and Economic Security for Working-Age Women." Commonwealth Fund. http://www.cmwf.org/programs/women/schoen_linkhealth&eco_ib_332.asp (retrieved Jan. 8, 2003).

Schofield, Toni, R.W. Connell, Linley Walker, Julian F. Wood, and Dianne Butland. 2000. "Understanding Men's Health and Illness: A Gender-Relations Approach." *Journal of American College Health* 48(6): 247–52.

Schooler, Caroline, E. Shyam Sundar, and June Flora. 1996. "Effects of the Stanford Five-City Project Media Advocacy Program." *Health Education Quarterly* 23(3): 346–64.

Schreiner, George E. 2000. "How End Stage Renal Disease (ESRD)—Medicare Developed." *American Journal of Kidney Diseases* 35(4): S37–44.

Schroedel, Jean Reith, and Daniel R. Jordan. 1998. "Senate Voting and Social Construction of Target Populations: A Study of AIDS Policy Making 1987–1992." *Journal of Health Politics, Policy and Law* 23(1): 107–32.

Schroeder, Patricia, and Olympia Snowe. 1994. "The Politics of Women's Health." In *The American Woman: 1994–1995,* edited by Cynthia Costello and Anne J. Stone, 91–109. New York: W. W. Norton.

Schwarcz, Steven L, Theodore Brown, Lowell M. Greenbaum, Herbert J. Kayden, and Richard Trumbell. 1981. "Nonscientist Participation in the Peer Review Process: Is It Desirable? Is It Implementable? Who Are the Nonscientists Who Should Become Involved? A Panel Discussion." *Annals of the New York Academy of Sciences* 368: 213–28.

Schwartz, Lisa M., and Steven Woloshin. 2002. "News Media Coverage of Screening Mammography for Women in Their Forties and Tamoxifen for Primary Prevention of Breast Cancer." *JAMA: The Journal of the American Medical Association* 287(23): 3136–42.

———, ———, William C. Black, and H. Gilbert Welch. 1997. "The Role of Numeracy in Understanding the Benefit of Screening Mammography." *Annals of Internal Medicine* 127(11): 966–72.

Seelye, Katharine. 2002. "Dean of the House Is Forced to Face Ex-Ally in Primary." *New York Times,* July 9, 16A.

Seydel, Erwin, Erik Taal, and Oene Wiegman. 1990. "Risk-Appraisal, Outcome and Self-Efficacy Expectancies: Cognitive Factors in Preventive Behavior Related to Cancer." *Psychology and Health* 4: 99–109.

Sharf, Barbara. 2001. "Out of the Closet and Into the Legislature: Breast Cancer Stories." *Health Affairs* 20(1): 213–18.

Shaw, David. 1987. "Coverage of AIDS Story: A Slow Start." *Los Angeles Times,* Dec. 20.

Shaw, Donald L., and Maxwell E. McCombs. 1997. *The Emergence of American Political Issues: The Agenda-Setting Function of the Press.* St. Paul: West.

Shen, Fuyuan. 2004. "Effects of News Frames and Schemas on Individuals' Issue Interpretations and Attitudes." *Journalism and Mass Communication Quarterly* 81(2): 400–416.

Shepherd, Melissa. 1997. "Prevention Marketing: A Framework Integrating Social Marketing and Media Advocacy." In *Social Marketing: Theoretical and Practical Perspectives,* edited by Marvin E. Goldberg, Martin Fishbein, and Susan A. Middlestadt, 284–87. Mahwah, N.J.: Lawrence Erlbaum.

Sherman, Janette. 1999. *Life's Delicate Balance: A Guide to Causes and Prevention of Breast Cancer.* New York: Taylor and Bacon.

Shilts, Randy. 1987. *And the Band Played On: Politics, People and the AIDS Epidemic.* New York: Penguin Books.

Shropshire, Susan. 2003. "Phoenix5: It Can Be Done." *Journal of Hospice and Palliative Care Nursing* 5(1): 12–14 .

Shubert, James N., and Gloria J. Shubert. 1997. "The Processing of Women's and Men's Health Policy Issues: Mass Screening Guidelines for Breast and Prostate Cancer." Paper presented at the Southern Political Science Association, Virginia Beach, 1997.

Silent Spring Institute. 2005. "About Us." http://www.silentspring.org/newweb/about/ (retrieved June 24, 2003).

Silverberg, Edwin. 1980. "Cancer Statistics, 1980." *Ca: A Cancer Journal for Clinicians* 30(1): 23–38.

Singer, Natashia. 2005. "Perplexing in Pink." *New York Times.* Oct. 5, 1E.

Siplon, Particia D. 2002. *AIDS and the Policy Struggle in the United States.* Washington, D.C.: Georgetown University Press.

Sisters Network, Inc. 2003. "About Us." http://www.sistersnetworkinc.org/about.htm (retrieved March 18, 2003).

Sledge, George. 2003. "Therapy of Breast Cancer: Past, Present and Future." Speech delivered to the National Breast Cancer Coalition Advocacy Conference. Washington, D.C., May 4.

Smigel, Kara. 1994. "Top Cancer Related News Stories Focus on Breast, Prostate and Colon Cancers." *Journal of the National Cancer Institute* 86(1): 10–12.

———. 1995. "Top Cancer-Related News Stories Focus on Fraud, Breast Cancer and Hope of Early Detection." *Journal of the National Cancer Institute* 87(1): 12–14.

Smith, Craig. 1994. "The New Corporate Philanthropy." *Harvard Business Review* 72(3): 105–15.

Soffa, Virginia M. 1994. *The Journey beyond Breast Cancer: From the Personal to the Political.* Rochester, Vt.: Healing Arts Press.

Sontag, Susan. 1978. *Illness as Metaphor.* New York: Farrar, Strauss and Giroux.

Sporn, Michael. 2003. "New Directions: Where Are We and Where Should We Be Headed?" Speech delivered to the National Breast Cancer Coalition Advocacy Conference. Washington, D.C., May 4.

Stabiner, Karen. 1997. *To Dance with the Devil: The New War on Breast Cancer, Politics, Power and People.* New York: Delacorte Press.

Steimle, Sabine. 1997. "NPCC Unifies Prostate Cancer Advocates." *Journal of the National Cancer Institute* 89(2): 117–18.

Stolberg, Sheryl Gay. 2002. "Confronting Cancer: Advocates Strive to Defeat Cancer but Disagree on Methods." *New York Times,* April 9, 2F.

Stone, Deborah A. 1989. "Causal Stories and the Formation of Policy Agendas." *Political Science Quarterly* 104(2): 281–300.

Susan G. Komen Foundation. 2003a. "About Komen: Facts and Figures." http://www.komen.org/sgk/facts.asp (retrieved Jan. 8, 2003).

———. 2003b. "New ACS Screening Guidelines Reinforce Komen's Breast Health Advice." http://www.komen.org/news/article.asp?ArticleID=306&print (retrieved June 24, 2003).

———. 2005. "About Komen: Facts and Figures." http://www.komen.org/sgk/facts
.asp (retrieved June 28, 2005).

Swift, Deborah Petersen. 2003. "A Most Important Part: The Mayor, the Senator and
the Coach Are All Talking about Prostate Cancer, but What Happens after the
Treatment?" *Hartford Courant,* March 23, 1.

Swissler, Mary Ann. 2002. "The Marketing of Breast Cancer." *Sacramento News and
Review,* Oct. 31 (electronic version, retrieved Dec. 18, 2006).

Tankard, James W., and Michael Ryan. 1974. "News Source Perceptions of Accuracy
of Science Coverage." *Journalism Quarterly* 51(2): 219–331.

"A Taste of Budapest." 2002. *Chicago Sun-Times,* May 24, 25.

Taylor, Elizabeth Johnston. 2000. "Transformation of Tragedy among Women Surviving Breast Cancer." *Oncology Nursing Forum* 27(5): 781–88.

Taylor, Humphrey. 1999. "Perceptions of Risks: The Public Overestimates the Risk of
Major Diseases and Types of Accidents—Breast and Prostate Cancer in Particular."
Harris Poll press release, Jan. 27. Louis Harris and Associates.

Terkildsen, Nayda, Frauke I. Schnell, and Cristina Ling. 1998. "Interest Groups, the
Media and Policy Debate Formation: An Analysis of Message Structure, Rhetoric
and Source Cues." *Political Communication* 15(1): 45–61.

Theodoulou, Stella Z., ed. 1996. *AIDS: The Politics and Policy of Disease.* Upper Saddle
River, N.J.: Prentice-Hall.

———, Gloria Y. Guevara, and Henrik Minnassians. 1996. "Myths and Illusions: The
Media and AIDS Policy. In *AIDS: The Politics and Policy of Disease,* edited by Stella
Z. Theodoulou, 48–67. Upper Saddle River, N.J.: Prentice-Hall.

Thompson, Ian M. 2005. "The Predictive Value of PSA for Prostate Cancer: Clinical
Insights and Implications." *Contemporary Urology,* May 17, 70–75.

"Traffic Safety Facts, 1998." *1998 Motor Vehicle Crash Data from FARS and GES,* 86.

Trumbo, Craig. 1995. "Longitudinal Modeling of Public Issues: An Application of the
Agenda-Setting Process to the Issue of Global Warming." In *Journalism and Mass
Communication Monographs,* edited by John Soloski. Columbia, S.C.: Association
for Education in Journalism and Mass Communication.

Turkington, Carol A., and Teresa G. Odle. 2003. "Toxic Shock Syndrome." *Gale Ency-
clopedia of Medicine* (retrieved July 7, 2005).

Ungar, Bernard L. 2000. "Breast Cancer Research Stamp: Millions Raised for Research,
but Better Cost Recovery Criteria Needed." United States General Accounting
Office Testimony before U.S. Senate Committee on Governmental Affairs, May
25.

United States Census Bureau. 2002. "Educational Attainment in the United States:
2002." Current Population Survey Data. http://www.census.gov/population/www/
socdemo/education/ppl-169.html (retrieved April 9, 2003).

———. 2005. "Historical Health Insurance Tables." http://www.census.gov/hhes/
www/hlthins/historic/hihisst1.html (retrieved June 26, 2005).

United States Department of the Army. 2003. "Breast Cancer." http://cdmrp.army
.mil/bcrp/ (retrieved April 3, 2003).

————, Congressionally Directed Medical Research Program. 1999. "FY99 CDMRP Annual Report." http://cdmrp.army.mil/pubs/annual_reports.htm (retrieved Aug. 12, 2005).

————. 2000. "FY00 CDMRP Annual Report." http://cdmrp.army.mil/pubs/annual _reports.htm (retrieved Aug. 12, 2005).

————. 2001. "FY01 CDMRP Annual Report." http://cdmrp.army.mil/pubs/annual _reports.htm (retrieved Aug. 12, 2005).

————. 2002. "FY02 CDMRP Annual Report." http://cdmrp.army.mil/pubs/annual _reports.htm (retrieved Aug. 12, 2005).

————. 2003a. "Consumer Involvement." http://cdmrp.army.mil/CWG/default.htm (retrieved April, 2003)

————. 2003b. "Why Get Involved?" http://cdmrp.army.mil/cwg/why.htm. (retrieved April, 2003).

United States Department of Justice, Bureau of Justice Statistics. 2003. "Crime in 1992." http://149.101.22.40/dataonline/Search/Crime/State/RunCrimeOneYearofData.cfm (retrieved June 24, 2003).

United States Department of State. 2001. "Biography: Nancy Goodman Brinker." May 9. http://www.state.gov/r/pa/ei/biog/6092.htm (retrieved June 24, 2003).

United States Department of Veterans' Affairs. 1996. "Diseases Associated with Exposure to Certain Herbicide Agents (Prostate Cancer and Acute and Subacture Peripheral Neuropathy)." *Federal Register* 61(217): 57586–89.

————. 1997. "VA Programs for Veterans Exposed to Radiation." VA fact sheet, Jan.

United States Equal Employment Opportunity Commission. 2003. "Sexual Harassment Charges EEOC and FEPAs Combined: FY 1992—FY 2002." http://www.eeoc .gov/stats/harass.html (retrieved July 24, 2003).

United States Postal Service (USPS). 2005. "Fundraising Stamps: Learn More about It." http://www.usps.com/communications/community/semipostals_print.htm (retrieved June 24, 2005).

University of California at Los Angeles. 2003. "Exercise, Dietary Changes Can Kill Prostate Cancer Cells, UCLA Scientific Report." Ascribe Higher Education News Service. Jan. 14. Infotrac, 719/0/44792121 (retrived Dec. 18, 2003).

US TOO! International. 2002a. "US TOO! International, Inc. Organization Introduction; Strategic Plan 2001–2003." http://www.ustoo.com/intro.html (retrieved Nov. 21, 2002).

————. 2002b. "Advocacy Program." http://www.ustoo.com/advocacy.html (retrieved Nov. 21, 2002).

————. 2005. "About US TOO!" http://www.ustoo.org/About_UsToo.asp (retrieved Aug. 11, 2005).

"Using Media Advocacy to Win Massachusetts Cigarette Tax Hike." 1994. *World Smoking and Health: An American Cancer Society Journal* 19(1): 15–17.

Varadarajan, P. Rajan, and Anil Menon. 1998. "Cause-Related Marketing: A Coalignment of Marketing Strategy and Corporate Philanthropy." *Journal of Marketing* 52 (July): 58–74.

Visco, Fran. 2002a. "Testimony of the National Breast Cancer Coalition Submitted to the House Subcommitte on Labor, Heath and Human Services and Education." May 9.

———. 2002b. "Testimony before the Senate Appropriations Subcommittee on Defense." June 12.

———. 2003a. Speech delivered before the National Breast Cancer Coalition Advocacy Conference. Washington, D.C., May 5–6.

———. 2003b. "Defense Subcommittee Hearing: Statement of Fran Visco." http://appropriations.senate.gov/subcommittees/record.cfm?id203938 (retrieved May 16, 2003).

———. 2005. "It's Time to Start a Revolution." Speech delivered before the National Breast Cancer Coalition Advocacy Conference. Washington, D.C., May 22.

Vucanovich, Barbara. 2000. *Roundtable: Women and Reflections on Congressional Life.* C-SPAN, April 20.

Wachter, R. M. 1996. "AIDS, Activism and the Politics of Health." In *AIDS: The Politics and Policy of Disease,* edited by Stella Z. Theodoulou, 27–35. Upper Saddle River, N.J.: Prentice-Hall.

Wadman, Meredith. 1996. "Clinton Woos Votes with Cancer Genetics Funds." *Nature* 383(6603): 753.

Wallack, Lawrence, and Lori Dorfman. 1996. "Media Advocacy: A Strategy for Advancing Policy and Promoting Health." *Health Education Quarterly* 23(3): 293–317.

———, ———, David Jernigan, and Makani Themba. 1993. *Media Advocacy and Public Health: Power for Prevention.* Newbury Park, Calif.: Sage Publications.

Walsh-Childers, Kimberly. 1994. "'A Death in the Family': A Case of Newspaper Influence on Health Policy Development." *Journalism Quarterly* 71: 820–29.

Walsh, Patrick, and Janet Worthington. 2001. *Dr. Patrick Walsh's Guide to Surviving Prostate Cancer.* New York: Warner Books.

Wanta, Wanda, and Joe Foote. 1994. "The President-News Media Relationship: A Time Series Analysis of Agenda Setting." *Journal of Broadcasting and Electronic Media* 38(4): 437–48.

Ward, Julie DeJager. 2000. *La Leche League: At the Crossroads of Medicine, Feminism, and Religion.* Chapel Hill: University of North Carolina Press.

Warlow, Charles, Peter Sandercock, Martin Dennis, and Joanna Wardlaw. 1999. "Research Funding." *The Lancet* 353(9171): 2250.

Weaver, David. 1990. "Women as Journalists." In *Women, Media and Politics,* edited by Pippa Norris, 21–40. New York: Oxford University Press.

Weinstein, Neil S. 1984. "'Why It Won't Happen to Me' Perceptions of Risk Factors and Susceptibility." *Health Psychology* 3(5): 431–57.

Weisman, Carol S. 1998. *Women's Health Care: Activist Traditions and Institutional Change.* Baltimore: Johns Hopkins University Press.

Weiss, Alice. 2005. "Advanced Policy Issues: Threats to Medicaid and the Breast and Cancer Treatment Program." Speech delivered to the National Breast Cancer Coalition Advocacy Conference, Washington, D.C., May 22.

Weiss, Rick. 1996. "War between the Sexes Rages over Research; Funds to Study Prostate, Breast Cancer at Issue." *Washington Post,* Aug. 6, A13.

Wells, Jane, Phillip Marshall, Barbara Crawley, and Kay Dickersin. 2001. "Newspaper Reporting of Screening Mammography." *Annals of Internal Medicine* 135(12): 1029–37.

West, Darrell M., Diane Heith, and Chris Goodwin. 1996. "Harry and Louise Go to Washington: Political Advertising and Health Care Reform." *Journal of Health Politics, Policy and Law* 21(1): 35–68.

———, and John Orman. 2003. *Celebrity Politics.* Upper Saddle River, N.J.: Prentice-Hall, 2003.

"White House Raps Pentagon for Not Spending Research Funds." 1995. *AIDS Weekly,* Feb. 27, 9–10.

Whiteman, Maura K., Yadong Cui, Jodi A. Flaws, Patricia Langenberg, and Trudy L. Bush. 2001. "Media Coverage of Women's Health Issues: Is There a Bias in Reporting an Association between Hormone Replacement Therapy and Breast Cancer?" 2001. *Journal of Women's Health and Gender-Based Medicine* 10(6): 571–77.

Williamson, David. 2002. "Long Island Breast Cancer Study Project Uncovers Small Risk from Hydrocarbons, nor Organocholorines." News release. University of North Carolina, Chapel Hill. http://www.unc.edu/news/newsserv/research/cancerstudy080602.htm (retrieved June 6, 2003).

Wingo, P. A., K. Newsome, J. S. Marks, E. E. Callie, and S. L. Parker. 1997. "The Risk of Breast Cancer Following Spontaneous or Induced Abortion." *Cancer Causes and Control* 8(1): 93–108.

Woliver, Laura R. 2002. *The Political Geographies of Pregnancy.* Urbana: University of Illinois Press.

Wood, Corinne. 2002. Statement before the National Breast Cancer Coalition Training Conference. C-SPAN II, April 29.

Woodruff, Katie. 1996. "Alcohol Advertising and Violence against Women: A Media Advocacy Case Study." *Health Education Quarterly* 23(3): 330–45.

Woolsey, Lynn. 2003. "Representative Lynn Woolsey: Fighting for Health Care." http://woolsey.house.gov/ (retrieved June 6, 2005).

Y-ME. 2003a. "About Y-ME: Mission Statement." http://www.y-me.org/about_yme/about_yme.php (retrieved March 17, 2003).

———. 2003b. "Earlier Detection Methods." http://www.yme.org/information/three_point_dectection.php (retrieved June 24, 2003).

———. 2003c. "Men's Match Program." http://www.y-me.org/cgi-bin/MasterPFP.cgi?doc=slf&bottom=self (retrieved July 29, 2003).

———. 2005. "National Programs and Services." http://www.y-me.org/about_yme/national_programs_services.php (retrieved Aug. 11, 2005).

Yalom, Marilyn. 1997. *A History of the Breast.* New York: Ballantine Books.

Yanovitzky, Itzhak. 2002a. "Effects of News Coverage on Policy Attention and Actions: A Closer Look into the Media-Policy Connection." *Communication Research* 29(4): 422–51.

———. 2002b. "Effect of News Coverage on the Prevalence of Drunk-Driving Behavior: Evidence from a Longitudinal Study." *Journal of Studies on Alcohol* 63(3): 342–51.

———, and Courtney Bennett. 1999. "Media Attention, Institutional Response and Health Behavior Change." *Communication Research* 26(4): 429–53.

———, and Cynthia L. Blitz. 2000. "Effect of Media Coverage and Physician Advice on Utilization of Breast Cancer Screening by Women Forty Years and Older." *Journal of Health Communication* 5: 117–34.

Yaphe, John, Richard Edman, Barry Knishkowy, and Joseph Herman. 2001. "The Association between Funding by Commercial Interests and Study Outcome in Randomized Controlled Drug Trials." *Family Practice* 18(6): 565–68.

Young, Jane M., Claire Davey, and Jeanette E. Ward. 2003. "Influence of the 'Framing Effect' on Women's Support for Government Funding of Breast Cancer Screening." *Australian and New Zealand Journal of Public Health* 27(3): 287–90.

Young Survival Coalition. 2002. "YSC Joins Forces with the American Cancer Society in New York City: Revised Reach to Recovery Program and New Brochure Will Address Young Women's Issues." *Young Perspective* (Spring): 6.

———. 2003. "YSC Mission." http://www.youngsurvival.org/?fuse=about.who .mission (retrieved March 18, 2003).

Zerbe, Michael J., Amanda J. Young, and Edwin R. Nagelhout. 1998. "The Rhetoric of Fraud in Breast Cancer Trials: Manifestation in Medical Journals and the Mass Media—and Missed Opportunities." *Journal of Technical Writing and Communication* 28(1): 39–61.

Interviews Conducted

Andrews, Cat. 2003. Breast Cancer Coalition of North Carolina. Personal interview, Feb. 24.

Atkins, Richard N. 2003. National Prostate Cancer Coalition. Personal correspondence, May 26.

Bachman, Robin. 2003. Aide to Representative Carolyn Maloney. Personal interview, Jan. 15.

Balma, Diane. 2003. Susan G. Koman Breast Cancer Foundation. Telephone interview, Sept. 12.

Berzok, Jennifer. 2003. National Breast Cancer Coalition. Personal interview, Jan. 16.

Biegel, Roberta. 2003. Society for Women's Health Research. Telephone interview, Jan. 30.

Botts, Dewey. 2003. Prostate Cancer Coalition of North Carolina. Telephone interview, Feb. 27.

Brenner, Barbara. 2003. Breast Cancer Action. Telephone interview, May 7.

Brinkman, Ann. 2003. Y-ME. Personal interview, Feb. 18.

Brooks, Rebekah. 2003. Y-ME Chicagoland Affiliate. Personal interview, Feb. 18.

Caputi, Anthony. 2003. American Foundation for Urological Disease. Personal interviews, May 20, July 16.

Coulter, Francis. 2003. Young Survival Coalition. Personal correspondence.

Dole, Robert. 2003. Telephone interview, June 3.

Frey, Scott. 2003. Personal interview, Jan. 14.

Gluck, Adam. 2003. Aide to Senator Tom Harkin. Personal interview, Jan. 15.

Hall, Cindy. 2003. Women's Policy Institute. Telephone interview, Feb. 21.

Hill, Heather. 2003. Young Survival Coalition. Email correspondence.

Isaacson, Orlie. 2003. Aide to Representative Carolyn Maloney. Personal interview, Jan. 15.

Kossover, Becky J. 2003. Arkansas Prostate Cancer Foundation. Personal interview, March 7.

McDaniel, Jane. 2003. Susan G. Komen Foundation–Central Arkansas. Telephone interview, March 7.

Miller, Jim. 2003. Marketing executive. Telephone interview, June 14.

Myrick, Sue (R-NC). 2003. Telephone interview, Jan. 23.

National Prostate Cancer Coalition. 2003. Personal interview, Jan. 14.

Oakar, Mary Rose. 2003. Telephone interview, Jan. 10.

Page, John. 2003. US TOO! International. Personal interview, Feb. 19.

Peres, Judy. 2003. Health reporter. Personal interview, Feb. 19.

Porter, Katie. 2003. Aide to Representative Sherrod Brown (D-OH). Telephone interview, Feb.

Rovner, Julie. 2003. Health reporter. Telephone interview, Feb. 14.

Sherman, Stephanie. 2003. National Breast Cancer Coalition. Personal interview, Jan. 16.

Simha, Joy. 2003. Young Survival Coalition. Telephone interviews, March 7, July 7, 2003.

Soule, Howard. 2003. CaP-Cure. Telephone interview, Feb. 13.

Volpe, Margaret. 2003. Y-ME. Telephone interview, May 13.

Weitzman, Gary. 2003. Congressionally Directed Medical Research Programs. Personal interview, May 21; telephone interview, June 27.

Wheeler, Susan. 2003. Aide to Senator Mike Crapo (R-ID). Telephone interview, Jan. 31.

Williams, Sarah. 2003. Breast Cancer Coalition of North Carolina. Personal interview, Feb. 24; telephone interview, May 15.

Wilson, Penelope. 2003. Susan G. Komen Foundation, Charlotte, N.C. Affiliate. Personal interview, Feb. 4.

Woolfe, Elizabeth. 2003. NABCO. Telephone interview, Feb. 11.

Index

ABC, 17, 84, 227; ABC News Women's Issues Poll, 99, 229–30
abortion. *See* breast cancer
absolute risk. *See* risk
Access to Cancer Therapies Act, 17
activists' movements. *See* specific disease
ACT UP. *See* AIDS
Adams, Abigail "Nabby," 19
Adweek, 192
African American Breast Cancer Alliance support group, 242n9
African Americans, 208, 217, 222, 233n2, 242n9
agenda-setting, 10–11, 158–59; AIDS, 11, 48; maintaining position on agenda, 162–83; media agenda, 91–92; policy agenda, 158–59
AIDS: activism, 26, 41–43, 207, 208; ACT UP, 40, 41, 42, 51; agenda-setting, 11; backlash, 207; cause-related marketing and, 187; death rates, 179; federal funding, 136–37, 167, 178, 203, 205, 206–7, 209; gay movement, 45, 47; Kimberly Bergalis and, 45; mortality, 44; National Hemophilia Association, 46; *New York Times* coverage, 48; red ribbon as symbol, 51
Akin, Todd, 150
Alliance for Lung Cancer Advocacy, Support and Education, 205
Altman, Roberta, 136

Alzheimer's Association, 43
American Cancer Society, 2, 3, 8, 175, 100, 120, 190, 221, 238n5, 240n10; Brother to Brother program, 32; Campaign for Early Detection, 234n2; Let's Talk About It program, 31; Look Good . . . Feel Better program, 24; mammography, 66, 68; Man to Man program, 58; Reach to Recovery program, 20, 22, 27; risk assessment, 100, 125n5; Side by Side program, 58; as source for media stories, 77, 88
American Chopper (television program), 191
American Express, 186, 187
American Foundation for Urologic Disease (AFUD), 30
American Prostate Society, 28, 30
American Society for Control of Cancer, 175. *See also* American Cancer Society
American Society for Plastic and Reconstructive Surgery, 17
American Urological Association, 8, 217
Anastasia (tweezers), 192
Andreason, Alan, 190
Andrews, Cat, 54, 55
Anita Hill–Clarence Thomas hearings, 145
Ansager, Julie, 69, 70, 98
Arkansas Prostate Cancer Foundation, 57, 239n8; Jim East and, 57
Arnold, R. Douglas, 94
AT&T (former), 186

Atkins, Richard, 124, 179, 181, 237. *See also* National Prostate Cancer Coalition

Atlanta Constitution, 17, 84, 106, 227

Atomic Energy Commission, 40

atomic testing, 40

autologous bone marrow transplants, 171–72

Avon, 189, 190, 192, 194, 195; Avon Foundation, 190, 195, 236–37n14, 240n1

Balma, Diane, 185

Barker, Mary, 146

Barker-Plummer, Bernadette, 75

Bateman, Herb, 151

Bathsheba's Breast (Olson), 19

Baumgartner, Frank, 163

BCRA1. *See* breast cancer

BCRA2. *See* breast cancer

Beltram, Kenneth, 214–15

Benford, Robert D., 233n4

benign prostate hyperplasia, 8

Ben and Jerry's Homemade Ice Cream, 186

Bergalis, Kimberly. *See* AIDS

Berger, Roy, 7

bills, introduction of, 153–57

Black Lung Association, 39–40, 45, 46

Black, Shirley Temple, 91

blue ribbon, as symbol of prostate cancer, 59, 198, 216, 217

Blunt, Roy, 150

BMW, 188

Bodai, Ernie, 143, 238n3

Bombeck, Erma, 127

Bonner, Frances, 235n3

Boodman, Sandra, 150

Booth, Karen M., 69, 97

Bordin, Ruth, 47

Bowles, Erskine, 146

Boxer, Barbara, 6

brain cancer, 205

breast cancer, 2–4, 19, 241n10; abortion and, 5; backlash against cause-related marketing, 194–98; BCRA1, 4; BCRA2, 4; as campaign issue, 145–46, 238–39n6; cause-related marketing and, 189–91, 192, 221–22; comparison with AIDS, 220; coverage of compared to prostate cancer coverage, 73–75; coverage of over time, 78–79; ductal carcinoma in situ (DCIS), 243n10; epidemic, 173–75, 182–83, 241n8; estrogen-receptive, 243n10; framing of

as a policy issue, 166–73; framing of as scientific neglect, 173–177; funding for research, 130–31, 136–37, 139–40, 142, 153–55, 167–71, 203, 208, 238n6, 241–42n1; genetic, 243n10; HER-2/neu receptive, 243n10; inflammatory, 222, 223, 243n9, 243n10; lumpectomy, 2; lympthedema, 2; mastectomy, 2, 17; media coverage of, 79, 84; metastatic, 222, 243n9; Paget's Disease of the breast, 243n10; patient blaming, 176–77, 182; pregnancy and, 104; risk factors for, 176; screening, prevention, and early detection, 175; study using men only, 139; support groups, 222. *See also* media coverage

Breast Cancer Action, 26, 171, 184, 194–95, 221

breast cancer activists: as assertive advocates, 133–34; on Capitol Hill, 137–46; collective action and, 183; on Long Island, N.Y., 176, 221; as maturing movement, 220–23; NORCAL, 26; peer review panel participation, 214–15; state-level activism of, 238n6; as survivors and surrogates, 217; testimony in hearings, 154, 169–170

Breast Cancer Awareness Month, 39, 145, 187, 196–97, 216

Breast Cancer Coalition of North Carolina, 42, 54, 55

Breast Cancer Control and Detection Program, 66

Breast Cancer Fund, 186

"Breast Cancer Marketing 24/7," 192

Breast Cancer Research Foundation. *See* Lauder Foundation

Breast Cancer: Society Shapes an Epidemic (ed. Kasper amd Ferguson), 174

Breast and Cervical Cancer Mortality Prevention Act, 139, 144

Breast and Cervical Cancer Treatment Act, 144, 172, 238n6

breast implants, 172

breast reconstruction, 171

breast self-examination (BSE), 175

Brenner, Barbara, 193, 194, 220, 221

Brinker, Nancy Goodman, 23, 145, 221. *See also* Susan G. Komen Foundation

Broder, David, 11

Brother to Brother program. *See* American Cancer Society

Brown Lung Association, 39–40, 44, 46–48;

Charlotte Observer and, 49; legal proce-
dures of, 49; Ralph Nader and, 49; wom-
en's role in, 51
Brown, Phillip, 45
Brown, Sherrod, 152
BSE. *See* breast self-examination
Burke, Wylie, 97
Burroughs Wellcome, 42
Burr, Richard, 146
Bush, George H. W., 140
Bush, George W., 146, 221; G. W. Bush
administration, 204n6
Bush, Laura, 221

Cagney and Lacy (television program), 57
California Breast Cancer Research Pro-
gram, 6
Campbell, Ben Nighthorse, 151
Canadian Periodical Index, 70
cancer. *See specific type*
Cancer Journals. See Lorde, Audre
CaP CURE, 30, 31, 55, 59, 191. *See* also Prostate Cancer Foundation
Caputi, Anthony, 53, 215
Carson, Rachel, 5
Carter, Linda, 127
Cartwright, Lisa, 70
Casamayou, Maureen, 25–25
casual stories, 165, 175–76
Caswell-Massey, 192
cause-related marketing, 16, 52, 184–99, 189,
216–17, 241n1; backlash against, 194–98;
breast cancer and, 189–92; CBS and, 17,
84, 227; "cherry picking" and, 194; defi-
nition of, 186; as different from philanthropy, 193–94; ethical concerns about,
193–94, 221–22; need to cultivate relationships, 188; overselling breast cancer, 194;
prostate cancer and, 191–93
CCWI. *See* Congressional Caucus for Wom-
en's Issues
CDMRP. *See* Congressionally Directed
Medical Research Program, Department
of Defense
CDPR. *See* Center for Prostate Disease
Research
celebrities, 126–27, 237n1
Center for Prostate Disease Research, 147
Centers for Disease Prevention and Control,
8, 139, 144, 179, 220, 233n3
cervical cancer, 203

Champion sports bra, 192
Chandliss, Saxby, 150
Chang, S., 11
Charlotte Observer. See Brown Lung Asso-
ciation
chemotherapy, 215, 243n10
Chicago Tribune, 4–5, 17, 66–77, 79, 84, 106,
227
Chodok, Jerry, 30
Clarke, James, 151
Clarke, Juanne, 69, 70
clinical trials, 180
Clinton administration health reform plan,
126
Clinton, Bill, 142, 145, 146, 173
Clinton, Hillary, 146
Club Mets-BC on-line support group, 243n9
CNN, 235n2
Cobb, Roger, 11, 12, 91, 93, 158, 165
Coca-Cola, 185
coding criteria, 227–29
Cohen, Peter, 47, 50
Cohn, Victor, 97
Colburne, Jane-Reese, 32
Committee of Ten Thousand, 47
Cone, Carol, 187, 195
Cone, Inc., 186
Congressional Black Caucus, 31
Congressional Caucus for Women's Issues,
138–40, 159, 238n2
congressional hearings, 130–31, 153–57,
239n12
Congressionally Directed Medical Research
Program, 142, 148, 170, 212–16, 241n12,
242n6
Connecticut Breast Cancer Coalition, 175,
240n7
consent laws, 23
consumer representatives on peer review
panels, 142, 210–16; cooptation, 211; defi-
nitions of consumer input, 211, 213; effectiveness of, 214–16; problems with, 210–11,
213–14; scientists' attitudes toward, 212,
214. *See also* breast cancer activists; prostate cancer activists
Conte, Silvio, 147, 151
Cook, Fay Lomax, 126
Corbett, Julie, 75, 91
corporate philanthropy, 185–86
Coulter, Francis, 93, 100, 235n
Cox News Service, 205

Craft, Stephanie, 75
Cranston, Alan, 73, 151
Crapo, Michael, 150
C-SPAN, 127
Cunningham, Randy "Duke," 150

D'Amato, Alphonse, 5, 141, 142, 144, 146, 201
Dartmouth-Hickcock Medical Center, 96
Dayton-Hudson (Target), 185
DCIS. *See* breast cancer, ductal carcinoma in situ
Dearing, James, 11
Department of Defense, 141–42, 147–48, 170, 202, 230. *See also* Center for Prostate Disease Research; Congressionally Directed Medical Research Program
Department of Veterans' Affairs, 147, 239n7
digital rectal examination (DRE), 181
Dimock, Susan, 30
Dingell, John, 146
disease groups, 201–3, 207–8
Dole, Robert (Bob), 3, 29, 68, 73, 127, 147, 151, 152, 160
Dorfman, Lori, 15
Downs, Anthony, 162
Dresser, Rebecca, 241n13
Dr. Susan Love's Breast Book (Love), 25
Drumwright, Minette, 190
drunk driving, 126

early detection, 175, 181
earmarking, 141, 147, 149, 202, 208
East, Jim. *See* Arkansas Prostate Cancer Foundation
Edelman, Murray, 164–65
Ehrenreich, Barbara, 21, 195, 198
Eisenstein, Zillah, 5, 55
Elder, Charles, 11, 12, 91, 158
end-stage renal disease, 94
English, Deidre, 21
Entertainment Industry Foundation, 190
Entman, Robert, 14
environmental pollution: asbestos, 126; breast cancer and, 143–44, 171; movements against, 40–41; radon, 126; Sisters Study, 6, 238n4; study of in Marin County, 238n3; uranium mining and lung cancer, 208. *See also* Long Island Breast Cancer Study Project; Love Canal
environmental racism, 48

Epstein, Samuel, 5
Epstein, Stephen, 235n4
erectile dysfunction, 9–10; Viagra and, 9–10
Estee Lauder, 59, 190, 192. *See* Lauder Foundation
Exxon, 186

Faircloth, Lauch, 143
Family to Family program, 58–59
Fan, David, 125
Farrakhan, Louis, 32, 57
federal research funding, 182, 201–10, 240n13; AIDS comparison of, 136–37, 167, 178; breast cancer, 130–31, 136–37, 139–40, 142, 153–55, 167–71, 203, 208; disease groups and, 201–3; military comparisons, 171, 178; prostate cancer and, 130–31, 136–37, 147–49, 156–57, 178, 203
Feinstein, Diane, 143
feminism, 183, 241n14
Ferguson, Susan, 174
Ferraro, Geraldine, 146
First You Cry. See Rollin, Betty
Fisher, Bernard, 5. *See Chicago Tribune*
Fletcher, Susan, 28
Florida Breast Cancer Coalition, 175, 240n7
Food and Drug Administration (FDA), 26, 42, 180
Ford, Betty, 21, 54, 91, 92
Ford Motor Company, 187, 188, 191, 193
Ford, Susan, 127
Foreman, Christopher, 43, 48–49, 52
Fosket, Jennifer, 69
foundations, corporate, 189. *See individual foundations*
framing, 14–15, 70. *See also* breast cancer, framing of; prostate cancer, framing of
Frey, Scott, 22
Fumento, Michael, 240n8

Gallo, Betty, 30
Gallo, Dean, 30, 151
Gamson, William, 233n4
Gandy, Oscar, 11
Gateway Arch, 145
Gay Men's Health Clinic, 241n
gender differences: collective action and, 217; in discussing health, 151–52, 218
General Accounting Office, 139, 143
genetic discrimination, 172–73, 180

Georgia Breast Cancer Coalition, 175, 240n7
Gephardt, Richard, 128
Gibbs, Lois Marie, 41. *See also* Love Canal
Gigerenzer, Gerd, 235–36n1
Gillette Company, 191–92, 193
Glamour, 177
Gleason scores. *See* Prostate-Specific Antigen test
Global Forum for Health Research, 209
Goldman, Debra, 192
Goodman, Susan, 174
Granath, Alan, 53
Grassley, Charles, 10
grassroots survivors' organizations (GSOs), 3, 200, 216–18; AIDS 41–43; cause-related marketing and, 188; changing public face, 131–33, 134; cancer movement and, 52–63; congressional activity, 153–57; definition, 38, 42–43; disagreement within movements, 194; educated, empowered activist base, 217; environmental health, 39–40; impact on funding, 203, 205–7, 209–10; maturing movements, 219–33; media advocacy, 128–30, 134; occupational health, 390–40; policy agenda, 185; survivors and surrogates, 217–18
Griswold, William, 63
Grove, Andrew, 52, 57
Guevara, Gloria, 157

Harelik, Larry. *See* US TOO! International
Halsted mastectomy, 17, 20–23, 234n3
Halsted, William Stewart. *See* Halstead mastectomy
Harkin, Tom, 141
Harper's Magazine, 105
Harris, Damon, 32
Harris poll, 229–30, 237n16
"Harry and Louise" advertisements, 126
Harvard School of Public Health, 100
Health Insurance Association of America, 126
heart disease, 137, 139
Heinz, John, 11
Helms, Jesse, 151
Herceptin, 134, 168, 170, 240n2
Hester, Susan, 25
Hill, Heather, 38, 234n
History of the Breast, A (Yalom), 174
Hobbs, Ellen, 27

Hodgkin's Disease, 203
Hooker Chemical Company. *See* Love Canal
hormone replacement therapy, 66
Houn, Florence, 65
House Energy and Commerce Committee, 138
House Select Committee on Aging, 138
House Ways and Means Committee, 138
Hudson, Rock, 92
Hurst, Stacey, 98
Hushpuppies, 192
Hyde, Henry, 150

IBC Support, 243n9
IBM, 186
Illness as Metaphor. See Sontag, Susan
Imperial Chemical Industries (AstraZeneca), 196
Inflammatory Breast Cancer Research Foundation, 243n9
informed consent, 21, 23, 138
institutional review boards, 210, 213
interest groups: media and, 124–26, 239n11; "outside" strategies, 124, 218; pluralist critiques, 210
issue: attention cycle for, 162–63; causal stories and, 165; definition and redefinition, 163–64; framing, 164–66. *See also* breast cancer, framing of; framing; prostate cancer, framing of
Ithaca Breast Cancer Alliance, 175, 240n7

Jaffee, Harry, 145
Johnson, Haynes, 11
Johnson, J. David, 68
Johnson, Ronald, 184, 199, 241
Jones, Bryan, 163
Journal of the American Medical Association (*JAMA*), 65, 77, 85, 227, 235n1
journalists: health reporters, 64–65; science and journalism, 62–71; women reporters, 75
Journey beyond Breast Cancer: From the Personal to the Political, The. See Soffa, Virginia

Kaiser Family Foundation, 100, 111, 236n6
Kaplan, Mimi, 22
Karren, Angela, 69
Kasper, Anne, 174

Keds, 192
Keebler's Wheatables, 192
Kelley, Virginia, 142
Kerry, John, 150
Kingdon, John, 163
King, Peter, 142
Komen Foundation. *See* Susan G. Komen
    Foundation
Korda, Michael, 33, 34, 35, 43
Kotler, Philip, 13
Kriegbaum, Hillier, 64
Kushner, Rose, 21–22, 24, 54, 138, 159, 212

LaFia, Christina, 69
Langer, Amy, 24, 25, 190, 202, 210. *See also*
    NABCO
Lantz, Paula, 69, 97
La Nueva Vida support group, 242n9
Lasser, Térèse, 20
Latinas, 222, 242n9
Lauder Foundation, 59, 187
Lazio, Rick, 146
Least Costly Alternatives policies, 180
Lee jeans, 192n
Legionnaires' disease, 43, 234n3
Leopold, Ellen, 176
lesbians, 222
Let's Talk About It program. *See* American
    Cancer Society
Leukemia, 205–6, 223
Levi-Strauss, 185
Lewis, Diocletan, 45
Lewis, James, 7
Lexis-Nexis Congressional Database, 17, 230
Libby Ross Foundation, 195–98
Life's Delicate Balance (Sherman), 144, 174
Lifetime Television, 191
liver cancer, 205
Lloyd, Marilyn, 140, 160
Loews Cineplex, 192
Long Island Breast Cancer Study Project, 5,
    6, 143–44, 201, 221, 240n4, 242n1
Longworth, Alice Roosevelt, 20
Look Good . . . Feel Better program. *See*
    American Cancer Society
Loomis, Burdett, 137
Lorde, Audre, 22, 23, 53, 55
Los Angeles Times, 84, 117, 227
Love Canal, 41, 43, 46, 48, 49, 212
Love, Susan, 6, 25, 140, 170–71, 220–21, 222

Lowey, Nita, 144, 146, 201
Luna Bars, 186
lung cancer, 205, 208, 223, 238n1
Lupton, Deborah, 69
lycopene, 7
lyme disease, 43, 234n2
lymphedema, 2, 222, 243n9

Mack, Connie, 151
magazine coverage. *See* media coverage
Major League Baseball, 191, 192
malaria, 223
Malecare, 32, 58
mammography, 96, 172, 174; media coverage
    of, 66; Medicare coverage and, 127, 138–39
Man to Man program. *See* American Cancer
    Society
March of Dimes, 39
Marcou, Ann, 22
Marin County Breast Cancer Watch, 175,
    240–41n7
Martin, Calvin, 32
Mary-Helen Mauter Project for Lesbians
    with Cancer, 25
Massachusetts Breast Cancer Coalition, 175,
    241n7
mastectomy, 2, 17, 171, 172
Matsunaga, Spark, 147, 151
Matuschka (artist), 27, 55, 70
McCain, John, 146
McCombs, Maxwell, 10
McKay, Susan, 235n3
M. D. Anderson Cancer Center, 178
media advocacy, 13, 15–16, 124–35, 126–31,
    157–58, 163, 218–19, 239n11; framing of,
    14; GSOs and, 126–28, 129–31; MADD, 15;
    news coverage, 128–31; Stanford Five City
    Project, 15
media agenda-setting 92
media and courts, 57
media coverage, 62–71, 92; difference by
    cancer, 71–78; of journalists and scien-
    tists, 62–65; in magazines, 68–70
Medicaid, 144, 171, 172
medical breakthroughs. *See* medical dis-
    coveries
medical discoveries, 228, 240n2; claiming
    credit for, 168–70; media coverage of,
    168–69, 179
medical licensure boards, 210

Medicare, 171–72; drug coverage of, 171, 172, 180; mammography coverage of, 127, 138–39; other screening coverage of, 148; prostate cancer screening coverage of, 148, 180

Medicare Catastrophic Care Act, 125, 138

melanoma, 203–5

Meloskie, Nikki, 58

Men's Health, 145

Men's Health Network, 29, 30

Menon, Anvil, 186, 188

methodology, 17–18, 227–32

Michael Simon sweater, 192

Milkin, Michael, 30, 57

Miller, Jim, 192–93

Minnassins, Henrik, 11, 157

Mitterrand, Francois, 106

Modigliani, Andre, 233n4

Molinari, Susan, 127, 143

Moran, Julie, 30

Morella, Connie, 146

Morgan, Sandra, 54

Mori, Motomi, 75, 91

Mothers Against Drunk Driving (MADD), 15

multiple myeloma, 205

Murphy Brown (television program), 57, 79, 191

Murray, David, 235n1

Murtha, John, 141

Myrick, Sue, 144, 146, 152, 160, 201

NABCO. *See* National Alliance of Breast Cancer Organizations

Nader, Ralph. *See* Brown Lung Association

Nagelhout, Edwin, 66

Nannery, Diane Sackett, 142

NASCAR Nextel Cup Circuit, 191

Natcher, William, 136, 141

National Alliance of Breast Cancer Organizations, 23–24, 190, 191, 202, 210, 221, 241, 242–43n9. *See also* Langer, Amy

National Breast Cancer Coalition, 19, 25–26, 27, 111, 139, 144, 145, 159, 170, 171, 172, 173, 198, 200, 202, 203, 208, 212, 221, 240, 240n4, 240n6, 241; abortion and, 5; annual advocacy conference, 128, 192, 230, 241n9; federal funding goals, 140, 167; letter writing campaign, 140; mammography, 235–36n1; "Not Just Ribbons"

campaign, 184, 194; Project LEAD, 212–13, 214, 216

National Cancer Institute, 30, 99, 137, 167, 149, 153, 167, 178, 182, 202, 203–7, 230, 238n5, 242n3, 242n4, 242n5, 242n6; public opinion polls, 116, 117, 120, 229–30

National Center for Infectious Diseases, 235n1

National Hemophilic Foundation. *See* AIDS

National Institutes of Health, 42, 136, 202, 203, 207, 209, 238n4, 241n12, 242n3; informed consent and, 23; Longitudinal Study of Aging, 139; neglect of women's health issues, 139, 208–9; recommendations on mammography, 4, 66

National Lymphedema Network, 243n9

National Prostate Cancer Coalition, 19, 30, 31, 32, 33, 55, 59, 134, 164, 178, 179, 191, 200, 203, 208, 219–20, 237, 241; advocacy conference, 128, 150, 180, 230; Families Fighting Prostate Cancer, 58; funding goals, 178; letter writing campaign, 148; mobile screening unit, 14, 128; Urban Challenge event, 33, 34

Nation, Carry, 45

NBC, 17, 84, 227

NBCC. *See* National Breast Cancer Coalition

NCI. *See* National Cancer Institute

nerve sparing surgery, 9

neurofibromatosis, 212

New Balance Athletic Shoe, Inc., 188

New England Journal of Medicine, 65, 77, 85, 137, 227

New York State Department of Health, 176

New York Times, 17, 48, 72, 84, 85, 91, 92, 97, 100–101, 126, 190, 218–19, 227

Ney, Lloyd, 28

Niagara Gazette, 41

NIH. *See* National Institutes of Health

Norem, Lois, 125

North Carolina Breast Cancer Coalition, 146

NPCC. *See* National Prostate Cancer Coalition

Oakar, Mary Rose, 22, 55, 127, 138–39, 141, 147, 159

O'Connor, Sandra Day, 67

Office of Men's Health, proposed, 29, 151

Office of Women's Health, 29

Ohio temperance activists. *See* temperance movement
Olsen, James, 19
100 Black Men of America, 31, 217
One Voice Against Cancer coalition, 208
One-in-Nine, 201
Orenstein, Susan, 191, 192
Our Journey Through Prostate Cancer (Miller and Miller), 192
outside lobbying, 124

PAACT. *See* Patient Advocacy for Advanced Cancer Treatment
Packer, Cathy, 63
Page, John, 35, 36–27, 59, 93, 193, 235n. *See also* US TOO! International
Palosky, Craig, 178
pancreatic cancer, 205
Panetta, Leon, 138
Patient Advocacy for Advanced Cancer Treatment, 28, 29
patient's bill of rights, 172–73, 180, 240n6
PCEC. *See* Prostate Cancer Education Cancer
peer review, 64, 235n1
Penny, Alexandra, 59
Pepper, Claude, 138
Perry, William, 142
personal is political definition of cancer, 134, 160
personal profiles, 94, 99; age of children in, 102–4
pharmaceutical industry: cause-related marketing and, 221–22; medical research funding and, 209
Phoenix5, 53, 58, 234
physician advertising, 63
pink ribbon, 59, 184, 198, 216, 217, 221; Avon products with, 189
Polaner All Natural Fruit Spread, 192
policy entrepreneurs, 137–38
policy equilibrium, 163
policymaking dilemmas, 200–16
policy process, use of language in, 164–66
Political Graveyard Web site, 239n9
political risk of illness, 151–52
Popular Health Movement, 50
postage stamps: for breast cancer, 33, 142–43; for prostate cancer, 33, 150, 238n4

Potts, Laura, 55
Powers, Angela, 69, 70, 98
Powers, Jean, 234n7
pregnancy and breast cancer, 104
Preventing Breast Cancer: The Politics of an Epidemic (Read), 174
Priest, Susanna Hornig, 64
problem definition: characteristics of, 165–66; importance of, 163–65
Proctor, Robert, 208
Proflowers.com/, 192
Project LEAD. *See* National Breast Cancer Coalition
prostate cancer, 6, 9, 241n10; cause-related marketing and, 191–93; civil rights and, 180; comparisons to breast cancer, 72–77, 134–35, 148; death rates from, 179; diet and, 7; digital rectal examination for, 8; framing as policy issue, 166, 177–80; framing science as salvation and, 181, 182–83; funding for, 130–31, 136–37, 147–49, 156–57, 178, 203; health-care access and, 179–80; as neglected, 178; risk factors for, 181; veterans and, 239n7; watchful waiting and, 9. *See also* media coverage
Prostate Cancer Action Network, 30, 31, 58. *See also* Roher, William
prostate cancer activists: on Capital Hill, 28–46, 146–52; effectiveness of, 152; individual action, 183, 217; maturing movement of, 219–20; peer review panel participation, 213–14, 215; piggybacking on breast cancer, 134–35, 157, 159–60, 182; quiet entrepreneurs as, 146–48; "reluctant champions" as, 150–52, 159, 217; state-level activism, 239n8; survivors and surrogates, 217–18; testimony in hearings, 154, 178–79
Prostate Cancer Awareness Month, 33, 196, 198, 216
Prostate Cancer Coalition of North Carolina, 32
Prostate Cancer Education Council, 28, 29, 60–61
Prostate Cancer Foundation, 30, 34, 36, 181, 191. *See also* CaP Cure
prostate specific antigen (PSA) test, 8–9, 97, 179, 180, 181, 220
PSA Rising (on-line magazine), 58
PSA test. *See* prostate specific antigen test

public face of cancer, 93–115, 131–33, 200; methodology, 228–29
public health campaigns: anti-drug, 12; Just Say No, 12; stop smoking, 12
public interest lobbies. *See* grassroots survivors' organizations
Public Opinion (Lippmann), 92
public opinion: Clinton health reform plan, 126; long-term care, 126; polling question convergence, 229–30; polls, 99
public policy measures, 230
Purnick, Joyce, 62, 235n

Quayle, Marilyn, 127, 140

Race for the Cure. *See* Susan G. Komen Foundation
raloxifene, 168
Ralph Lauren, 190
Reagan, Nancy, 67–68
Reach to Recovery program. *See* American Cancer Society
Read, Cathy, 174, 176
Real *e* Marketing, 192
red ribbon, 51
relative risk. *See* risk
Revlon, 190, 192
risk, 94–98, 177; absolute risk, 96; relative risk, 96
Rivers, Lynn, 146
Rochefort, David, 93, 165
Rockefeller, Margaretta Fitler Murphy "Happy," 21, 54, 91
Rockport Shoes, 186
Roe v. Wade, 21
Rogers, Everett, 11
Roher, William. *See* Prostate Cancer Action Network
Rollin, Betty, 21, 91
Roper Center, 236n6
Rosenthal, Cindy Simon, 237
Rostenkowski, Dan, 151
Roth, William, 151
Rousseau, Jean-Jacques, 186
Ryan White Care Act, 42

Saks, 190–91
Samuels, Robert (Bob), 62, 148, 241, 234n5, 235n

Sarbanes, Paul, 150
SBRL. *See* Social and Behavioral Science Research Laboratory
Schattschneider, E. E., 162, 166, 240
Schmitz, John, 151
Schneible, Cindy, 195
Schumer, Charles, 146, 152
Schwartz, Joel, 235n1
Schwartz, Lisa, 66
Schwarzkopf, Norman, 127
selenium, 7
self-efficacy, 93
Semi-Sovereign People: A Realist's View of Democracy in America (Schattschneider), 166
Senate Aging Committee, 148
Senate Defense Appropriations subcommittee, 170
Sephora, 190
Sharf, Barbara, 67
Shaw, D. L., 10
Shelby, Richard, 150
Sherman, Jeanette, 144, 174
Shoe Carnival, 192
Side by Side program. *See* American Cancer Society
Silent Spring Institute, 6
Silk Soymilk, 192
Simha, Joy, 54, 94, 104. *See also* Young Survival Coalition
Sisters Network support group, 26, 242n9
skin cancer, 233n1
smallpox, 63
Snowe, Olympia, 139
Social and Behavioral Science Research Laboratory, 229–30
social construction, 16–17, 183, 241n14
social marketing, 13, 51
Soffa, Virginia, 25, 174, 176–77
Sokolof, Peter, 15
Soloman, Gerald, 151
Sontag, Susan, 22
Soule, Howard, 181
sponsorships: corporate, 189
Stabiner, Karen, 136, 173
Stanford Five-City Project, 15
Stevens, Ted, 36, 146, 147, 149, 150
stomach cancer, 205
Stone, Deborah, 11, 165, 175

St. Petersburg Times, 178
Strax, Jacqueline, 58
stroke, 137, 223
survivors: role of, 160–61. *See also* breast
    cancer activists; prostate cancer activists
Susan G. Komen Foundation, 23, 24, 208,
    213, 221, 240n1, 240n3, 240n63; cause-
    related marketing and, 185, 187, 188, 190,
    194–95; Race for the Cure, 26, 140, 145,
    188, 189
Symbolic Uses of Politics, The (Edelman),
    164–65

Talent, James, 145
tamoxifen, 168
Tampa Tribune, 178
television coverage: of breast cancer, 85; of
    prostate cancer, 85
temperance movement, 45, 47, 49
Temptations, The, 32
"10/90 gap," 209
Theodoulou, Stella, 11, 157
Torricelli, Robert, 145–46
toxic shock syndrome, 43, 234–35n3
Trumbo, Craig, 11
tubular sclerosis, 212
Tuskegee syphilis experiment, 208

United Colors of Benetton, 187
United States Postal Service, 143
United Way, 186
University of Texas-Houston School of
    Medicine, 97
uranium mining, 208
Urban Challenge. *See* National Prostate
    Cancer Coalition
US TOO! International, 30, 31, 32, 36, 193, 219
uterine cancer, 139

Vanderbilt Television News Archive, 17, 227
Varadarajan, P. Rajan, 186, 188
Varmus, Harold, 202
Viagra. *See* erectile dysfunction
Visco, Fran, 13, 56, 124, 136, 142, 162, 169,
170, 173, 203, 208–9, 221, 237, 240. *See also*
    National Breast Cancer Coalition
Vitamin E, 7
Vucanovich, Barbara, 136, 145, 160, 238

Wadler, Joyce, 94
Wallack, Lawrence, 15, 163
Walsh-Childers, Kim, 11
Walsh, Patrick, 6, 147
Wanta, Wayne, 75
Washington, Mary, 19
Washington Post, 17, 84, 85, 92, 106, 227
Waxman, Henry, 139
Weisman, Carol, 50
When Science Offers Salvation (Dresser),
    241n13
Woloshin, Steven, 66
Willard, Francis, 17
Williams, Sara, 42, 215
Wofford, Harris, 11
Women's Basketball Association, 191
women's health, 139, 208–9; women's health
    movements, 50, 217; women in GSOs, 57
women in medical school, 50
women journalists. *See* journalists
Women's Christian Temperance Union. *See*
    temperance movement
Women's Policy Institute, 238n2
Women's World Daily, 190
Woolfe, Elizabeth, 184, 241
Woolsey, Lynn, 6

Yalom, Marilyn, 174
Yanovitsky, Itzhak, 126
Y-ME survivors' organization, 20, 22, 26, 32,
    25, 58, 59, 172, 190, 208, 221
Yoplait, 195
Young, Robert, 38, 66, 234
Young Survival Coalition support group, 26,
    55, 59, 100, 126, 171, 221, 236n9, 243n9. *See
    also* Simha, Joy.

Zaltman, Gerald, 13
Zerbe, Michael, 66

KAREN M. KEDROWSKI is professor and chair of the political science department at Winthrop University, where she conducts research in the areas of public policy and political communication. She is the author of *Media Entrepreneurs and the Media Enterprise in the U.S. Congress* and coauthor of *Breastfeeding Rights in the United States.* Her articles have appeared in *Political Communication, Perspectives on Politics, Armed Forces and Society, Teachers College Record,* and the *Journal of Political Science.*

MARILYN STINE SAROW is an associate professor of mass communication and coordinator of the integrated marketing communication program at Winthrop University. She is the coauthor of *Integrated Business Communication in the Global Marketplace* and has worked in public relations and marketing in higher education and in the medical field. Her work has appeared in several anthologies and has been presented at national and regional conventions.

The University of Illinois Press
is a founding member of the
Association of American University Presses.

———————————————————————

Composed in 10.5/13 Adobe Minion
with Meta display
by Celia Shapland
at the University of Illinois Press
Manufactured by Thomson-Shore, Inc.

University of Illinois Press
1325 South Oak Street
Champaign, IL 61820-6903
www.press.uillinois.edu